FROM WEIMAR TO HITLER

Also by E. J. Feuchtwanger

AIR POWER IN THE NEXT GENERATION
   (*editor with R. A. Mason*)
DEMOCRACY AND EMPIRE: Britain, 1865–1914
DISRAELI, DEMOCRACY AND THE TORY PARTY
GLADSTONE
PRUSSIA: Myth and Reality
SOCIAL CHANGE AND POLITICAL DEVELOPMENT IN
   WEIMAR GERMANY (*editor with R. Bessel*)
SOVIET MILITARY POWER AND PERFORMANCE
   (*editor with John Erickson*)
THE SOVIET UNION AND THE THIRD WORLD
   (*editor with Peter Nailor*)
UPHEAVAL AND CONTINUITY: A Century of
   German History (*editor*)

From Weimar to Hitler

Germany, 1918–33

E. J. Feuchtwanger

former Reader in History
University of Southampton

St. Martin's Press   New York

DD
2 40
· F46
1993

© E. J. Feuchtwanger 1993

First published in the United States of America in 1993

Printed in Great Britain

ISBN 0–312–09588–0

Library of Congress Cataloging-in-Publication Data
Feuchtwanger, E. J.
From Weimar to Hitler : Germany, 1918–33 / E. J. Feuchtwanger.
p.   cm.
Includes bibliographical references and index.
ISBN 0–312–09588–0
1. Germany—Politics and government—1918–1933.   2. National
socialism.   I. Title.
DD240.F46   1993
943.085—dc20   92–44734
                                             CIP

Contents

Preface

The history of the Weimar Republic is overshadowed by the catastrophic consequences of its collapse. No account of these years can avoid explanation and analysis of the failure of German democracy. In writing the present book I have, however, tried to prevent the question of ultimate failure from being too predominant. The problems of German society between the end of the First World War and Hitler's coming to power deserve to be discussed on their own terms and in the context in which they presented themselves to contemporaries. My choice of themes is designed to bring out the interconnections which seemed important at the time and which help towards an understanding of events and decisions. In history the illogical simultaneity or dissimultaneity of things is often significant. There are many aspects I have had to neglect or to explore merely in passing: for example the cultural scene, which has been dealt with in easily accessible books more fully than is possible here. There is a huge literature on the Weimar Republic, especially in German, to which the end-notes in this volume offer a selective introduction. A separate note gives hints on further reading in English.

E.J. FEUCHTWANGER

Abbreviations

ADGB   *Allgemeiner Deutscher Gewerkschaftsbund* (Association of Free Trade Unions).

AfA   *Allgemeiner freier Angestelltenbund* (Association of White-Collar Employees, affiliated to ADGB).

BVP   *Bayerische Volkspartei* (Bavarian People's Party, the Bavarian counterpart of the Catholic Centre Party).

DDP   *Deutsche Demokratische Partei* (German Democratic Party, the left-wing liberal party).

DNVP   *Deutschnationale Volkspartei* (German National People's Party, the conservative party).

DVP   *Deutsche Volkspartei* (German People's Party, the right-wing liberal party).

Gedag   *Gesamtverband Deutscher Angestelltengewerkschaften* (General Association of White-collar Unions, more right-wing than AfA).

IMCC   (IMKO in German) Inter-Allied Military Control Commission.

KPD   *Kommunistische Partei Deutschlands* (the Communist Party).

MICUM   *Mission Interalliée de Contrôle des Usines et des Mines.*

NSBO   *Nationalsozialistische Betriebszellenorganisation* (National Socialist Factory Cells Organisation).

NSDAP   *Nationalsozialistische Deutsche Arbeiterpartei* (National Socialist German Workers' Party, the Nazi Party).

OHL   *Oberste Heeresleitung* (Supreme Command).

RDI   *Reichsverband der Deutschen Industrie* (Association of German Industry).

RGO   *Revolutionäre Gewerkschafts-Opposition* (Communist trade union organisation).

SPD   *Sozialdemokratische Partei Deutschlands* (the Social Democratic Party, between 1917 and 1922 sometimes known as MSPD, *Mehrheits-SPD*, majority SPD).

USPD   *Unabhängige Sozialdemokratische Partei Deutschlands* (Independent Social Democratic Party, split from MSPD between 1917 and 1922).

Vestag   *Vereinigte Stahlwerke A.G.* (United Steelworks Ltd).

ZAG   *Zentralarbeitsgemeinschaft.*

1 The Revolution

WAR, DEFEAT AND THE COLLAPSE OF THE MONARCHY

The German revolution of 1918 remains unique in the twentieth century as a major upheaval in a large and highly-developed country. It is still a matter of dispute whether this upheaval deserves the label 'revolution' or if it was only an aborted revolution. Judgments on its complex course are coloured by the knowledge that the regime for which it laid the foundations ended catastrophically with Hitler's Third Reich. The question is bound to loom large whether different decisions could have been taken and a different outcome been achieved by the revolution's leading figures, but this is judging with hindsight. Taking a long perspective the German revolution looks less like a violent break and is seen more in the continuity of German developments. The tensions released in 1918 had been building up in Germany for many years. Had it not been for war and defeat, gradual solutions to some of the problems might well have emerged. The outbreak of war in August 1914 had temporarily transcended the deep divisions in German society. The key event was the decision of the SPD to vote for war credits in the Reichstag on 4 August 1914 and thereby to give their support to the war.[1] From the point of view of German nationalism it was an unforgettable moment of unity and enthusiasm. From the perspective of the international socialist movement it was a moment of great disenchantment. The class solidarity of the proletariat across the frontiers turned out to be an illusion.

The decision of the SPD, the foremost party in the Second International, to support their own country in the war was itself the culmination of many years of internal party strife, which had turned a party of revolution increasingly into a party of reform. The programme and the rhetoric remained revolutionary, but the practice was becoming evolutionary. The party spanned a wide political spectrum. On the left there were those like Rosa Luxemburg, who continued to believe in revolution and sought

1

to advance it with tactics like the mass strike. On the right the most extreme revisionists, for example Joseph Bloch and the *Sozialistische Monatshefte*, advocated adaptation to the nationalist–imperialist ideology of the Wilhelmine establishment. The centrist party leadership kept the party together with difficulty. Unity was maintained by the charismatic figure of August Bebel, the emperor of German socialism, who died in 1913. Karl Kautsky, the prestigious theorist of the party, papered over the ideological cracks with formulae, such as 'the SPD is a party of revolution but not a party that makes revolution'. The vote of 4 August 1914 split the party, but for the moment the imposition of party discipline prevented the minority from making itself heard. Given the mood of the party in the country, the pro-war line was probably inevitable. Bethmann Hollweg, the chancellor, had been successful in giving the German public, including the working class, the impression that Germany was compelled to fight a defensive war, above all against reactionary Russia. A Tsarist victory would be a catastrophe for the German proletariat no less than for other sections of society.

The SPD was marked for ever by its decision to support the war. The leaders of the party, men like Friedrich Ebert and Philipp Scheidemann, stood by the decision to the bitter end, for first and last they were patriotic Germans. They were hardly ever prepared during the war to express any criticism, let alone opposition to official policy. They were not willing to risk anything that might jeopardise the successful prosecution of the war, for in their minds the well-being of German workers was totally bound up with a German victory. Even a long-standing goal of the whole labour movement, the abolition of the Prussian three-tier franchise, was pressed only halfheartedly for fear of breaching the political truce. By 1917 this attitude of the SPD and trade union leaders had tried beyond endurance the patience of the minority who had opposed the war from the beginning. They moved to an open split and founded the Independent Social Democratic Party, the USPD. Arguably this split came in the wrong place and at the wrong time. The USPD was not the left wing of the SPD, but was held together only by opposition to the war. The father of revisionism, Eduard Bernstein, and the centrist ideologue Kautsky, found themselves in the USPD because of their internationalism, pacifism and revulsion against war. The split occurred at the very moment when the SPD was itself moving to a recognition that an outright German victory was no longer possible. It might have been just the time when the more moderate USPD leaders could have influenced the SPD more effectively from within. The extreme left, mainly represented by the Spartakus League, with Rosa Luxemburg and Karl Liebknecht as the most prominent personalities, sheltered for tactical reasons within the USPD until they turned themselves into the German Communist Party, the KPD, in December 1918. Their numbers never exceeded more than a few thousand, but their presence further aggravated the lack of coherence in the USPD.

In the heady days of August 1914 the SPD's patriotic stance ended the divisions of prewar Germany and ushered in a truce between the parties, the *Burgfrieden*, the peace within the castle. The Kaiser proclaimed that he no longer saw parties, only Germans, when not so long ago he had called the socialists 'unpatriotic fellows'. For the great mass of nationalist middle-class Germans August 1914 was a myth-making experience, when the national community, the *Volksgemeinschaft*, became a reality. It was a mood that could not last, as the war became protracted and imposed severe hardships, but support for the war and the *Burgfrieden* held out tangible benefits to the SPD and trade union leaders. Without the full cooperation of the workers and their leaders a total war could not be fought and therefore the labour movement could no longer be kept in a political ghetto. The leaders of the SPD and the unions had to be brought in from the cold and their organisations used for the mobilisation of the people. A movement previously regarded as beyond the pale became integrated into the machinery of government. This development, however, caused growing alienation between the leaders and the rank and file. The expectations of the leaders that they would acquire influence on policy and make progress towards constitutional change were mostly disappointed. Decision-making passed in fact to an annexationist, right-wing military leadership, after August 1916 to the quasi-dictatorship of Ludendorff. There was no political advance and even the end of the Prussian three-tier franchise was only a vague promise in the Easter Message of 1917.

The rank and file of the working class, on the other hand, experienced growing deprivation, aggravated by the inability and unwillingness of the authorities to enforce equality of sacrifice.

The gulf between the classes widened. The important role played by military officers in the administration of the home front focused popular resentment on the military hierarchy and its prominent place in the imperial power structure. Large numbers of newly recruited workers, often from the countryside, unskilled, many of them female, were drawn into the burgeoning war industries. Squeezed into inadequate urban housing they provided fertile ground for political radicalism. The Auxiliary Labour Law, passed in December 1916 at the behest of OHL, the Supreme Command, gave the authorities draconian powers over labour and epitomised the inequality of sacrifice.[2] Carl Legien, the chairman of the General Commission of the Trade Unions, gave this law his consent. He secured important concessions for labour, such as elected works councils in all enterprises with over fifty employees and arbitration councils composed equally of representatives of employers and workers. For the first time the place of trade unions in official bodies governing employment and social policy was enshrined in law. Nevertheless Hugo Haase, a chairman of the SPD in the Reichstag in 1914 and by 1917 the leader of the USPD, felt compelled to exclaim at the founding congress of the USPD: 'Nothing has stirred me so deeply during the whole of my life as the attitude of the majority and the party presidium in this affair [the Auxiliary Labour Law]. That social democrats could ever have brought themselves to help forge the chains for the proletariat!'[3] Not surprisingly the leaders of the SPD and the unions became obsessed with the threat posed by the left to their hold on the rank and file. It was an obsession that sometimes overshadowed even before the revolution their traditional confrontation with the imperial authorities.

The fall of Bethmann Hollweg and the passage of the peace resolution in the Reichstag in July 1917 aggravated the impasse in the German political situation. The collaboration between the SPD and the bourgeois parties enhanced the feeling among workers that the SPD was now part of the political establishment. Yet the Interparty Committee (*Interfraktioneller Ausschuss*) which formalised this collaboration was unable to achieve any of the political advances so long promised. On the contrary the formation of the Fatherland Party (*Vaterlandspartei*) with its links to OHL (*Oberste Heeresleitung*, Supreme Command) strengthened the forces of resistance to change at home and boosted annexationism abroad.

The outbreak of the Russian revolution moved left-wing opinion in the opposite direction. There were big strikes in major centres like Berlin, first in April 1917, and then in a more politicised form in January 1918. The leaders of the SPD could only retain their control over the rank and file by associating themselves with the January strikes. Alternative organisations like the USPD and the Berlin Committee of Revolutionary Shop Stewards were already claiming the allegiance of militant workers.

Nevertheless these divisions did not weaken the electoral strength of the SPD and this was to be an important factor during the revolution. German workers had become more radical, but they were not interested in factional disputes and wanted a united front against the hated imperial authorities. To many the outcome of the war was no longer relevant. Yet the majority of the German public retained their faith in victory and saw it renewed when Ludendorff's spring offensive started in March 1918. The peace treaties of Brest-Litovsk with Soviet Russia and Bucharest with Romania were still largely shaped by the annexationist outlook of OHL and the Fatherland Party, with the parties of the Interparty Committee unable to exert much influence. Soon the failure of the spring offensive to achieve decisive results was undermining the morale of the army, as is evident from the growing number of deserters, absentees and soldiers reporting sick and disappearing while on leave.[4]

By the spring of 1918 opinions about Germany's prospects were profoundly divided. On the one hand it seemed more plausible to expect an all-out victory than it had ever been since the Battle of the Marne in September 1914. It seemed realistic to believe that the military stalemate in the West might be ended in favour of Germany by the use of the forces released by Russia's collapse. This favourable prospect was admittedly counterbalanced by America's entry into the war, but it was felt that American forces could hardly make a decisive impact on the Western front before 1919. The position of France and Britain in 1917 was distinctly precarious and their peoples might well reach breaking point before the Germans did.

If this assessment was correct there could be no thought of compromise for Germany. To aim for anything less than total victory was tantamount to treason. This was the view of Ludendorff, the quartermaster-general of the army and virtual dictator of Germany. Hindenburg, the chief of the Supreme Command, gave the Ludendorff dictatorship an impressive and trustworthy public image. Against Ludendorff and Hindenburg neither emperor nor chancellor nor Reichstag could prevail and the will of OHL was decisive down to the smallest detail. A majority of the German people, reaching well into the working class, still put their faith in Hindenburg and Ludendorff and in consequence these two military leaders could prevail against all other power centres in the German system. The Fatherland Party, still advocating a *Siegfrieden*, a peace based on total victory, had more members in 1918 than the SPD. It was a mass mobilisation of chauvinism exceeded only, in due course, by the Hitler movement.

There was an equally plausible pessimistic view of the German situation. After three or four years of war against enemies with superior resources the nation was near the end of its tether. The strikes of January 1918, linked to demands for an immediate peace, were an alarm signal. Class divisions had become dangerously aggravated, disaffection and defeatism were spreading among previously loyal sections of the population, even among the middle classes and the peasantry. When unrestricted submarine warfare had failed to bring Britain to her knees and had brought America into the war, a Reichstag majority had passed the peace resolution. Even after Bethmann Hollweg's fall there were influential officials who saw the need for a negotiated peace. Kühlmann, the state secretary at the German foreign office, fought in vain to make the peace imposed on Russia more acceptable to international opinion. In July 1918 OHL brought about his fall.

In 1918 a defensive military strategy with the aim of securing a negotiated peace without annexations might still have had a chance. Instead Ludendorff pursued an all-or-nothing policy almost as extreme as that of Hitler in the Second World War. Even after his spring offensive had failed to achieve a decisive breakthrough he did not change course. The reason was domestic as much as military, for anything less than outright victory would profoundly shake the political and social fabric of Germany. Ludendorff, the Fatherland Party and all on that side of the political divide were therefore determined to banish all thought of compromise. Colonel Bauer, Ludendorff's principal assistant in domestic affairs, put the alternatives starkly in early 1918: 'The princes, governments, parliaments and people must stand up and be counted. It is a struggle between two ideologies. 1. Do they want . . . a strong peace, worthy of our sacrifices, which makes us militarily strong, facilitates great economic development, and probably a long and secure peace, with firm, purposeful government at home. 2. Or are we to resign, to drop militarily and politically out of the concert of great powers, decline into economic misery and drift towards a bolshevik regime. . . . Both systems are embodied in a number of names, here Hindenburg, Ludendorff . . . there Haase, Scheidemann, Erzberger.'[5]

Bauer produced one analysis after another advocating extreme measures of mobilisation and proposals of sheer repression against all signs of defeatism and opposition. Ludendorff, like Hitler, believed that an exercise of will could master all problems, but the reality was that by July and August 1918 the position of the German army had gravely deteriorated. The plans to mobilise more reserves and increase the supply of weapons became ever more frantic and desperate. The continued discussions about annexations and puppet regimes in Eastern Europe took on the air of fantasies. Having staked everything on outright victory Ludendorff was facing total defeat.

This was the background to the headlong rush of events that began on 23 September 1918, when the news of Bulgaria's request for an armistice and separate peace reached German head-quarters at Spa. The collapse of Germany's allies had begun. Up to this point Ludendorff had obstinately refused any admission of defeat. It had, however, become obvious to his immediate entourage that his nerve was failing and that his ability to make decisions had become paralysed. There was now a move by his subordinates to force the issue before the German army was totally overwhelmed. The state secretary for foreign affairs, von Hintze, the successor of Kühlmann, was urgently asked to come to Spa. He brought with him a plan which outlined the essentials of the scenario that was now to be enacted. Hintze rightly judged that the existing imperial government of Chancellor von Hertling had lost all credibility abroad. Therefore a new German government was to be formed, based on the parties that had passed the peace resolution in 1917. This new government would then request the American president, Woodrow Wilson, to arrange an armistice on the basis of his fourteen points. The only alternative would have been a military dictatorship pledged

to resist to the bitter end, but even Ludendorff had now lost the
will to play such a role. Hintze's plan was accepted at Spa with
surprising speed on 29 September. The Emperor, deeply shaken,
did not dare to disagree; Ludendorff, now that the die was cast,
insisted on the utmost speed; Hertling tried in vain to delay his
own fall.

Although the political leaders on the Interparty Committee
had been aware of the precariousness of the military situation for
some weeks, they were horror-struck when the full extent of the
disaster was revealed to them. When a week earlier the SPD
leaders had discussed the possibility that the party might be asked
to join a new government coalition with the bourgeois parties,
voices were raised against taking on 'a bankrupt enterprise'.
Ebert's view prevailed that it was a burden that the party could
not, for the sake of the proletariat and indeed of the whole nation,
refuse to shoulder. It was essentially a continuation of the view
that had governed the attitude of the SPD since August 1914. The
fear that the alternative might be a military dictatorship also
swayed opinion. Had the full gravity of the military situation been
known at the time, it is by no means certain that a majority for
entry into government would have been found in the leading
decision-making bodies of the SPD.

Ebert's influence remained crucial in holding the SPD to this
course with all its fateful consequences. When a week later the full
truth was revealed all the leading Reichstag politicians were
stunned and for the moment paralysed, in spite of the warning
signals they had had earlier. They were unable at short notice to
agree upon a new chancellor and for the last time the Emperor
and his advisers had to make the choice. It fell upon Prince Max
of Baden, who had been mentioned as a successor to Hertling for
some weeks. He was the heir to the throne of Germany's most
liberal state, a man with generous convictions, but not ideally
suited to the exercise of power at so critical a moment.[6]

Prince Max found himself immediately subject to extreme
pressure from Ludendorff to dispatch the armistice request
without delay, when he would have preferred to proceed more
cautiously. The public request for an armistice meant an
admission of defeat which could not be revoked and was to seal
the fate of the monarchy. The military defeat itself was not in
doubt. The defection of Bulgaria, and even more that of Austria-
Hungary, about to occur, left gaps that Germany could not

possibly plug. On the Western front the German army was steadily retreating and its strength was continuously declining through desertions and lack of reserves.

There was thus no truth in the legend, so damaging later on, that it had not been defeated. There was, however, not yet a rout and it is possible that vestiges of the defensive strategy that should have been adopted much earlier could still have delayed the Allies sufficiently on the German frontier to improve conditions for an armistice. Ludendorff's pressure for an immediate cessation of hostilities was due to his fear that the Allies would break his front, in many places only thinly held by officers without men. The Allies for their part still overestimated the remaining German powers of resistance and did not want to risk heavy casualties in an unnecessary offensive. In Germany there were calls for a last-ditch levée-en-masse to defend the fatherland and rally the population against revolution and bolshevism. Supporters of annexationism and of the Fatherland Party, who had but recently execrated social democrats and even Progressives, were now appealing to their former enemies to save the country from the enemy at the gates and from the bolshevik threat at home. Even if the reality of defeat had come upon the German people less suddenly, it seems unlikely that the deep divisions of German society could have been bridged at this late hour and in these desperate circumstances.

There was another reason for Ludendorff's sudden admission of defeat. He wanted to off-load the responsibility for it on to the parties and politicians of the Reichstag, whom he regarded as guilty of undermining the German people's will to fight. In announcing the request for an armistice to the members of his military staff he said: 'I have advised His Majesty to bring those groups into the government whom we have in the main to thank for the fact that matters have reached this pass. We will now therefore see these gentlemen move into the ministries. Let them now conclude the peace that has to be negotiated. Let them eat the broth they have prepared for us.'[7] Ludendorff thus laid the ground for one of the most damaging legacies left to the Weimar Republic, the 'stab in the back' myth.

The German request for an armistice precipitated events which no one could control. The government of Prince Max proved unable to steer a clear course between the conflicting pressures to which it was exposed. In successive notes President Wilson demanded clear signs that Germany now had a democratic government and had turned its back on authoritarianism and militarism. The German masses were impatient for peace and took Wilson's notes as evidence that the Kaiser and the military leaders were blocking the path to it. The Kaiser himself and much of the imperial establishment were still reluctant to recognise that their role was played out.

The changes made in October 1918 to the German political system were real enough and amounted to the introduction of a fully-fledged parliamentary democracy, but they passed largely unnoticed. The most important change was that in future the chancellor needed the confidence of the Reichstag and bore the responsibility for all the political actions of the Emperor. Members of the Reichstag could hold ministerial office without giving up their seats, so that governments could now be based on the Reichstag. The imperial power of military and naval command was restricted: appointment of officers and officials required the approval of the chancellor or the Prussian minister of war. Declarations of peace and treaties with foreign states required the consent of Bundesrat and Reichstag.[8] It was a constitutional revolution bringing in a parliamentary monarchy and in essentials anticipated the Weimar constitution adopted ten months later.

Had these changes been accompanied by the abdication of the Kaiser their impact would have been much greater and events might not have moved towards open revolution. As it was, the radicalisation of the masses proceeded apace throughout October. In spite of the refusal of the military authorities to give up press censorship some newspapers of the left were calling openly for the Kaiser's abdication. The mood at the growing number of mass meetings and demonstrations, often addressed by leaders of the USPD, was unmistakably and impatiently for immediate peace and for the removal of all obstacles to it. No obstacle seemed more obvious than the continuation of the Kaiser as head of the German state. Wilson's note of 23 October strengthened this impression and thereafter the personal abdication of Wilhelm II became urgent if there was to be any chance of saving the monarchy as an institution. Instead the Kaiser left Berlin on 29 October for General Headquarters at Spa, against the wishes of the government and in order to escape the pressures that could be brought to bear on him in the capital.

The drift towards revolution was accelerated by the refusal of sections of the armed forces and the imperial state apparatus to support the new government in its quest for an armistice. After Wilson's note of 23 October Ludendorff reversed his stand and demanded a resumption of hostilities. Even the Kaiser realised that this was unrealistic and agreed with the government's demand that the quartermaster-general should be dismissed. At an interview on 26 October with Hindenburg and Ludendorff the Kaiser ordered the former to stay and the latter to go. At crucial moments Hindenburg now and later, as president of the republic, failed to live up to his public image of unshakeable loyalty. He abandoned Ludendorff, the architect of his fame, and stayed on.

Ludendorff's defiance of the government's quest for peace thus failed, but in the meantime the Naval High Command was also preparing a challenge that would cut right across the request for an armistice. The fleet was to be sent into a last battle with the British navy, a plan which became the final detonator of revolution. The German battle fleet had fought only one major engagement, the battle of Jutland in 1916. In the intervening two years morale on the lower deck had declined steeply. There had been a mutiny in 1917, for which blame was falsely put upon members of the USPD. Ten death sentences were imposed, of which two were carried out, but many of the participants were still in prison in October 1918. The sudden order to put to sea for what was virtually a suicide mission was seen by the sailors as a deliberate act of defiance of the government's policy of ending the war. The sailors did not think of themselves as revolutionaries but as loyal followers of the legitimate government. The Naval High Command and the officers had a variety of motives. The desire to save the honour and reputation of the navy through a last act of defiance was undoubtedly widespread, but less vainglorious though futile calculations also played a role. The navy might protect the flank of the army in northern France and action by the battle fleet might compensate for the cessation of submarine warfare.

The Kaiser shared the long-cherished belief that this ocean-going fleet, which he had done so much to create, should be saved for a final strike. Admiral Scheer, the chief of the navy, may have believed that a bold stroke could still change Germany's situation or that he could topple the government of Prince Max. The chancellor did not know in detail of the battle plans, though he could hardly have been totally ignorant of them.[9]

Once the sailors' mutiny faced attempts at violent suppression by the officers, the uprising became self-perpetuating. A week after the mutiny began, on 4 November, Kiel was in the hands of the sailors and all ships were hoisting the red flag. Prince Max's government sent Conrad Haussmann, of the Progressive Party, and Gustav Noske, the naval spokesman of the SPD in the Reichstag, to Kiel to calm the situation. Noske was elected governor of Kiel by the local soldiers' council and promised an amnesty for the mutineers. In the meantime delegates of the sailors had spread the uprising to other naval bases and ports and inland to many major cities in north Germany. Often the sailors linked up with soldiers' and workers' councils already formed. By 8 November many cities, as far south as the Main and further, were controlled by councils.

In Munich King Ludwig III had fled his throne on 7 November. He was the last ruler of the house of Wittelsbach, one of the oldest German dynasties. In Bavaria the hardships of the war had caused growing discontent among all classes. The peasants were angered by the requisitioning of scarce food supplies. There was a recrudescence of anti-Prussian sentiment, which had virtually vanished when Bavaria had become a partner in imperial Germany's success. In Munich, the Bavarian capital, new armaments factories had been established during the war. They employed men and women from all over Germany and formed them into a volatile proletariat. Many radical intellectuals had their haunts in Schwabing, Munich's *Quartier Latin.*

This was the milieu in which Kurt Eisner moved, a Jewish intellectual from Berlin. He had worked as a journalist in the SPD press in Bavaria and opposition to the war had brought him into the USPD, a small minority in Bavaria. In the closing weeks of the war Bavaria was threatened by the possibility of an Allied invasion from the south, the consequence of Austria-Hungary's capitulation. A big demonstration, sponsored by the SPD and USPD, was held on 7 November to protest against the war and demand the abdication of the Kaiser. It was taken over by Eisner and his followers, aided by the radical wing of the Bavarian Peasant League (*Bauernbund*). Within hours Eisner had gained control of barracks, arsenals and ministries and was able to proclaim a Bavarian republic. Countermeasures foundered on lack of resolution and reliable troops. The King was advised to leave his capital, which he did with only a cigar box under his arm.[10]

THE REVOLUTION IN BERLIN AND THE COUNCIL OF PEOPLE'S COMMISSARS

News of these events from all over Germany heightened the critical atmosphere in Berlin. Ebert, Scheidemann and their leading colleagues wanted nothing more than an orderly transition to peace so that the immense problems facing the government of a defeated Germany could be tackled. Although republicans by conviction they were prepared to accept the constitutional monarchy that had just been established. They were 'monarchists by reason', just as many monarchists later became 'republicans by reason'. At this juncture the SPD leaders had in fact a preference for the continuation of the monarchy, for this would make it easier to maintain law and order, keep the loyalty of the bulk of the nation and retain the cohesion of the Reich.

Events had, however, reached a point where the monarchy could only be saved if both Emperor and Crown Prince, equally discredited, abdicated in favour of some other Hohenzollern prince or a regency. On 6 November the leaders of the SPD and the trade unions had a meeting with General Wilhelm Groener, Ludendorff's successor as quartermaster-general. Groener, a key figure now and in the later years of Weimar, was a Württemberger, not a Prussian. As a desk general administering the war effort he had gained the confidence of the labour leaders. His administration of the Auxiliary Labour Law had been based on the realisation that the war could only be won with the collaboration of the workers. Yet on this occasion he still categorically refused to entertain the abdication of the Kaiser. As Ebert left the meeting he declared portentously: 'We thank your Excellency for your frankness and we will always remember our collaboration with you during the war. From now on we have to go our separate ways. Who knows if we shall ever meet again?'[11]

The main task now facing the SPD leaders was to stay in control of the masses and avoid supersession by the USPD and forces further left. Ebert and his colleagues had to show their followers that they had the measure of the Emperor and his military officers, who were blocking the way to an immediate peace. On 7 November the SPD leaders threatened to resign from Prince Max's cabinet. The following day, a Friday, the Prince, faced by the continuing refusal of the Kaiser to abdicate, himself threatened to resign. In the meantime the revolutionary wave, which had already brought so many places under the sway of the council movement, was breaking over Berlin.

Attempts by military commanders to beat back the revolution failed because troops thought to be loyal proved to be so no longer. It was a significant moment when in Berlin early on the morning of 9 November the Naumburg Chasseurs, considered especially reliable, asked the party executive of the SPD to send someone to explain the political situation to them. As that day progressed vast demonstrations of workers moved from the suburbs to Berlin's centre. By midday Prince Max at last announced the Emperor's abdication. At Spa, Groener, with Hindenburg's consent, had made it clear to the Kaiser that any plan to march home at the head of the army to crush the revolution was doomed to failure. 'The Army will march home under its leaders and commanding generals with discipline and order, but not under the command of Your Majesty, for it no longer follows Your Majesty . . .', he declared. For a while Wilhelm hoped to hang on as King of Prussia, but he was finally persuaded, for his own safety, to leave for Holland. Three years after celebrating the quincentenary of its rule in Brandenburg the Hohenzollern dynasty passed into history.[12]

Prince Max's announcement of the abdication in Berlin, though slightly preempting the Kaiser's decision, came too late. The SPD leadership had in the meantime decided that they must ask for a transfer of the office of chancellor to Ebert. Prior to this decision they had secured the agreement of some of the USPD leaders to enter a purely socialist government. This seemed the best way of meeting the conflicting pressures of the moment: on the one hand to secure as much continuity as possible in the hand-over of the state apparatus; on the other to remain in control of the mass uprising. The continuation of the monarchy could now no longer be a priority for the SPD.

When, at around 1 pm on Saturday 9 November, Prince Max handed his office over to Ebert he was acting unconstitutionally in a strict sense, but the element of continuity was sufficient to ensure the loyalty of the imperial bureaucracy to the new masters. When about an hour later Scheidemann proclaimed the republic from a window of the Reichstag building, one of his motives was to preempt the proclamation of a socialist republic by Karl Liebknecht from a balcony of the Schloss. Ebert was furious for he would still have preferred to preserve, however thinly, the veneer of monarchy, or at least to leave the decision to the constituent assembly to be elected. It was too late.[13]

A more pressing concern for Ebert on the afternoon of 9 November was how to retain the SPD's hold on the masses, against whom no effective force could now be mobilised. This meant completing his pact with the USPD and the forces to the left of it. Without their presence in the government it was unlikely that Ebert and his SPD colleagues could have survived in office at this moment and indeed during the next few weeks. Until now the SPD leaders had been inclined to continue in coalition with the bourgeois parties, but with Ebert instead of Prince Max in the lead. Events were overtaking this possibility. If the USPD, let alone representatives from further left, were to be brought into the government this could only be done on the basis of an all-socialist coalition and without the participation of bourgeois politicians. As it was there was strong feeling on the left against combining even with the SPD in a traditional governmental structure. The vision on the left was of a new, revolutionary system receiving its authority from the workers' and soldiers' councils that had arisen spontaneously all over Germany. Ebert's problem therefore was to achieve enough of a compromise with the moderates in the USPD to bring them into the government, so that its authority could be sustained until the election of a constituent assembly. He was prepared to make far-reaching concessions and even to bring Karl Liebknecht into the government. There was overwhelming pressure for socialist unity from the masses, who had no interest in the differences between their leaders. The outcome was the formation of a Council of People's Commissars (*Rat der Volksbeauftragten*), in which SPD and USPD held three seats each. The SPD commissars were Ebert, Scheidemann and Otto Landsberg; from the USPD came Hugo Haase, the chairman of the party, Wilhelm Dittmann and Emil Barth, representative of the Berlin Revolutionary Shop Stewards. The 'Russian' flavour of the titles was meant to proclaim the revolutionary credentials of the new government.[14]

The speed of events had sidelined the Berlin Revolutionary Shop Stewards, who, earlier in the week, had still hesitated to fix a date for an uprising in the city. Two reasons may account for the relatively late entry of Berlin, a radical stronghold, into the revolutionary movement: during the January strikes many of the most militant ringleaders had been arrested and sent to the front and the majority SPD had then taken great pains to restore its grip in the big Berlin factories. Now the Revolutionary Shop Stewards tried to regain control by convening a meeting of representatives from soldiers' and workers' councils, to be held on 10 November in the Zirkus Busch. The SPD organisation in Berlin managed to ensure that this meeting was not dominated by the radicals. Nevertheless there were stormy scenes and threats, but Ebert and the SPD leaders were left in possession of the field. The SPD–USPD coalition in the Council of People's Commissars was confirmed. An Executive Council (*Vollzugsrat*) of the workers' and soldiers' councils of Greater Berlin was established, which in theory was to control the Council of People's Commissars. In practice it never came anywhere near to exercising such an ambitious function. Its fluctuating membership included many moderates and non-party members, particularly from the soldiers' councils. It had no realistic chance against Ebert and his colleagues, backed by the whole apparatus of the bureaucracy.[15]

Ebert and the SPD had thus gone a long way in consolidating their power. Their position in radical Berlin was, however, far from secure and they had to act out a charade until they could acquire reliable forces to protect them. The Prussian minister of war Scheüch, who had retained his office, assured Ebert that he could provide protection, but he was soon to be proved wrong. Ebert and his SPD colleagues did not seek confrontation and bloodshed, but knew that they could not survive in Berlin by simply playing for time and appeasing the left. In the meantime an event had occurred that increased Ebert's confidence that the real levers of power would soon be at his disposal. On the evening of 10 November contact had been established between Ebert and Groener. We owe the account of the famous telephone call between the two men, along the secret wire linking the chancellery with GHQ, to Groener himself and it is tempting to overdramatise it. It did not foreclose any options about civil–military relations in the new regime. The phone call assured Ebert that the military apparatus was at his disposal, provided he could ensure the continuing authority of the general staff and the officer corps.[16]

There was nothing surprising about such an arrangement. The orderly return of the field army and its eventual demobilisation was one of the most pressing tasks facing the government and it was entirely natural for Ebert to think that it could only be discharged with the full cooperation of OHL. It was unthinkable to allow large numbers of German soldiers to become prisoners of war on the western front. This was a real danger if the expertise of the general staff was not available to bring the troops back to Germany within the tight timetable imposed by the Allies. OHL for its part needed the cooperation of the Council of People's Commissars to maintain its control over the troops and over discipline. The officers of the general staff and other regular officers who remained in the army saw themselves as guardians of a national continuity that transcended the particular form the state had assumed for the time being. The Kaiser's departure had released them from their personal loyalty to him and to the monarchy. They did not consider themselves as owing more than a temporary and pragmatic allegiance to the Council of People's Commissars and to the republic which succeeded it.

One of the first fruits of the understanding between Ebert and Groener was a telegram sent by the Council at the request of OHL asking the latter to order the army to respect the authority of officers, proclaiming the duty of soldiers' councils to prevent disorder and mutiny and giving them an advisory role only in matters of supply, leave and discipline.[17] This telegram was sent with the agreement of the USPD commissars, except Barth. Initially the relationship between the Ebert government and OHL was therefore one of mutual dependence. Ebert and his SPD colleagues are, however, open to criticism for their lack of attention to the civil–military problem in the ensuing weeks and for the naïvety of their trust in the good faith of OHL. Their preoccupation was with the escalating conflict with the radical left, barely disguised by the show of unity in the first few days after the revolution. In contrast most SPD leaders saw the right as so thoroughly beaten that it could pose no threat. Talk of counter-revolution was in their minds only a propaganda ploy by the left. In this divergence of perceptions the position of OHL and the officer corps became the central issue. A vicious circle became established: the SPD leaders were suspected by the left of being in league with the military remnants of the old regime and were branded as class traitors; as the rhetoric of the left became more venomous, the SPD leaders felt more threatened.

The military problem was not the only factor in the reemergence of the deep division in the German working-class movement, a division which came to dominate the course of the revolution. Another major issue between the Ebert government and the left arose from their different views of the workers' and soldiers' councils.[18] The name itself, conjuring up analogies with Russian models, was misleading and unnecessarily frightening. Councils sprang up spontaneously, their membership was mostly moderate, with the majority SPD in the ascendant, and in general they collaborated smoothly with the existing authorities. A major motivating force of the council movement was the anti-chaos instinct of the population, itself a factor severely limiting the scope of revolutionary change. The radical left dominated the councils only in a few of its strongholds. In places remote from the great industrial centres the councils were often controlled by middle-class officials and were mainly instruments for the maintenance of public order.

The soldiers' councils had many non-party members. With the progress of demobilisation their membership tended to fluctuate and their influence to wane. Insofar as any coherent aim or purpose can be attributed to so diverse and diffuse a movement, the councils were an expression of the widespread desire for a more democratic, less authoritarian and hierarchical society, and above all a wish to end the prevalence of military values. It is argued that they represented a valuable potential for democratisation that could have been used in the early phase of the revolution to lay firmer social foundations for the republic. There is much vagueness in such arguments. Socialisation of industry, the parcelling up of the great East Elbian estates, these were policies that were on the agenda, but for various reasons were not implemented. It is far from clear how the councils could have advanced such policies, all of which required legislation. It was not easy for the councils to initiate changes of personnel and get rid of officials of the *ancien regime*; they were too conscious of their lack of expertise.

The role of the councils was therefore difficult to define, but it was also the case that the SPD leaders had no concept whatsoever of such a role. Thus it was the radical left who came up with a council ideology and used it as a weapon in their struggle with the right. 'All power to the councils' was a slogan virtually synonymous with the dictatorship of the proletariat. For the extreme left this became the alternative to the election of a constituent assembly, seen by them as a recipe for counter-revolution. What was left of the councils by the end of 1918 reflected the dominance of the radicals. Not surprisingly this made Ebert and the SPD more determined than ever to reach the safe haven and the legitimacy of a constituent assembly elected by universal suffrage. The councils, always considered marginal, increasingly an embarrassment and eventually part of the threat from the left, no longer had a place in their scheme for the future.

From the perspective of the late twentieth century the rigorous reliance of the SPD on the democracy of the ballot appears correct and inevitable. Dictatorship of the proletariat and Leninism, let alone Stalinism, have proved historical dead ends which have exacted a high price in human happiness. In an advanced industrial society like Germany, where male workers had had a vote for half a century, the dictatorship of the proletariat would have meant regression not progress and was never a realistic option.

Ebert and the SPD may have been right in fundamentals, but they did not always cope well with their difficult situation. For many weeks they were condemned to follow an uneasy policy of appeasement towards the left, including the three USPD members of the government. They saw themselves as interim administrators for the period up to the election of the assembly. They referred to themselves as commissioners in bankruptcy for the defunct imperial regime. They therefore felt justified in postponing decisions, such as the socialisation of industry, that should properly be left to a democratically legitimated government. Such an attitude could easily become an alibi for an absence of ideas and for a failure of will. They genuinely hoped that a socialist majority would emerge from elections to be held as early as practicable and that socialist policies could then be implemented.

During the interim period the problems were daunting enough and the achievements of the Ebert government considerable. Armies had to be brought home and demobilised, work had to be found for the returning soldiers and industries converted to peacetime production. In a country still subject, till March

1919, to Allied blockade food supplies had to be secured and channelled to the great urban centres. Law and order had to be maintained and the cohesion of the Reich, threatened from many quarters, had to be safeguarded.

Everything was overshadowed by the question of whether a tolerable peace could be obtained from the Allies. A bare and incomplete recital of such problems shows the enormous difficulties and the constant pressure for major decisions faced by the Council of People's Commissars. It was hardly surprising that Ebert and his colleagues gave high priority to smooth collaboration with the officials inherited from the imperial regime and low priority to implementing socialist policies. The quasi-legal transfer of power on 9 November was recognised throughout the central bureaucracy and even if Ebert had doubts about the deeper and longer-term loyalties of these men he could only welcome their immediate willingness to work with his government.

Nevertheless important steps were taken, even in the first rush of revolution, signalling the intention of the new government to remove the many obstacles to full working-class emancipation inherited from the empire. The foundations were laid for the progressive social policies that became one of the hallmarks of the Weimar republic. Restrictions on the trade union rights of civil servants and state employees were removed in a proclamation of 12 November 1918, as were the restrictive conditions affecting workers on the large landed estates. The following day a decree about unemployment provision was promulgated, and in due course this was extended and refined in further decrees.[19] Nine years later the law for unemployment insurance was to become one of the most notable achievements of the republic.

In the meantime a series of meetings had taken place between prominent trade union leaders and industrialists which resulted in the announcement on 15 November 1918 of the establishment of a central committee between representatives of workers and employers (*Zentralarbeitsgemeinschaft*).[20] The announcement outlined a settlement between capital and labour which reflected the compromise upon which the new regime rested. The rights of the trade unions to represent the workers were fully recognised and the employers undertook to refrain in future from giving support to so-called yellow unions. There were to be legally binding wage agreements, compulsory arbitration and arbitration tribunals composed equally of representatives from both sides. Enterprises with more than fifty employees were to have a representative works council. The most important concession made by the employers was the eight-hour day. The *Zentralarbeitsgemeinschaft* was to institutionalise permanently the collaboration between capital and labour which force of circumstances had imposed on both sides.

The leaders of the free trade unions had, if anything even more than the politicians of the SPD, become involved with official policy during the war and had staked everything on a German victory. Their suspicion of the left and distrust of radicalism among their followers was no less profound than the same sentiments among SPD leaders. The revolution had taken them just as much by surprise. The employers, in the past fiercely anti-union and committed to the *Herr im Haus* (master in the house) attitude, were alarmed and chastened by defeat and revolution. They feared socialisation and expropriation and, with all their traditional sources of support collapsing around them, an agreement with the unions seemed the only escape route left by October 1918. Carl Legien, the foremost figure in the free trade union movement, and others knew that any concessions the employers might make in their moment of panic might later be whittled away. Nevertheless they thought an agreement worth while, fearful as they were of losing control of the radicalised workers. They acclaimed the concessions made to them as a great success, as they undoubtedly would have been before October.

The central committee agreement was thus the exact counterpart in the industrial sphere of the moderate course that was the essence of SPD policy. It was ominous that even a right wing union leader in the Ruhr, when given his first hint of the negotiations with the industrialists, including the notorious Hugo Stinnes, exclaimed 'With Stinnes? Are you mad? He will be hanged!'[21]

CONFRONTATION WITH THE LEFT AND SPARTACIST UPRISING

Whatever violence the future might hold, the initial changes following 9 November had been accomplished in most parts of Germany with surprising ease and little bloodshed. The kings and

princes had departed, but the state apparatus over which they
had presided was still there. Only the military part of it seemed to
be on the way out. Some symbols and insignia had been hastily
removed and others substituted according to taste. Officers were
wary of appearing publicly in uniform. Arthur Rosenberg, an
active member of the radical left, wrote in the late 1920s an
analysis of the revolution and Weimar which has much influenced
later historiography. His verdict was: 'The Government of 10
November was in fact the rule of the old Reichstag majority,
extended by the right wing of the USPD and with a slight socialist
ornamentation.'[22] Apart from those who had actively participated
in the revolutionary events, little enthusiasm could be detected
among the masses. For them it was the deserved collapse of the old
order, but no vision of an exciting future. Above all there was a
desire that the severe economic hardships of the war should be
quickly eased. There was a determination to make up for lost time
by hectic pursuit of pleasure and entertainment.

The atmosphere of business and pleasure as usual was
deceptive. However effective the Ebert government might be in
keeping chaos at bay and ensuring an orderly transition from war
to peace, nothing could avoid the continuation of severe hardship,
great dislocation and accelerating inflation. With the Allied
blockade still in place for the time being, it would take a long
time for Germany to recover her place in the international
economy.

It was against this unpromising backgound that the events of
the next few weeks unfolded. They were dominated by the
growing confrontation between the Ebert government and the
radical left, while the right, the bureaucracy, the middle classes
and not least OHL recovered their breath. In Berlin the tussle
between the Council of People's Commissars and the executive
council set up on 10 November institutionalised this clash. The
cards were stacked in favour of the government, backed by the
resources of the bureaucracy, while the *Vollzugsrat* often dege-
nerated into farce. Its chairman, Richard Müller, on the left of the
USPD, declared that the path to the constituent assembly would
be over his dead body. This earned him the nickname 'Müller the
Corpse'. Ebert dominated the government, but its three USPD
members had constantly to look over their shoulders at their
heterogeneous, radicalised followers. On 29 November Scheidemann wrote in his diary: 'Ebert, Landsberg and I repeatedly

faced the question whether we should allow matters to come to a break with Haase, Dittmann and Barth. It was at times intolerable to deal with these cowardly sitters-on-the-fence, who out of fear of Spartakus do not dare follow their own convictions, who in everything first look over their shoulders at the paper tigers around Liebknecht. In the long run it is quite insupportable that for every minute detail we have to engage in wrestling matches with the three gentlemen from the USPD – day after day, hour after hour, which must always end in compromise if there is to be no breach.'[23] December was to bring these tensions to a head and the role of the military became central in escalating them.

The bargain struck in the telephone call between Ebert and Groener had been between equals, but the situation quickly tilted in favour of OHL. Groener and the officers of the general staff worked with determination to recover their position as a major centre of power. They experienced great difficulty in amassing a body of troops on which they could rely, but they finally succeeded. Against this Ebert and his colleagues were not only unable to give the military problem much attention, but their attempts to set up a force with reliable republican loyalties met with little success. They discussed the formation of a republican guard and on 6 December promulgated a law for the formation of a voluntary people's militia. This project was largely stillborn because OHL, charged with its implementation, had no interest in pursuing it.

The real obstacle to the formation of a reliable republican force was the deep-seated and long-standing anti-militarism and pacifism of the socialist movement, greatly reinforced by the recent experience of war, militarism and defeat. There was no enthusiasm among workers for joining such a force and no clear ideas among the leaders about the constitution of it. The current deep divisions in the labour movement would have made the practical problems of recruiting it almost insoluble. Thus the Ebert government, increasingly under threat in the radicalised capital, had little alternative but to rely for protection on such forces as OHL could make available. There is no sign in the recorded discussions of Ebert and his colleagues that they were alarmed by the speed with which this situation brought about the resurrection of OHL as a major power factor. In the circumstances the Ebert government had to take on trust the manner in which the troops were used and where their real loyalties lay.[24]

An early indication of the shifting power balance were the bloody events of 6 December in Berlin. Troops moved in on to the chancellery and tried to proclaim Ebert president. Others tried to arrest the Berlin *Vollzugsrat*. Behind these moves were officials in the foreign office and the chancellery, among them Colonel von Haeften, the representative of OHL at the chancellery. The Spartakus League called a counter demonstration and in the ensuing clash 16 demonstrators were killed and 12 were seriously wounded. On 10 December troops returned to Berlin from the front, a prospect which aroused deep suspicion among the left. Ebert, when welcoming the troops, said 'no enemy has defeated you', a remark which could easily be interpreted as an early version of the stab in the back myth. In fact any hopes OHL might have had that these troops could be used to maintain order in Berlin proved illusory. Most of them melted away, so great was the urge of the returning soldiers to go home.

It looked unlikely that OHL would be able to maintain control over any part of the returning field army. In early December a congress of soldiers' councils at Bad Ems had demanded far-reaching changes in military discipline, the abolition of salutes and of separate officers' messes, and the right of participation by the councils in all economic, social and disciplinary questions as well as full trade union rights.[25] Although these demands were relatively moderate, OHL campaigned desperately against them, insisting on the maintenance of military discipline as called for in the order of the Council of People's Commissars of 12 November.

The next major moment of decision was the meeting of the first general congress of workers' and soldiers' councils, held in Berlin from 16 to 21 December. It had been called by the Berlin executive committee on the basis of one delegate per 200 000 inhabitants and per 100 000 soldiers. Elections had been held at *Land*, provincial and district meetings of the councils. Out of over 500 delegates about 300 belonged to the SPD and about 100 to the USPD. Neither Rosa Luxemburg nor Karl Liebknecht received a mandate and a proposal to admit them as guests with a consultative voice was rejected. The numerical weakness of the Spartakus League and other extreme left-wing groups was thus again strikingly revealed. This did not diminish the psychological impact of their propaganda, nor the fears aroused by their verbal violence among the middle classes and on the right wing of the SPD.

Nevertheless this congress proved to be a milestone in the Ebert government's success in moving with all due speed to the election of a constituent assembly. A decisive vote of 344 to 98, on 19 December, rejected a proposal to base the future of the country on a council system and by an even larger majority adopted the early date of 19 January 1919 as the day for national elections to the constituent assembly. Ebert's overall strategy was powerfully reinforced. Fear of 'Russian conditions', the realisation that only a universally elected government could hope to conclude a tolerable peace, such fundamental perceptions prevailed.

On the military problem the congress was, however, much closer to the views of the extreme and even of the moderate left. There was widespread fear of the growing pretensions of the military and of their counter-revolutionary intentions, reinforced by the underlying anti-militarism that had fuelled the whole revolutionary movement. These feelings were strengthened by the fate of the Marine division, which had been brought to Berlin in the early days of the revolution to protect the new government and which was quartered in the Berlin Schloss. It had proved unreliable and its disbandment was demanded by the military authorities. The sailors were accused of stealing art treasures from the castle, but they refused to move until they had been paid. By Christmas Eve this situation was to lead to violent clashes which precipitated the departure of the three USPD commissars from the Council of People's Commissars. At the congress the emotions aroused led to the endorsement of the so-called Hamburg points regarding the control of the military. As a symbol 'of the destruction of militarism and the abolition of blind obedience' all insignias of rank were to be abolished. Soldiers would elect their own leaders and discipline was to be a matter for the councils. There was to be no standing army, only a popular militia.

The congress also opposed the dilatory policy of the Ebert government in the socialisation of industry, by instructing it to proceed to the immediate socialisation of all industries suitable for such treatment, especially the coal mines. The adoption of the Hamburg points and the socialisation demands showed that even among the SPD delegates there was a strong feeling that the fruits of revolution had not been fully secured and that there was a danger of counter-revolution reinforced by military power. The passage of these resolutions had, however, virtually no practical consequences. The treatment of socialisation continued to be a long drawn-out affair which eventually ran into the sand.

In the more pressing and vital matter of military control Ebert found himself immediately confronted by the categorical refusal of OHL to accept the Hamburg points and by the threatened resignations of Hindenburg and Groener. The failure of the Ebert government to develop a policy for a republican army now came home to roost. Ebert had to accept what OHL could scrape together – *Freikorps* without any loyalty to the republic and which quickly became hotbeds for counter-revolution and renascent chauvinism.

Before the council congress dispersed it established a central council (*Zentralrat*) which was to exercise that control over the Council of People's Commissars which the Berlin *Vollzugsrat* had so signally failed to maintain. The terms under which the central council was to exert its control became a matter of dispute between the SPD and the USPD. The paradoxical result was that the USPD, stretched to breaking point by its inherent incompatibilities, voted to boycott the central council. It was therefore composed entirely of SPD members and all attempts by the councils to exert some control over Ebert's government effectively collapsed.[26]

By late December 1918 the strategy pursued by Ebert and the SPD after the military collapse of the empire was thus still being vindicated by events. Only the final endorsement, due to be given by the constituent assembly elections on 19 January 1919, was still lacking. Nevertheless disillusionment with the limited results of the revolution was rising among the workers. Economic hardship soon began to produce strikes, uprisings and conditions amounting to civil war in many parts of the country. This second, more violent, phase of upheaval began with the clashes round the Berlin Schloss at Christmas 1918 and did not end until the Ruhr uprising after the Kapp Putsch of March 1920, or the communist risings in central Germany and Hamburg in the spring of 1921. Even the attempt at a German 'October' in the autumn of 1923 can still be seen as an effort to revive a revolution that had not lived up to its promise.

All these attempts to produce belatedly the revolutionary results that had not materialised in the first flush were doomed to failure. Violence had been at a remarkably low level in the first few weeks, for the forces of resistance were demoralised and discredited, but this phase was now definitely over. The divisions on the left deepened, the mood of compromise and new beginning, which had produced cooperation between middle and working classes, evaporated. Among much of the population a feeling arose that the revolution and the republic had arisen from a temporary moment of defeat and disorientation that had best be forgotten. For many Germans the emergence from the post-revolutionary dreamland was completed when the terms of the Versailles treaty became public.

In Berlin the attempt to dissolve the Marine division and storm the Schloss turned into a fiasco for the troops OHL had mustered to crush the radicals in the capital. The episode heightened the hostility of the left wing of the Berlin workers towards the Ebert government. The funeral of the sailors killed in the fighting turned into a demonstration against the SPD leaders. Differences over the handling of the incident by Ebert and his failure to control the military authorities led to the long-awaited breach with the USPD. Their three representatives resigned from the Council of People's Commissars on 28 December 1918. The long balancing act in which the SPD leaders had been involved was at an end. There was, in their view, no longer any point in compromising with the radicals and the only course open was to confront them.

Some commentators, notably Arthur Rosenberg in his classical analysis of Weimar's failure,[27] have argued that it would have been better if the moderate USPD leaders like Haase and Dittmann had given up their struggle to remain linked to the extreme left and had remained inside the government. By resigning they lost what was left of USPD influence and perpetuated 'the split in the wrong place' started in 1917. Gustav Noske became one of the two new members of the government, with special responsibility for military and naval affairs. He emerged as the unambiguous exponent of the policy of working without qualms with the existing officer corps, asking no questions as to their loyalty and using the forces made available by them without compunction to suppress the radical left.

This policy was put into effect during the January disturbances in Berlin, known as the Spartacist uprising. At the end of December 1918, just as the USPD was leaving the government, the extreme left split off from the USPD and formed the Communist Party of Germany (KPD).[28] There were at least two distinct sections of the extreme left, the Spartakus League on the one hand and various smaller groups, mostly based in Bremen and Hamburg, on the other. The policy adopted in 1917 of staying within the USPD had been mainly that of Spartakus. It hoped to acquire through the USPD access to the mass following which it lacked. Events in November and December 1918, particularly the poor support for the extreme left at the council congress, showed that this was an illusion. Those who felt, like Liebknecht, that nothing was to be gained by remaining in the USPD, got the upper hand. At a congress of Spartakus, also attended by delegates from groups like the Bremen and Hamburg radicals, the decision was taken to found a separate party and the title *Kommunistische Partei Deutschlands* was adopted.

Rosa Luxemburg was, apart from Liebknecht, the leading figure in Spartakus, and much superior to him in intellect. She had regarded the foundation of a separate party as premature. A central point in her creed was the importance of spontaneity in mass action and therefore the need to develop the maturity of the masses. She had welcomed the Russian revolution and recognised the duty of all proletarians to support it. Nevertheless she was very critical of the Leninist concept of a cadre party, rejected its undemocratic implications and considered it totally unsuited to German conditions. 'Spartakus is not a party that seeks power through or over the proletariat. The Spartakus League is only the most purposeful section of the proletariat, which reminds the proletariat at every step of its historical task, which at every stage of the revolution upholds the final socialist goal . . . Spartakus will never take power except through the clear unambiguous will of the majority of the proletariat, never except by virtue of the conscious consent of the proletariat to the views, aims and methods of Spartakus.'[29]

Paradoxically these views meant that Luxemburg had to go along with actions which she knew to be doomed to failure and which would shortly lead to her death. Among those who made up the new KPD utopian expectations and revolutionary impatience were rife. They paid little attention to the reservations and caution implicit in the Luxemburg programme. Against her advice and that of the central leadership they decided to boycott the elections to the constituent assembly, thus depriving the new party of a means of mobilising a larger following. Their fury against the right-wing socialist leaders, fanned to white heat by the bloodshed in Berlin at Christmas, made them eager for another revolutionary push to overthrow the traitorous Ebert-Scheidemann government. The infant KPD did not follow the mature revolutionary ideology of Rosa Luxemburg, but it was even further removed from the Leninist-Stalinist cadre party which it later became.

The new KPD was certainly not the instigator or leader of the January uprising. It was precipitated by the removal from office of the Berlin police chief, Emil Eichhorn, a member of the USPD and of the KPD, on 4 January 1919. This was a natural consequence of the departure of the USPD commissars from the government, paralleled by a similar departure of USPD members from the Prussian government, which controlled the Berlin police. It seemed an immense provocation to the whole of the Berlin left. The USPD and the Revolutionary Shop Stewards issued an appeal for a demonstration, which the KPD had to join if it was not to be sidelined. 'Workers, comrades! You cannot, you must not tolerate this! Come out on mighty mass demonstrations. Show the tyrants of today your power; show that the revolutionary spirit of November has not died in you!' The demonstrations took on a momentum of their own and led to the spontaneous occupation of newspaper and printing offices, including that of *Vorwärts*, the SPD party organ. The control of the party press by the right wing had for a long time been a symbol to the left of the betrayal of the masses and the fabrication of false consciousness.

The Ebert government tried to protect itself by calling for a massive counter-demonstration in the Wilhelmstrasse. The wording of their appeal conveys something of the mood: 'For a second time armed bandits of the Spartakus League have occupied the *Vorwärts* building. The leaders of these bandits have proclaimed in public speeches the violent overthrow of the government, murder, bloody civil war and establishment of a Spartakus dictatorship . . . Anarchy and hunger would be the consequence . . . our patience is at an end!'[30]

The spontaneous action of the masses and an over-optimistic assessment of the military position had indeed induced the hastily formed revolutionary committee to widen the protest against Eichhorn's dismissal into an attempt to overthrow the government. Once again the leaders followed the masses, none more so than the Spartakus leaders, now absorbed into the KPD. Liebknecht could never resist the scent of revolution, Luxemburg had to follow the spontaneous move of the masses, however ill-

timed it was in her view. The Ebert government had grown
thoroughly tired of its exposed position in Berlin, which had on
occasions compelled Ebert and his colleagues to leave their offices
by fleeing over roof tops and through back gardens.

Only now was the Ebert–Groener pact fully consummated.
OHL, which had for weeks tried unsuccessfully to cleanse Berlin of
the radical left, was now given the opportunity to use some of the
'loyal' troops it had been gradually assembling. The recruitment
of volunteer forces, *Freikorps*, was gathering momentum. It had
not been OHL's first choice to recruit such irregular, mercenary
formations whose very nature contradicted the traditional notions
of the Prussian army. Yet the idea of recruiting them was born at
the very moment of revolution, as the unreliability of what
remained of the regular army became clearer by the day.

The Freikorps varied considerably in size and permanence and
there is no complete record of them. Generally they were recruited
by former imperial officers and were known by the names of their
commanders, for example the Brigade Ehrhardt or the Freikorps
Rossbach. Front line officers and NCOs from the imperial army
were common in their ranks, as were university students.
Although one of their main tasks was to defend the republican
government, contempt for the republic and its politicians was rife
in their ranks from the beginnning. The type of the *miles perpetuus*
was characteristic of the Freikorps: many who had fought in the
trenches in daily confrontation with death found themselves
permanently alienated from civil society. There was deep hatred
of the cowardly and complacent bourgeois, which could lead to
sympathy with the proletarian enemy in the civil war of 1919.

Similar contradictions could be seen in the many Freikorps
established in the Baltic and the eastern provinces. Although
fighting Bolsheviks was one of their main tasks they were attracted
by the apparently new revolutionary society of the east and were
virulently anti-western and anti-democratic. The quarter of a
million men eventually in the Freikorps constituted a highly
volatile, unstable element, where the extremes of right and left
often came close to each other. Theirs was a spirit more easily
conjured up than dispersed again.[31] A newspaper of the SPD
aptly described the danger posed by the Freikorps in an article
entitled 'Are we willing to let militarism throttle the revolution ?':
'The Freikorps are tight formations along the old model and
methods, in which officers and NCOs displeased with the

revolution have come together in military service. At present they serve the Social Democratic government in the protection of the eastern borders and at home. What guarantee have we that tomorrow they will not turn their machine guns against the revolution and the government?'[32]

In the Berlin area these forces were now under the command of General von Lüttwitz, who was later to play a leading role in the Kapp Putsch. Noske was in political control of the operations, a task which according to his own testimony he accepted with the words 'So be it! Someone must be the bloodhound – I don't shirk the responsibility!' Desperate attempts were made to end the occupation of the newspaper buildings by negotiation, but when they failed Noske determined to crush the left with a decisive show of force. He accepted the arguments of the generals and officers around him that anything less would damage the morale of the newly recruited forces. Much of the fighting was in fact done by republican volunteer forces available in Berlin, but most of the acts of brutality and terror were committed by the Freikorps unleashed at a stage when, had a policy of minimum force prevailed, they were mostly no longer needed. The most notorious atrocity was the murder of Liebknecht and Luxemburg on 15 January, four days after the *Vorwärts* building had been retaken. It is said that when Ebert heard the news he was more deeply shaken than at any time during the tumultuous events of those weeks. Deep damage had been done to the reputation of his government and ineradicable scars had been inflicted on the German labour movement. The damage was not mitigated by the inadequate judicial proceedings subsequently taken against the suspected murderers and their superior officers.[33]

The January rising in Berlin was paralleled by similar events in other parts of Germany. These formed the beginning of that second and more violent part of the revolution, often amounting to civil war, which continued at least until 1920. The events of January 1919 have been called the revolution's Battle of the Marne. On 13 January Karl Kautsky wrote: 'From a purely military point of view the government was entitled to refuse to negotiate. It was in the stronger position and could be sure of crushing the uprising, but quite apart from considerations of humanity, it has lost the firm political ground it held. No doubt the government will be victorious and will gain in strength, but the bourgeois and military elements, with whose aid it has triumphed, will gain even more power ... as a socialist proletarian government it has become weaker. The bourgeois element and the officers are again feeling their weight, the danger of counter-revolution is now real. Unfortunately it is a danger brought on by the Spartacists who set out to fight against it . . . . There is now a danger that the logic of events will drive the government further to the right.'[34]

THE PARTIES AND THE ELECTIONS TO THE CONSTITUENT ASSEMBLY

Within days of the crushing of the Berlin uprising the elections to the constituent assembly (*Nationalversammlung*) were held on 19 January 1919 and a week later the Prussian Landtag was elected. There were also elections to the parliaments of many German *Länder*, including Bavaria. After the violent confrontation in the streets the politics of the ballot box once again became crucial.

Another continuity had maintained itself across the upheavals of the previous weeks: the party system of the imperial era. It was broadly a five-party system, comprising the conservatives, the Catholic Centre Party, the National Liberals, the Progressives or left liberals and the socialist left. This party landscape did not change fundamentally. The new foundation on the left, the KPD, was not of immediate electoral importance, since it had decided to boycott these elections. It was not until 1922, when it acquired most of the mass following of the USPD, that it became a significant electoral force.

On the right the two conservative parties of the imperial period and some right-wing National Liberals formed themselves into the *Deutschnationale Volkspartei* (DNVP).[35] All leading Conservatives had right up to the revolution fought against an electoral law based on equality and had tried to save what they could of the three-tier electoral system in Prussia. On the basis of this system the two conservative parties had in the last Prussian Landtag elections in 1913 obtained 200 out of 443 seats, while the SPD had only nine. Yet the SPD had in the Reichstag elections of 1912 obtained nearly 35 per cent of the vote and 110 out of about 400 seats.

There were thus some features of the new regime, such as universal suffrage, which imposed fundamental changes of attitude on conservatives. This can be seen from the fact that they now had to call themselves a *Volkspartei*. They refused, however, to accept some of the other major changes of the great upheaval of 1918–19. They remained an avowedly monarchist party. Their strongholds continued to be in the agricultural areas east of the Elbe and they were a Protestant party, though not to the extent that the Centre Party was a Catholic one. The DNVP took over much of the ideological stock-in-trade of German conservatism, such as emphasis on private property and enterprise, but with some reservations towards pure market capitalism. Farmers and the *Mittelstand* were singled out as constituencies particularly worthy of respect, while in keeping with the spirit of the times much was made of social policy in the Bismarckian paternalist tradition.

The leaders of the former Free Conservative Party, or *Reichspartei*, who in contrast to the *Deutsch-Konservative* came from industry rather than from the big Junker estates, were most concerned to adjust the new party to republican realities. The DNVP also gave house room to the racialist, anti-Semitic section of opinion and was linked to organisations like the Pan-German League, though in 1922 some of these leaders and supporters split off to form the *Deutsch-Völkische Freiheitspartei* (German Racialist Freedom Party, DVFP).

Thus the DNVP, for all its attempts at a popular image, could not shake off its links with the discredited past. As the mood changed, it became the main receptacle for the reaction against the revolution and the republic and from 1924 to 1928 it was the second largest party. This confronted the party with a dilemma, for many of the interest groups that were linked to it now wanted the party to participate in republican politics. The DNVP thus entered several coalitions after 1924 and used its position in government to press for policies such as protective tariffs on agricultural commodities. Yet its fundamental opposition to the republic itself and to many of its policies remained strong. This dilemma weakened the electoral position of the party and in 1928 it lost about a third of its support. This eventually benefited the more extreme right in the shape of the Hitler movement.

The Centre Party (*Zentrum*) was along with the SPD the party that maintained most continuity through the revolutionary period.[36] It had long ceased to be the oppositional force it was when the *Kulturkampf* brought it to maturity in the 1870s. Those

Catholics who gave it their allegiance, about half the nominal
Catholic population, wanted to leave any suggestion of second-
class citizenship behind them. The rise of secularism and the
consequent gradual decline of the Centre Party vote had led some
prominent figures in the organisation to advocate turning it into
an interconfessional party. These efforts had succeeded only in
causing fierce strife in the party, with the Vatican ranged against
the reformers. During the war the Centre Party was second to
none in its professions of patriotism and even annexationism.
Under the influence of its most highly profiled leader, Matthias
Erzberger, on the left of the party, the Centre Party did, however,
join the SPD and the Liberals in the Interparty Committee and
voted for the peace resolution in July 1917.

The coalition which had come into being under Prince Max of
Baden, and which was resumed after the constituent assembly
elections, had existed therefore in embryo since 1917. It was,
however, not certain that this disposition to collaborate with the
SPD and the Progressive Party would survive the revolutionary
turmoil. Although the Centre Party had a strong working-class
wing, particularly in the Rhineland, most of its followers were
essentially conservative and monarchist.

Immediately after the revolution the anti-republican sentiments
in the Centre Party were strengthened by the activities of the
naïvely atheist USPD Prussian minister of culture, Adolph
Hoffmann. He, and to a lesser extent his SPD colleague
Haenisch, had issued decrees affecting the place of religion in
schools. These decrees were deeply offensive to Catholics and
Protestants alike. Prayers were to be abolished and there was to be
no religious element in school festivities; teachers and pupils were
freed from any obligation to give or take part in religious lessons
and religion ceased to be an examinable subject. The storm of
protest aroused by these measures helped greatly to keep the
Centre Party in existence without even a change of name, when
some of the leaders had wanted to resume the prewar effort of
turning it into a non-denominational Christian–Social party. This
was not to happen until after the Second World War.

The anti-religious campaign also added momentum to a
campaign to separate the Rhenish provinces from Prussia and
set up a separate Rhineland state within the Reich.[37] One major
change did occur: the Bavarian wing of the party turned itself into
a separate party, the Bavarian People's Party (BVP), which from

1920 formed a separate parliamentary group in the Reichstag. It was more conservative than the Centre Party and opposed collaboration with the SPD. Political Catholicism always faced a dilemma in the Weimar period, for pluralist democracy was fundamentally incompatible with the exclusive claims of Catholic doctrine. More specifically, the marriage between the Centre Party and the SPD, a cornerstone of the republic especially in Prussia, could never be unclouded. Catholicism and 'godless Marxism' were irreconcilable.

The Progressive Party (*Fortschrittliche Volkspartei*) was the third component, in addition to the MSPD and the Centre Party, in the parliamentary coalition that had begun to form in 1917. The National Liberal Party, the other party nominally liberal, cooperated with this coalition from time to time, but did not enter the government formed by Prince Max. After 9 November there was widespread feeling among Progressives and even some National Liberals that it was time for a new beginning based on a wholehearted acceptance of the regime. Only in this way could the middle classes play the political role that was their due.

These were the sentiments in the appeal for the foundation of a new party issued on 16 November. Among the signatories were personalities such as Theodor Wolff, the editor of the *Berliner Tageblatt* and a prominent critic of imperial policies, and Alfred Weber, the more radically democratic brother of Max. The appeal not only unreservedly accepted the democratic republic, but also envisaged measures of socialisation in 'monopolistic' areas of the economy and steps to limit large landholdings. It expressed the middle-class mood of the moment that the time had come to extend the hand of friendship to the working class. The founders of the new party did not want to be tainted by being associated with men who had until recently supported annexationist policies. This put a question mark over the inclusion in the new party of Gustav Stresemann, the powerful leader of the National Liberals in the Reichstag. While in domestic affairs Stresemann was prepared to back the demands of the parties on the Interparty Committee for a reform of the Prussian franchise, in foreign affairs he had acquired the reputation of being a henchman of Ludendorff.

Thus policies and personalities finally frustrated the foundation of a united liberal party. Instead there came into existence on the left the Democratic Party (*Deutsche Demokratische Partei*, DDP) and on the right the oddly named People's Party (*Deutsche Volkspartei*, DVP).[38] The DDP was initially strongly placed to catch the mood of fear and panic combined with repentance and idealism that gripped the German middle classes on the morrow of the revolution. Therefore it emerged as one of the three major parties from the elections of January 1919, but less than eighteen months later it had lost more than half of that support.

Some of this failure may be due to ideological and organisational shortcomings evident from the beginning. Many of the academics and journalists who had given the DDP its initial stock of ideas were strongly committed to an honest attempt to bridge the gap between bourgeoisie and proletariat that had bedevilled German society. Most of these idealists and intellectuals soon left the party or were marginalised. The professional politicians who took over, mainly former Progressives, could not overcome the lack of a broad popular base that had long weakened German liberalism. The party became an increasingly ineffective interest party representing civil servants, academics, teachers, small farmers, shopkeepers and similar groups. Some of the DDP's losses initially, in 1920, benefited the DVP, but soon the latter also shared in the general decline of liberalism in the Weimar period.

At the outset the DVP was reserved in its acceptance of the republic and less willing to build bridges to the left. Some of the industrialists who supported it would have preferred to form a unified party with the DNVP. Later the DVP gained advantage from the strong leadership of Stresemann and from his realistic accommodation with the facts of life at home and abroad. The DVP was the party par excellence of industry and business. The divergence between the views of this interest group and the need, in the Stresemann era, to play a central role in republican politics in cooperation with the SPD placed a great strain on party unity.[39] Liberalism as an ideology had lost most of its power to fuel a political movement by the time of Weimar. As organisations the two liberal parties of the republic were still too reliant on *Honoratioren*, or notabilities, a condition that had already weakened them in the imperial era.

The electoral law under which the constituent assembly was elected was an early version of the pure proportional representation system in operation throughout the Weimar period. It produced a fairly precise correspondence between the percentage of the vote obtained by a party list in the country as a whole and the proportion of seats in the assembly allocated to it. There was no way then or later for the voter to record a preference for any specific name on a list. The voting age was lowered from 25 to 20 and women were given the vote equally with men. The result of the election was an overwhelming endorsement of the parties that had formed the Interparty Committee in 1917 and were about to form the Weimar coalition. The SPD (37.9 per cent), the Centre Party and the BVP (19.7 per cent) and DDP (18.5 per cent) together had more than 76 per cent of the vote and 329 out of 421 seats. The socialists, with 45.5 per cent of the vote, were well short of a majority; the radical left on its own, the USPD, only obtained 7.6 per cent. Ebert's constitutional and democratic course was thus endorsed by the voters.

The USPD was, however, strong in some industrial areas, central Germany, the Ruhr and Berlin, and in a few constituencies, for example Leipzig, it surpassed the SPD. If there was going to be further disillusionment among the industrial proletariat with the fruits of the revolution and with the bourgeois coalition entered into by their leaders, then much greater numbers of working-class voters might move further left. The SPD could not count on compensating for such losses by drawing support from other social groups. In January 1919 it markedly improved its showing, compared with 1912, in a few predominantly agricultural areas in the eastern provinces of Prussia. More agricultural workers now probably voted for the SPD. Such support proved fickle and soon drifted back to parties much further to the right and this was also true of small farmers, among whom the SPD may have made some converts in 1919.

Most of the middle classes, including much of the *petit bourgeoisie*, voted for the DDP. Such a vote seemed to them 'a life insurance policy against the dreaded St. Bartholomew's Night'.[40] The strength of the Centre Party varied according to the denominational configuration of different regions. In the Protestant areas of Prussia east of the Elbe it was below 5 per cent, in the Catholic Rhineland, for example in Cologne, it reached nearly 60 per cent. In the Catholic areas of Bavaria the BVP, the Centre Party's sister party, averaged 40 per cent.

The result of the constituent assembly elections could have been anticipated from some of the Landtag elections held before 19 January 1919. As early as 22 December elections in the small duchy of Brunswick, with half a million inhabitants, had left the

USPD the smaller of the two socialist parties, with 24.3 per cent, against the SPD's 27.7 per cent and 21.8 per cent for the DDP. This was in spite of the fact that the USPD had become predominant in the Brunswick social democratic movement during the war and had assumed sole power in November 1918. In Baden, traditionally moderate, liberal as well as confessionally mixed, a coalition of the SPD, the Centre Party and the two liberal parties had taken office in November 1918. In the Landtag elections of 5 January 1919 the Centre Party became the largest party with 36.6 per cent, ahead of the SPD with 32.1 per cent and the DDP with 22.8 per cent. In Bavaria Eisner's USPD suffered a crushing defeat on 12 January with only 2.5 per cent of the vote; the BVP emerged as the largest party with 35 per cent, followed by the SPD with 33 per cent. In the important Prussian Landtag elections of 26 January the results were very similar to the Reich elections a week earlier: the SPD got 36.4 per cent, the USPD only 7.4 per cent, the Centre Party 22.3 per cent and the DDP 16.2 per cent.

While these elections showed support for the radical left to be very modest, except in a few strongholds, the same was true of the anti-republican parties of the right. The DNVP received only 10.3 per cent nationally and did significantly better only in a few areas of East Elbian Prussia. Stresemann's DVP, whose attitude to the republic was at this stage still equivocal, obtained 4.4 per cent nationally, an average exceeded only in a few areas like the Palatinate, which was part of Bavaria but had a Protestant majority. Overall these elections encouraged the hope that the German people were strongly behind a moderate, republican, democratic course.

THE DRAFTING OF THE WEIMAR CONSTITUTION

Weimar was chosen as the seat of the constituent assembly because of the insecure state of Berlin, and its sessions opened on 6 February. Its two principal tasks were to adopt a constitution and to conclude a peace treaty. It had to carry on its work against a background of civil war in many parts of Germany and in the knowledge that the cohesion of the Reich was under threat. On 10 February an interim constitution was adopted which formally ended the rule of the People's Commissars and re-established continuity with the parliamentary regime that had come into existence the previous October.

Rarely can a body of men who derived their authority from a revolution have surrendered it as willingly as Ebert and his colleagues. He himself was elected president, an office which gave him as much if not more authority than being head of the executive. Scheidemann became Prime minister in a cabinet of SPD, Centre Party and DDP ministers. A state committee (*Staatenausschuss*) was also formed to represent the separate states, roughly on the basis of their population, in the interim legislative process. All these steps to a considerable extent prejudged the shape of the constitution about to be considered.

It was also significant that as early as 15 November the People's Commissars had placed the preparatory work for the constitution in the hands of Hugo Preuss, a liberal academic strongly committed to the concept of a unitary democratic parliamentary state in the tradition of 1848, but who was in no way a socialist or an advocate of a council system. A Progressive and a Jew, Preuss had been denied a chair at a university and was a professor at the Berlin *Handelshochschule*. A socialist constitution, let alone a dictatorship of the proletariat based on councils, was never on the agenda nor were there any ideas around in the SPD or even the USPD on how such a system might look. It was only as the confrontation with the radical left developed that the notion of a council system as an alternative to a democratic parliamentary state took on a strong life of its own. Preuss and those who worked with him, including Max Weber, were concerned only with the details of the democratic parliamentary system.

The establishment of a unitary state to end the long history of German particularism was one of the main points in the early drafts put out by Preuss and his collaborators. This would have meant splitting up Prussia into a number of provinces, so as to give the unitary state provincial sub-units of roughly equal size. It would have fitted in with the widely held view that many of the faults of the second Reich derived from the predominance of Prussia with its archaic monarchical, militaristic constitution. It would also have facilitated the expected adhesion of Austria to the new state.

Events quickly overtook these aspirations. The different governments brought to power by the revolution in the various German states acquired a vested interest in their own survival.

Socialists of all persuasions had always believed in a unitary state
to overcome Germany's age-old divisions foisted on her by her
ruling dynasties, but when they were themselves in power they
began to feel differently. Eisner in Bavaria, for example, had need
to preserve his independence and distance from Berlin. Even the
SPD ministers who held office in the Prussian government no
longer wanted to see the end of their state. It was also argued that
the abolition of Prussia would facilitate the dismemberment of
Germany by the Allies. By the time the constituent assembly met
this mood was firmly established and found expression in the
formation of the state committee mentioned earlier, as well as in
the provision in the interim constitution that territorial changes to
the states required their consent. In the event the existence of the
historic German states continued in the Weimar Republic, but
with some modifications. The most considerable of these was the
amalgamation of the tiny former Saxon states into the Land of
Thuringia. The central government acquired greater powers in
the course of the Weimar period, particularly in matters of
taxation and finance. Nevertheless the governments of the larger
Länder remained significant factors, with their control of education
and the police. By an ironical twist of history, the Prussian
government, made up of the Weimar coalition parties for most of
the time till 1932, was an important bulwark of the republic. The
Bavarian government, by giving aid and comfort to the extreme
right between 1919 and 1923, had the opposite effect.[41]

In addition to the continued federalism three major features
became particularly characteristic of the Weimar constitutional
system. They are the strong position of the president, the electoral
system based on proportional representation and the provision of
a whole section concerned with the fundamental rights of citizens
and the social aims of the state. The president of the Reich
(*Reichspräsident*) was elected for a seven-year term by the whole
electorate. If no candidate obtained an absolute majority in the
election, there was a second ballot in which a mere plurality of
votes was sufficient to secure election. It was possible to introduce
new candidates in the second round. This was how Hindenburg
became a candidate when the procedure was used for the first
time in 1925.

A number of considerations led to the establishment of this
strong elective presidency. There was much discussion of the
French and American models. The Third Republic's method of

choosing a president through election by the two parliamentary chambers was thought to produce a head of state too weak for German circumstances. Therefore the American method of direct election by the people was preferred, but not enough attention was paid to the role played by a well-established party system in the election of an American president.

Another consideration which favoured a strongly legitimated presidency was the fear of leaving too much power with a parliament based, alone among all institutions of state, on popular sovereignty. Such 'parliamentary absolutism' was again judged unsuitable for German conditions. Men like Preuss believed in a balance of power and a president directly elected by the people would be a strong counterweight to a parliament also directly elected. There were a few warning voices raised against resurrecting 'a republican monarchy'. It was, however, precisely this long German tradition of looking up to an authority figure that made it seem dangerous to leave a vacuum at the top. In fact the president, though strong in popular legitimacy, could in normal times exercise his considerable executive powers only with the consent of the chancellor and his ministerial colleagues. There was thus a discrepancy between the formidable electoral process from which the president emerged and the fairly limited tasks required of him. He was in one respect like the American president, in another like the French president.[42]

There was, however, in case of emergencies, article 48 of the constitution. It enabled the president to intervene by armed force against a *Land* which failed to fulfil the obligations imposed upon it by the constitution and the laws of the Reich. It was therefore in the first instance a provision to cope with possible dangers arising from the continued federal structure of the Reich. Article 48 did, however, also empower the president to restore public law and order in the Reich as a whole, if necessary by armed force. To this end he could temporarily suspend some of the basic rights guaranteed by the constitution. Any such measures had, however, to be immediately notified to the Reichstag, which could render them invalid by voting against them.

In 1919 article 48 did not occasion a great deal of discussion or uneasiness. It was felt that such emergency powers were necessary and that the safeguards against abuse were sufficient. During Ebert's presidency over 130 emergency decrees were issued under article 48, including many dealing with economic rather than law and order problems. It was only when the Reichstag became deadlocked in 1930 that article 48 came into use as a permanent extra-constitutional way of governing. It then acquired its quasi-dictatorial significance because it was used by Hindenburg in conjunction with the presidential power of dissolving the Reichstag. Between his election in 1925 and the summer of 1930 Hindenburg did not, however, exceed his formal executive powers under the constitution and exercised them, when appropriate, with the consent of chancellor and cabinet.[43]

The president's considerable political importance, even in times of relative normality, stemmed mainly from the short-lived nature of Weimar cabinets. When Hitler formed his cabinet on 30 January 1933 it was the twenty-first cabinet since Scheidemann's on the morrow of the constituent assembly elections almost exactly fourteen years earlier. Between Scheidemann and Hitler eleven different men had held the office of chancellor. The main reason for this governmental instability was the multiplicity of parties produced by the system of proportional representation.

Many commentators have seen in this system one of the major causes of Weimar's failure.[44] The constitution itself did not lay down the details of the electoral system, only the principle of proportionality; the precise operation was defined in a law which went into force in time for the Reichstag elections of June 1920. Its main features were that for every 60 000 votes cast a seat in the Reichstag was allocated, so that the total number of seats in the Reichstag varied from election to election and depended on the degree of electoral participation. Votes which were insufficient to qualify for a seat in one of the 35 constituencies could ultimately be combined at the national level. A minimum of 30 001 votes could then gain one seat. The intention was to ensure that no votes would be lost and all votes would count equally. A slight barrier against very small splinter parties was built in: a party which did not get at least 30 000 votes in a single constituency could not have its votes aggregated at national level, and the number of seats obtained by national aggregation could not exceed those obtained at constituency level. Large parties and small parties regionally concentrated had thus a slight advantage over nationally dispersed small parties.

Otherwise the system was open to any party, however small, that satisfied the legal requirements. These provisions arose from an understandable reaction against the unfairness of the system in force before 1918. In Imperial Germany there had been no adjustment of constituency boundaries since 1871, in spite of the huge movements of population that had occurred. This in itself gravely disadvantaged the SPD, whose support came mainly from recently enlarged urban centres. Any party, such as the SPD, which stood outside the established consensus, suffered a further disadvantage in the pre-1918 system: it could not on the second ballot enter into alliances with other parties. There could be no such distortions under the Weimar system. On the other hand the new system minimised the link between the individual voter and his representative and maximised the power of party bureaucracies in controlling access to the Reichstag. The voter was confronted by a choice between a large number of different party lists. He was usually only dimly aware of the personalities that figured on these lists and could not make a choice between them. The name of a local candidate might appear on the ballot paper under the party name, but it was not a legal requirement. The voter had no control over the personalities that might stand for the party of his choice at local level. In any case the constituencies were far too large to make such personal links very meaningful.

There was never any possibility of the emergence of a two-party system in the Weimar period, since, as we have seen, much of the party system of Imperial Germany had survived the revolution. A country with as many religious and regional divisions as Germany was unlikely to find political expression in only two major parties. The electoral system adopted in 1920 did, however, encourage splinter parties and put little obstacle in the way of the further subdivision of parties. Nor did the electoral system itself put any barrier in the way of a rapid rise or decline of parties. Electoral trends were immediately translated into parliamentary seats.

None of this might necessarily have proved damaging in a country less shaken by crisis and with a more established democratic tradition. The number of genuine splinter parties in the Weimar Republic was no greater than in Imperial Germany and they were not the main cause of governmental instability. A more persistent difficulty in reaching compromises necessary to the formation and conducting of coalition cabinets lay in the rigidity of the larger parties. This ideological immobility might even have been reinforced if splinter parties had not provided a certain fluidity in the system. The reabsorption of the USPD into the SPD in 1922 made it, for example, more difficult for the reunited SPD to enter into coalition governments.

A fair electoral system, based on strict proportionality and including women, had been demanded by the SPD in its Erfurt programme of 1891. Although the party might have gained an absolute majority in 1919 if it had stuck to the imperial dual ballot electoral system, the refusal of the SPD leaders to abandon their long-cherished principles was part and parcel of their commendable determination to reach the safe haven of democratic legitimacy without equivocation. Both contemporary and subsequent commentators often blamed the electoral system too exclusively for the weaknesses of the republic as a whole.

Originally Preuss had wanted to make only limited reference to basic rights in the constitution. He was mindful of the prolonged discussions on this subject which had bogged down the assembly in Frankfurt in 1848. In fact the constitution emerged with a wide-ranging section of over sixty articles which not only defined the basic rights of citizens, but also gave constitutional expression to aspirations such as the sanctity of marriage or the equal rights of illegitimate children. Some of the economic aspirations of the left, which had become sidetracked in the course of the revolution, re-emerged in the constitution. Thus article 165 provided for the establishment of a Reich Council of Labour and a Reich Economic Council. This was given legislative expression in the controversial works council law of 1920, all that remained of the ambitious socialisation plans discussed in the earlier phases of the revolution. Even if many provisions in this part of the constitution remained only aspirations, they were not without importance in raising expectations. In its constitutional prospectus the Weimar Republic proclaimed itself as a state designed to satisfy the social needs of its citizens to an extent unprecedented in Germany. Even in an international context it was a progressive manifesto ahead of its time.[45]

In pursuit of democratic perfection the constitution also provided procedures for direct plebiscitary participation by the people in the legislative process. There was a preliminary process called a 'people's request' (*Volksbegehren*): if a tenth of those entitled to vote supported a properly worked out legislative proposal, by inscribing their names in the appropriate lists, then such a proposal had to be submitted to the Reichstag. If the Reichstag rejected the proposal, then it had to be submitted to a referendum (*Volksentscheid*). In practice a majority of the whole electorate, not merely of those actually voting, was required to turn the proposal into law. It was therefore very difficult for this procedure to achieve any result and it never did throughout the Weimar period.

It could, however, be used as a weapon of agitation, particularly by extremists. In 1926 the communists derived considerable advantage from promoting a proposal to expropriate the property of the former German ruling houses and forced the SPD into following their lead. In 1929 the NSDAP gained national prominence in agitating, alongside the DNVP, for a law imposing penal sanctions on any member of the cabinet or their plenipotentiaries who signed the Young Plan decisions. Thus these provisions, which on paper added an element of direct democracy on the Swiss model to the Weimar constitution, in practice served the purposes of the most determined enemies of that democracy.[46]

THE TREATY OF VERSAILLES AND THE BATTLE OVER ITS ACCEPTANCE

The deliberations on the constitution in the constituent assembly were relatively low key. Since the establishment of a parliamentary democracy was common ground between all the main parties, controversy centred on details.

A much more important matter in the eyes of the public and of the political establishment was the impending peace treaty. The implications of military defeat had overshadowed developments in Germany from the moment when at the end of September 1918, Ludendorff had pressed for an immediate armistice. Those forces in Germany that had asked for more moderate war aims and an approach based more on international cooperation and less on power were vindicated.

Even before 1914 there had always been a strand of opinion that was fully aware of Germany's growing links with the world economy and of the mutual interdependence of the advanced industrial countries of the world. Export-oriented industries like chemicals or electricals, which in Germany were technologically advanced, had always been open to such considerations. There was naturally no clear dividing line between such a point of view and the position held by so many representatives of heavy industry and the agrarian sector, who believed in autarky and the acquisition of markets, if necessary by conquest.

Even among German liberals nationalism was deeply embedded before 1914. Stresemann, who had started his career as an official of the trade association of export-oriented industries, became as a leading National Liberal an advocate of annexationism during the war. Eventually his policy as Weimar's long-serving foreign minister was based on the political and economic reintegration of Germany with the community of nations, provided it was combined with a full restoration of Germany as a great power.

Such a vision of the future was in essence what the Reichstag parties voting for the peace resolution in 1917 were trying to proclaim and it was these parties, in the shape of the Weimar coalition, that had now to cope with the consequences of defeat. Well before September 1918 German foreign policy makers like Kühlmann and, in the final phase, Hintze had perceived that the United States, so disastrously underestimated by the traditional élite, would have to become Germany's principal diplomatic interlocutor if military success proved unattainable. Secret contacts with American diplomats had gone on throughout 1918.

All this was obscured for the great mass of the German public by the last flare-up of exaggerated annexationist victory expectations following Brest-Litovsk and Ludendorff's spring offensive. The precipitate course of events in October 1918 left no time to prepare the wider public for a grand reorientation of German policy. Wilson's own successive notes to the German Government did not help. While the American president did have the ultimate aim of a peace without victors or vanquished, he was not unreasonably suspicious about the genuine nature of the change that had taken place in Germany. By dilatory tactics he hoped to weaken further the German position and drive the new but still suspect German government of Prince Max into a corner.

The Lansing note of 5 November 1918, which finally set in motion the departure of the German armistice delegation led by Erzberger, was with minor modifications based on the Fourteen Points. On any realistic assessment this was going to impose heavy territorial and material losses on Germany. Point VIII required the restoration of Alsace-Lorraine to France; point XIII called for an independent Polish state, a demand which was bound to impose territorial sacrifices on Germany. The Lansing note declared that evacuation of occupied territories must include compensation for all damage done to the civilian population.

Even if the situation in October 1918 had been better managed on the Allied as well as on the German side, the psychological readjustment required of the great majority of the German population was too great and the time for making it too short. A simplistic expectation was created among the masses that if they divested themselves of their discredited rulers with all possible haste, they would be spared the consequences of defeat. The prevailing view was that the armistice had been requested on the basis of Wilson's Fourteen Points and that anything that fell short of the German interpretation of the points represented unacceptable trickery. Thus a thoroughly unrealistic mood of illusion and aggrieved sense of national honour pervaded both the political establishment and public opinion at large as the process of peacemaking began.

The armistice agreement of 11 November 1918 anticipated many aspects of the ultimate peace settlement. In the West there was to be a return of all German-occupied territories and the permanent cession of Alsace-Lorraine was envisaged. The German areas on the left bank of the Rhine were to be occupied by the Allies. As a means of pressure the blockade was continued and there were to be far-reaching handovers of assets such as gold, foreign currency and railway rolling stock, anticipating later reparation demands. German forces were to be disarmed and demobilised to a low level. In the East the treaties of Brest–Litovsk, with Russia, and Bucharest, with Romania, were declared invalid, but German troops were to evacuate their current positions in former Russian territory, such as the Baltic states, only when the Allies demanded it. Indeed one of the major problems faced by the peacemakers was how to unravel the German hegemonial position in Eastern Europe, created as a result of the Russian collapse, without allowing the westward spread of Bolshevism. The armistice hardly fell short of a total submission of Germany to the victorious Allies. It came as a cold douche to the German government and a public high on illusions.[47]

Nevertheless the German government made extensive preparations for the peace negotiations in which they now hoped to engage. Presiding over these efforts was Count Brockdorff-

Rantzau, who took charge of German foreign policy in December 1918.[48] He was a liberal aristocrat, a professional diplomat with an internationalist outlook. He also had somewhat old-fashioned ideas of national honour. Brockdorff-Rantzau engaged a wide circle of advisers, prominent among them businessmen and bankers of again liberal and internationalist outlook, such as the Hamburg banker Max Warburg. All this was fuelled by the perception that German rehabilitation would have to begin with her economic recovery and that the restoration of the German economy was of international interest, above all shared by the United States and also Great Britain. It proved, however, very difficult to make such a vision effective in the existing political and military situation, particularly if it emanated from defeated Germany.

The course of the peace conference from its first meeting in January 1919 gave the Germans virtually no opportunity to engage in serious negotiations with their former enemies. The divisions on the Allied side, between Wilson's vision of a new world order on the one hand and the French requirement for security against a German revival, were so great that the hammering out of some kind of agreed settlement formed the main theme of the negotiations in Paris. If the Germans had been allowed to engage seriously in these negotiations the task of peacemaking would have become almost impossible. German hopes of separate and detailed talks with major and minor allies therefore never became a reality.

On 7 May 1919 the German delegation was asked to receive a completed draft of the treaty and invited to make written comments only. On this occasion Brockdorff-Rantzau delivered a speech from a seated position to express his utter contempt for the way the German delegation was being treated. He voiced perfectly the mood of impotent rage and the profound sense of injustice that was sweeping the German nation. The same sentiment was expressed by the chancellor Scheidemann when he declared a few days later that 'the hand must wither that put such shackles on itself and on us'. Even the most representative organ of the liberal press, the *Frankfurter Zeitung*, declared, on 8 May 1919, that 'in this document the delusions of an all-conquering materialism had reached ... their peak. If this draft, or a similar one, should be put into operation, then it is time to despair of the future of mankind.'[49]

The depth and unanimity of revulsion in Germany from the proposed treaty was above all due to article 231, the war guilt clause. It did not explicitly proclaim Germany's war guilt. Its wording was: 'The Allied and Associated Governments declare, and Germany acknowledges, that Germany and her allies are as perpetrators responsible for all the losses and damages suffered by the Allied and Associated Governments and their citizens, as a result of the war forced upon them by the attack of Germany and her allies.' The main purpose of the article was to pin on Germany the responsibility for reparations and to provide a moral justification for this responsibility.[50]

The reparations question had loomed increasingly large during the peace negotiations. The final and unfortunate outcome, which was to poison international relations for over a decade, was the product of the difficult economic and fiscal situation which a war of unprecedented destructiveness had created in most of the combatant nations. The leading politicians were under great pressure to mislead their public into thinking that the defeated enemy could be forced to make good these losses.

The notion that the Germans should be made to pay 'until the pips squeak' figured prominently in the British general election of 1918. National interests clashed on the definitions of damage and compensation. The French might initially have been satisfied if they had received a large measure of help in repairing the physical damage to their economically crucial northern departments. This could hardly have suited the British who had suffered great financial losses, but not much physical damage. The Americans were not prepared to forgo repayment of the loans which they had provided for the European belligerents, which in turn reinforced the need of the Europeans for heavy reparation payments. The British and American reluctance to support fully the French security requirements motivated the French into using reparations as a means of controlling the situation of Germany. Through reparations the German economy, still much stronger than the French, could be kept in a position of dependence while being brought back to full recovery. The differences over reparations and the complexity of the question made for a wide definition of German liability, which, given the climate of public opinion, had to be based on a moral responsibility. Even so it proved impossible to arrive at concrete figures, which were to be left to a future reparations commission. Meanwhile Germany was

obliged to make an interim payment of 20 billion gold marks by
May 1921.

The war guilt clause clinched the almost universal call for the
rejection of the treaty in Germany, unless it could be substantially
modified. Even on the left it was seen as an attempt to enslave the
German worker in perpetuity and the SPD party congress voted
for rejection. Brockdorff-Rantzau unleashed an avalanche of
counter-proposals, the tone of which struck even some members
of the cabinet as misconceived. On 16 June 1919 an Allied
ultimatum cut through all these illusions. A resumption of
hostilities would have been difficult for the Allies, but there was
a high degree of probability that the unity of the Reich, which the
treaty left intact, would not have survived it. The Scheidemann
Government fell, because the DDP was adamant on rejection and
left the coalition. Erzberger, who had all along been critical of
Brockdorff-Rantzau's way of making the German case and had
advised greater flexibility, played a decisive role in swinging his
own party, the Centre Party, towards acceptance. Another
decisive factor was that Groener emphasised the hopelessness of
military resistance. This counterbalanced indications that sections
of the army, particularly in the east, would revolt if the treaty was
accepted.

In the last resort the vote for acceptance was a vote for the
continuing unity of the Reich. It was ominous that this final vote
had to be accompanied by an acknowledgement from its
opponents that its supporters had acted from patriotic and
honourable motives. That this should have been judged necessary casts a lurid light on the circumstances in which the young
republic had to take up its poisoned inheritance. The conditions
under which Germany had to sign the treaty made it all too easy
to argue that it was in no sense an agreed peace settlement but an
imposition. Versailles was rarely referred to other than as a *Diktat*
or *Gewaltfrieden*, a dictated peace imposed by violence.[51]

Leaving aside the emotional issues of war guilt and reparations
the provisions of the treaty fall into four main categories:
territorial cessions, occupation of territory subject to time limits
and without permanent loss of sovereignty, limitation of forces
and armaments and demilitarised zones, and cession of economic
assets over and above reparation liabilities.

In the west the principal territorial cession was Alsace-
Lorraine, a forgone conclusion, which aroused relatively little

immediate resistance. There were minor adjustments of the German–Belgian frontier around Eupen and Malmedy. The future of Schleswig was subject to plebiscite, which in 1920 gave North Schleswig to Denmark and left the south with Germany. Much more deeply resented were the losses to Poland, West Prussia and Posen, which gave Poland direct access to the sea and left East Prussia separated from the main body of Germany by the so-called Polish corridor. It was a slight alleviation that Danzig remained a free city and that Upper Silesia's future was to be subject to a plebiscite, one of the two major changes to the original draft treaty secured by the German delegation. The other major change was that the Saar was only to be temporarily detached and its permanent future to be decided after fifteen years by plebiscite.

Any border line between Poland and Germany would have left sizeable ethnic groups on the wrong side and this settlement certainly left more than a million Germans under Polish sovereignty. The frontiers chosen did, however, have some historical validity, in that they were similar to the dividing line of 1772 between the rising state of Prussia and the then Polish state. The depth of German resentment can only be understood in the light of the tradition, going back at least into the nineteenth century, of growing hostility between German and Polish nationalism, tinged on the German side with racial contempt.

The German grievance about the eastern borders was aggravated by the fact the principle of national self-determination, central to Wilson's Fourteen Points, was here applied to Germany's disadvantage. Where it might have worked in her favour, in the case of Austria and the Sudeten areas, it was not applied. The Austrian provisional assembly had voted in November 1918 to join the German Reich. Even among German social democrats this evoked echoes of the dream of *Grossdeutschland* which had foundered in 1848. There was, however, sufficient realism in Berlin to dictate caution in the practical implementation of the step. Others saw such realism as cowardice and advocated confronting the Allies with a *fait accompli*. The veto on the *Anschluss* implicit in article 80 of the treaty of Versailles and formalised in the Treaty of St Germain with Austria reinforced the sense of injustice felt among virtually all sections of German opinion. It was claimed that German territorial losses had deprived the country of 14.6 per cent of its arable land, 74.5 per cent of its iron ore, 68.1 per cent of its zinc ore, and 26 per cent of its coal production.[52]

The main area of temporary occupation was the left bank of the Rhine, with bridgeheads at Mainz, Coblence and Cologne. That this area was not permanently detached from Germany was probably the single most important outcome of the peace negotiations. In conjunction with the failure of the American and British security guarantees for France to become valid, it left France at a permanent long-term disadvantage against Germany, in spite of victory and so many of the other treaty provisions. It explains the desperate French attempts during the next five years to secure the permanent safety which the treaty had failed to give her.

Nevertheless if these, albeit temporary, zones of occupation and demilitarisation are taken in conjunction with the drastic limits placed on German forces and armaments, Germany was effectively barred for the foreseeable future from becoming a great power again in a military sense. The major force limitations were a ceiling of 100 000 men on the army, of 15 000 on the navy, the prohibition of conscription and the abolition of the General Staff. Offensive weapons, such as tanks, aeroplanes and submarines, were not permitted. The reduction of the army presented the German government with an immediate problem, for it required the disbandment of what remained of the regular army and of the Freikorps which were still being recruited to fight the republic's internal battles and to fight, legitimately or otherwise, on Germany's eastern frontier.

The speed of demobilisation required by the Allies was a factor in the first major attempt to overthrow the republic from the right, the Kapp Putsch of March 1920. It is also often argued that in the longer run the creation of a small professional army, with a tightly-knit officer corps recruited mainly from the traditional Prussian military élite, contributed to making the Reichswehr a state within a state with only a conditional loyalty to the republic.[53]

Finally, the surrender was required of many economic assets: merchant marine, patents, overseas investments and property. The Allies were to be granted most-favoured-nation treatment and there was a five-year ban on protective tariffs. The loss of all German colonies was seen as a special attack on German honour, for it seemed to impugn Germany's ability to act as trustee for less developed peoples. Although many Germans regarded the League of Nations with suspicion as one more example of Wilsonian trickery and illusionism, Germany's exclusion from it was seen as another instance of the Allied determination to degrade their former enemy to a power of the second rank.

The extradition of German political figures seen in Allied countries as war criminals, led by the Kaiser, was regarded in Germany as a totally vindictive, dishonourable and insupportable demand. It caused the first major tussle between the Allies and the German government. The Dutch government in any case refused to hand over the Kaiser and official Germany remained totally adamant in its refusal to comply with this aspect of the treaty. All that was conceded was that proven war crimes, such as firing on civilians in lifeboats after a submarine sinking, would be tried in German courts. If there had been less pressure from without the republican elements in Germany might have been more inclined to bring to trial those who bore political responsibility before 1918. This would have helped to counter the myth of the 'November criminals'.[54]

The cliff-hanging drama around the rejection or acceptance of the peace terms in June 1919, personified in many people's minds by Brockdorff-Rantzau and Erzberger, highlighted the atmosphere of hysteria and unreason which engulfed most of the German public. The grand reorientation of Germany's vision of herself in the international community received a setback from which it never fully recovered, even if in due course underlying realities were bound to reassert themselves. An acute observer, the liberal theologian and sociologist Ernst Troeltsch, caught something of the prevailing total loss of composure: 'grim community of people, but the old legends about defeat due to Jews and SPD surface again . . . Prof. X calls the peace a catastrophe which could only happen to a people whipped up by Jews and SPD . . . Anglo-Saxon predominance, also Anglo-Saxon individualism . . . The European peoples will become bi-lingual and retain their own languages as dialects . . . . Brockdorff-Rantzau's no would only have been possible with a united nation, not with a heap of garbage sodden with decomposition and rottenness.' Even pacifists joined in the universal chorus of condemnation and self-pity. A German historian speaking on 16 June 1919 in commemoration of students fallen in the war said portentously: 'Our misfortune is boundless and we cannot reach its limits in our lifetime.'[55]

TURMOIL ON THE EASTERN BORDERS

The utter consternation of the moment completely obscured in most German minds two major underlying factors which were in due course to prove much more important and enduring than many treaty provisions that appeared for the time being to strip Germany of her status as a great power. These two factors were the continuing unity of the Reich and the weakness of her former great eastern antagonist, Russia. The agonising decision whether to sign or reject appeared itself to threaten the continuing unity of the Reich. There were rumours that Bavaria, with French encouragement, might go her own way. There was the separatist movement in the Rhineland, mainly directed against control from Berlin, which might, however, with French help become a movement to break away from the Reich.[56]

Even more menacing was the threat from the German forces strung out along the eastern borders from the Baltic to Silesia to form a separate *Oststaat* which would refuse to recognise the treaty. That such a threat could be made at all arose from the murky and uncertain situation on the eastern marches of the Reich from the moment that the armistice was signed. Article XII had permitted the German forces holding parts of former Russian territory a continuing role in keeping the Red Army out. It was part of the negotiating stance of the new republican government to present itself as a bastion against Bolshevism and this fitted in well with its domestic battle against the extreme left. On 5 November 1918 the Soviet ambassador in Berlin, Joffe, had been expelled because of financial and propaganda links that had come to light between him and the extreme left. The governments of Prince Max of Baden and of Ebert both wanted in principle to break with the previous policy of territorial acquisition in the Baltic. They realised that German policy could not in future be based on ensuring a privileged position for the Baltic Germans and that it was necessary to come to terms with the emerging nationalism of the Baltic nations.

With regard to Poland a highly confused and complicated position arose when the military collapse of the central powers became obvious. The policy of creating a satellite Poland, in which a great deal of effort had been invested by OHL and the imperial authorities right up to the moment of collapse, was clearly doomed. Nevertheless the Ebert government had to negotiate with the emerging pro-Allied Polish government of Pilsudski and Paderewski for the return of the German troops from the Ukraine. No German government, whatever its political colour, was willing to hand over large tracts of German territory, inhabited by hundreds of thousands of Germans as well as Poles, to the new Poland.

The Ebert government had by January 1919 been persuaded to sanction the recruitment of Freikorps for service in the Baltic. Groener moved his headquarters to Kolberg to be nearer the action on the Polish border and in the Baltic. The Berlin government had only imperfect control over these eastern forces, just as it could not control in detail the conduct of the forces used against left-wing risings elsewhere in the Reich. The Socialdemocrat August Winnig, who as *Reichskommissar* was put in charge of an orderly withdrawal from German responsibilities in the Baltic area, connived with local commanders who were trying to maintain the German position. Winnig belonged to the nationalist right of the party and left it in 1920.

Local Allied commanders in the Baltic also at times worked with the German commanders, when it seemed they could be used against Bolsheviks, but in general these efforts, particularly when directed against Poland, could only feed Allied and particularly French suspicions about German intentions. They therefore ran counter to German efforts to get into a dialogue with the Allies during the peace negotiations.

A flagrant example of this go-it-alone policy by German commanders in the east was the overthrow of the Latvian provisional government in favour of a government dominated by Baltic Germans in April 1919. The commander responsible was General von der Goltz, one of the many senior military figures still in positions of authority, whose loyalty to the republican government was tenuous. Von der Goltz and others like him dreamt of maintaining the German imperial position in Eastern Europe, linking up with White Russia and eventually using this position to remove the left-wing government in Berlin, defy the

Entente and overthrow the Versailles system. The links between
the Freikorps operating in the Baltic area and extreme right-wing
groups already plotting to overthrow the republic was soon to
become only too clear. The SPD was suspicious of the reactionary,
counter-revolutionary complex, connected with East Elbian
Junkerdom, that was operating on Germany's eastern marches.

Nevertheless the attitude of the Scheidemann government, and
particularly of influential ministers like Noske, remained ambivalent, nor could they give this matter, amid their many other
pressing preoccupations, much attention. German forces failed to
secure the province of Poznan from a Polish rising and Erzberger
signed, on 16 February 1919, the Trier armistice convention,
according to which German forces pulled back behind a
demarcation line west of the province.

On 24 April 1919 there was a discussion in the cabinet on the
situation in the east, following events in Latvia. Erzberger was in
favour of resurrecting links with the Lenin government, but
Brockdorff-Rantzau wanted, in view of the position in Paris, to
maintain the anti-Bolshevik stance. Groener tried to reassure
ministers that there was no counter-revolutionary threat from the
eastern forces and that it was inadvisable to withdraw and
demobilise prematurely. Groener was also attempting, through
military contacts with the Americans, to work for a solution that
would have maintained German sovereignty over what was to
become the Polish corridor, while still giving Poland, through
specially privileged road and rail links, direct access to the sea. In
the Baltic von der Goltz carried on with little control from Berlin.
His defeat of Soviet forces at Riga on 22 May 1919 undoubtedly
helped the cause of Baltic independence, but it could not salvage
either the German position in the Baltic or the future of the Baltic
Germans as a ruling class. Needless to say, German nationalists
saw this as one more betrayal of the German cause by the left.

In the meantime the Allies gradually reached the decision to
give up active intervention against the Bolshevik regime and
instead to maintain a *cordon sanitaire* in Eastern Europe against
both Russia and Germany. It was by no means a tidy decision and
left many loose ends. Nevertheless it put an end to any German
military role in that area and made Poland into the central factor
in the French alliance system of the interwar period. The fantasies
of German military hotheads about erecting a separate eastern

state as a counter to the acceptance of Versailles by Berlin evaporated. The repatriation and demobilisation of the German eastern forces became inevitable, but reinforced the putschist threat from the right within the Reich. In the longer run it was almost equally inevitable that German foreign policy would at some stage play the Russian card again in its efforts to revise Versailles and regain great-power status.[57]

LEFT-WING UPRISINGS AND THE BAVARIAN SOVIET REPUBLICS

The imposition of the peace treaty gave rise to profound disillusionment right across the German political spectrum and powerfully reinforced the anti-republican mood on the right. On the left, in the meantime, the disillusionment with the fruits of the revolution deepened. The second and more violent phase of revolution, of which the Spartacist rising in Berlin in January had been an early and spectacular harbinger, was sweeping across Germany in the first half of 1919. In place of the utopia that decades of socialist rhetoric had promised the working class, the German worker was experiencing growing hardship and, when he rose in protest, brutal repression by counter-revolutionary troops sent by his own leaders. At any rate this was the view that the variously assorted forces to the left of the SPD were encouraging him to take. The strikes and uprisings in many parts of Germany in 1919 were marked by many local variations, but violent social protest against economic hardship was their underlying motivation.[58]

The political groups tried to give a focus to this protest, by calls for the replacement of the parliamentary republic by a council system (*Räterepublik*), by demands for the socialisation of key industries, especially mining, often in a syndicalist, direct worker-control form. In general the left-wing groups, whether USPD or KPD, were following rather than leading the masses. The three most significant arenas for the revolutionary wave were the Ruhr, central Germany, and some big cities, of which Berlin and Munich were the most important.

In the so-called 'wild west' part of the Ruhr, with its major industrial centres of Duisburg, Mühlheim, Essen and Hamborn, a strike movement had started in December 1918, particularly round the town of Hamborn. This centre of coal mining, the population of which had increased from 11 000 in 1895 to 120 000 in 1914, starkly exhibited the social ills and the alienation of breakneck industrialisation. Yet the presence of large numbers of Catholic Poles among the recently arrived miners and the strength of the Centre Party left the SPD relatively weak before 1914. The German Mineworkers Union, usually known as the *Alte Verband* (Old Association), had been in the ascendant before the war in Hamborn and other radical areas of the 'wild west', but the cooperation between the union leaders and the authorities during the war and the disillusionment with the course of the revolution had estranged the rank-and-file from their leaders.

The eight-hour day agreed by the *Zentralarbeitsgemeinschaft* in November carried little conviction among the workers. They wanted shorter hours still and direct workers' control of the mines. By January 1919, when the crushing of the Berlin rising made emotions run high, over 80 000 miners, 15 per cent of those in the whole Ruhr, were on strike; by late February the figure was 180 000. The workers' and soldiers' council of Essen set up a Commission of Nine to negotiate with the Berlin government about the socialisation of the mines. In spite of their rivalries, all the three left-wing parties, SPD, USPD and KPD, were represented on the commission, for they knew that unless the spontaneous movement of the masses was canalised it would lead nowhere.

It was the basic dilemma inherent in all syndicalist aims that in the essentially post-revolutionary situation of 1919 only legal changes sanctioned by the government could change the facts of ownership. The Scheidemann government's response was governed by the overriding priority attached to economic survival. Coal production was indeed a key element in the German economy at that moment and the losses due to the strike movement were heavy. The government therefore took refuge behind the work of the socialisation commission, which had been established in November, and which by February 1919 had reached the conclusion that some form of social control of the coal mines was desirable.

Such vague commitments, which even if they had been carried out would have been far removed from the syndicalist aspirations of the workers, were insufficient to calm the storm of social protest spilling over into a near-civil war situation. In February 1919 the newly appointed commander of the Münster military district, General Watter, had clashed with the local soldiers' council, which wanted to enforce the Hamburg points, and had forcibly dissolved it. Further violent clashes between Freikorps' forces and workers' militias followed. These events precipitated the big strike movement in late February, but on the other hand loyalty to their colleagues in Berlin and the increasing radicalisation of the situation forced the local SPD leaders to drop their support for the strike. This for the moment condemned it to failure, but the underlying economic pressures from the workers, always now coupled with syndicalist demands, in no way subsided. The old Mineworkers Union tried in vain to control the demand for shorter hours, while such political control as was attempted increasingly came from the USPD and the KPD.

In April 1919 the strike movement reached a new peak, with nearly three-quarters of the miners on strike on one day. Carl Severing, destined to be one of the strong men of the SPD, was sent to the Ruhr as state commissioner, with the task of bringing the strike to an end and establishing some control over the military. He succeeded rather better in the first than the second of his allotted tasks. Further deep wounds were inflicted on the body of the German labour movement, from which it never fully recovered for the remainder of the Weimar period.[59]

The central German industrial area, with major centres like Halle and Merseburg, had already during the war become a stronghold of radicalism. By early 1919 the left wing of the USPD was dominant in this area, so that more than in the Ruhr the aims of the militant workers were politically focused around the demand for socialisation. There was little difference between the programme of 'socialisation from below' articulated by the central German USPD leader Wilhelm Koenen and the points put forward by the Essen Commission of Nine. At the end of February 1919 about 75 per cent of the work force in this region were on strike behind this programme. The response of the Scheidemann government was again a mixture of repression and apparent accommodation. The military occupation of Halle left 29 dead and 67 wounded among the population. Government proclamations made the most of the works councils already promised in earlier negotiations with the Essen Commission. For the time being this put an end to the central German general strike.[60]

In early March 1919 Berlin also became again the arena for fierce conflicts. Here the focus was almost entirely political, because with its varied industries and differentiated proletariat socialisation was not as powerful a slogan as in other industrial areas. Recognition of the council movement, application of the Hamburg points, the formation of a workers' militia, the release of political prisoners, all these were demands which indicated the deep disappointment of the Berlin workers with the way the revolution had developed and their profound suspicion of the SPD-led Scheidemann government. The Berlin SPD had to bow to these sentiments among their own followers and go along with a general strike. As elsewhere, promises by the government about the socialisation of mines and the future rights of the council movement enabled the Berlin SPD to change tack and after a few days the strike collapsed. Street fighting continued, however, and produced Noske's notorious order that 'every armed person found fighting against government troops was to be shot immediately'. The death toll in Berlin amounted to 1200.[61]

The revolutionary wave of the spring of 1919, a confusing amalgam of social protest, economic demands, utopian expectations and emotional backlash against counter-revolutionary excesses by the Freikorps, saw several local attempts to set up soviet republics, in Bremen, Brunswick and other centres of radicalism. All of them were short, utopian experiments, crushed with excessive force. Munich had the most lasting impact and arose out of the special and exceptional Bavarian circumstances.

The rise of Kurt Eisner to the leadership of the Bavarian revolution was itself the result of a wholly unusual constellation. The exceptional nature of the role he was briefly able to play was starkly revealed by the crushing defeat suffered by his party in the Landtag elections of 12 January 1919. Eisner adopted a fearless and idealistic, but sometimes also unrealistic, approach to many issues. He advocated, for example, an unreserved opening up of the German archives, so that the war guilt of Germany's imperial rulers might be fully revealed. Such attitudes earned him fierce hatred from the nationalist right. When he was assassinated on 21 February 1919 by Count Arco-Valley, a young army officer, he was about to announce, somewhat belatedly, his resignation. However great the hatred that Eisner had attracted, his violent death also revealed the deep and wide support his revolutionary endeavour had evoked among the population. Hundreds of thousands attended his funeral and the murder directly led to a period of confusion in Bavarian affairs which by April produced the short-lived attempts at setting up a soviet republic. The Bavarian establishment, when fully restored, preferred to forget and to suppress the memory of the profound impact of Eisner's personality, which was enhanced by his murder.[62]

An aspect of Eisner's impact was that the council movement, treated as an irrelevance by the SPD leaders at national level, was in Bavaria more conscious of its political mission. Although Eisner had failed dismally in the Landtag elections, his murder made the left more determined to back a council system as a real alternative to parliamentary rule. The Landtag, in which the SPD had 61 and the Bavarian People's Party 66 seats, was deadlocked and the coalition government formed by Hoffmann in mid-March 1919, made up of the SPD, the USPD, the Peasants' League and the DDP, had little strength. On the right much real power remained with the old bureaucracy, with citizen militias and fragments of the old Bavarian army under von Epp. Growing economic hardship, disillusionment with their leaders in the USPD and the SPD, the apparently successful proclamation of a soviet republic in Hungary, gave the slogan of 'all power to a council republic' increasing attraction. The call provided a political focus in a situation of great confusion and explosive discontent, just as the socialisation call had done in the Ruhr and Central Germany.

The young KPD, initially led in Bavaria by Max Levien and later by Eugene Leviné, sent from the Berlin party centre, tried to capitalise on the mass movement for its own purposes. That two Russian-born Jews should have played a role in these events soon became grist to the mill of extremist demagogues like Hitler. The KPD had in fact no part in the initial proclamation of a soviet republic on 8 April 1919. Some SPD leaders, on the other hand, judged it expedient to swim with the prevailing current. For the first few days the soviet republic was dominated by an oddly assorted crew of anarchists and idealists, some of them habitués of Schwabing coffee houses. The whole enterprise was highly unrealistic and irresponsible. A comic opera touch was not lacking: capitalism was to be abolished by 'free money'; the regime's foreign minister broke off relations with Berlin and informed Lenin by telegram of the unity of the Upper Bavarian proletariat. There was a positive aspect: idealists like the writers Gustav Landauer and Ernst Toller saw themselves lighting a torch for human freedom and emancipation, even if it should end in their own martyrdom.

On 13 April minor military successes by the Red Guards convinced Leviné, initially sceptical, that the time had come for the KPD to take over and elbow out the amateur anarchists. For the next three weeks a more repressive, but hardly more competent, tone prevailed. The Hoffmann government, which had taken refuge in northern Bavaria, in its turn came to the conclusion that only a serious military effort would crush the soviet republic. Reluctantly it sought outside aid, over which in the event it could exercise little control. With the help of Noske a force of 35 000 men was collected together and under the leadership of von Epp, to become 14 years later Hitler's *Reichsstatthalter* (governor) of Bavaria, entered Munich on 1 May 1919. Terrible vengeance was exacted and the white terror, with over 600 killed, far exceeded the red terror. More important in the long run was the trauma which afflicted the profoundly conservative and predominantly Catholic population of Bavaria. An atmosphere was created in which many were prepared to tolerate the excesses of the extreme right as a lesser evil. Among the urban working class the events produced, as elsewhere in the Reich, a swing to the left, of which the USPD was the beneficiary.[63]

The collapse of the soviet republic in Munich marked for the moment the end of open rebellion from the left. The deep discontents that had given rise to this second revolutionary wave were in no way eased. In spite of repression sporadic outbreaks of unrest and strikes continued. Of the three political parties of the left, the SPD was the most serious loser. Apathy and disillusionment afflicted its followers and for the time being the USPD was the beneficiary. The electoral strength of the SPD, which had survived so remarkably across all divisions engendered by war, defeat and revolution, began to crumble. The USPD became a large mass party, but this only made the task of giving itself coherence even more difficult. What has been called 'the senseless policy of abstention', upon which the party had embarked when its representatives left the central control council and the Council of People's Commissars in December 1918, continued to deprive it of the capacity to influence the course of events. The KPD tried opportunistically to mobilise the mass following it so far lacked by jumping on to every rolling bandwagon. Revolutionary activism and putschism were rife in its ranks anyhow and the problem of discipline and coherence was aggravated. For the aims of the left as a whole the balance sheet remained almost wholly negative. The second revolutionary wave could not move the state of affairs beyond where it had been left in November 1918.[64]

THE WAVE FROM THE RIGHT; SOCIAL AND FINANCIAL REFORMS

The drama of the dictated peace of Versailles, as the majority of Germans saw it, followed immediately upon the collapse of the violent and bloody second wave of revolution. In November 1918 the supporters of the old order had been in such a chastened mood that they were prepared to accept almost anything as the price of sheer survival. In the words of Thomas Mann, up to this point himself a man of the old order, they were '*windelweich*', as soft as a nappy. The willingness to give the new order a chance was reflected in the election results of January 1919. Outside the ranks of the working class, defined as the followers of the left-wing parties, they were still not converted to socialism, but they were prepared to collaborate with moderate socialists in a democratic, parliamentary order, which many of them had traditionally despised. After the summer of 1919 this mood had passed and gave way to bitter resentment. Since among the proletariat in a narrower sense there was also deep disillusionment with their leaders, the base of support for the republic was narrowing dangerously on the left as well as on the right.

In the autumn of 1919 there was universal talk of a 'wave from the right'. The right-wing opponents of the new order regained their breath and attacked the republic and its personalities with a brazenness unthinkable only a few months earlier. To quote Troeltsch again: 'It is again as in the days after the Bethmann crisis [in July 1917] and the immense sharpening of the domestic conflicts that followed. Nothing has been learnt and nothing forgotten. But now, since it is no longer possible to take it out on the enemy, one wants at least to force one's fellow citizens of a different persuasion to their knees, to take revenge on the revolution and on the defeatists, to justify the former holders of power and prepare for the new elections. The same blind obstinacy and irresponsible short-sightedness, which previously insisted on an impossible war policy, now wants total domestic confusion and subversion, to pave the way for the return of the old order or at least to pull the old enemy along into a common abyss . . . . The DNVP believes it can reappear as the former Conservative and the former Fatherland Party and can dispense with the veneer of a "people's party", which initially it thought it owed to the new order and which is now confined to a daily growing anti-Semitism. A section of the universities is now electing the sharpest war propagandists as *Rektors*, the students for the most part collect around their old associations and ideologies. The Protestant church prepares to become the conservative counterpole to the state founded by the revolution. In short, the in part deliberately planned, in part instinctively chosen foundations of the counter-revolution are becoming visible.'[65]

The Weimar coalition government which had to cope with this dangerous erosion of support was now headed by the Socialdemocrat Bauer. The DDP, having left the coalition over the acceptance of the peace treaty, rejoined it in October. When the new constitution came into force in August, elections were required for the presidency and for the Reichstag. Detailed electoral laws had, however, to be promulgated first and this was only done after much delay. The simple prolongation of Ebert's term of office did not cause too much controversy. The failure to hold early elections for the first Reichstag was, however, seen by the enemies of the republic as a sign of waning confidence among the coalition parties and further weakened the government's legitimacy. It was in such inauspicious circumstances that the Bauer government had to deal with three vital areas of uncompleted business: the question of socialisation and, connected with it, what, if any, form of worker participation was finally to be adopted; the reform of the financial and fiscal structure, where the absence of sufficient tax revenue at the Reich level had bedevilled German affairs since the 1870s; and the future shape of the armed forces, where the drastic reductions demanded in the peace treaty imposed heavy strains.

In spite of the promises made to insurgent workers in the spring, the government remained deeply reluctant to interfere with existing ownership arrangements in the mines and in industry and to grant anything more than strictly limited rights of codetermination to workers. Fear of production losses, fear of

'Russian conditions', fears among trade union leaders that their organisations might become redundant, all this inhibited meaningful action. As in so many other areas, the SPD and union leaders had not developed any practical ideas beyond the long ossified slogans of common ownership originally formulated by Marx.

The economics minister Rudolf Wissell advocated a form of corporatism. He was much influenced by the state secretary in his ministry, Wichard von Moellendorff, who had collaborated with Walther Rathenau during the war in bringing industry into partnership with the state. Moellendorff and Rathenau were men of affairs, who felt the need, in the German tradition, to be philosophers as well and who had read their Kant. They saw in corporatism, or *Gemeinwirtschaft*, tested in the war, the means of solving society's most crucial problem, bridging the gulf between capital and labour. There was a strange resemblance between such ideas and the picture sketched in 1920 by Oswald Spengler in his book *Prussianism and Socialism* (*Preussentum und Sozialismus*). Spengler, scanning the horizon for social forms to counter the decadence of the Weimar 'non-State', extolled the soldier-king Frederick William I and his capacity to make his subjects work for the greatness of his fledgling kingdom. Such authoritarian concepts came oddly from a socialist minister like Wissell.

A more positive interpretation of such an overlap of ideas between left and right would be to see it as an aspect of the consensus prevailing in the twilight period before the full rigours of defeat were borne in on the German public. Capital and labour, working and middle class seemed to be coming together. It could have been the foundation stone of a 'social republic', but there was also an element of fantasy in such a vision of social harmony. Nevertheless, in line with these ideas, two laws were passed in the spring of 1919 to regulate the coal and potash industries. These did little more than consolidate cartel arrangements for the sale of these products going back to the beginning of the century and strengthened during the war. They did nothing to give more say to the workers in these industries.

A general socialisation law also promulgated at this time was proclamatory and entailed no practical steps. The socialisation commission which had been set up the previous November resigned at this purely cosmetic treatment of its recommendations. Wissell eventually also resigned, for his colleagues found his ideas too much at variance with what they had always been taught to regard as socialism. But no progress was made with socialisation in this traditional sense. An argument constantly put forward by government ministers was that industries taken over by the state offered the Allies ready-made targets for seizure. There was no indication from the Allied side that such arguments had any substance.

The Weimar coalition government would undoubtedly have found it difficult to enact anything amounting to a clear-cut change of industrial ownership, for this would have met with opposition from the non-socialist partners in the coalition. The Centre Party, for example, had put opposition to socialisation and expropriation at the heart of its programme. The SPD, however, accelerated its loss of support among its traditional followers by doing so little to meet the demand for more worker participation. Constant appeals to maintain production, with the activities of the Freikorps in the background, were no substitute.[66]

Lack of action on the question of industrial ownership still left open the problem what was to become of workers' councils in so far as they were functioning at shop floor level. The general development was, as we have seen, that as the councils became radicalised official policy ceased to see any place for them in the scheme of things. Since elective democracy prevailed at all levels, from national to local, there was in practice no room for the duplication of representation. As the council movement declined in real significance, there was some attempt by radicals to revive it at the shopfloor level. The trade unions, initially hostile to works councils, gradually adopted a more flexible attitude. The bourgeois parties in the Weimar coalition, while never moving from their determination to maintain the private ownership of industry, were compelled to pay at least lip service to the notion of worker participation. The notion that there should be at the national level some institutionalisation of the corporate interests of capital and labour, producers and consumers, also gained general acceptance.

All these notions were sufficiently vague and overlapping to leave considerable room for manoeuvre. When a 'national chamber of labour' was advocated at a central congress of workers' and soldiers' councils in April 1919, critics from the left spoke of a 'stew from the kitchens of Bismarck'. Eventually it proved possible to insert into the constitution article 165 which stipulated that workers and white-collar employees were entitled to take part equally with employers in the regulation of wages and conditions of work as well as in the total economic development of the productive forces. Institutions at local and national level were envisaged to give effect to these aims. This article belonged to that part of the Weimar constitution which set out a catalogue of social aspirations. Agreement on such an article between the parties was possible because the actual implementation was left open.

When it came to concrete steps, the Bauer government promulgated, in February 1920, a works council law, and established three months later a Reich Economic Council. The latter was uncontroversial and never became more than a discussion forum. The former was the final legal remnant of the council movement and of all the massive conflicts that had surrounded it. Enterprises with more than twenty employees had to have a works council, with separate representation of workers and white-collar employees, where appropriate. The councils had in the main advisory functions, but were to be informed of the firm's balance sheet and to have representation on the board.

The detailed consideration of this law occasioned sharp controversy, the hyperbolic tone of the arguments indicating the deepening gulf in German society left by the events of 1919. The Prussian minister of trade, from the DDP, spoke of 'organised bolshevism'; the *Reichsverband der Deutschen Industrie* (RDI, the new unified representative body of German industry) claimed that the representation of works councils on boards represented the gravest danger to German economic life. More seriously, a debate on the law in the national assembly in January 1920 was used by the Berlin USPD to rekindle the revolutionary mood in the capital. Shooting broke out in front of the Reichstag building leaving 42 dead and 105 wounded. The government reimposed the state of siege in Berlin and Brandenburg and Noske was again given special powers. The works council law was not simply a tool of capitalism, as the left claimed, but on the other hand it was a meagre outcome considering the high expectations and aspirations that had collected around the council movement.[67]

The financial reforms associated with Erzberger, who had taken over as finance minister in the Bauer government, were important and to some extent permanent, even though they proved ineffective in solving Germany's grave financial problems.

They were built on those articles in the constitution giving the Reich priority in the raising of taxation, when previously it had been 'the lodger', as Bismarck put it, of the *Länder*. It was the most important step towards the unification of the Reich taken since the early years of the Bismarck era. In introducing his proposals Erzberger claimed no less than the intention to reverse the destruction of sound finance wrought by the war. He declared that the income of the Reich would have to be raised by 900 per cent, compared with the prewar level, and that of the *Länder* and communes by probably 100 per cent. To this end a financial administration for the Reich was created, with sub-offices in the *Länder*.

A progressive income tax with a top rate of 60 per cent, a level previously unheard of in Germany, a corporation and a capital gains tax, a sales tax and various other taxes on consumption were eventually enacted. Real bitterness was injected into the debates by the proposal of a national emergency levy on capital, rising to 65 per cent on sums of over two million marks. The DNVP and the DVP predicted total ruin for both agriculture and industry, massive evasion and flight of capital abroad. They did not hesitate to claim that the Allies might confiscate the proceeds of such a levy. The clashes showed again a high degree of exaggeration and posturing, revealing the deep fissures in German society. The fact was that Germany's propertied classes were not prepared to shoulder the burden of mitigating the ruinous financial legacy of the war.

Nevertheless it proved possible to raise the percentage of Reich expenditure met from taxation from 30 to 44 per cent between 1919 and 1921. This improvement in the public finances might have provided a window of opportunity for getting on top of the inflation which the war had caused in Germany. Up to the time when Erzberger announced his reforms in July 1919 this inflation had been severe. It had been aggravated by the failure of the German imperial authorities to finance a sufficient proportion of war expenditure by taxes, rather than by loans and increases in the unfunded part of the national debt. Germany's position was, however, not exceptional among European belligerents and by 1919 Italy and France had experienced an even higher rate of inflation.

Hyperinflation was still a long way off and avoidable. In the German case the mark had fallen against the dollar by 89 per cent between the armistice and the signing of the treaty. The index of wholesale prices, calculated on a base point of one in 1913, had risen to 2.34 in November 1918 and a further 32 per cent to 3.08 by June 1919. From July 1919 to the Kapp Putsch in March 1920 the mark fell a further 465 per cent from 15.08 marks to the dollar to 83.89 marks to the dollar. In the same period wholesale prices leapt by 404 per cent from an index figure of 3.39 to 17.09. Then there was a period of relative stabilisation: between April 1920 and May 1921 the mark fell only 7 per cent against the dollar, from 59.64 to 63.53 marks to the dollar, and its exchange value remained therefore substantially stable. Between April 1920 and April 1921 the index of wholesale prices actually fell by 15 per cent, from 15.67 to 13.26.[68] In part this stabilisation was due to the Erzberger reforms, which were by then bringing in revenue to the Reich. In the spring of 1920 the defeat of the Kapp Putsch and hopes of a reparations settlement had also revived confidence in the German economy. A year later the course of events at home and abroad put an end to this brief opportunity for bringing inflation under control. Erzberger himself became for the nationalist right the most-hated man among Weimar politicians. The part he played in the passage of the July peace resolution in 1917, his signature on the armistice agreement and his support for the acceptance of the Versailles treaty had already earned him virulent hostility.

THE KAPP PUTSCH

The future of Germany's armed forces had become an acute question as a result of the limits imposed by the treaty of Versailles. Immediately after the acceptance of the treaty the government ordered a reduction of the numbers in the army to 200 000 by 1 November 1919. It was a difficult target to achieve, as the number under arms in the summer of 1919 in Germany and on her eastern borders was over 650 000. About 400 000 men had been taken into the temporary Reichswehr legally embodied in March 1919. This force incorporated the various volunteer bodies and Freikorps providing security in the Reich and involved in the suppression of the second revolutionary wave. Noske as *Reichswehrminister* was in overall control, but worked through what remained of OHL and of the old General Staff. OHL from its headquarters at Kolberg controlled the units fighting or guarding the Polish border, the *Grenzschutz Ost*. The most difficult problem was posed by the Freikorps in the Baltic region. Extravagant promises of land had been made to these volunteers, yet the overall international situation in the autumn of 1919 dictated their return to Germany and their demobilisation.

There had all along been considerable tension between many Freikorps elements and the general staff officers trying to build up a disciplined army. The two sides had been kept together by their common aim of crushing the revolution and saving Germany from what they saw as bolshevism. Pressure from the Allies for a speedy implementation of the Versailles limits made the dismissal of large numbers of men inevitable. Senior officers like Groener and Seeckt, soon to become the chief of the Reichswehr, were particularly reluctant to keep the highly politicised *Baltikumer* in the army. Many of these men were given refuge on the estates of Pomeranian and east Prussian landowners, sometimes taking the place of agricultural workers who had joined trade unions after the revolution and had been dismissed.

The energetic Prussian agriculture minister Otto Braun, later Prussian prime minister, did succeed in enforcing the right to join trade unions, but many aristocratic land owners found it hard to come to terms with such a challenge to their traditional paternalism. Land reform was shelved and the local administration in the rural areas of eastern Prussia was still in the hands of the Junker landowners, as in imperial days. The SPD Prussian minister of the interior, Heine, was prepared to work with *Landräte* from the traditional élites just as Noske was with army officers from the same background. With men and weapons being collected the preparations for a right-wing putsch were evident in late 1919.[69]

Soon the supporters of the republic were pushed further on to the defensive. The constituent assembly had established a commission of enquiry into the causes of the German defeat. It was a move by the coalition parties to place the responsibility where it ought always to have lain, with the power élites of imperial Germany. Eventually the commission accomplished some solid work, but some of its early meetings turned into propaganda triumphs for the discredited old order. On 18 November 1919 Hindenburg was called as a witness. He drove through cheering crowds and the witness stand was decorated with a bouquet of flowers tied with a ribbon of black, white and red, the imperial colours symbolising opposition to the republican black, red and gold. Hindenburg refused to reply to the chairman's questions and read a prepared statement. It ended with a frequently quoted passage, which was music to the ears of all Germans who wanted to believe that their country had never been defeated in open battle, but had succumbed to treason by the left: 'Our repeated requests for strict discipline and strict laws were never met. Thus our operations were bound to fail and the collapse had to come: the revolution was only the last straw. An English general rightly said: "The German Army was stabbed in the back." The sound heart of the army is without blame . . . . Where the guilt lies is clearly proven. If further proof were necessary, it lies in the quoted remark of the English general and in the boundless astonishment of our enemies at their victory.' The English general, Major-General Malcolm, had actually not given his own opinion, but had merely asked, in reply to a question during an interview with Ludendorff: 'You mean you were stabbed in the back ?' Whatever the origins of the remark, the stab in the back myth had been sanctioned by the highest authority.[70]

Another blow against republican confidence was struck when Erzberger was forced to bring a libel suit to defend himself against severe defamation in a pamphlet published by the former imperial vice chancellor Helfferich, now a member of the DNVP. He and Erzberger were long-standing political enemies, a hostility recently aggravated when Erzberger, in introducing his financial reforms, had blamed the parlous state of German public finances on Helfferich's lax management during the war. For the German middle class, who wanted to believe the worst of the republic, Erzberger made a particularly apposite target. This was not only because of the key role he had played in so many crucial events, but because they saw him as a renegade from their own side. He was in appearance the petit bourgeois personified, yet he was also totally identified with the ruling Weimar coalition, which from 1917 he had largely helped to bring about. Among the accusations which Helfferich had flung against his enemy were: 'a sordid mixing of political activity with his own pecuniary advantage . . . at the crucial moment of the war, acting for his Habsburg-Bourbon patrons, he cowardly attacked German policy from the rear with his July action, and thereby destroyed in the

German people the belief in and therefore the will to victory . . .
his signature rightly seals the miserable armistice . . . he led us to
Versailles and during the negotiations indicated to our enemies
that he was willing to sign without conditions the treaty of shame
and servitude'. All this was the stock-in-trade of right-wing
nationalist demagogy, repeated endlessly until fourteen years
later Hitler made it orthodoxy in the Third Reich.

The Helfferich trial, which started in January 1920 and ended
on 12 March, the day before the Kapp Putsch, showed all the
lamentable political bias of which so many of the judges of the
Weimar period were guilty. These judges were protected against
political interference by the republican constitution and could not
be removed. Most of them were survivors from the imperial age
and were deeply prejudiced against the republican order, which
they regarded as fundamentally illegitimate. They had no
sympathy for the new political class of which Erzberger was a
conspicuous representative. Most of Helfferich's accusations were
found to be false, but there were a few cases in which Erzberger
had acted unwisely and had failed to keep his personal and official
affairs sufficiently separate. Only a minor fine was imposed upon
Helfferich, whose 'patriotic motives' were acknowledged by the
court. When a student severely wounded Erzberger on his way to
the court, he was only given a sentence of 18 months imprisonment for grievous bodily harm and was prematurely released.
Helfferich's slogan 'Away with Erzberger!' had been an incitement and eighteen months later Erzberger was, like several
leading politicians, assassinated. The verdict in the Helfferich
trial was seen by the nationalist public as a clear indictment of the
republic and led to Erzberger's immediate resignation as minister
of finance.[71]

It was the eve of the Kapp Putsch. The immediate cause was
the need to comply with the Allied demand that the Reichswehr
should be reduced to 200 000 men by 10 April 1920. In
consequence Noske had issued an order which entailed, among
others, the disbandment of the Marine Brigade Ehrhardt, located
at this moment near Berlin. It was one of the more effective
Freikorps and had in its ranks many former Baltic volunteers. On
10 March General von Lüttwitz, who commanded the Berlin
Reichswehr, confronted Ebert and Noske with a series of
demands: revocation of the disbandment order, immediate
dissolution of the constituent assembly and Reichstag elections,

non-party experts to be put in charge of the ministries of foreign affairs, economics and finance, Lüttwitz himself to be made commander of the whole Reichswehr in place of the pro-republican General Reinhardt. Ebert and Noske naturally rejected these demands. Noske asked Lüttwitz to retire and sent him on leave. Somewhat belatedly he ordered the arrest of Kapp, about to become the titular leader of the plot, as well as of Colonel Bauer, Ludendorff's former assistant and Captain Waldemar Pabst, responsible for the murders of Liebknecht and Luxemburg. These men had been deeply implicated in the plotting of which the government had received many warnings.

It centred on an organisation called *Nationale Vereinigung* (National Association), of which Ludendorff was patron, which had wide ramifications among Freikorps and Junker landowners and which received financial support from industry. Wolfgang Kapp, a founder of the *Vaterlandspartei*, an East Prussian official and member of the presidium of the DNVP, was a leading light. The plotters were by no means united on the aims or the timing of a coup. There was an obvious difference between the immediate and narrower aims of the military plotters and the broader counter-revolutionary goals of the politicians, but it was through the actions of Lüttwitz they were now prematurely forced to move.

It was characteristic of the insidious weakness of the republican authorities that the reports they had received about these putschist machinations on the right often deliberately minimised the danger. Some of the officials charged with surveillance were themselves sympathetic to the plotters. Bauer and Pabst received a tip-off about their impending arrest from police sources. In the early hours of 13 March the Brigade Ehrhardt moved into Berlin and occupied the government quarter. During a hastily convened meeting in the early hours Noske, who now wanted to meet force with force, was told by his military advisers that resistance would be useless. Only General Reinhardt was prepared to stand and fight.

It was at this meeting that General von Seeckt is said to have made the famous remark: 'Reichswehr does not shoot on Reichswehr'. Seeckt was head of the *Truppenamt* (troop office), the title under which the old general staff was now disguised. Whatever he exactly said, there is no doubt what he meant. He considered it unlikely that any forces the government would be able to muster would in fact oppose Ehrhardt's troops. It was not a matter which Seeckt or any of the officers present, other than Reinhardt, wished to put to the test. Although they considered the putsch ill-conceived, their main concern was not to defend the republican government, but to keep intact the forces they controlled. These forces might again, as so often during the past year, be needed to defend the country against bolshevism. In their eyes the Reichs-wehr represented the continuity of the state, while the republic was only a temporary phenomenon which might not survive.

As dawn broke the cabinet met in the presence of Ebert. They had little choice but to endorse the decision not to resist by force and in order to retain their freedom of action they reluctantly decided that president, chancellor and most ministers would have to leave the capital. Only Schiffer, the vice-chancellor from the DDP, and a small group of ministers would stay in Berlin. While these decisions were being taken, the press officer of the chancellery drafted a proclamation calling for a general strike: 'Workers, Party Comrades! The military putsch has started. The Baltic mercenaries, fearing the command to dissolve, are trying to remove the republic and to form a military dictatorship. Lüttwitz and Kapp at their head . . . . The achievements of a whole year are to be smashed, your dearly bought freedom to be destroyed. Everything is at stake! The strongest countermeasures are required. No factory must work while the military dictatorship of Ludendorff and Co. rules! Therefore down tools! Come out on strike! Deprive the military clique of oxygen! Fight with all means for the Republic! Put all quarrels aside! There is only one way against the dictatorship of Wilhelm II: paralysis of all economic life! No hand must move! No proletarian must help the military dictators! General strike all along the line! Proletarians unite! Down with the counter-revolution!'[72]

The proclamation carried the signatures of the social demo-cratic members of the government headed by Ebert and Bauer and of Otto Wels on behalf of the presidium of the SPD. It has never been clearly established whether Ebert, Bauer and their colleagues sanctioned this proclamation. They knew, however, that the SPD had to be firmly associated with the general strike, which was bound to start in any case, if it was not to lose even more ground among the working class than it had already done.

Ebert, Bauer and the other ministers withdrew in the first instance to Dresden. They had been advised by Noske that the commander there, General Maercker, was reliable. Maercker had been at the head of an officially established early volunteer corps, had crushed the radical left in Halle in the spring of 1919 and had protected Weimar and the constituent assembly. When Ebert and the government ministers arrived in Dresden Maercker made it clear that he disapproved of the general strike and that he was taking up a mediating position between the old and the new government of Kapp, in the meantime installed in Berlin. Although Ebert and his SPD colleagues immediately distanced themselves from the general strike call they no longer felt secure in Dresden and on 14 March retreated further south to the safer atmosphere of Stuttgart.

In Berlin Kapp found it difficult to establish himself. The coup was ill-prepared and even many of those who sympathised with its general thrust felt it was mistimed. It soon became clear that the high ministerial bureaucracy in Berlin was disinclined to collaborate with a venture so lacking in legal veneer. Although the general strike could not make an immediate impact, since the putsch started at a weekend, the massive support for it showed the more sober-minded supporters of the right that the time to get rid of the unloved republic had not yet arrived. This did not mean that there was much unequivocal support for the republic outside the Weimar coalition parties. Even Stresemann's DVP initially adopted an ambivalent position. As it became clear that Kapp and his associates were unable to act effectively as a government, it became a matter of negotiating a face-saving retreat for them. Schiffer and other ministers started to negotiate and party leaders like Stresemann also took a hand. Many concessions were offered to bring the putsch to an end quickly. By 17 March Kapp and Lüttwitz were at the end of their tether and there was not much face-saving left. Kapp fled to Sweden and Lüttwitz, having had his pension rights recognised, took refuge on a Pomeranian estate.[73]

This was by no means the end of the matter. The trade unions, particularly their central body, the ADGB, under the chairmanship of Carl Legien, had during the past eighteen months been a mainstay of the opposition to radicalism in the labour movement. They were, however, now less restricted in their freedom of manoeuvre than the SPD, whose leaders were members of a coalition government. The union leaders were also aware of the deep disappointment of many of their members with the fruits of the revolution. They saw themselves as the trustees of the unity of a politically divided labour movement. The ADGB had taken an unaccustomed leading role in calling for the general strike.

After the collapse of the putsch they again took the lead in exploiting the discomfiture of the right to fulfil some of the frustrated expectations of the left. A nine-point programme demanded a decisive influence for the free unions on the restructuring of Reich and *Länder* governments and on social and economic legislation. More specifically the cleansing of anti-republican elements from all bureaucracies was demanded, as well as the resignation of Noske and Heine. Further demands included the socialisation of the coal and potash industries, the expropriation of landowners holding back food supplies, the dissolution of counter-revolutionary military forces and the formation of security forces by the organised workers. Legien was successful in securing the support of the USPD for this programme, which otherwise had taken the line of resisting the putsch but refusing to cooperate with the 'traitorous Ebert–Noske–Bauer clique'.

It was now a question to what extent the government, still in Stuttgart, would be willing to accept such a programme. It constituted the minimum that would enable the ADGB to call off the strike and to prevent it from slipping into the control of the radicals. On the other hand the non-socialist parties in the coalition, the Christian and Liberal trade unions linked with them, even the moderate SPD leaders, including Ebert himself, could not accept such a programme in its entirety. Insofar as the programme implied the establishment of a 'workers' government' or a 'trade union state' it could hardly be constitutional or acceptable to the bourgeois parties. In the end there was sufficient agreement between the ADGB and its allies and representatives of the government to enable the former to call off the strike on 20 March, exactly a week after the start of the putsch. This call could not, however, at a stroke end the underlying tensions. The huge masses of workers who had come out on strike would not simply return to work without assurances that the stalled revolution had really been revived. In many areas the call to end the strike was not followed and in the Ruhr it escalated into another full-scale rising.

Even before agreement had been reached between the unions and the government on ending the general strike, Noske and

Heine, the two men judged by most SPD members to have been guilty of the grossest negligence in failing to guard against the putsch, had handed in their resignations. Ebert was very reluctant to let Noske go and considered resigning himself. The SPD could not find anyone to take the post of minister of defence and, almost with a sigh of relief, let it pass to Otto Gessler, from the DDP. When Gessler, previously mayor of Nuremberg, told Ebert that he still felt loyalty to the Bavarian Wittelsbachs and was only a *Vernunftrepublikaner*, the president replied that this particularly fitted him to turn the Reichswehr into a force loyal to the new state. Gessler held the post for nearly eight years and saw it as his main task to shield the new small professional Reichswehr from political attack and control. He thus made a crucial contribution to turning it into a state within a state.

Even more important in determining the future role of the army was the appointment of Seeckt as its commander (*Chef der Heeresleitung*). In line with the part he had played during the putsch his allegiance was less to the republic than to the continuity of the German state.[74] The arrival of Otto Braun and Carl Severing in the posts of Prussian prime minister and Prussian minister of the interior was a more positive development for the republic. Both held their respective offices for much of the time till 1932. They were the strong men of moderate social democracy.

In consequence there were now considerable personnel changes particularly in the eastern provinces of Prussia, where the putsch had been strongly supported. Three provincial presidents (*Oberpräsidenten*), three district commissioners (*Regierungspräsidenten*) and 88 *Landräte* were retired or moved because they had favoured the putsch.[75] In Bavaria events took an opposite course. The local Reichswehr commander, von Möhl, without supporting Kapp directly, took the opportunity to remove the Hoffmann Government from office and to install Gustav von Kahr, a senior official with conservative–monarchist leanings, as commissioner. A few days later these moves were legalised by the election of Kahr as prime minister in a government based on the BVP and excluding the SPD.

In these developments the Bavarian civil guards (*Einwohnerwehren*) played a major part. Such bodies of part-time armed men existed all over Germany. They were almost entirely recruited from the middle classes and it was made difficult for members of the SPD to join them. In Bavaria their complexion was particularly counter-revolutionary, because of the shock caused by the short-lived soviet republics in the spring of 1919. The success of the local version of the Kapp Putsch turned Bavaria henceforth into a stronghold of the right, often prepared to defy efforts of the Berlin government to protect the republic.[76] In general the aftermath of the Kapp Putsch collapse proved deeply disappointing to those who hoped that the 'wave from the right' would be reversed and that some of the expectations raised by the revolution would be belatedly realised.

The terms on which the general strike had been called off were thus to a large extent not implemented. One of the main reasons for this was that in some regions of Germany, notably the 'wild west' of the Ruhr, the strike turned into an uprising even more fiercely fought than a year earlier. The government, which had been nearly overturned from the right, almost immediately saw itself threatened again from the left. The Ruhr uprising can be regarded as the third of the revolutionary waves, after November 1918 and the spring of 1919. The motives may have been more clearly political than a year earlier. There was a residue of bitterness among the Ruhr proletariat from the brutal Freikorps repression of the previous year. It was aggravated by the clearly counter-revolutionary nature of the Kapp Putsch. To contain this bitter protest the government once again had no remedy other than more repression by the very forces that had just tried to overthrow it. The situation is symbolised by the figure of General Watter, the local commander, who had imperfectly cooperated with Severing the previous year. He had declared himself neutral when the putsch began and only after prompting from Noske reaffirmed his allegiance to the government. In March 1920 he was again only partially controlled by Severing, the Reich commissioner.

Not surprisingly those sections of the Ruhr proletariat who fought in the so-called Red Army were in a mood of blind fury, prepared to die in a fruitless enterprise. Estimates of the size of the Red Army vary, but a figure around 50 000 seems plausible. There were big fluctuations in the numbers out on strike, which on some days exceeded 75 per cent among the miners. Nevertheless it cannot be claimed that anything like the whole working population in the Ruhr was involved in the uprising. The initial successes of the Red Army owed something to the fact that in the zone about to be demilitarised under the Versailles treaty the German security forces had already been thinned out. The uprising cut across party lines and all three left-wing parties, the SPD, the USPD and the KPD, were associated with it.

The USPD had pursued a wavering line over the putsch, for its rapidly increasing size had merely aggravated its internal divisions. Its membership had risen from 300 000 to 750 000 between March and December 1919. The KPD had initially refused to join the general strike 'to save the murderers of Liebknecht and Luxemburg', but had then jumped on the bandwagon. At this moment it was in a particularly weak position, for the attempt by the party leadership to clamp down on putschism and adventurism had lost the party about half its 100 000 members at the beginning of 1920. Many ultra-leftists joined an alternative party, the KAPD (*Kommunistische Arbeiterpartei Deutschlands*). Thus neither the USPD nor the KPD could lead in the Ruhr uprising, they could only try to take advantage of an uncontrollable grass roots movement and the SPD in the Ruhr had for a time to go along with it.

A central council established in Essen never had effective control throughout the region; on the local councils party strengths and the degree of radicalism varied. The aim of the more extreme elements, to erect a soviet republic and spread it to the whole of Germany, was never realistic. For the government there was little option but to separate the moderate from the extreme elements and thereby contain the uprising with as little bloodshed as possible. They had some success with the Bielefeld agreement, negotiated on 24 March 1920. It repeated the settlement reached with the ADGB nationally four days earlier, but with additional points concerning the surrender of weapons, release of prisoners and amnesties. The ultra-radicals became more isolated and where they held sway conditions were increasingly anarchical.

On the other hand efforts to make the military retribution more restrained and less provocative failed. Watter's troops were now reinforced by Freikorps elements that had only just taken part in the Kapp Putsch. The white terror much exceeded the red: there were over a thousand proletarian casualties, many of them shot after being taken prisoner. About 250 soldiers and police died. It was the largest working-class revolt in Germany and deepened further the wounds and divisions of the labour movement.[77]

Another consequence of the military action was that the French government considered the use of German troops in the demilitarised zone a breach of the Versailles treaty and, in spite of British and American protests, temporarily occupied Frankfurt, Hanau and three other towns on the Rhine. It was also a moment when the Soviet advance on Warsaw heightened fears of bolshevism.

The task of the government was made no easier by the fact it faced an uprising similar to that in the Ruhr in Thuringia. It was on a smaller scale, but it was supported by the radical government of Saxe-Gotha, against which action under article 48 had to be taken. The amalgamation of the central German dwarf states into the *Land* Thuringia had not yet taken place. A characteristic incident during the crushing of the central German revolt occurred when a volunteer battalion of Marburg students shot without trial fifteen villagers whom they suspected of participation in the uprising. When the students were found not guilty by a court martial, confirmed on appeal, there were widespread protests.[78]

ELECTIONS: THE WEIMAR COALITION LOSES ITS MAJORITY; THE PROBLEM OF FORMING A GOVERNMENT

The ignominious failure of the Kapp Putsch had shown that it was not possible to remove the republic by unconstitutional action. The attempt, for the most part equally unconstitutional, to realise working-class aspirations that had failed to materialise at an earlier stage of the revolution, also failed. A stalemate existed which was in constant danger of spilling over into civil war. Vigilante groups, *Einwohner-und Bürgerwehren* (civil guards), were the response to proletarian uprisings and they went underground when an attempt was made to dissolve them.

One cause of the republic's weak legitimacy was, however, about to be remedied. The reconstructed Weimar coalition government, now led by the former foreign minister Müller, at last finalised the electoral law and elections were to be held on 6 June 1920. The spectacular failure of the right-wing putschists made it seem unlikely that there would be as much of a swing to the right as was anticipated before the putsch. It was a vain hope.

The elections cut the support of the Weimar coalition parties from over 70 per cent to less than 45 per cent. The Centre Party suffered least: in January 1919 it had, without the BVP, obtained 15.1 per cent of the vote; this now dropped to 13.6 per cent. The losses of the DDP were devastating: it dropped from 18.5 per cent to 8.4 per cent. Much of its support moved to the DVP, which rose from 4.4 per cent to 13.9 per cent. The SPD also lost heavily and dropped from 37.9 per cent to 21.7 per cent. Much of this vote went to the USPD, which rose from 7.6 per cent to 17.8 per cent. In many of the radical strongholds of Germany it overhauled the SPD. The KPD, which had boycotted the 1919 elections, obtained only 1.7 per cent of the vote. The DNVP saw its vote rise from 10.3 per cent to 15 per cent. These figures were later subject to slight revisions: impending plebiscites delayed the elections in East Prussia and Schleswig-Holstein till 20 February 1921 and in the Upper Silesian district of Oppeln till 19 November 1922.

Even if the vote of the three left-wing parties, the SPD, the USPD and the KPD, are simply added together there was a decline of some 4 per cent in their combined percentage of the vote. The KPD's boycott of the 1919 elections can only partially account for this. Some explanation may be found in the loss to the DNVP of the rural labour vote, which in 1919 had for the first time inclined to the SPD. For example in East Prussia the two left-wing parties had obtained over 50 per cent of the vote in 1919, whereas the three parties of the left got only just over 36 per cent in 1920. In Schleswig-Holstein, the subject of a pioneer electoral study,[79] agricultural workers and those working in industries processing agricultural and fishery products appear to have switched from the SPD to the DNVP. The tendency for a switch from the SPD to the DNVP was greater in areas with large estates than in areas where small farms predominated, thus adding weight to the argument that many agricultural workers went from their short-lived attachment to the SPD straight over to conservative nationalism.

The switch of many middle-class voters from the unequivocally republican DDP to the largely still monarchist DVP, which had prevaricated at the beginning of the Kapp Putsch, can be seen as a symptom of the decline of liberalism. If fear for their lives had driven them into the DDP in 1919, fear for their property now drove them into the DVP. The party's rhyming campaign slogan in 1920 was 'from red fetters will make you free, a vote cast for the DVP'. A simple addition of the DDP and DVP percentages showed even in 1920 a diminution which, except for the election of December 1924, continued relentlessly. Membership figures show this trend even more clearly.

The result of the 1920 Reichstag elections confirmed the stalemate that the failure of the Kapp Putsch had brought into the open. The quip that Weimar was a republic without republicans was not true, but it was not a state that could count on general acceptance. One of the Kapp conspirators, von Jagow, as Berlin police chief before 1914 notorious for his persecution of social democrats, was nominated minister of the interior by Kapp. When asked by an official of his ministry by what right he was taking over, he replied: 'By the right of 9 November 1918.'[80] This remained the attitude of many Germans to the republic.

The outcome of the elections of June 1920 immediately created a problem from which the republic could never thereafter escape, in fair weather or foul. It was the question of how to form a government. The parties of the Weimar coalition no longer had a majority. A socialist government was even less of an option than it had been since December 1918. The SPD and the USPD were too divided and even combined did not have a majority. When the KPD succeeded to the USPD's mass vote, the divisions on the left became even more unbridgeable. The great coalition, stretching from SPD to DVP, was an option and was put into practice for a few months in 1923 under Stresemann and from June 1928 to March 1930. It had to span the gulf between left-wing socialists and right-wing heavy industry and its effectiveness was therefore limited. This left the possibility of various minority combinations, of which the bourgeois block, the DDP, the DVP, the Centre Party, and in the middle years of the republic sometimes also the DNVP, was the most frequently used version.

From June 1920 to June 1928 all governments were minority governments, except for Stresemann's in 1923 and Luther's first government from January 1925 to January 1926, when BVP and DNVP were in the cabinet. A strain was put on all coalitions by the potential divergence between those members of a party who held ministerial office and their backbenchers or parliamentary party (*Fraktion*). The *Fraktion* often chafed under the decisions taken by their colleagues as members of the Reich cabinet. The *Fraktion* and the party organisation were constantly looking over their shoulders at the reaction of their followers in the country (the *Basis*). Unpopular decisions taken in government might make sections of the *Basis* slide away to a neighbouring party. Least affected by this tendency was the Centre Party, which in spite of being always in government, held its vote steady. The bulk of its voters were Catholics, whose vote was determined by their religious allegiance and who had nowhere else to go. Even in the Centre Party there was often much criticism of the compromises entered into by the party in the Reichstag.

A particularly flagrant case of divergence between the *Fraktion* and members of the government afflicted the SPD, when it entered and led a great coalition in 1928. The party had campaigned in the elections of that year against the building of a new battle cruiser (*Panzerkreuzer A*), which would have led to further ships of the same type being built in subsequent years. The SPD was particularly vulnerable on this issue, for the KPD was exploiting to the hilt the argument against 'guns before butter'. In October 1928 a 'people's request' (*Volksbegehren*) was promoted by the KPD on behalf of a proposition that 'the building of all battle ships and cruisers is illegal'. This was yet another example of the exploitation of the constitution's plebiscitary provisions for demagogic purposes. The SPD instructed its members to abstain and less than 3 per cent of the electorate, instead of the required 10 per cent, signed the lists.

This was by no means the end of the quandary in which the SPD found itself. The SPD *Fraktion* in the Reichstag, under pressure from the *Basis* and the KPD, and mindful of its campaign pledges, introduced a motion to suspend the building of *Panzerkreuzer A* and devote the money to school meals. Under the rules of party discipline (*Fraktionszwang*) the chancellor, Müller, and the three SPD members of the cabinet supported this motion. Yet three months earlier they had supported the cabinet decision to build the battle cruiser. Unless they had done so, the great coalition, only just formed with difficulty, would have immediately broken up again and the Reich would have been left virtually ungovernable two years earlier than it actually was. The spectacle of ministers voting against their own decisions undermined the fragile confidence in Weimar's parliamentary processes in no uncertain manner.[81]

This case was only one example of tensions which constantly afflicted the system, but which in this instance were carried to their logical conclusion. Stresemann, the strong man of Weimar's middle years, hastened his death in the constant struggle to keep his DVP *Fraktion* in support of his foreign policy, when particularly the heavy industry wing of the party would have preferred a more aggressively anti-Versailles stance. The most consistent support for his foreign policy came from the SPD, even when it was not in the government. Similarly, the Centre Party could agree with DDP and SPD on foreign policy, but clashed with them on issues such as denominational schools. All this made the formation of stable governments very difficult.

The case of Prussia shows, however, that the situation was by no means incapable of cure. Relatively minor constitutional and attitudinal differences facilitated the formation of the stable coalitions in Prussia that proved so elusive in the Reich. The crucial difference in constitutional machinery lay in the absence of a head of state in Prussia. There had been much discussion about the need for a *Staatspräsident* (state president) in Prussia, for the makers of the Prussian constitution were, like their counterparts in the Reich, obsessed by a fear of 'parliamentary absolutism' and by the vain search for a neutral power above parties. For various reasons a state presidency could not be established in Prussia nor could a substitute for his allegedly neutral function be found. In practice the Prussian Landtag had to elect the prime minister (*Ministerpräsident*) and once it had done so found it difficult to topple him.

There were prolonged governmental crises in Prussia in 1921 and 1925, but the constitutional situation forced the parties to reach an understanding eventually and the resulting coalition lasted for the term of that Landtag. It was virtually impossible to dissolve the Prussian Landtag except with the consent of its majority. It could be done through a referendum, but this device was no easier to bring to a successful conclusion in Prussia than it was in the Reich. In 1931 Nazis and Communists combined in an attempt to force the premature dissolution of the Prussian Landtag by referendum and failed. The only time there was a premature dissolution was in 1933 and then it was part of the process of creeping illegality that was about to put an end to German democracy.[82]

It was, however, not only constitutional technicalities that ensured stable parliamentary government in Prussia. The SPD and the Centre Party, both former outcasts in the Prussian

context, were more pragmatic and ready to cooperate in the
Landtag than they were in the Reichstag. A new genuinely
republican political élite emerged in Prussia, though derided by
their opponents as placemen (*Bonzen*). Leaders like Ernst
Heilmann in the SPD and Josef Hess in the Centre Party
facilitated the relationship between parliamentary parties and
ministers that proved so unsatisfactory in the Reichstag. It also
helped that the Prussian government did not have to deal with
foreign affairs, where defeat, Versailles and reparations imposed
their heavy mortgage on the politics of the Reich.

Governmental and parliamentary stability was also achieved in
many other *Länder*, though its centre of gravity might be on the
right rather than on the left. This was the case in Bavaria,
especially after 1924.[83] No democratic arrangements can be made
proof against the electorate and when Papen removed the
Prussian government in July 1932 it had already been fatally
weakened by the elections of the previous April, in which Nazis
and communists together obtained nearly half the vote.

In the formation of a new coalition in the Reich after the
elections of June 1920 the president had to play a key role and it
therefore tilted the balance of power in the constitution towards
him and away from the Reichstag. On this occasion an extension
of the Weimar coalition either to the left or to the right could
theoretically have produced a majority government. Ebert therefore charged the out-going chancellor Müller with the task of
trying to bring the USPD into the government. Crispien, the
leader of the USPD, declared the party unwilling to ally itself with
parties that had favoured counter-revolution and betrayed the
working class. It was a decision by no means uncontested within
the USPD; for example Kautsky was in favour of entering either a
bourgeois coalition or forming a socialist minority government.
He considered it important for the proletariat that its representatives should share in the control of state power. In practice the
USPD leaders had no alternative but to stay out, for their party
would have split even sooner and more thoroughly than it did.

The SPD was unwilling to remain in the coalition if it was
extended to the right by the inclusion of the DVP and had made
this clear. In any case neither of the SPD's Weimar coalition
partners, the Centre Party and the DDP, were willing to work
with a USPD still strongly committed to the proletarian
revolution. There were great sighs of relief in the SPD when

Müller gave up the task Ebert had placed upon him. There was a widespread opinion in the SPD that a spell out of government could do the party nothing but good and would enable it to reverse the disastrous haemorrhage of voters to the left. Events were to some extent to prove this expectation correct, but there was a heavy price to pay for shedding the burden of power. No party was more completely identified with the Weimar republic than the SPD and its withdrawal from government weakened the republic itself. Nor was it possible to withdraw completely from responsibility. For the next eight years, when the SPD was most of the time out of government, it remained a consistent supporter of the foreign policy of successive governments, the policy which in varying degrees implied an acceptance of the Versailles system combined with peaceful revision. The SPD therefore could not, even out of government, avoid shouldering what was the heaviest burden Weimar had to carry.[84]

When the impossibility of extending the coalition leftwards had been demonstrated, Ebert commissioned a member of the DVP to explore a right-wing coalition including the DNVP. This attempt was not much more than a formality. It then fell to the Centre Party to form a minority government with the DDP and the DVP. It included some non-party figures, most significantly General Groener as minister of transport. Its head was Konstantin Fehrenbach, a respected Centre Party politician who had been president of the Reichstag before 1918. He was in his late sixties and in indifferent health. The Fehrenbach cabinet, like many of its successors, could not base itself upon a positive vote of confidence from the Reichstag, but merely upon a motion implying toleration. The SPD voted for it and the DNVP abstained. It made specific reference to the reparation negotiations at Spa, the imminence of which had made it necessary to form a government by hook or by crook. This kind of pressure arising from Germany's foreign political environment was crucial in the formation of many Weimar cabinets and when the immediate necessity passed such coalitions often fell apart again. It was the weak minority government of Fehrenbach that had now to face the *damnosa hereditas* that war and defeat had left.[85] The elaborate quadrille that led to its formation was to be repeated many times in the next few years. It aroused the contempt of the many Germans who still craved a man on horseback to rescue them from their predicament.

2 The Time of Troubles

GERMANY AND THE INTERNATIONAL SITUATION

It was only in the summer of 1920, after the elections which deprived the Weimar coalition of its majority, that the full burden of the interconnected problems facing the German republic became evident. The treaty of Versailles had left the final determination of the German reparation payments open and had for the time being decreed transfers in kind, above all of coal. The Spa conference, which met from 5 to 16 July 1920, was to be a first step towards settling the economic legacy of the treaty.

It was in itself a matter of significance that a settlement was now approached through the medium of an international conference. It had been the French point of view that the full execution of the treaty was not negotiable. Any German departure from the letter of the treaty was to lead to immediate sanctions. For this reason France had occupied Frankfurt and other West German towns in response to the westward move of German troops in the aftermath of the Kapp Putsch.[1] France was still trying to recover the position of security which she had failed to obtain at Versailles. It was a failure reinforced by the refusal of the US Senate to ratify the treaty. The proposed Anglo–American guarantee never became operative.

There was, however, also another prong to French policy, an alternative to the threat of sanctions. It was to bind German heavy industry, located in the Rhine–Ruhr area and now deprived of direct access to Lorraine ore, more closely into an economic system dominated by France. The extraction of coal deliveries, the most important reparation in kind obtained by France since the signature of the treaty, played a crucial role in such schemes. A further strand in French policies, often in conjunction with the economic offensive, was the encouragement of separatism in the Rhineland. At the best of times it was difficult to tread the line between extracting the maximum economic advantage, reviving Germany as a junior partner without a renaissance of her economic hegemony, and yet ensuring her permanent subordination to French security. Not surprisingly French policy failed to deal with these insoluble dilemmas.

The British position was somewhat different. Increasingly the main British preoccupation was the economic restoration of Europe and of the international trading system. This involved the economic recovery of Germany, a prerequisite also for the extraction of reparations. On British insistence the Spa conference was to be the first occasion when a German delegation would become a partner in negotiations. Lloyd George, the British prime minister and chief protagonist of this approach to international problems, had to pay a price for this. He had to agree to the French position that any German failure to meet obligations would entail sanctions, including the occupation of more territory. There were fundamental tensions between Britain and France, because, true to her traditional balance of power policies, Britain did not want the German defeat to be followed by a French hegemony in Europe. There was, however, also a limit beyond which the British were unwilling to risk their entente with France, a limit which was not always clearly perceived by the Germans. Moreover Britain was dependent on French goodwill in the Near and Middle East. British confidence in the Versailles settlement, particularly its economic aspects, was already waning. The arguments against many aspects of the Versailles settlement put forward by J. M. Keynes in his famous book *The Economic Consequences of the Peace* were widely accepted in Britain.[2] In Germany Keynes became as popular as he was execrated in France.

Reparations thus became crucial in German politics. All Germany's ills flowing from defeat and Versailles were encapsulated in the reparations question. The nationalist right regarded all these impositions, as much as the republic itself, as intolerable. They were ever more inclined to heroic gestures of repudiation and martyrdom and it became fashionable to flirt openly with catastrophe. Those who retained a modicum of reason, in the moderate centre and left, advocated a policy of fulfilment to demonstrate Germany's good intentions, but even for them the main object of fulfilment was to show how impossible it would be to meet such demands. Reparations thus became closely linked with Germany's domestic economic problem. They were a principal reason why the window of opportunity for stabilising Germany's inflationary situation passed in 1921.

The social situation in Germany was also inextricably linked with this question. The almost insuperable problems of demobilisation, while still under Allied blockade, had been relieved by the printing of money to cover ever-increasing public deficits. The collapse of the empire had also created among the dominant economic classes, above all the employers, a disposition to be accommodating. The *Zentralarbeitsgemeinschaft* and the eight-hour day were a product of this spirit of accommodation. In official circles there was a strong awareness that there had to be an active social policy to alleviate the transition from war to peace and to enable the working population to cope with the reality of Germany's impoverished state. It was essential to maintain employment even at the risk of deepening deficits. When in the autumn of 1920 the temporary stabilisation of the currency caused a rise in unemployment, many politicians and civil servants insisted on more public expenditure.[3]

The reparations question impinged on these problems in a variety of ways. The initial spirit of accommodation symbolised by the *Zentralarbeitsgemeinschaft* was already diminishing among industrialists and reparations reinforced the trend. The question of socialising the coal mines, back on the agenda after the Kapp Putsch, could be side-tracked by the argument that coal production had to be maximised under reparation agreements. In the same breath it could be claimed that the mines under public ownership might more easily be seized by the Allies under the terms of the treaty.

Men like Hugo Stinnes had lost patience with conciliatory policies either abroad or at home. On the whole Stinnes and other leading figures in Ruhr heavy industry responded negatively to French attempts to make them junior partners in a French-dominated continental economic system. In common with many sections of the German public the course of events had confirmed them in thinking in terms of competitive power politics rather than interdependence. German industrialists seemed to be in the forefront of the fight to preserve Germany's power against the world's hostility and this restored to them some of the influence in domestic affairs they had lost in 1918.[4]

Stinnes was merely the most prominent of the many industrialists who profited greatly from the failure to arrest inflation. This was also broadly true of many other types of property-owners and substantial taxpayers. The Erzberger reforms had attempted to

narrow the deficit in the German public budget by putting
burdens on property and on the more affluent. Such taxes were,
however, made progressively less productive by accelerating
inflation, for by the time they were assessed and collected they
had lost much of their value. This did not apply with equal force
to taxes immediately paid by wage and salary earners. This
problem led to a tug-of-war between left and right which was
again directly affected by reparations. It was easy for the right to
argue that nothing could be done until the reparations burden
was known, that the inflation itself was primarily due to the
depreciation of the external value of the mark rather than to the
budget deficit and that this was in turn caused by reparations and
by the threat of even higher payments in the future. There was a
positive incentive not to cope with the internal deficit, even if a
majority could have been found in the Reichstag to do so, for thus
it could be demonstrated that the treaty was in fact incapable of
fulfilment.

A further twist to the complex situation was added by developments in Eastern Europe. The fluctuating fortunes of Poland and
Russia in the war that raged in 1920 offered opportunities and
risks to Germany. The plebiscites that were to take place in
various territories on the Polish–German border, most impor-
tantly in Upper Silesia, would determine the future of the German
population in these regions. A bitter struggle was going on
between irregular forces on both sides. It was widely believed in
Germany that Poland was the most immediate enemy and that in
spite of ideological differences German policy should be based on
collaboration with Russia. If the new Polish state could be wiped
off the map a central feature of the Versailles system would
collapse and the French position in Europe would be fatally
weakened. This strategy was strongly supported by Seeckt and the
Reichswehr and insistently advocated by the Russian section of
the German foreign office. Such open defiance of the Allies did not
seem realistic to most moderate politicians. Social democrats like
Ebert were more alarmed by the possible domestic risks of
bolshevism arising from an eastern orientation than many
conservatives bent on the destruction of Versailles at all costs. It
became an on-going paradox of German politics that the
nationalist right, driven to hysteria by the alleged threat of
bolshevism at home, was broadly in favour of using Soviet Russia
to cock a snook at the hated West. Anti-Westernism, its roots deep

in German history, lost none of the virulence it had acquired during the war. On this the right had common ground with the extreme left, most of which was about to be taken over by an increasingly Moscow-orientated Communist party.[5]

THE REPARATIONS PROBLEM AND ITS IMPACT ON DOMESTIC POLITICS

Immediately before the Spa conference met an Allied meeting at Boulogne had come up with the figure of 269 billion gold marks, to be paid in 42 annual instalments, as the German overall liability. This figure caused a storm of indignation in Germany, but it had no real significance, other than whetting appetites in Allied countries and temporarily calming disputes about the division of the spoils. At Spa itself the reparations question was sidestepped, but there were limited agreements about coal deliveries and the time allowed for reducing the Reichswehr to 100 000 men was extended to 1 January 1921. As a result the German foreign exchange situation, vital to propping up the external value of the mark, was marginally improved and a first step taken towards restoring Germany's international credit-worthiness.

The dissolution of internal security forces, particularly the *Einwohnerwehren*, was also stipulated. The continued existence of these forces fed the suspicion that Germany was trying to evade the disarmament obligations of the treaty. The attempt to dissolve the *Einwohnerwehren*, already under way after the failure of the Kapp Putsch, became a matter of dispute between Berlin and the right-wing government in Munich. The more extreme nationalist paramilitaries were in fact more dangerous underground than in the open.

Thus Spa set a pattern. The German delegation hovered uneasily between appearing to make an honest effort to fulfil treaty obligations and demonstrating the impossibility of fulfilment. The Allies were divided between conciliation, mainly a British attitude, and exasperation at German intransigence. The Germans did little to help British efforts to moderate French pressure on Germany. The limited alleviations achieved met with little enthusiasm in Germany. The advocates of realism, moderation and conciliation received virulent vituperation from the nationalist right. These attitudes were reinforced when the reparations liability was at last discussed in concrete terms early in 1921.[6]

In late October 1920 Joseph Wirth, the finance minister soon to become chancellor, estimated that the cost of implementing the treaty would in the current financial year be more than the entire ordinary budget of the Reich. When the financial year was completed in March 1921 the actual cost of treaty payments accounted for only 18 per cent of the budget. The method of closing the budget deficit continued to be bitterly disputed between right and left. The SPD from outside the government demanded a more effective collection of taxes on the wealthy, especially the *Reichsnotopfer* (National Emergency Levy). From the right Helfferich proclaimed that any increase in taxation to meet reparation demands was impossible. Within the government coalition the DVP jealously guarded the interests of industry and of the more affluent taxpayers. Wirth had to concede in January 1921 that no large-scale tax programme was possible as long as the reparations problem remained unsettled.

The failure of Spa to move nearer to a settlement had undermined the mark on the foreign exchanges and most of the improvement that had followed the collapse of the Kapp Putsch was temporarily lost. The renewed hope of agreement and of the restoration of Germany's credit early in 1921 led to a rebound in the dollar value of the mark. The index of wholesale prices, another important indicator of inflation, did not follow the external value of the mark except to a limited extent, so that the period of relative price stability that had started in the spring of 1920 continued until the summer of 1921. In the year to March 1921, however, only 35 per cent of Reich expenditure was met by tax revenues. This turned out to be, in due course, a powerful engine for accelerating the inflation.[7]

The resolution of the reparations problem was subject to a deadline, 1 May 1921. In December 1920 Jacques Seydoux, the French official primarily concerned with the reparations question, put forward a plan based on deliveries in kind and German participation in French reconstruction. Seydoux was aware of Germany's limited capacity to pay and of the need to promote her economic recovery. An agreement of this kind probably presented the best opportunity before the Dawes Plan of 1924 to arrive at a provisional reparations settlement. It would have taken the question off the agenda, which was the most that could be done in any case, and thus opened the way towards other measures of international economic reconstruction.

At this juncture a multitude of political and economic pressures frustrated a settlement along these lines. German industry feared French domination, French industry feared German competition, the British feared Franco–German control of the European economy and wanted a global sum stated to help in settling the financial markets. In January 1921 the Allied Supreme Council committed itself to the fanciful figure of 226 billion gold marks plus 12 per cent of the value of German exports as the global sum of German obligations. The outcry in Germany further limited the room for manoeuvre of the weak Fehrenbach coalition. As the May deadline approached the figure of 132 billion gold marks finally emerged as the extent of the German global liability. As 82 billion of this was to be relegated to the distant future in the form of so-called C Bonds, only the A Bonds of 12 billion and the B Bonds of 38 billion were really relevant.

The total of 50 billion was in fact close to a German offer that had earlier been promoted with the help of the United States and the Vatican. The annual payment by Germany was to be two billion gold marks plus 26 per cent of the value of her exports. Payments were to be made in quarterly instalments with a first payment of one billion gold marks due on 31 May 1921. The immediate payments, and these were the only ones that mattered, represented a considerable reduction on previous fanciful figures and for this reason had to be wrapped up in future expectations, however unreal. The immediate burden on Germany, even if her finances had been in better shape, would still have been very great and scarcely capable of fulfilment except through generous international loans.

A great deal of posturing for the sake of national electorates continued to motivate the whole reparations process. Lloyd George, the real driving force towards a settlement that would allow economic reconstruction to proceed, was forced by German intransigence to allow the imposition of sanctions in the form of the occupation, on 8 March 1921, of Düsseldorf, Duisburg and Ruhrort. He managed, however, on this occasion to avert an occupation of the entire Ruhr. Finally, on 5 May 1921, the Germans were presented in London with an ultimatum. The Fehrenbach government resigned and a resuscitated Weimar coalition government under Wirth then accepted the London ultimatum.[8]

Throughout the winter of 1920–1 the atmosphere surrounding the reparation talks had been crucially affected by the German–Polish struggle over Upper Silesia ahead of the plebiscite scheduled for 20 March 1921. In July 1920 a Soviet army had appeared at the gates of Warsaw, raising the hopes of all those who saw in the collapse of Poland the prospect of overturning Versailles. The 'miracle of the Vistula' in August 1920, when the Russians were in turn chased eastwards by Pilsudski, put paid to such hopes in the immediate future. The Polish victory precipitated an uprising in the Polish areas of Upper Silesia designed to pre-empt the plebiscite.

In spite of the presence of Allied forces German irregular forces infiltrated the disputed territories. These German forces included Freikorps elements and substantial numbers of men from the *Orgesch*, the predominantly Bavarian-based civil guards, whose dissolution had been demanded both by the German government after the Kapp Putsch and by the Allies at Spa. Seeckt warned the cabinet that the Polish army might intervene on the side of their irregulars and in principle the decision was taken to send in Reichswehr units. In fact both the Polish and German governments held back from official intervention, though both sides gave much support short of sending their regular armies. In the plebiscite nearly 60 per cent voted to stay with Germany, but this did not finally settle the matter. According to the treaty the plebiscite commission was instructed to take into account the vote in each community. In the meantime fighting continued and the storming of the Annaberg by the German forces at the end of May 1921 was hailed in Germany as a great national victory. The final settlement by a conference of ambassadors in October 1921 was severely criticised in Germany and gave fresh impetus to nationalist agitation. A quarter of the territory and 44 per cent of the population went to Poland, roughly in line with the plebiscite, but this territory comprised 80 per cent of the Upper Silesian coal production and the total German zinc production.[9]

The fall of Fehrenbach and the renewal of a Weimar coalition government, now in a minority, under Wirth had been almost a re-run of the events nearly two years earlier, when the signature of the Versailles treaty itself was at issue. This time it was the refusal of the DVP, among the parties in the Fehrenbach coalition, to accept the London ultimatum that made a change of government necessary. Stresemann declared that his party would only accept the London terms if Upper Silesia remained German. He said that the acceptance of conditions that could not be fulfilled would not save Germany from fresh extortion. Even a majority of the reduced DDP *Fraktion* still voted against accepting the London ultimatum.

A realistic appreciation of Germany's immediate possibilities in the international context was only slowly gaining ground. Koch-Weser, the minister of the interior from the DDP in the Fehrenbach cabinet, who had been in favour of rejecting the treaty in 1919, was now for acceptance of the London ultimatum. He did not want a collapse, 'when nine-tenths of the way back had been accomplished', he noted in his diary. But it was for him also a matter of 'squeezing one's way through, if necessary by telling lies – the path begun at Versailles'.[10] The leader of the DNVP, Hergt, called for rejection of the London ultimatum and for a defiant assertion of the national will.

There were plenty of more extreme and less responsible expressions of opinion. The *Deutsche Zeitung*, an organ close to the *Völkisch* groups, while tacitly admitting that there was no alternative to fulfilment, proclaimed 'but we turn red with shame at the sight of a chancellor . . . boasting to the world how obediently he has done everything, how punctually he is paying the billion marks . . . how conscientiously he is turning us into slaves . . .'[11]

At the end of May 1921 Walther Rathenau accepted the post of minister of reconstruction. He and Wirth, close friends, became the central figures in the making of German policy. The first instalment of reparations due on 31 May was transmitted to the reparations commission by the purchase with paper marks of gold and foreign exchange to the value of 150 million gold marks and by the remission of three-months' treasury bills to cover the remaining 850 million. Similar operations were necessary to finance subsequent instalments. At one stage the abnormally low flow of water in the rivers Rhine and Elbe during that summer halted the barges transporting the huge quantities of silver required to be exported.

Foreign exchange was being hoarded in Germany on an increasing scale, aggravating the problem. As a result the index of the dollar/mark exchange rate, which had stood at one in 1913 and had hovered around 15 at the beginning of 1921, plummeted to nearly 63 by November 1921. Hyperinflation was still some way off, because the index recovered to around 46 in December 1921 and remained below 50 in the early months of 1922.[12]

Only a combination of internal financial discipline with massive foreign assistance could have arrested Germany's slide into virtual bankruptcy. A foreign loan would only become feasible when there was evidence that Germany was putting her own financial house in order. Yet the chicken and egg argument, whether the reparations question or Germany's internal budget problem should be settled first, continued unabated. Wirth, who had held on to the finance portfolio when he became chancellor, presented his budget for 1921–2 in July 1921. He forecast an expenditure of around 150 billion paper marks, nearly half of it treaty expenditure including reparations, and a revenue of only 80 billion paper marks. There may have been a propaganda element in these figures, but none could doubt the yawning gap in Germany's public finances.

There was, however, a continuing gulf between right and left on ways to tackle the deficit. The left wanted appropriation of property values, possibly outright confiscation. The right objected even to minor measures to make the collection of the National Emergency Levy (*Reichsnotopfer*) more effective. Nevertheless the Wirth–Rathenau government continued with its 'fulfilment offensive' to demonstrate simultaneously German good faith and inability to pay.

In October 1921 Rathenau and his French counterpart Louis Loucheur concluded the Wiesbaden agreement, which, similar to the Seydoux Plan, provided for direct German assistance in kind with French reconstruction over a period of years. It was in the main a public relations exercise, for French industry was not prepared to accept a large influx of German goods. Rathenau's calculation was that one more demonstration that the transfer of reparations, either in cash or goods, caused almost insuperable difficulties could only strengthen the German case. This was increasingly recognised, because in 1921 a sudden and severe slump hit the major industrial countries and only Germany, because of her inflationary policies, escaped. In 1921 average unemployment was 41 per thousand in Britain and 47 per thousand in the United States, but only six per thousand in Germany.

In the autumn of 1921 there were indications that German industry, whose representatives in the Reichstag, mainly in the DVP, had steadily refused to make taxation on property more effective, was preparing to come to the government's assistance through a loan. The moderate view in the RDI (*Reichsverband der deutschen Industrie*) was that the relative political and economic stabilisation of 1920–1 should be maintained and that Germany should regain her position as a trading nation in collaboration with the West. Internally the concessions made to the workers in 1918 should not be reversed, so that social peace would help to underpin the republican political compromise. There was also a more extreme view, held mainly in heavy industry, which wanted to undo much of what had been agreed with the trade unions, particularly the shorter working week. Raised production, especially in the mines, better productivity and rationalisation would form the basis for a more aggressively revisionist foreign and reparations policy. The conditions which came to be attached to the proposed industrial loan would have undermined the social compromise and were politically unacceptable.

The efforts to make reparations and fulfilment more viable, internally or externally, received a severe set-back when the Allied decision to partition Upper Silesia was formally announced. The policy of fulfilment appeared to have been proved futile. Wirth and Rathenau had at times tried to make the policy more palatable and to prove their own patriotic credentials by holding out the hope that the future of Upper Silesia would be resolved in Germany's favour. They had connived at assistance to the German irregular forces fighting there, when elsewhere they were committed to their disbandment. In the West there had been no evacuation of the areas on the Rhine occupied as sanctions in the spring.[13]

Upper Silesia entailed the resignation and reconstruction of Wirth's cabinet. Any hope that the DVP might join, widely entertained during the negotiations about an industrial loan, were now dashed. Even the DDP distanced itself, though Gessler, the defence minister and formally a member, remained at his post. Rathenau, also a formal member of the DDP, left the government for three months but continued to play an important role in reparations negotiations. He rejoined in January 1922 as foreign minister, a post he had coveted and which he held until his assassination on 24 June 1922. Wirth's second government was therefore even more in a minority. It had to rely on picking up support from case to case, on the right from the DVP or even the DNVP, and on the left from what remained of the USPD. This made it less likely than ever that Germany's finances could even begin to be set in order. In November 1921 official estimates put the German budget deficit at 110 billion paper marks, of which 60 billion were attributed to the treaty.

In early 1922 the international financial and political situation offered Germany little incentive to put her house in order and stop the rush towards hyperinflation. The new republican administration of President Harding made it clear that it could not induce Congress to cancel the Allied debts. Britain could not be generous to her continental allies if her American debts had to be repaid. French realism about reparations could thus make little progress. The Wirth government's request for a reparations moratorium in December 1921 seemed to the French a deliberate refusal to pay, the failure to tackle domestic inflation a wilful attempt to make payment impossible.

All the while the inflationary boom induced heavy investment by German industry and the recovery of production in many fields, pig-iron, crude steel, shipping, even coal supplemented by lignite, to pre-war levels. For a time the rapid external devaluation of the mark, while the internal price level moved upwards more slowly, enabled German industry to mount an export offensive.

In France a German economic revival without the shackles of a reparations settlement was seen as a danger signal, while in Britain it was seen as a necessary prelude to such a settlement and to a revival of the international economy as a whole. Given these wide differences, the Cannes conference in January 1922 failed to find a satisfactory substitute for the stalled schedule of payments agreed nine months earlier in London. Shortly afterwards the conciliatory Briand was replaced by the hardliner Poincaré in the French premiership.[14]

RAPALLO AND THE BEGINNING OF HYPERINFLATION

In spite of all adverse signals Lloyd George continued to place faith in international conferences as a means of resolving the many interconnected political and economic problems. Time was running out for him, for the economic slump of 1921 was undermining the popularity of his coalition government. Among the many big problems crowding in upon him, the Near East, with its impact on Anglo–French relations, had become particularly controversial.

Russia's future place in the community of nations was another great question. Lenin's New Economic Policy was raising hopes that the capitalist West might after all have a role in the economic reconstruction of Russia, but there would also be competition among the powers, including Germany, for a share in the Russian trade. Both Britain and Germany had concluded trade treaties with Russia in the spring of 1921.

The Wirth government was under great domestic pressure after the Upper Silesian verdict had revealed the meagre fruits of fulfilment and the development of relations with Russia seemed to offer some compensatory benefits. Wirth himself was attracted by the Russian schemes of Seeckt and of Ago von Maltzan, the head of the Russian section in the German foreign office. He knew about and sanctioned the secret contacts between the German and Russian armies. This military collaboration might help Germany to circumvent the disarmament clauses of Versailles. Rathenau did not regard Russia as capable of compensating Germany for the difficulties in her relations with the Allies. He had a more sceptical and realistic view than many in Germany or in the West of the commercial value of the Russian market. He was on the whole disinclined to take any risks in Western relations for the sake of Russian favours.

Such was the background to the Genoa conference and its spectacular disruption by the signing of the treaty of Rapallo between Russia and Germany.[15]

Three weeks before the Genoa conference convened on 10 April 1922 the German government received the proposals of the reparations commission for payments in the current year. Cash payments were to amount to 720 million gold marks and payments in kind to 1450 million. The German government was ordered to enact legislation by 31 May to raise an extra 60 billion paper marks in revenue. This direct intervention in Germany's fiscal affairs caused a storm of indignation. It seemed to add close financial supervision to the control of disarmament exercised by the Military Control Commission (IMKO), which was already deeply resented. Disillusionment with the policy of fulfilment was now so bitter that even its protagonists like Rathenau were leaning to a more aggressive stance.

When Chicherin, the Russian foreign minister, passed through Berlin on his way to Genoa in April, preparations for a treaty dealing with outstanding issues in Russo–German relations were all but completed. The Genoa conference itself was intended to produce a wide-ranging settlement of problems inhibiting international political and economic reconstruction. The course of events in the weeks leading up to it had further reduced the chances of such a comprehensive settlement, which were never good. Almost straightaway the position of Russia assumed a central importance, since the intransigent French position left little room for manoeuvre on reparations and the related economic issues.

Rumours reached the German delegation, which felt itself isolated and insufficiently consulted by Lloyd George and the British, that an Allied accord with the Russians might be in the making. In fact Western insistence, in their discussions with Chicherin, that the Soviet government should honour Tsarist debts inclined the Russians towards a deal with Germany. This enabled Maltzan to persuade Rathenau, in spite of his scepticism about Russia and to some extent against his better judgment, to meet the Russian delegation at the neighbouring resort of Rapallo. Within hours, on 16 April, the treaty was signed for which the groundwork had already been laid. The contents were not spectacular: resumption of diplomatic relations, mutual renunciation of compensation claims, most-favoured nation treatment of trade.

Nevertheless the Russo–German agreement to wipe the financial slate clean was impressive when contrasted with the inability of the Allies to reach a similar understanding with their former enemy. The immediate effect of Rapallo was sensational and destroyed any chance there might have been of the Genoa conference producing results. France was more than ever convinced of German bad faith. Rapallo was a step towards the French occupation of the Ruhr nine months later. It has remained to this day a symbol for the Eastern orientation in German policy, an alternative option for Germany if she felt rebuffed by the West.

The immediate effect for Germany was almost entirely negative. The policy of fulfilment, however painful and meagre in its results, was in ruins.[16]

The German government did its best to play down the significance of Rapallo, claiming that it was no more than a completion of agreements already initiated. It was to no avail, for the intractability of the external and internal political situation, highlighted by the assassination of Rathenau in June 1922, caused a massive loss of confidence and ushered in the phase of hyperinflation in the summer of 1922. Whereas at the end of 1921, 36 per cent of the deposits in major German banks were still owned by foreigners the proportion dropped to 11 per cent in the course of 1922.

Measures to show the serious intent of the German government, for example the law of 25 May 1922 making the Reichsbank independent, were counteracted by the evident impossibility of raising an international loan for Germany. The loan committee of the reparations commission suspended its work on 10 June 1922.

The flight from liquid into real assets had by early 1922 created a severe shortage of credit. In order to keep commercial life going from day to day the Reichsbank, in spite of all professions to the contrary, was forced to expand the monetary base. The dollar/mark exchange rate index, which had remained below 70 in the spring of 1922, began to go through the roof after June: in July it was 117.49, in August 270.26, in October 757.53, in December 1807.83. A dollar could be bought for 439.22 marks in July, but cost 7589.27 marks in December, a rise of 1539 per cent. The rise in German internal prices no longer lagged much behind the fall in the external value of the mark and the advantage conferred on German exports by the difference began to disappear. The index of German wholesale prices had risen from one in 1913 to 70.3 in June 1922, but by December 1922 it stood at 1475.

The increasing likelihood in the autumn of 1922 that the deadlock on reparations would propel the French into an occupation of the Ruhr had a day to day impact on the exchange value of the mark. The chicken and egg argument between right and left, whether reparations or the domestic printing press were to blame for the collapse of the currency, continued, but ceased to have any practical relevance.[17]

THE REALIGNMENT OF THE LEFT: THE REUNIFICATION OF THE SPD AND THE RISE OF THE KPD

Even before the policy of fulfilment had plumbed the depths of disappointment the parliamentary position of the Wirth coalition had been weak. A major reason for this lay in the changes in the political landscape that had taken place since 1920. The rise of the USPD at the expense of the SPD had been sensationally illustrated by the election results of June 1920. At last the electoral strength of the SPD, which had been sustained in the face of all difficulties, was being sapped by profound working-class disillusionment and bitterness. The drift to the USPD occurred among traditional areas and groups of socialist support, like the miners in the Ruhr; among workers in the industries newly created during the war, like the chemical industry in central Germany; and among young and previously unpoliticised workers outside the major industrial basins. In Leipzig, where the percentage of the poll in January 1919 was 20.7 for the SPD and 38.6 for the USPD, the respective percentages in June 1920 were 9.1 and 42.1. In Upper Bavaria the USPD's percentage of the poll rose from 3.7 in 1919 to 11.9 in 1920; in Württemberg from 2.7 to 12.8; in Pomerania from 1.9 to 16.7.

The USPD proved unable to integrate more than fleetingly this huge and diverse surge of support. The party was fundamentally divided between authoritarian and libertarian socialism, between support for a soviet and a parliamentary system and for and against affiliation to the Moscow-controlled Third International. The dividing line left most of the leadership and parliamentary party on the moderate side and the representatives of the radicalised mass following on the other. Hugo Haase, the party leader who had never wanted to destroy all the bridges back to a reunified socialist movement, was assassinated in November 1919. After him the chairmanship of the party was divided between Ernst Däumig, one of the radical leaders of the revolutionary Shop Stewards, and the more moderate Arthur Crispien.

In August 1920 the Comintern, the Third International, promulgated its twenty-one conditions for affiliation. They implied total subordination to the Russian party, the one socialist party that had made a successful revolution. For German socialists it would have been unthinkable before 1917 that they should accept the leadership of a party formed in much more primitive and backward conditions. For the radicalised mass following now supporting the USPD the revolutionary rigorism emanating from Moscow proved attractive.

The election of delegates to the USPD party congress convened in Halle in October 1920 showed a majority for acceptance of the twenty-one conditions and the congress itself voted 236 to 156 for affiliation to the Comintern. The minority left the congress and set up a separate party which, after the fusion of the left-wing majority with the KPD two months later, remained as the USPD. In the Reichstag it retained 59 of the 81 USPD members elected in June 1920, while the other 22 joined the KPD, giving it for the first time a sizeable *Fraktion*. The rank and file membership of the USPD divided very differently. Before the split in October 1920 it had risen to nearly 900 000. Around 370 000 joined the KPD, while about 340 000 remained with the USPD. The rest retreated from active politics, so that there was a loss from radical left-wing politics compared with the high-water mark of 1920.

On the other hand the KPD for the first time acquired a mass following. The first big electoral test after these events were the Prussian Landtag elections of 20 February 1921. In their strongholds, for example in Berlin and Bremen, the USPD and the KPD together lost over 10 per cent of their vote, compared with the Reichstag elections of the previous June. About half of this loss benefited the SPD, but the three working-class parties together also had a slightly reduced share of the vote. On the other hand the KPD for the first time gathered a sizeable vote, 7.4 compared with 2.1 per cent eight months previously.[18]

The rise of the KPD occurred just when the party was in process of being turned into a Moscow-orientated cadre party. In 1919 Paul Levi, an intellectual from a Jewish middle-class background, had become leader. Following in the tradition of Rosa Luxemburg's stress on spontaneous mass action, he tried to rid the party of putschism, adventurism and anarchism, even at the cost of a heavy haemorrhage of support. In the KPD merged with the USPD it was now his turn to be cast out. He and his associates resigned from the party's central committee in February 1921. Supporters of the Moscow line of imminent revolution, men like August Thalheimer, Heinrich Brandler and Wilhelm Pieck, later the first President of the DDR, came to the fore, with Karl

Radek frequently acting as the wire-puller sent from Moscow. Some of these men later became the victims of purges, as the Moscow line shifted in the transition from Lenin to Stalin. Paul Levi found his way back to the left of the SPD via the USPD.

The KPD line itself veered between revolutionary activism, attempts to undermine the SPD and the trade unions under slogans like 'union from below', and 'union from above'. An immediate consequence of the leadership changes in the KPD was an uprising in central Germany, of which the Leuna synthetic oil refinery near Merseburg was the main focus. The left had pressed for such revolutionary activism, hoping that it would act as the catalyst for a renewed revolutionary wave. While Levi was in control this type of ill-prepared action was discouraged, but the new central committee gave its backing.

Emissaries from Moscow, including Bela Kun, gave their blessing, perhaps because of the severe crisis in which the Soviet regime found itself at this moment. It was thought that the Fehrenbach government might be toppled and a more pro-Soviet course in German foreign policy might follow. The uprising in March 1921, led by the proletarian Robin Hood figure Max Hölz, received some support in other centres of radicalism like Hamburg, but in the Ruhr only about 200 000 workers participated in the general strike proclaimed by the KPD. The rising may well have started ahead of its planned date, because the Prussian authorities had themselves initiated police action against left-wing extremism in the central German industrial area.

Within a few days the ill-timed venture was crushed by the regular police forces, leaving at least 145 dead.[19] Its most important general impact was to heighten middle-class fears of a left-wing putsch. Resistance was stiffened to the government's efforts to comply with Allied demands for the disbandment of the civil guards, a central factor in the negotiations leading up to the London ultimatum of May 1921.

The fiasco aggravated internal disputes in the KPD. Along with Levi and the 'Levites' other well-known figures left the party, among them Ernst Reuter, known as 'Friesland', who had been the party's general secretary and ended up as social democratic mayor of West Berlin during the Russian blockade of 1948–9. Although Lenin expressed agreement with some of Levi's criticism of the March uprising, the twists and turns of the KPD were increasingly influenced and finally determined by the requirements of the Comintern's Executive Committee in Moscow. These were in turn governed by the perceived foreign policy interests of the Soviet Union and by the power struggle inside the Soviet Communist Party.

The KPD suffered a heavy loss of members as a result of disillusionment and the exclusion of successive waves of deviationists. By June 1921 the number of members was down to 180 000, less than half what had been reported at the beginning of the year. In 1924 the figure was back to about 100 000, not much more than it had been before the split in the USPD turned the KPD into a mass party. The loss of members and the subservience to Moscow did not, however, in the long run diminish the ability of the KPD to function as the electoral receptacle for left-wing radicalism.

When the SPD was in government in the hectic days of 1918 and 1919 it was hardly able to pause and take stock of its position. There was more energy and inclination to do so in opposition after the electoral setback of June 1920. The disadvantages of opposition were soon evident to the party leaders, especially when the party could not escape sharing responsibility for many unpopular decisions in foreign policy. Nevertheless a resolution was passed at the party congress in October 1920 which effectively prevented the party from going into coalition with the DVP. For the SPD rank and file Stresemann's party was now the principal instrument of the bourgeoisie and fundamentally antagonistic to the interests of the workers. Its republican credentials were dubious.

After the Prussian Landtag elections of February 1921 the DDP and the Centre Party insisted that the DVP should join the SPD-led coalition of Otto Braun, but the SPD refused. It temporarily left the government in Prussia and this was one of the reasons for its willingness to join the Wirth coalition in the Reich a few weeks later. The party could not afford to give up too many of the levers of power. By the autumn of 1921 the entry of the DVP into the Wirth coalition was under active discussion. It was part of the package deal which was to include a loan from industry to meet reparations, and a tax compromise to impose effective taxation on property as well as on consumption.

This was the political background against which the SPD party congress met at Görlitz in September 1921. There was a general feeling that the changed circumstances required a new statement of aims and principles, to take the place of that adopted at Erfurt in 1891. Eduard Bernstein, the father of revisionism, was a member of the committee which prepared the new programme. Some of the basic Marxist concepts that had inspired the Erfurt programme were toned down, if not discarded. Progressive pauperisation, the polarisation between a small number of monopoly capitalists and a vast undifferentiated mass of proletarians, had not occurred as expected. If the SPD was to make converts in a democratic parliamentary system, it had to attract groups like small farmers and shopkeepers, who were not in the least inclined to see themselves as part of a mass proletariat. The disappearance of such intermediate groups in the armageddon of class confrontation had therefore to be played down. The class war itself had to be stripped of its aura of violence and the party portrayed as a left-wing people's party rather than as a class party. Rhetoric about socialising property had to be muted.

The Görlitz programme was the closest the SPD got to revisionism in its official ideology during the Weimar period. The transformation was, however, strictly limited. The party was not likely to make wholesale conversions among farmers and the lower middle class and it could not afford to let the more radical left-wing parties make the running among its traditional working-class constituency. The most important practical political issue was to maintain the ability of the party to form coalitions in defence of the republic. It might have been easier to be in partnership with the DDP than the DVP, but the latter was now the more important party. There were voices warning that if it was the DVP today it might be the DNVP tomorrow. At the other end of the political spectrum there were realistic prospects that the rump of the USPD might find its way back to the SPD and coalition with the DVP might hinder these prospects.

The Görlitz congress passed a resolution proposed by the leadership rescinding the bar on a great coalition including the DVP. At the Reich level the formation of such a coalition came to nothing after the Upper Silesian partition and the failure of industry to come up with a loan. In Prussia, however, where the reparation and tax issues mattered less, Otto Braun resumed the premiership in November at the head of a coalition stretching from SPD to DVP. In the Reich Wirth's precarious second coalition was on several occasions in 1922 supported by the

USPD. After the Rathenau murder the SPD and USPD Reichstag *Fraktionen* entered into a formal collaboration and the reunification of the two parties was completed in the autumn of 1922.

At this time the USPD was in a very weak position. Landtag elections had shown the erosion of its electoral support: for example in Mecklenburg-Schwerin the USPD vote had declined from 7.7 per cent to 0.8 per cent between June 1920 and March 1921, in Baden from 10.9 per cent to 3.0 per cent between June 1920 and October 1921.

The support the USPD gave to Wirth was in part due to its fear of precipitating a Reichstag dissolution. In the joint party programme with which the two socialist parties marked their reunification the USPD gave up much of its uncompromising stand on war guilt and internationalism. The reunited party remained tied to the patriotism that had all along hamstrung the ability of the SPD to nail the enemies of the republic and the stab in the back myth. On the other hand the SPD gave up some of the revisionism it had taken on board at Görlitz. There was a reversion to the rhetoric of class war and revolution.

Some who were to play a leading role in the SPD in the next decade now re-entered the party, among them the two Rudolfs, Breitscheid and Hilferding. The latter became the principal theoretician of the party in the 1920s, with perceptive ideas about the evolution of organised capitalism. He was Reich finance minister in 1923 and 1928–9.

Theoretically the reunified SPD gave the Wirth government a broader parliamentary base, for with over 170 seats it was again much the largest party in the Reichstag. In fact the leftward extension of the SPD made collaboration with the bourgeois parties in the coalition much more difficult. The Centre Party, in an effort to broaden its support beyond the Catholic part of the population, was itself moving to the right.

These changes in the party landscape played a part in the final collapse of Wirth's government in November 1922. In the longer run the reunification of the socialist parties was a factor in keeping the SPD out of government between November 1922 and May 1928, except for the brief interlude of Stresemann's great coalition at the height of the crisis of 1923. It also made it more difficult for the party to break out of its proletarian ghetto.[20]

THE RADICAL RIGHT AND THE RISE OF THE HITLER MOVEMENT IN BAVARIA

The deepening crisis of the republic over reparations and inflation also transformed and radicalised the right wing of German politics. The DNVP had been formed as an amalgam of many elements: old Prussian Conservatives, Free Conservatives and some National Liberals, Anti-Semites, Christian Socialists and Pan-Germans and *Völkische*. Some of these groups overlapped and the ideological differences were fluid, but personal and sectarian infighting could also aggravate the differences.

The elections of June 1920 had established the DNVP as the major right-wing nationalist party. It now had considerable support outside its traditional East Elbian Protestant strongholds. Many interest groups became linked to the party, among them the Agrarian League, now renamed *Reichslandbund*, the important association of artisans, small traders and white-collar employees, *Deutschnationaler Handlungsgehilfen-Verband*, and some industrial interests.[21]

In essence the DNVP was totally opposed to the republican regime, but it was no easier for the German right wing to play the role of opposition than it was for the SPD to assume the mantle of government. The vested interests linked to the party had specific aims more likely to be obtained by participation in government than by opposition. After June 1920 the possible entry of the DNVP into government came within the realm of discussion. The two most prominent leaders of the party, Oscar Hergt and Karl Helfferich, both of them in high office before 1918, wanted to exercise influence either through reponsible opposition or from within a coalition. The gulf widened between this attitude and the violent and revolutionary radical right, constantly reinforced by crisis and chaos. In 1922 three of the party's 71 Reichstag members became separated and formed the *Deutsch-Völkische Freiheitspartei*. This was symptomatic of the constant growth and radicalisation of the radical-right or national-revolutionary spectrum of politics.

There was nothing new in the ideas and attitudes of the many sects and parties on the radical right. Even in Imperial Germany organised chauvinism, racism and anti-semitism had been formidable and deeply enmeshed with orthodox conservatism.

The new factor after the defeat of 1918 was profound psychological disorientation and alienation among many who had
previously been the most unquestioning supporters of the existing
order. The only way to cope with unacceptable reality was to take
refuge in myth. The stab in the back myth offered an explanation
of the unacceptable and conveniently tied together the external
enemy, who for the moment was unassailable, with the internal
enemy, revolution, Marxism, Jewry, the republic, fulfilment.
Added weight was given to this form of extremism by the support
of large sections of the intelligentsia. Again there was a formidable
ancestry, German romanticism, anti-modernism, the iconoclastic,
aphoristic, often misunderstood utterances of Nietzsche. Passion-
ate opposition to democracy, parliamentarism, liberalism and
reason itself came from fashionable writers of the moment, men
like Oswald Spengler and Ernst Jünger. Reaction to the day-to-
day problems of disarmament, reparations, inflation and continuing revolutionary spasms on the left therefore took on a hysterical
counter-revolutionary guise on the right.

The violence of the radical right was powerfully reinforced by
the speed-up of demobilisation of all types of forces after the Spa
conference. The Allied requirement to bring down the size of the
German army to 100 000 left a whole stratum of displaced officers
who could not or would not find a place in civilian society.
Successive attempts to dissolve *Einwohnerwehren* and Freikorps
radicalised and drove underground many of their members and
organisations. Most of these men saw an ongoing need to protect
German society from 'bolshevism'. The spirit of the Freikorps had
been dangerous enough when there had been obvious internal
and external enemies to fight in the days before the Kapp Putsch.
Since then the growing threat of redundancy brought resentment
against the republic to boiling point. Yet the attitude of the Reich
government, even under Wirth, had not entirely lost its
ambivalence towards the use of such elements, for example in
Upper Silesia. Seeckt was suspicious of the Freikorps spirit and
anxious to make the Reichswehr politically neutral. Nevertheless
links were maintained with remnants of dissolved Freikorps in
establishing secret stores of arms and in the border guard against
Poland.

The Prussian government was the most forthright in controlling
and when necessary suppressing politically compromised irregular

forces, under whatever name they appeared. Severing was
Prussian minister of the interior from March 1920 until October
1926, except for just over six months from April 1921, and
dissolved organisations like the *Orgesch* in Prussia. He shared the
suspicion that had grown up between the SPD and the Reichswehr after the Kapp Putsch, but had to make concessions to
Seeckt on questions such as the border guard in East Prussia.[22]

In Bavaria the climate was favourable to the radical right,
particularly after the Kapp Putsch. From March 1920 to
September 1921 Kahr was head of a coalition of the BVP and
DNVP.[23] The idea began to gain ground that Bavaria was a focus
of order, *Ordnungszelle Bayern*, which stood out against the spread
of chaos and bolshevism elsewhere in the Reich. Eventually a cure
for the German malaise would come from Bavaria. Munich, the
Bavarian capital, was particularly fertile ground for *völkisch*
groups after the episodes of the Soviet republics of April 1919.

Hitler's movement grew from one of these groups and rapidly
made its impact as the most extreme and radical among them.
The BVP, always the largest single party in Bavaria, and the
Catholic Church could not bring themselves to offer clear and
active opposition to Hitler and his party when they became a
threat to law and order. The fear of revolution and of
'bolshevism', a broad term in their book, had entered so deeply
into their outlook that even the furthest extremes of the right had
to be tolerated as possible allies in another time of troubles. It was
only after the Beer Hall Putsch of November 1923 that they learnt
their lesson.

The National Socialist German Workers Party (*Nationalsozialistische Deutsche Arbeiterpartei*) moved out of the pack of *völkisch*
sectarianism entirely because of the personality of Hitler. The
twenty-five point programme adopted early in 1920, along with
the name of the party, was a conflation of aims and aspirations
current among extreme nationalists in Germany and Austria
before and after the First World War. Even the mixture was not
particularly original. Its most obvious characteristic was to
combine the radical nationalism of the extreme right with
some of the anti-capitalism of the left. In making this combination
anti-Semitism provided a readily available and easily exploitable
link.

Such a concoction would have remained unremarkable if
Hitler had not found the means of projecting his specific version

of it on to an ever widening public. It is said that when Hitler attended his first meeting of the German Workers Party in September 1919 and spoke, the then leader of this tiny sect, the railway worker Anton Drexler, whispered to his neighbour in broad Bavarian dialect: 'Man, he's got a mouth, we could do with him'. Hitler was at this time awaiting demobilisation from the army. He was being used by his officers for political education among the troops and to gather information on political activities in the city. Like so many soldiers he could not see himself returning to ordinary civilian life. Even before 1914 he had not been able to fit into it and had been a drifter. Thus political agitation offered a way out.

It was not long before Hitler's performances became a by-word among the frequenters of Munich's beer halls, something that had to be experienced, if only as 'a bit of a lark'. The hallmark of Hitler as a speaker in this kind of ambience was his ability to sense the mood of his audience, to articulate their frustrations and give vent to their resentments and hatreds. He acted like a medium. No one else could use extreme verbal violence, in due course accompanied by physical violence, so effectively. Less immediately apparent was Hitler's remarkable ability to dominate and his great tactical skill, fuelled by a powerful political instinct. It was this sure instinct that enabled him adapt his ideological stock-in-trade, in itself entirely second hand, to whatever the immediate tactical situation required.

In the radical right camp, with its great diversity of organisations, ideological nuances and precise programmes did not matter much. In the early days the NSDAP had to seek its adherents mainly among those who suffered from a sense of dispossession, not only the working and lower middle classes, but the many declassé members of the middle class. Therefore the anti-capitalist elements in the Nazi ideology figured quite prominently in Hitler's speeches and propaganda. A central feature of the 25-point programme was the abolition of interest payment and of unearned income. Such economic crankiness was promoted by Gottfried Feder, an important figure in the early party, but insignificant in the Third Reich. Hitler exploited anti-capitalist resentment to the full in his early speeches, but always combined it with virulent anti-Semitism by equating capitalists with Jews, just as he was at the same time identifying Jewry with bolshevism. A distinction could thus be maintained between legitimate property and productive capital and exploitative, internationalist, Jewish finance capitalism, a distinction long familiar to German conservatives.

National socialism began to receive patronage from the establishment because, while posing no real threat to property, it could yet prove more attractive to the masses misled by socialism than other organisations on the radical right. Hitler himself was anxious from the start to distinguish his movement from other *völkisch* organisations, for example the *Deutsch-Völkischer Schutz-und Trutzbund* (German Racial Defensive and Offensive League), one of the more considerable among the many extreme nationalist groups. He claimed that they were ineffective, élitist discussion circles, while the NSDAP was a potential mass movement. Hitler's radical anti-Semitism, which put the 'Jewish question' always at the centre of his propaganda and made the Jews the incarnation of all evil, also distinguished his approach from that of other *völkisch* groups. All of them were anti-Semitic, but mostly attempted to maintain some rationality in their attack. Other enemies and causes usually ranked higher in their catalogue of evils than the Jews. The totality of Hitler's anti-Semitic offensive was beyond reason, but its cutting edge derived from this very irrationality. Words like 'fanatical', 'ruthless', 'brutal', and 'barbaric' lost their normal pejorative meaning in Hitler's rhetoric and took on a positive ring.[24]

A meeting in the Munich Hofbräuhaus on 24 February 1920 came to be regarded in the mythology of Nazism as the moment of foundation. Shortly afterwards Kahr came to power. He worked closely with Ernst Pöhner, a strongly nationalist judge, who had been appointed police president of Munich by the Hoffmann Government after the collapse of the Soviet republics in May 1919. Wilhelm Frick, minister of the interior in the Third Reich and executed at Nuremberg in 1946, was head of the political section of the police under Pöhner. These men deliberately refrained from suppressing the budding Nazi movement because they considered it a useful counterweight to the socialist parties among the proletariat.

An equally important protector was Captain Ernst Röhm, through whom Hitler maintained his links with the Reichswehr after his official demobilisation in March 1920. Röhm was one of the most radical younger officers in the Bavarian Reichswehr, a fervent believer in a nationalist, revolutionary regeneration of German society, but he retained a sentimental attachment to the Bavarian Wittelsbach dynasty. Another indigenous Bavarian, the nationalist writer Dietrich Eckart, had much influence on Hitler and introduced him to his friends in Munich society, including the family of the piano manufacturer Bechstein.

Röhm and Eckart helped with the purchase of the party newspaper, the *Völkische Beobachter*, at the end of 1920, and Eckart became the editor. Men who were to accompany Hitler on the road to power made their appearance, among them Rudolf Hess, a student at Munich University of the geopolitician Haushofer. Alfred Rosenberg, one of a group of Baltic Germans drawn into the movement, saw himself as the ideologue of the party and succeeded Eckart as editor of the *Völkischer Beobachter* in 1923.[25]

In February 1921 the Nazi party was sufficiently well established to fill the tent of the Zirkus Krone with an audience of 6000. Hitler himself took great interest in the choice of the party's symbols: the swastika was well known in *völkisch* circles, but it came to be used in a specific form on the party's flags and emblems.

At this time Hitler officially only held the position of the party's propaganda chief (*Werbeobmann*). It was therefore a highly significant development when in July 1921 he imposed his overall leadership by threatening to resign. Drexler and some of the other earlier members had no alternative but to accept his terms, for only his demagogical skill and enormous will power had made the party into a considerable force.

The use of violence was always an essential part of Hitler's tactics. The breakup of hostile political meetings, the ejection of opponents from one's own meetings with deliberate brutality, street brawling to show domination and to provoke, such tactics had helped to give his movement publicity and to spread fear among opponents. For this purpose a gang of strong-arm men and bodyguards had been collected from which the SA (*Sturmabteilung*) grew during 1921, when especially after the end of the fighting in Upper Silesia many fighters were looking for a new home. Hitler's concept for his paramilitary formation was that it should be a political and propaganda force, a second prong to the party. Disreputable characters did not deter Hitler; in fact he believed the more disreputable a man was in his private life the more suitable he might be for the movement, provided he was sufficiently dedicated and fanatical.

Developments in 1922 and 1923 brought it about that the SA became assimilated to the military associations that were playing an increasing role in German politics. It acquired a dynamic of its own and circumscribed Hitler's room for manoeuvre. This problem of control was one of the reasons for the ill-timed beer hall putsch and in a different form surfaced again in the tensions that led to the Night of Long Knives in 1934.[26]

When Hitler had finally put himself in untrammelled control of the NSDAP in July 1921 and was taking first steps to recruit an enlarged paramilitary formation in the shape of the SA, a year had elapsed since the Spa agreement. During that time the Kahr Government had dragged its feet over the dissolution of civil guards and security police forces. For a time it seemed that the *Orgesch* would provide the means of maintaining the civil guards in legal form in Bavaria and in the Reich as a whole. The organisation was named after the Bavarian *Forstrat* (forest official) Georg Escherich and the membership was mainly mainstream conservative and nationalist. In North Germany the suppression of the *Orgesch* caused the torch of nationalist military preparedness to pass chiefly to the *Stahlhelm* and the *Jungdeutscher Orden, Jungdo* for short.[27] Both were destined to play a considerable role in the republic for the rest of its days. The *Stahlhelm* (steel helmet) was in form a veterans' association; the *Jungdo* was inspired by the romantic, nationalist, anti-bourgeois ideology of the prewar youth movement.

In Bavaria the government came under growing pressure in the spring of 1921 to comply with the disarmament obligations. As a result a new cover organisation emerged as the main rallying point for the orthodox right, which eventually assumed the title *Bund Bayern und Reich* (Bavaria and Reich League). The label itself demonstrates the mixture of German nationalism and Bavarian particularism that also characterised the policies of the Kahr Government and of the BVP under its powerful leader Dr Georg Heim. These men were Bavarian monarchists, who remained loyal to the House of Wittelsbach, but they were not outright separatists. At most they contemplated a temporary separation from the Reich, in conjunction with other Catholic regions like the Rhineland, and also with Austria, to save the Reich from the bolshevism that was threatening to engulf it from Berlin and Prussia. They cultivated some French links, which gave their opponents a chance to accuse them of high treason.

Organisations like *Orgesch* and *Bund Bayern und Reich* also saw themselves as protecting the middle classes against the powerful and militant organisations of the left. They were the unions of the *Mittelstand* confronting the trade unions of the proletariat. There continued to be a clear ideological difference between them and the radical, revolutionary right, but under the pressure of events the dividing line often became indistinct. Among the more extreme elements there were, besides the NSDAP, the *Bund Oberland*, which took part in the fighting in the Ruhr in 1920 and in Upper Silesia, and the remnants of the Ehrhardt Brigade, who with their leader had found refuge in Bavaria after the Kapp Putsch. Hitler received much help from Captain Ehrhardt in setting up the SA after August 1921. The Ehrhardt Brigade also spawned the secret Organisation Consul (OC), dedicated to terrorism and assassination. After a lull following the collapse of the Kapp Putsch these more extreme organisations played a part in re-igniting the endemic civil war and in brutalising and militarising German politics until the climax of 1923.[28]

THE MURDERS OF ERZBERGER AND RATHENAU

The first big blow struck by the clandestine forces of the radical right was the assassination of Erzberger on 26 August 1921. The perpetrators were members of the Organisation Consul, young ex-officers who had figured in various phases of the internal and external postwar violence. They were typical of the displaced soldiers whose only satisfaction was in continued fighting. Erzberger's assassins escaped to Hungary via Munich, returned to Germany in 1933 and were put on trial after 1945.

After the murder Ebert and the Reich government issued an emergency decree for the protection of the republic under article 48 of the constitution. The Bavarian government challenged the validity of this procedure, though condemning the murder of Erzberger. The conflict between Berlin and Munich led to Kahr's fall. With him went his DNVP Minister of Justice, Roth, under whose aegis Bavarian judges, even more than elsewhere in the

Reich, had meted out heavy punishment for any transgression from the left, while letting off right wing offenders lightly, if the police had brought them to book at all.

Kahr was succeeded by Count Lerchenfeld, whose BVP-led coalition pursued a policy not essentially different from its predecessor. There was, however, an attempt to maintain better relations with Berlin and to keep a firmer grip on the radical right. Pöhner and Frick left the Munich police presidency and Hitler was threatened with deportation as an Austrian.

None of this could stop the growth of the Nazi movement and the general advance of political radicalisation. Hitler remained, however, a lesser player, with only a limited ability to dictate to other more powerful but less fanatical actors on the Bavarian stage. Ten months later the murder of Rathenau provided an even more dramatic replay of the events following Erzberger's death.[29]

Rathenau was frequently warned that he would be the target of an assassination attempt, but he refused to take precautions. On 24 June 1922 he left his home in West Berlin to drive to his office in an open car and his assassins gunned him down from another car which drew alongside. It is probably going too far to claim that Rathenau deliberately incurred martyrdom, but the policy of fulfilment was in deep crisis after his deal at Rapallo. It is equally difficult to be too precise about the motives of his killers, other than that they wanted to hit a prominent representative of the republic and of fulfilment, and that they came from exactly the same quarter as the assassins of Erzberger. Kern and Fischer, the two principal perpetrators, were again young ex-officers with links to the Organisation Consul. Blind, nihilistic activism drove them on. Rathenau was particularly in their sights as a Jew, doubly hated because he was so German as well and had played so significant a role in German affairs. It is more speculative to claim that the murderers and their circle also saw him as a renegade representative of the imperial bourgeois ruling elite.

Rathenau's murder shook the German public deeply, for he commanded much respect among the moderate middle classes. The left saw the murder as another right-wing outrage directed against the very fabric of the republic. As was the case after the Kapp Putsch, the official representatives of the right, for example the DNVP leadership and particularly Helfferich, were put very much on the defensive. Even so it may be doubted if Wirth's famous remarks in the Reichstag: 'The enemy is on the right – here are those who drip poison into the wounds of the German people!' were entirely wise. It became relatively easy for the right to claim that the new decrees for the protection of the republic were aimed primarily at them.

These decrees and the law subsequently passed by the two-thirds majority required by the constitution, for Weimar an almost unique case of consensus, were more effective and longer lasting than those passed after the murder of Erzberger. They involved the Reich government in an even fiercer clash with the Bavarian government than had occurred nearly a year earlier following Erzberger's murder. Munich declared the law for the protection of the republic invalid and passed its own law for the security of the state. The criminal investigation into Rathenau's murder was obstructed in Munich. Lerchenfeld, the Bavarian prime minister, found himself under pressure from huge demonstrations of the right wing political and paramilitary organisations and threatened with a putsch. Hitler felt deeply let down when it did not take place and fulminated in private against 'counts and generals' without the true revolutionary fanaticism. Prolonged negotiations between Munich and Berlin led to a compromise which left the law for the protection of the republic largely ineffective in Bavaria, where it was most needed.[30]

THE OCCUPATION OF THE RUHR

The upsurge of republican sentiment after Rathenau's murder was impressive, but it made virtually no impact on a rapidly deteriorating situation, most obvious in the catastrophic collapse of the German currency from July 1922. The downward slide could only have been halted if there had been the prospect of unravelling the whole tangled web of interlocking problems, reparations, Germany's huge budget deficit, international debts, French security and British and American foreign policy goals.

The fierce nationalist agitation against reparations and fulfilment left the Wirth cabinet little room for manoeuvre. Although Germany did not in fact pay much more in cash or kind in the autumn of 1922, there was no agreement on a moratorium. Just before its fall in November 1922 the Wirth government had succeeded in obtaining a broad measure of agreement, stretching from industry and the DVP to the now reunited SDP, on a German negotiating position. In a note to the Allies there was a detailed offer for the stabilisation of the mark in return for a three- or four-year moratorium on payments and an international loan of 500 million gold marks.

This position was part of a deal that would have led to the entry of the DVP into the government, turning it into a great coalition. The bourgeois partners in the coalition wanted such a widening to the right to counteract the weight of the reunited and more leftward-orientated SPD and had entered into formal cooperation with the DVP during the summer. In October the DVP agreed to an extension of Ebert's term of office till June 1925, thus avoiding the necessity of a presidential election. The SPD leaders were in favour of broadening the coalition, but the SPD *Fraktion* refused to follow their leaders, as so often in Weimar. It was hardly surprising that they baulked at linking themselves to the DVP, for Stinnes had only just demanded publicly that the eight-hour day, the symbol of the revolution's social achievements, should be scrapped. Also typical for political life in Weimar was the fact that minor irritants, like changes in grain-price subvention, against which the SPD had voted a few days earlier, contributed to these decisions of major significance.

The reunited SPD preferred to relinquish its hold on power rather than run risks with its new-found unity. Ebert picked Wilhelm Cuno, a director of the Hamburg–America Shipping Line, formerly a member of the DVP but currently without party ties, to head a bourgeois coalition of the DVP, the DDP, the Centre Party and the BVP. In form it was a cabinet 'above parties' and the SPD did not oppose it.

One of the new cabinet's first acts was to transmit a reparations memorandum similar to Wirth's final offer. Neither was seen in Paris as offering anything concrete. It contained no guarantees about the size and timing of reparations. The new British Conservative government under Bonar Law, formed after Lloyd George's fall on 19 October, did not, in the course of its meetings with Poincaré in December 1922, offer any new concessions, nor was a way out of the deadlock indicated by Washington. The French prime minister had pinned himself into a corner, for his political position was based on the claim that he would make

Germany pay and on the hidden agenda that through the reparation lever France might after all obtain the security that had eluded her at Versailles.

To retain his credibility Poincaré had to carry out his threat to extract productive pledges. On 9 January 1923 the reparations commission voted, with Britain abstaining, that there was deliberate default on coal deliveries, having already registered a default on timber and telegraph poles. This provided the legal cover for the military move into the Ruhr by France and Belgium. Although the move had been so long in the making, it was so cautiously embarked upon that it took place in three stages on 11, 15 and 17 January. It ushered in a tragic year in European history and brought the Weimar Republic to the verge of collapse.[31]

In Germany the response to the French move was a mighty upsurge of nationalist outrage. Many commentators perceived a national unity comparable to that of August 1914, but if there was a *Burgfrieden* it was very short-lived. All the antagonisms that had already approached a level near civil war became even more acute. The German government declared a policy of passive resistance in the Ruhr and undertook to provide the necessary financial underpinning. Billions of paper marks were made available in credits to industry in the Ruhr and in subvention of wages. Even so the uneven distribution of the burden, with real wages among many groups of workers dropping to less than half their 1913 level, caused great bitterness and reduced the chances that passive resistance could be sustained for very long.

The vast cost of keeping the Ruhr financially afloat, while tax revenues and export earnings were lost, was bound to reduce the already deeply shaken finances of the Reich to total chaos. On 2 January 1923 one dollar cost 7260 marks; on 11 January it had risen to 10 450 marks and on 31 January to 49 000 marks. The Reichsbank then embarked on a support operation for the mark, using its remaining reserves of gold and foreign currencies. These were no longer needed for reparations, for in retaliation against the French action the German government had stopped all payments and deliveries. The mark stabilised around 20 000 marks to the dollar until 18 April when the domestic and external political stalemate caused a further slide. Thereafter the Reichsbank confined itself to occasional interventions which were also given up at the end of June. This was the result:[32]

Average price of the dollar in Berlin
(in brackets: exchange rate index, 1913 = 1)

May	47 670	(11 355)
June	109 996	(26 202)
July	353 412	(84 186)
	In millions	
August	4.62	(1.1)
September	98.86	(23.5)
	In billions (= 1000 million)	
October	25.26	(6)
November	2193.60	(522)

The paper mark was officially stabilised on 20 November 1923 at a rate of 4200 billion marks to the dollar. The total internal war debt of the German Reich of 154 billion marks was then worth a mere 15.4 pfennigs.

These developments, with their catastrophic social and political consequences, made it impossible for Germany to sustain the policy of passive resistance beyond the autumn of 1923. The German mood when the Ruhr was occupied in January 1923 made any other policy for the time being impossible. The official rationalisation for passive resistance was that it would deprive the occupiers of any economic benefit from their move. There was a solid basis for the German calculation, for deliveries in kind, above all coal deliveries vital to French industry, fell off sharply. They gradually recovered, as the French authorities found means of getting deliveries out of the Ruhr. Support for passive resistance was solid among railway workers who were state employees. The French and Belgians had to bring in their own railway workers to move the coal from the pitheads and even by May 1923 deliveries were only about a third of the average monthly reparation deliveries in 1922. There were thus considerable economic pressures on both sides to get back to the negotiating table, but they were much greater and more immediate on the German side. In the longer run the damage to the French economic and financial position was, however, sufficient to cause the failure of the operation and the fall of Poincaré.

The Franco–German struggle and the international context surrounding it were not fundamentally changed by the Ruhr occupation, but there was a hostility not far removed from open war, while the stakes were even higher than before. On the French side the ring round the Ruhr was only gradually tightened, with exports of coal to unoccupied Germany prohibited on 30 January and a customs barrier being set up on 15 February. A large number of uncooperative Ruhr inhabitants were expelled, including 46 000 officials and their dependants. There were some serious incidents. In a clash between workers and French troops at the Krupp works in Essen on 31 March 13 workers were killed and 30 wounded. Gustav Krupp von Bohlen und Halbach, head of the firm, and other Krupp directors were put on trial and condemned to long terms of imprisonment and heavy fines. The execution of Albert Leo Schlageter on 26 May for acts of sabotage created a martyr for German nationalism, whose memory was still being officially celebrated in the Third Reich. He was an ex-Freikorps fighter who may have been a member of the NSDAP. The sabotage troop to which he belonged had links with the Reichswehr and the ministry of transport. His case shows how thin was the dividing line between passive and active resistance and how close the German government came to overstepping it.[33]

French policy was, however, hardly less ambivalent. Officially restraint had to be exercised and limited aims professed in order not to widen even further the gulf between France and the Anglo-Saxon powers, especially Britain. Behind the scenes there was much discussion of more ambitious goals, an autonomous Rhineland, a divided Germany, as the German chaos deepened. There was also much uncertainty among French decision-makers about what was feasible and in the real interests of France. The encouragement of separatism, in the Rhine area and in Bavaria, had long been an element of French policy, but there was disagreement how far this could be taken.[34]

In Germany the Cuno government and industrial interests were still casting around for a diplomatic solution. These culminated in a new reparations note on 2 May, but it came no nearer to offering either a solution to the internal problem of stabilisation or an overall figure acceptable to France. It did not give any real incentive to the British to step up the pressure on France. The failure of this initiative ended hopes of an early negotiated solution to the Ruhr stalemate.

At home the weak Reich government was exposed to the rising tide of nationalist extremism, still strongest in its Bavarian redoubt. Cuno had been chosen as chancellor because of his international financial contacts, particularly with Britain, which it was hoped would lead to a diplomatic solution of the reparations tangle. This politically naïve businessman was unable to stand up to the hypernationalism that was sweeping the country.

Even those most likely to suffer in such an atmosphere, the SPD and even the KPD, could not simply contract out of the chauvinist outrage. The KPD increasingly took a 'national bolshevist' line, that the bourgeoisie could not be trusted to defend Germany and that only after a successful revolution, in which all the dispossessed would form up behind the proletariat, would French imperialism be defeated. Only through the defeat of Stinnes and Krupp would Poincaré and Loucheur be defeated. In his famous 'Schlageter' speech on 21 June 1923 Karl Radek made a thinly veiled appeal to the revolutionaries of the radical right: 'Schlageter, the courageous soldier of the counter-revolution, deserves to receive honest manly honour from us, the soldiers of the revolution . . . . If the circles of the German fascists, who sincerely want to serve the German people, do not understand the meaning of Schlageter's fate, then Schlageter died in vain . . .' Radek and his masters in Moscow were increasingly convinced that a German October was at last about to happen, based on the strong proletarian position in central Germany. The pressure of the Ruhr occupation and the collapse of the currency were raising the German civil war not only to a new pitch of intensity, but the regional strongholds of the opposing camps were threatening to tear the Reich apart.[35]

In Bavaria the pressure of the paramilitary associations and of the *völkisch* movement brought about the resignation of Lerchenfeld in November 1922, because he was felt to have been too accommodating towards Berlin in the aftermath of the Rathenau murder. Von Knilling, from the right wing of the BVP, became prime minister. The relationship between the Bavarian government and the military associations remained more than ever ambivalent in the tense situation of 1923. The government could not dispense with them, but was itself threatened by them.

Within the nationalist right and among the military associations the divisions between moderates and radicals, often also a generational divide, could only be thinly disguised. An overall organisation created in 1922, United Patriotic Associations (*Vereinigte Vaterländische Verbände*), had little influence. The Ruhr occupation had the effect of strengthening the more extreme and dynamic elements. Since the NSDAP, the SA and Hitler were undoubtedly the most active, their influence grew. They were, however, even now only one group in the radical right, *Völkische* movement. Ludendorff had made his home in Munich and in 1923 he could be regarded as the most prominent and prestigious personality among the *Völkische*.

Ideological and personal disagreements were potentially limit-less among all these groups, but they mattered less because the immediate sense of crisis pushed them into the background. When the Ruhr occupation began Hitler took the line that resistance to the occupier must still take second place to the overthrow of the 'November criminals' at home. It was the mirror image to Radek's contention that the road to the overthrow of French imperialism led through a successful proletarian revolution in Germany.

Hitler's idiosyncratic line did not prevent his collaboration with other radical right activists like the *Bund Oberland* in another umbrella organisation in early 1923, later known as the *Kampfbund* (fighting league). The party and the SA were too important to be left out and their extreme radicalism brought them ever more recruits. In a trial of strength at the end of January 1923 Hitler forced the Bavarian government to give up their attempt to ban a big party rally in Munich, in the party mythology the first of the rallies later to be held at Nuremberg. The government had declared a state of siege to prevent serious disorder, but the intervention of Röhm with von Lossow, now the commander of the Bavarian Reichswehr, enabled Hitler to go ahead. Lossow, a Bavarian, had been appointed to the Munich command by Seeckt in order to cope with the delicate situation in which the Reichswehr found itself between the Bavarian government, the paramilitaries and the increasing need to prepare for mobilisation in case of further French encroachments. It was a role of such complexity that even a general with more political sense would have found it hard to play.

Although the many operators on the Bavarian scene had to take the Nazi movement increasingly seriously, Hitler was still only a bit player on this crowded stage. As the German chaos deepened, his view was that a unique opportunity to overthrow the republic should not be missed and that it was his mission to bring about the national counter-revolution. Mussolini's march on Rome the previous October would be paralleled by a march on Berlin.

Hitler greatly overestimated the extent to which he could control events. The *Bund Bayern und Reich* remained the largest of the paramilitary leagues in Bavaria and was clearly at odds with the radicalism of the Nazis and the other more extreme groups. In the atmosphere of 1923 its relative moderation may have led to a loss of members to the SA, but made relations with the government and the Reichswehr easier.

On 1 May Hitler suffered a serious set-back when he had assembled a large number of SA and other formations to disrupt the May day parades of the left-wing parties in Munich. Lossow and the Government forced him to abandon an armed attack and the parades went ahead peacefully under the protection of the police. Hitler had come near to a putsch, but he could not risk it with the army and the Bavarian police against him. It was only the relentless aggravation of the crisis that enabled him to recover from the fiasco.[36]

Seeckt had met Hitler in Munich in March 1923 and remained unimpressed. Outside Bavaria the Reichswehr had, however, to strengthen its links with the paramilitary forces of the right in the same way as Lossow was doing in the south. The Stahlhelm and the Jungdo were the biggest available reservoirs of patriotic manpower. Following the Rathenau murder the Prussian government, through its minister of the interior Severing, had banned these organisations, but they became legal again in January 1923. Thus were the protective devices of the republic undermined by the external pressure.

The NSDAP and later the *Deutsch-Völkische Freiheitspartei*, the radical right group split off from the DNVP, were, however, banned in Prussia. No amount of patriotic solidarity in the face of the French enemy could prevent the nationalist right from regarding the SPD-led Prussian government as treasonable and as an enemy within. The removal of the Braun–Severing government ranked high among the priorities of even the more respectable right.

The Prussian government was at this stage a great coalition including the DVP, while the Cuno government was making advances to the DNVP and flirting with the radical right. The whole parliamentary merry-go-round was increasingly an abomination to large numbers to the right of centre. The constant promulgation of decrees under article 48 only went to confirm the utter bankruptcy of parliamentary democracy in their eyes. There were widespread calls for a dictatorship or directory and Seeckt's name was often mentioned in this connection. Seeckt himself did nothing to discourage such talk, but he was far too cautious to act prematurely. Nor did he show much enthusiasm for the relationship between the Reichswehr and the nationalist paramilitary elements. He did not wish to be dragged into irresponsible adventures by Freikorps elements. In the situation of 1923 the need to cultivate such forces, now generally known as the Black Reichswehr, to supply them with arms and to set up secret weapons depots, had, however, become inescapable in Seeckt's eyes. Gessler as Reichswehr minister defended the policy in the Reichstag and between him, Seeckt and Severing there were discussions and agreements to define the status of the Black Reichswehr.[37]

Saxony and Thuringia were, now that the Ruhr was cut off, the principal strongholds of the left. Here the USPD had always been strong and therefore the reunited SPD leant to the left. In Saxony an SPD government took office in March 1923 under the pacifist Erich Zeigner. It had the support of the KPD and the two parties signed an agreement to set up defence organisations against fascism which became known as 'proletarian hundreds'. Such bodies were also set up in Thuringia, but the Prussian government, in its balancing act, banned them. The proletarian hundreds were defensive and lightly armed, but they did have secret fire arms depots.

For the KPD the justification for entering into collaboration with the SPD, a policy regarded with suspicion on the communist left, was that a revolutionary uprising could eventually be organised from this base. In fact the KPD derived considerable advantage from the united front in Saxony, which did not preclude it from continuing to attack the half-heartedness of the SPD. The entry of the KPD into the Saxon government and the attempt at another uprising was, however, delayed until the German crisis reached its zenith in October.

For the SPD the collaboration with the KPD in Saxony was a considerable liability at the national level. It lent credibility to those on the right who accused the SPD of treasonable cosmopolitanism. The Bavarian government was confirmed in its determination to protect its northern frontier in collaboration with the paramilitaries of the radical right. Tensions within the SPD were running high. The collapse of the currency in the summer of 1923 was putting its followers under severe pressure and many of them were deserting to the left and to the right. In Landtag elections in the small state of Mecklenburg-Strelitz on 8 July 1923 the KPD, which had not contested the previous elections in 1920, got 20.4 per cent of the vote. The SPD got 22.7 per cent against 42.9 per cent in 1920. Elections in the Berlin Metal Workers Union at about the same time showed a sharp swing from SPD to KPD.

The leading parliamentary figures of the SPD could see no way out of the crisis but the formation of a great coalition, which had failed narrowly in November 1922, but they were in no hurry to grasp the poisoned chalice. A meeting of the left of the SPD *Fraktion* on 29 July committed itself to a diametrically opposed course: immediate negotiations with France, an end to hyperinflation by heavy taxes on property and capital, strong measures against the radical right and the Black Reichswehr, all this to be achieved by a socialist government in cooperation with the KPD. There was a danger that the recently reunified SPD might split again.[38]

STRESEMANN'S HUNDRED DAYS: THE END OF PASSIVE RESISTANCE AND CRISIS IN BAVARIA AND SAXONY

The days of the Cuno government were in any case numbered. It managed to make some progress on the reparations question, sufficient to induce the British government to make a formal declaration on 11 August 1923 that the French–Belgian occupation of the Ruhr was illegal. The German government was, however, still unwilling to end passive resistance unconditionally, as the French demanded. It was a step which the British government, not prepared to make a real break with France, regarded as inevitable. Cuno was personally at the end of his tether and resigned on 12 August.

Nobody could be in any doubt that the social crisis caused by hyperinflation was now so profound that Germany was threatened by a revolution that might put the events of 1918–19 into the shade. A general strike called by the Communists in Berlin to topple Cuno was a failure, but when in the course of it the Reich Printing Works were stopped for a day, the shortage of bank notes made itself felt immediately.

A great coalition under Gustav Stresemann, long talked about, was now formed. The hundred days of its existence covered a period of chaos more severe than anything yet experienced since the formation of the republic. Stresemann himself remained foreign minister until his death in October 1929 and emerged as the republic's strongest political personality. He had travelled a long way since he was known as Ludendorff's blue-eyed boy. He was above all a realist with an exceptional capacity to come to terms with realities however repugnant and unpleasant. As leader of the DVP he also enjoyed an exceptional personal position. The party represented German industry, but it lacked a solid mass basis and was therefore very dependent on the prestige and appeal of its leader.

When the Stresemann cabinet was formed on 13 August 1923 it was already becoming clear to well-informed observers that only an unconditional end to passive resistance could provide a way out of the stalemate and save Germany from disintegration. It was, however, a very difficult step to take, for all the pent-up fury and frustration of German nationalism had found an expression through resistance to the occupier, however ineffective and self-destructive. Anybody advocating an end to passive resistance would find himself branded a traitor and risked the fate of Erzberger and Rathenau. Even an end to passive resistance would only create the preconditions for tackling hyperinflation and the threat of civil war and disintegration.[39]

At the moment when Stresemann took office the signs were multiplying that in the Ruhr itself passive resistance was reaching its limits. The feeling among the working classes and the less well-off generally was that they were bearing the brunt of the sacrifices. This was in spite of the fact that by this time salaries and wages were constantly being adjusted by agreed multiplication factors to the rapid decline of the currency. Even weekly adjustments were soon overtaken by the speed of the currency collapse. The separatist movement in the Rhine–Ruhr area, which had lain dormant for some years, was reviving with the help of the occupying authorities, although it never managed to take firm root. More significant was the fact that the industrialists and managers were beginning to believe that the area would as an economic unit become permanently separated from the Reich and that they would have to work in close relationship with France. Such views were being brought to the notice of Stresemann and the government in Berlin.[40]

Early in September 1923 the chancellor had a conversation with the French ambassador in Berlin, who had been kept in diplomatic isolation since the start of the Ruhr occupation. Stresemann still hoped for some face-saving gesture from Poincaré, but it did not come. A meeting between Baldwin, now British prime minister, and Poincaré on 19 September, showed that the British disapproval of the French position would remain limited in its effects. Thus the German government had to swallow the bitter pill and declare an unconditional end to passive resistance on 26 September. Before this policy could show any positive results Germany had still to pass through events which came close to causing a three-way disintegration of the Reich.[41]

The most serious challenge came again from Bavaria. The government in Munich had preempted the end of passive resistance by several hours and declared a state of emergency. Kahr was recalled and given special powers as general commissioner. It was a clear case of poacher turned gamekeeper, for there were close links between Kahr and the military associations. The Reich government had now in its turn to take special powers under article 48 of the constitution, to be exercised by Gessler, the Reichswehrminister, and under him by Seeckt. At the hastily convened cabinet meeting in Berlin Ebert asked Seeckt where the Reichswehr stood in this threatening situation. Seeckt's famous reply was: 'The Reichswehr stands behind me, Mr. President'.

Rumours of a putsch and a march on Berlin were rife in Munich. Knilling, the Bavarian prime minister, tried to reassure Stresemann about the Bavarian move by telling him that it had been taken to preempt possible 'stupidities' in a highly emotional situation. This was part of the truth, for the radical *Völkische* were poised for action and the appointment of Kahr cut across their plans. Hitler, his party and above all the SA were now a sufficiently important element in the Bavarian situation to make their thirst for revolutionary action crucial. Hitler was the recognised political leader of the *Kampfbund*, the radical wing of the military associations.

The position of the Bavarian government of the BVP and of Kahr himself was much more ambiguous. They were fighting on two fronts: above all against bolshevism, which in their book might include the Berlin government and certainly the SPD; and in this struggle the radical right were allies. As Bavarian particularists and monarchists, sometimes coming close to separatism, as a part of the 'black' international of the Catholic church, they were potential enemies of the *Völkische*.

Such simplification hardly does justice to the infinite complexities and mutual suspicions. Each camp was subdivided by ideological nuances and personal rivalries. Kahr and the Bavarian government looked forward to the establishment in Berlin of a national directory with dictatorial powers that would lead to a national revival. The most likely candidate to head such a directory was Seeckt and a march on Berlin might help to bring it about. The collaboration of the patriotic associations in Bavaria was essential, but to keep the more extreme elements and personalities under control was difficult for Kahr. No one was more difficult to control than Hitler.

Within hours of the Munich and Berlin governments declaring their separate states of emergency, Gessler and Seeckt asked von Lossow, their Bavarian commander, to ban the *Völkischer Beobachter*, the newspaper of the Nazi party. The paper had published a violent anti-Semitic attack on Stresemann and Seeckt. Stresemann's wife was Jewish and Seeckt's half Jewish. For Hitler and the extreme right Stresemann was at this point the principal traitor who had ended the fight against France. Seeckt was the man who should have taken over to lead the German revival, but who had so far declined to act illegally. Kahr refused to have the *Völkischer Beobachter* banned at this stage, partly because he did not want to get into a premature confrontation with Hitler, but even more because he refused to tolerate this heavy-handed interference by Berlin in the delicate Bavarian situation. Lossow, who also had a responsibility to the Bavarian government as Bavarian *Land* commander, was caught in a conflict of loyalties and preferred to obey Munich rather than Berlin.

Out of this case arose the third major conflict between Bavaria and the Reich in three years. Eventually Lossow was relieved of his command by Berlin, but ordered to stay on by Munich. It was this conflict between Bavaria and the Reich that gave some plausibility to Hitler's attempt in the beer hall putsch six weeks later to induce Kahr and Lossow to join him in the overthrow of the Reich government. Yet Kahr's relations with the extreme wing of the *Völkische* movement represented by Hitler remained as ambiguous as ever and he imposed his own ban on the *Völkischer Beobachter* for advocating violent civil war. Hitler in his turn tried to mend his fences with Seeckt and published an apology. Even at this stage of his career he knew that there was no future in a confrontation with the Reichswehr.[42]

The Reichswehr was itself in a state of confusion and Ebert's question to Seeckt about its loyalty was well justified. Joachim von Stülpnagel was an officer from a military family, one of whom was to meet his death in the aftermath of the unsuccessful attempt on Hitler's life on 20 July 1944. He wrote in his diary at this time about the army's conflicting loyalties: 'Our duty is to protect the constitution, but it is a sick system. Our duty is to prepare the war of liberation, which this sick system is preventing . . .'[43]

No one could be sure how much sympathy there was, especially among the younger officers, for the *Völkische* movement and for a coup against 'the system'. In Munich it was widely believed that the army had been infiltrated by Hitler sympathisers. Ernst Röhm had been forced to retire from the army after the events surrounding the May Day demonstrations in Munich, but Lossow, a pliable man, had maintained his contacts with all elements of the military associations. So much weaponry was and had been deliberately allowed to remain in irregular hands that the Reichswehr felt it could not do without these allies, whatever the mutual suspicions.

The first putsch attempt following the end of passive resistance occurred in fact in North Germany and not in Bavaria. Its leader was a Major Buchrucker, who had been employed by the Reichswehr in the command around Berlin to organise so-called labour commandos. These were typical examples of the Black Reichswehr, ex Freikorps soldiers and members of paramilitary organisations, who were kept in training and had secret stores of weapons. Buchrucker planned to occupy the government quarter in Berlin, but the assumption of special powers by Seeckt under the state of emergency foiled him. The pressure of his activists was such that Buchrucker was then forced into an attempt, on 1 October 1923, to capture the fortresses of Küstrin and Spandau near Berlin. Seeckt and the local commanders crushed this putsch.

The coup might have had more effect if it had occurred in conjunction with the putsch expected in Bavaria, but for the moment prevented by the appointment of Kahr. The firm suppression of putschism in the north lessened the chances of any successful putsch and march on Berlin from the south. The relations between Seeckt and the Black Reichswehr had much in common with the relationship between Kahr and Hitler, but it was also true that with respect to Seeckt Kahr played a role similar to the role Hitler played vis-à-vis the Bavarian State Commissioner, the role of prompter.

Throughout October the threat from Bavaria remained real enough and there was much coming and going between nationalist and *Völkische* figures north and south. Stresemann, Gessler and others maintained that it was impossible and impolitic to act decisively against Munich. This caused tension in the cabinet with the SPD and nearly brought about its fall in early October. It was a major grievance within the SPD that a much more energetic policy was being pursued against the SPD-led government in Saxony. Matters moved rapidly to a head after the KPD joined the Zeigner government on 10 October. The Saxon prime minister had become highly obnoxious in the eyes of the Reichswehr, because he constantly publicised and attacked its links with the right-wing paramilitaries.

Within days of the formation of the SPD–KPD Saxon coalition the local Reichswehr commander dissolved the proletarian hundreds. These events put further strain on the position of the SPD in the Stresemann coalition. In the KPD there was now a strong belief that the moment for a German revolution had come and that Saxony was to be its starting point. This belief was encouraged by Moscow, where fears of an international counter-revolutionary attack on the Soviet Union were running high. A successful German 'October' would also have had a major influence on the infighting round the succession to Lenin. It would probably have helped Trotsky and at least hindered the advance of Stalin.

A conference of works councils at Chemnitz on 21 October was under pressure from KPD leaders to call a general strike and battle against the Reichswehr. The call was strongly opposed by the SPD representatives and fell flat. The only uprising which actually occurred, two days later, was at Hamburg and was quickly crushed. The failure of the German 'October' had, however, the consequence that within the KPD the influence of those totally committed to the Moscow line was further strengthened. The failed Hamburg rising was used to lend a heroic aura to Ernst Thälmann, a Hamburg dock worker who emerged as the Stalinist leader of the party.

It had always been among the fevered calculations of the extreme right that by provoking a coup by the extreme left an appropriate signal for their own takeover would be given. Something like this now happened in Saxony. More troops were moved in and on 27 October Stresemann issued an ultimatum to Zeigner demanding the resignation of his SPD–KPD coalition. Two days later Ebert appointed a commissioner for Saxony under article 48 and Zeigner's government was removed. A minority SPD government was elected by the Saxon Landtag and this brought the Reich execution against the country to an end after two days. Little had been done to save the faces of the SPD members of Stresemann's government and there was still no majority in the cabinet for action against Bavaria. On 2 November the SPD Reichstag *Fraktion* voted to remove its ministers from the coalition. Stresemann's chancellorship lasted only another three weeks. The SPD was out of the Reich government for the next four and a half years.[44]

HITLER'S BEER HALL PUTSCH

On the face of it the action against Saxony and the departure of the SPD from the Stresemann coalition lessened the likelihood of a coup from Bavaria. In early November Colonel von Seisser, the head of the Bavarian police, was in Berlin to find out how matters stood with regard to the formation of the much discussed national directory. Seisser was the third of the triumvirs, with Kahr and Lossow, who held the real power in Munich. In Berlin he found a great deal of caution. There was little disposition to act against the Reichswehr or illegally and Seeckt, the key figure, remained cautious.

On Seisser's return to Munich there was a meeting on 6 November with representatives of the military associations at which Kahr warned against any putsch. The establishment of a national government in Berlin independent of the Reichstag remained the aim, but it had to be attained legally or with the minimum of illegality.

Hitler and those in the *Kampfbund* associated with him now decided to cut through all the prevarications in Munich as well as Berlin. It was undoubtedly becoming very difficult for them to hold their men who had been led to expect action ever since the beginning of the year. Many of them were suffering severely in the prevailing economic chaos and were looking for release from an intolerable situation. Hitler himself had always believed in his revolutionary mission, in the power of sheer activism, in the need to go to extremes. Until his end in the Berlin bunker twenty-one years later he put his faith in the exercise of will. More realistically, the attitude of the triumvirs, especially of Lossow and Seisser, the controllers of armed power, remained so ambivalent that it still seemed plausible that they could be forced into action.

It was decided to unleash the putsch on the night of Thursday, 8 November. A meeting had been called at the *Bürgerbräukeller*, one of Munich's largest beer halls, at which Kahr was billed to make a speech explaining his policy. All the prominent men of Munich, ministers, generals, police officers, would be there. It was rumoured that Kahr might use the occasion to proclaim the Bavarian monarchy. To pre-empt such an eventuality would have supplied the *Völkische* with another motive for immediate action. Once the decision was taken by the *Kampfbund* leaders to act at the *Bürgerbräukeller*, they prepared a takeover throughout Bavaria and the proclamation of a national government including Ludendorff and Hitler for the Reich. The assumption was that the Munich triumvirs would be carried along and that neither Reichswehr nor police would oppose the coup.

Initially all went according to plan for Hitler. The *Bürgerbräukeller* was surrounded by SA and *Kampfbund* formations. Hitler forced Kahr, Lossow and Seisser into a side room. At first he apparently had some difficulty in persuading the triumvirs to go along with him. Ludendorff's arrival and Hitler's own speech to the audience changed the atmosphere. He proclaimed a Reich government led by himself, with Ludendorff as commander-in-chief, Lossow as minister of defence, and Seisser as police minister. In Bavaria Kahr would be viceroy on behalf of the Wittelsbachs, and Pöhner prime minister.

The triumvirs filed back on to the platform and made speeches accepting their respective roles, as did Ludendorff and Pöhner. There was much invocation of national honour and of divine blessing. Lossow later claimed that he had throughout these proceedings whispered to his colleagues to 'play-act' and Kahr appears to have displayed the greatest reluctance. In his speech he declared himself to be acting as regent for the monarchy.

Then matters quickly went wrong for the plotters. Hitler left the meeting to deal with the takeover of military installations, which had been only partially successful. Ludendorff allowed the triumvirs to leave the *Bürgerbräukeller*. This undoubtedly helped countermeasures against the coup to gather momentum. Several members of the Bavarian government had in any case escaped the net. Countermeasures were also being taken in Berlin, where Seeckt was given the emergency powers previously exercised by Gessler. Hopes of widespread support for the putsch in the Reichswehr and the police were disappointed. The one military establishment where there was clear sympathy for the putsch was the Infantry School in Munich, a national institution where young officers and cadets were on training courses.

When morning dawned on 9 November the putsch had effectively failed, but Hitler and Ludendorff were slow to recognise it. Although Kahr normally enjoyed much popular respect and support, he had clearly cut a poor figure during the night's events and the putschists could count on a certain amount of sympathy and anti-establishment feeling among the population of Munich. Hitler and Ludendorff also still cherished the illusion that no army or police units would fire on Ludendorff. Thus it was decided to organise a big demonstrative march from the *Bürgerbräukeller* to the government buildings in the centre of the city. When the marchers were about to enter the broad boulevard where the prime minister's office was located, they were fired upon and sixteen men were killed. These became martyrs of the Nazi movement and an annual celebration attended by Hitler himself was built around them during the Third Reich.

Even if the coup had succeeded in Munich, it seems doubtful if it could have done so in Bavaria as a whole, let alone elsewhere in Germany. For the Reich Hitler's success would have been catastrophic, because the French had already made it clear in Berlin that they would intervene. In the highly volatile situation of 1923 conservative nationalists and *Völkische* extremists marched together, but the coup's failure reopened the fault line between them. Kahr's flirtation with the radical right was discredited in Bavaria. When the Nazi threat revived even more menacingly six years later, the BVP regime in Bavaria held out longer against it than many others.[45]

CRISIS RESOLVED: THE ENDING OF INFLATION AND THE CONSEQUENCES

The Rhine–Ruhr area was the third region in Germany that seemed to be going its own way in the autumn of 1923. There were two distinct forces at work: separatist movements, some of whose leaders were prepared to contemplate total separation from the Reich; and a more respectable and significant movement prepared to accept at least temporary separation from the Reich in order to get economic life in this great industrial region going again.

The leaders of the separatist movement were dubious figures and the majority of the population was hostile to them. They suffered from the fact that no clear French policy ever emerged, even at the height of the crisis. Tirard, the French High Commissioner, actively supported the separatists and believed in the possibility of an autonomous Rhenish republic under French tutelage. Degoutte, the French military commander, tried to cultivate relations with the political and industrial élites of the region and with the representatives of the working class. He thought in terms of forming another state within the Reich, but independent of Prussia, which would have close economic and political links with France. Poincaré did not follow a clear line, but at the height of the crisis in October and November 1923 he probably believed that a total break-up of the Reich was imminent.

The separatist coups in late October 1923 all failed ignominiously. The one place where there appeared to be the possibility of some success was the Bavarian Palatinate, where even many social democrats were keen to break away from the reactionaries in Munich, though they also wanted to stay within the Reich. This attitude received little sympathy from the SPD nationally, which did not want to provide any ammunition to those accusing it of lack of patriotism. Britain took a strong line against France over support of separatism, calling it a breach of the Versailles treaty. The Belgians followed the British line and all this acted as a restraining influence on Poincaré.[46]

As early as August 1923 there was evidence that Ruhr industrialists were making approaches to the French authorities and this became a factor in ending passive resistance. By October many negotiations and communications were going on between Ruhr industrialists and politicians, the occupying authorities, MICUM (Mission interallié de contrôle des usines et des mines) and the Reich government. Even superpatriots like Stinnes were now actively engaged in this process. Confusion and divided counsel were just as prevalent on the German as on the French side. If the ending of passive resistance was to lead to the ending of German inflation, then payments from the Reich to the occupied territory had to cease. The danger was that German policy would itself bring about the separation of the Rhine–Ruhr area from the Reich. There were advocates of a 'morass policy' (*Versackungspolitik*), namely that the French should be left to sink in the morass of their own making, the responsibility for feeding the population and resuscitating the economy of the region. A more nationalistic version of this course would be to combine it with a renunciation of the Versailles treaty. From the German point of view it was dangerous to concede to Ruhr politicians the right to engage in official negotiations with the occupying power, but eventually Stresemann had to accept this.

Among those who took a leading part in these negotiations was Konrad Adenauer, the mayor of Cologne. He was sometimes accused of being a separatist, particularly when after the Second World War he became the founding father of West Germany. In fact he was reluctant to accept *Versackungspolitik* with its implied abandonment of the Rhinelanders. When he was told that the new currency about to be introduced would go the way of the old unless payments to the occupied region ceased, he is supposed to have replied that the Rhineland was worth more than two or three new currencies. The crucial question was whether a separate Rhenish currency should be created. Adenauer was prepared for this and for a Rhineland sufficiently autonomous to satisfy French security needs.

The close links between French and German industry, so often talked about in the previous five years, would come about in such a framework. In the negotiations with the industrialists their demand for an end to the eight-hour day figured prominently, just as it had in all the German domestic political wrangles. Neither the French nor the German authorities were prepared to concede this in the context of these negotiations, though in Germany legislation was about to allow a longer working day. On 23 November 1923 an agreement was concluded between MICUM and the representatives of West German industry about the delivery of reparation coal. This was hailed as a great success by Poincaré, who appeared to have secured the 'productive pledges' his policy was designed to obtain. A further step seemed to have been taken towards the separation of the Rhine–Ruhr area from the rest of the Reich and towards its closer integration with France.

At this moment the new German currency, the *Rentenmark*, had been in circulation for just a week and it was still uncertain whether it would gain acceptance. Shortly it was seen to be a resounding success, while the attitude of London and Washington put the French franc under strain. A separate Rhenish currency or an autonomous Rhineland quickly ceased to be an option.[47]

More by accident than by design German payments to the Ruhr never completely ceased. In the meantime the international diplomatic machinery had gradually edged back to the proposal, originally advanced at the end of 1922 by the United States Secretary of State Hughes, that Germany's ability to pay should be examined by a committee of experts. This proposal was at the centre of a German note to the reparations commission sent on 24 October. Britain and America reacted positively, but the big surprise was that France also indicated guarded acceptance. This was at the very moment when France was still playing the separatist card, although its failure was every day becoming clearer. By accepting an international discussion of the reparations question by experts French policy was in fact turning its back on the whole occupation strategy pursued for the previous ten months. The way was opened towards the Dawes Plan. Poincaré's domestic political position was weakening and it gradually became apparent that he had managed to snatch defeat from the jaws of victory.[48]

The great crises which nearly tore the Reich apart in the autumn of 1923 were aggravated by a common underlying factor: severe economic dislocation owing to the collapse of the currency.

Stresemann's main purpose in ending passive resistance was to re-establish a stable currency in Germany. Any advantage that had arisen for sectional interests from the inflation had disappeared. Through the hoarding of foreign currency earned from exports many businesses had been able to insulate themselves from the inflation and the political deadlock had made it impossible for the state to tax or control such holdings.

The collapse of production in the Ruhr and the imposition of trade barriers between the occupied area and the rest of the Reich caused severe dislocation in the whole German economy. The decline was then further aggravated by the total collapse of the currency in the summer of 1923. There was also a sharp rise in unemployment in the autumn of 1923. Although the statistics are imprecise, for the year 1923 gross national product dropped back to somewhere near the levels at the low point after the war. The threat of upheaval and social disintegration was now so obvious that no one could any longer rationally oppose drastic steps towards a stable currency.

For a long time inflation had worked against reparations, meant a virtual dumping of German goods in foreign markets and had kept the domestic battle about the distribution of the national cake from becoming a civil war. By the summer of 1923 at the latest further inflation ceased to be an option. Industry's export advantage had gone, investment could no longer be financed by worthless paper credits, the trade unions were losing members, their coffers were empty, the strike weapon blunted. Among many proposals the plan for a currency based on rye, advanced by Helfferich, came closest to the one eventually adopted.

In order to introduce a new currency it was necessary to pass an enabling law. When this was being finalised, the SPD's position in the Stresemann coalition was already weakened by the government reconstruction of early October. The left-wing socialist Hilferding had been replaced by the non-party conservative Hans Luther as finance minister. As part of a package deal the SPD came close to giving up the symbolic eight-hour day to ensure the passage of the required enabling act. The fear was that otherwise the imposition of a dictatorship of Seeckt or a business directory was imminent.

On 15 October the *Rentenbank* was set up and a month later the *Rentenmark* was issued. It was secured by a mortage on agricultural and industrial property. This was really a fiction because these values could not be realised, but the confidence trick worked. The total issue was strictly limited and on 20 November the parity was fixed so that one *Rentenmark* equalled 1000 billion paper marks and was therefore also equal to 1 gold mark. The *Rentenmark* was a purely domestic currency which operated until the Dawes Plan settled the international reparations and debt questions and a fully convertible currency could be introduced. When the acceptability of the *Rentenmark* became apparent, people could only satisfy their need for cash by disgorging vast quantities of paper marks. It was a brutally deflationary stabilisation, backed by drastic measures, such as the dismissal of large numbers of civil servants, to bring public revenue and expenditure into balance.[49]

Conventional wisdom has it that the inflation ruined the German middle classes. Marxist historians have emphasised the immiseration of the proletariat. Undoubtedly everybody who owned money-denominated assets and did not in good time take part in the 'flight into real assets' was a loser. The statistics show a steep decline in income from financial assets, broadly speaking rentier income. Whereas in 1913 such income formed about an eighth of German national income, after 1923 it had dropped into the 2–4 per cent range. Sections of the middle class who lived on income or pensions from cash savings, or relied on life insurance policies, were effectively wiped out financially.

It was common in middle-class households squeezed by the inflation to sell off family heirlooms, antiques, silver and paintings. There is a short story by Stefan Zweig in which an art dealer visits a well-known but now elderly and blind collector of lithographs during the inflation. The collector knows his precious pieces so well that he can describe them without being able to see them any longer. The daughter of the old man whispers despairingly to the dealer on his arrival that the whole collection has been sold off and that he should help her to keep up the pretence that it is still there, for that is what her father thinks. The old man lovingly describes each empty page as it is turned and the dealer leaves with the silent gratitude of the daughter.[50]

The plight of those stripped of their possessions, like Stefan Zweig's collector, was exploited by smart wheeler-dealers, in popular parlance *Raffkes* (greedy ones), who often flaunted their new-found wealth and added to the bitterness. There was a general decline in honesty and moral standards and a rise in delinquencies of all kinds. Many members of the traditional

middle class did well out of the inflation, for example houseowners
or small farmers with mortgaged properties, whose debts simply
disappeared. Yet house-owners might also suffer from the fact that
many rents had been fixed by law during the war and were only
slowly if at all adjusted for inflation. The devastating effect of the
inflation on small savers from whatever social background may be
gauged from the fact that a municipal savings institution like the
Sparkasse Frankfurt had deposits of 8120 billion marks distributed
between 153 423 depositors. After stabilisation these deposits were
worth 8.12 marks. It was unrealistic to suppose that such losses
could ever be made good, although the introduction of the
Rentenmark precipitated a long and politically significant battle
over the revaluation of debts.[51]

There is now general agreement that wage earners suffered a
severe loss of real income in the later stages of the war. Some of
these losses were made good after 1919. The rapid decline of the
currency after the end of the war helped in the process of
demobilisation and reintegration into the civilian labour market.
The brief respite in the progress of inflation in 1920 produced an
upsurge of unemployment, but the resumed decline of the currency
kept unemployment at exceptionally low levels in Germany until
1923. The onset of hyperinflation in the summer of 1922 had a
depressing effect on real wages. They began to fluctuate wildly,
depending on the frequency and effectiveness of inflation adjustments. The following table (see p. 141) is based on official
statistics[52] (1913 = 100; lowest and highest months in brackets).

These figures, whatever their technical limitations, show the
decline in working-class living standards with the onset of
hyperinflation in 1922 and the severe hardship in the second
half of 1923. They also show the wild fluctuations caused by
inflation, with the railway workers as state employees benefiting
from slightly more effective adjustment. They give evidence of a
compression of differentials, with unskilled workers maintaining
their position somewhat better than the skilled. Other figures also
show this decline of differentials: in 1913 the wages of skilled
workers were 145.8 per cent of those of the unskilled, while in
1923 they were only 105.5 per cent.

A similar tendency can be seen at work in civil service salaries:
in 1923 higher civil servants received 38 per cent of the 1913
salaries, middle ranks 49.55 and lower ranks 69.9 per cent. Civil
servants as a whole suffered a steep drop in their real income

	Railway workers			Printers		Ruhr miners	
	skilled		unskilled				
1920		66.7	89.1		60.8		77.6
March	(52.3)		(69.9)	April	(43.5)	March	(62.7)
Sept.	(75.3)		(99.8)	Sept.	(69.9)	Oct.	(91.6)
1921		74.5	100.0		68.9		89.1
July	(67.3)		(90.1)	Aug.	(63.1)	Aug.	(81.9)
Oct.	(90.3)		(121.1)	Dec.	(76.6	Nov.	(97.5)
1922		64.2	87.6		60.9		69.9
Oct.	(53.3)		(73.5)	Nov.	(44.4)	Oct.	(51.6)
June	(78.4)	Sept.	(114.4)	June	(74.1)	Jan.	(83.3)
1923		50.9	69.1		54.2		70.1
July	(42.9)	Oct.	(60.8)	Oct.	(35.7)	July	(47.6)
March	(59.6)		(82.4)	March	(74.6)	March	(86.2)

relative to those of wage earners as a result of the war, a development which reached a low point in 1919. The inflation period did not further aggravate this tendency, but there were severe fluctuations until an effective adjustment system was in operation. From April 1920 civil service pay was linked to the pay of a specific public service manual grade, itself related to pay in private industry. There was thus for a time a community of interest between all Reich employees and manual workers. This situation started to unravel again in the final phase of hyperinflation from November 1922. Civil service pay was paid quarterly in advance and only its nominal value held against the ever more frequent inflation supplements. When stabilisation finally came manual workers and civil servants, typical for many middle-class households, held the position which they had attained in the immediate postwar situation and before inflation took off. This still meant that differentials across the board, among manual workers, among civil servants, and between manual workers and civil servants, were reduced from what they had been before the war.[53]

If the whole chain of events from war through revolution and inflation to stabilisation had a certain levelling effect this did not apply to industry. Business did well out of inflation and the bigger the better. The most famous or infamous beneficiary of inflation was Hugo Stinnes, who built up a huge vertical conglomerate that proved short-lived after his death in 1924. Large companies could buy up real assets and retain foreign currency earned through exports. When hyperinflation came the bigger firms found it easiest to carry on their business in foreign currency terms, clearly impossible in the day-to-day transactions of the small shopkeeper. In the absence of an agreement to tax real assets, bigger firms, just like wealthier individuals, provided a decreasing proportion of the total tax revenue. There is also general agreement that in the early 1920s Germany, unlike the other major industrial nations, enjoyed a great investment boom.

In this way the German economy managed to catch up on some of the investment backlog caused by the war. It is, however, also frequently argued that a good deal of this investment was misdirected and that this accounts for the relatively low growth rates after the stabilisation of 1924 and also for the severity of the rationalisation process in the middle and late 1920s. In the period 1926 to 1929 Germany's share of world industrial production was 11.6 per cent compared with 14.3 per cent before 1914, taking into account territorial changes. Great Britain was an even bigger loser, dropping from 14.1 to 9.4 per cent, while the USA's share rose from 35.8 to 42.2 per cent. It is debatable whether Germany would have performed better without the inflationary boom of the early 1920s.[54]

The introduction of a new currency was prepared by the Stresemann government when it was still a great coalition. Once the SPD left Stresemann's position was tenuous. As rumours of the Bavarian putsch thickened, a takeover by Seeckt moved closer and even after Hitler's failure the possibility of a national directory with dictatorial powers remained. Relations between Stresemann and Seeckt were never good and now became tense. The chancellor decided to put his position to the test in a vote of confidence. He lost it on 23 November because the SPD voted against him, still on the grounds that his government had acted in Saxony and Thuringia but had failed to do so in Bavaria. On this occasion Ebert made the frequently quoted remark to his SPD colleagues that 'the reasons that induced you to bring this chancellor down will be forgotten in six weeks, but the consequences will haunt you for ten years'. The SPD continued to be faced with a dilemma: it would risk its unity and lose voters to the KPD if it supported measures at home and abroad to save the republic and preserve it from a right-wing dictator. Even by retiring into opposition or voting against a bourgeois coalition it could not escape from this dilemma. Its support was still needed in the Reichstag for the policies of stabilisation at home and reconciliation abroad.

The fall of Stresemann did not bring about the abrogation of parliamentary government and the establishment of a dictatorship that had been so long feared and predicted, but which was also ardently desired by large sections of the German people. Stresemann's successor was Wilhelm Marx from the Centre Party, an unexciting figure, whose total tenure of the chancellorship was longer than anybody's in the Weimar period. Any hope that the DNVP might join this coalition was nullified by Stresemann's continuance as foreign minister. It was an indication that the efforts to find a way out of the international deadlock by negotiation would continue and that there would be no self-destructive gestures of nationalist machismo. Some time was yet to elapse before the DNVP would bring itself even tentatively to support Stresemann's policy of negotiation and revision by conciliation.

Yet the SPD, even though out of the government, had no alternative but to support such policies. It was more difficult for the SPD to vote for the new enabling law which the Marx coalition, made up of the Centre Party, the DDP, the DVP and the BVP, had to bring in, the previous one having lapsed when the SPD left the Stresemann government a month earlier. It was only when Ebert threatened to use his powers under article 48, which would have deprived the Reichstag of even the degree of control it had under an enabling act, that a sufficient number of SPD deputies could be induced to ensure the passage of the act. While this act still affirmed the principle of the eight-hour day, it left the way open to the abolition in practice of what was left of it. The eight-hour day continued to be regarded as the most important social achievement of the revolution, but even its erosion by no means put an end to the social dimension of the republic. By early 1924 this republic had survived, unheroically, from hand to mouth. Perhaps a majority of Germans at this moment had nothing but contempt for it and were looking for a strong man. His time had not yet come.

3   The Golden Years

THE STABILISATION OF THE MARK AND THE DAWES PLAN

It was not immediately obvious at the beginning of 1924 that Germany was about to enter a calmer and more stable phase. There was a great deal of unfinished business and the all-important economic problems remained unresolved. The success of the new currency was still uncertain and the expert committees had still to find solutions to the reparations problem. The Reich government, deprived of unlimited credit from the Reichsbank, now had to balance its books.

The political problems remained equally unresolved. For the moment the parliamentary system was still incapable of taking the many urgent steps required to make the new currency stick. Therefore the establishment of a dictatorship in some guise remained on the agenda. Seeckt who still exercised emergency powers had caused deep disappointment on the right and in the Reichswehr by not seizing the helm. Yet Seeckt himself, as his adjutant noted, hated the parliamentary system and found the constant cabinet changes demeaning.[1]

On the left the SPD remained more than ever torn between incompatible policies. Even out of government it had to support measures necessary to preserve the republic and stave off a right-wing dictatorship. Yet its supporters faced extreme hardship in the closing months of 1923 and felt that they were being asked to carry the burden of stabilisation by surrendering such hard-won advances as the eight-hour day. This was grist to the mill for the left wing of the party who thought a minority government with the KPD, if necessary backed by extra parliamentary action, preferable to the preservation of the existing bourgeois state. Those SPD or former USPD supporters who shared these views could always transfer their allegiance to the KPD, as indeed many did in the Reichstag elections of May 1924. They were not deterred by the KPD's constant changes of party line; nor by the fact that these changes were dictated more by the in-fighting in Moscow after Lenin's death than by any objective consideration of the German situation.

It was a stroke of luck for the success of the *Rentenmark* that on the very day when its rate of exchange with the paper mark was fixed at 1000 billion, Dr Havenstein, the President of the Reichsbank, died. Under his aegis the Reichsbank had been willing to discount treasury bills to an unlimited extent and had kept the printing presses rolling. This process had only stopped five days before his death. Since it was not possible to remove Havenstein, the man chosen to supervise the introduction of the new currency, Dr Hjalmar Schacht, had to be given the title of currency commissioner. By December 1923 he had taken Havenstein's place. Schacht does not deserve the reputation as the wizard who single-handedly stopped inflation, a title which he claimed and which popular opinion has allowed him. He was, however, technically highly competent in supervising the process by which the *Rentenmark* was used to pave the way for the return of a gold-based currency, the *Reichsmark*, in 1924. An important factor in these developments was the good relationship established by Schacht with the City of London and the Governor of the Bank of England, Montagu Norman. Schacht was an original member of the DDP and had the reputation of being a staunch supporter of the republic. He was rigorous in sticking to the refusal of the Reichsbank to print any more money, in forcing the redemption of emergency money by the originators and in forcing speculators to disgorge foreign currency to the Reichsbank.[2]

At the same time Luther, the finance minister, proceeded with the measures to achieve a balanced budget. In the later months of 1923 revenue had not paid for even 5 per cent of expenditure. By the early months of 1924 this proportion rose to an average of 85–90 per cent. A rigorous programme of cutting the number of civil servants was embarked upon. The Reich dismissed about 150 000 and altogether about 750 000 public employees lost their jobs. The cuts fell least heavily on fully established civil servants, of whom about one-sixth were laid off; more heavily on manual workers in the public service, of whom nearly a third were dismissed; and most heavily on white-collar public employees, whose numbers were nearly halved. Any solidarity among public servants that may have existed at an earlier phase of the inflation was at an end. Established civil servants made much of their right to tenure for life and of their professional superiority and party-political neutrality.[3]

In spite of the powerful pressures that produced this wholesale dismissal of public employees, German payments to the Rhine–Ruhr area, for example unemployment relief, were not suspended, though the *Rentenmark* did not circulate in the occupied areas. Hardship, particularly unemployment, continued to be severe in these areas in early 1924. In the tough tug-of-war over this all-important industrial powerhouse the Germans tried to make sure that the plans for a separate currency and bank of issue did not come to fruition. Schacht reassured the Ruhr magnates that their credit requirements would receive favourable treatment from the new gold discount bank which he established.[4]

Against this background the two committees of experts to assess German capacity to pay met in January 1924. One was chaired by the American financial expert, Charles G. Dawes, and three months later issued the Dawes Plan. The United States government had been reluctant to get too closely involved in the European imbroglio and Dawes was not acting as its official representative. By the autumn of 1923 the American business and financial community had, however, become so concerned about the damaging economic effects of the Ruhr struggle that they pressured Washington to adopt a more positive line. This was of great importance to Germany, for it meant that both Anglo-Saxon powers, though not always in agreement, were now acting as a brake on French policy.

It was a further bonus from the German point of view that a minority Labour government came into office in Britain in January 1924. Its head, Ramsay MacDonald, had a great personal interest in the peaceful resolution of international conflict, in the League of Nations and disarmament. On the other hand the French position was weakened by the decline of the franc, the failure of the separatist movements and the fact that in the reparations commission Belgium and Italy now generally sided with Britain. Against this the operation of the MICUM agreements went ahead, an indication that France still had something to bargain with. The German foreign office, under the guidance of Stresemann and Carl von Schubert, the influential official who became state secretary in December 1924, had to extract from this international constellation whatever advantage it could.[5]

German foreign policy had to be made from a domestic context which continued to be very fragile. The enabling act under which the currency stabilisation programme had been pursued ran out on 15 February 1924. The minority government of Marx had no chance of renewing it and therefore asked Ebert to dissolve the Reichstag. Its statutory term would in any case have ended in the summer of 1924. At this point Seeckt also gave up his emergency powers, as it had become imperative to disengage the Reichswehr from its compromising involvement with the nationalist paramilitary formations.

The failure of the beer hall putsch had been the signal for the suppression of the more extreme organisations, such as the NSDAP and the *Deutsch-Völkische* party.[6] None of this could end the fierce debate between those who wanted to deal with the continuing national humiliation by sheer defiance, however unrealistic, and the supporters of the official policy of seeking a way out by negotiation. The elections held on 4 May 1924 showed that at least a third of the German electorate supported parties that professed total opposition to the republic and to its policy of seeking international rehabilitation.

By joining with the *Landbund* the DNVP emerged as the largest *Fraktion* and its vote was only marginally behind that of the SPD, 19.5 against 20.5 per cent. To its right the joint list of NSDAP and *Deutsch-Völkische* received 6.5 per cent of the vote and had 32 deputies, of which about one-third were Nazis. On the left the KPD was the beneficiary of the virtual demise of the USPD and of the radicalisation of the workers, particularly in the occupied area. The voters had thus refused to follow the reunification of SPD and USPD carried out by most of the leaders of the latter. In the West the KPD scored some remarkable successes. In Westphalia South the KPD had 1.5, the USPD 19.7 and the SPD 20.8 per cent of the vote in 1920; now the KPD had 21.9 and the SPD 16.1 per cent. In Düsseldorf East the KPD had 1.2 the USPD 32.8 and the SPD 10.0 per cent of the vote in 1920; now the KPD had 24.9 and the SPD 11.4 per cent. The KPD also did well in the former USPD strongholds in central Germany. It scored its highest percentage in Merseburg, where the figures were 25.7 for the KPD and 15.5 for the SPD; in 1920 the percentages had been 1.6 and 8.8 respectively while 45.2 had gone to the USPD.

The arrival of the KPD as a mass party did not mean that it could in the next few years recapture the revolutionary potential which the extreme left had mobilised intermittently from 1918 to 1923. It did, however, confront the SPD with the electoral competition that the USPD had only fleetingly been able to mount in 1920. There is some evidence that the decline in the combined left-wing vote, from nearly 42 per cent to just under 34 per cent nationally, benefited the extreme right in some places. For example in Hof in Franconia, a textile centre with a high proportion of women in the labour force, the combined left-wing vote in 1920 was over 60 per cent. In May 1924 it dropped to 40 per cent, while the *Völkische*-NSDAP list, which had not contested the election in 1920, achieved almost exactly the same proportion. At least half of this upsurge of the extreme right must have come from former left-wing voters, the other half from the steep decline of the DDP. Franconia was an early stronghold of the Nazis and voted for them at an above average rate in all subsequent elections, but beyond this there was evidence that the party could prove attractive to workers whose roots in the traditional labour movement were shallow.[7]

The rise of the DNVP was the major political problem created by these elections. The party claimed a leading role in the government, which in its existing form now only commanded about 150 out of 472 Reichstag deputies. In the middle of the election campaign the Dawes committee had issued its report and the Marx government had indicated its willingness to cooperate with its plans. The DNVP unleashed a ferocious campaign against the Dawes proposals, calling them a second German enslavement after Versailles. A new version of fulfilment and cooperation with the West was undoubtedly implicit in the Dawes Plan.

In nationalist circles a completely different concept of German foreign policy prevailed: repudiation of Versailles and of the affront to German honour and great power status, cooperation with Russia, possibly with other powers in south-east Europe. Such a vision still had much support in the Reichswehr and had always appealed to Seeckt. In Germany's current predicament it was a highly unrealistic prescription.

The DNVP also had domestic demands: an end to the great coalition in Prussia and the exclusion of the SPD from the Prussian government; the resignation of Stresemann from the foreign office. The lack of realism in nationalist circles can be gauged from the DNVP's demand that Admiral von Tirpitz should become chancellor. It would have been an obvious affront to British public opinion at a moment when Britain was playing a crucial role in bringing the whole complex of reparations and the Ruhr occupation back to the negotiating table. Nothing came of the attempt to bring the DNVP into government after the May 1924 elections.

Ironically the negative outcome, from the point of view of an international settlement, of the German elections was followed a week later, on 11 May, by the positive outcome of elections in France. Poincaré fell from power and was succeeded by Edouard Herriot at the head of a more conciliatory left–centre coalition.

In Germany Marx resumed office with a minority government, this time even without the BVP and with the support of only 138 out of the 472 deputies. To have any chance of getting the Dawes Plan through the Reichstag the government needed the support of the SPD; even this was not enough if some of the package required a two-thirds constitution-changing majority. Fortunately the DNVP's opposition to the Dawes Plan and to much of the subsequent foreign policy initiatives, like the Locarno treaties, was not as monolithic as it appeared. The party comprised a heterogeneous collection of interests, agrarian and industrial, which for the most part did not want to be excluded from the political and economic horse-trading of the republic.

Some prominent figures in West German heavy industry, including Stinnes just before his death in April 1924, had at this moment abandoned their hope of a national directory or dictatorship, but they had also shifted their support from the DVP to the DNVP. Stresemann's collaboration with the SPD was not to their liking. They wanted to see the DNVP in the government representing their interests and they could also see the advantages of the Dawes Plan and the flow of American capital into Germany that might result from it. When the Dawes proposals came to be voted on in the Reichstag at the end of August 1924, nearly half the DNVP voted for the restructuring of the German Railways, thus providing the two-thirds majority required for this part of the Dawes Plan.

This set a pattern for the operation of the political process for the next four years. DNVP rhetoric opposed the Stresemann policies of revision by negotiation, but in practice the party allowed them to go ahead and joined coalitions for most of 1925 and again from January 1927 until the election for the fourth

Reichstag of the republic in May 1928. SPD rhetoric opposed much of the domestic agenda of the bourgeois state during this period, but sustained the foreign policy that was the framework of this state. All big issues were fought over inch by inch, the outcome frequently a cliff-hanger. Much, though not all, of this would have had to occur in any pluralist democracy, but large numbers of Germans thought it demeaning and contemptible. A pluralist society filled them with alarm and they looked back with nostalgia to the imperial era.[8]

The most important aspect of the Dawes Plan was that it took the reparations question out of the vicious circle of refusals to pay, sanctions and threats. In future Germany was to make payments to a reparations agent, who significantly was an American, Parker Gilbert. He was to supervise the payment, monitor German capacity to pay and transmit money to the recipient countries in such a manner that Germany's external payments position would not be damaged. German obligations to pay were now real enough, if modest: under a five-year plan payments were to to rise from a billion marks to 2.5 billion. Even this latter figure seemed at the time somewhat speculative and no attempt was made to assess any final overall liability. An 800 million gold mark international loan was to give the German economy an initial boost to help it cope with these obligations. There were productive pledges, such as the mortgage on the German railways which required the two-thirds majority in the Reichstag. Specific liabilities were borne by German customs and tax receipts and the degree of control over German economic affairs from the outside was considerable.

On the other hand France was finally deprived of the possibility of using reparations as a lever on Germany. Herriot was induced to agree that the Ruhr was to be evacuated within a year. A cycle of international payments was created in which German reparations enabled the United States' European debtors to repay their debts. In the absence of a German trade surplus the inflow of private American capital into Germany enabled the transfer of reparations to be made. It was not a permanent settlement nor an ideal solution and as events were to show it carried many dangers, above all increasing dependence of the German economy on American credits. For the time being it enabled the German economy to function more normally.[9]

THE ECONOMY AND SOCIAL POLICY: COMPULSORY ARBITRATION, HOUSING, UNEMPLOYMENT INSURANCE

The internal and external measures to normalise economic life produced a sharp fall in unemployment from April 1924 onwards. After a temporary blip in the summer of 1924, caused by the tight credit policies of the Reichsbank when the new Reichsmark was being introduced, the fall in unemployment continued until late 1925 when there was another steep rise resulting from a drop in economic activity. There was a recovery in late 1926 and the years 1927 and 1928 saw German production broadly back to prewar levels.

It remains a matter of debate whether the German economy, during these so-called 'golden years', was really performing well, or whether it was already suffering from the sickness that was devastatingly exposed in the great depression. None of the major European industrial powers could approach the growth rates of extra-European countries like the United States and Japan after the First World War and their share of world industrial production and world exports of industrial goods therefore declined. Germany and Britain were the most obvious losers. Germany was at a low point in terms of gross national product and real wages at the end of 1923, but it then recovered fairly strongly.

Nevertheless at the end of the period of stability, in 1929, Germany's gross national product exceeded the prewar base by rather less of a margin than was the case in Britain and France, let alone the United States. If the level of 1913 is taken as 100, approximate figures for 1929 were 106.2 for Germany, 122.8 for Britain, 130.6 for France and 164.5 for the USA, but in 1925 the German figure had been only 90.3. A comparison of industrial production in 1913 and 1929, however, shows Britain to have been a bigger loser than Germany (see appendix, p. 330). The rise in real wages between 1925 and 1929 in Germany (1913 = 93; 1925 = 81; 1928 = 100; 1929 = 102) was proportionally somewhat faster than that of the gross national product or of productivity in industry (1913 = 100; 1925 = 95.9; 1929 = 107.1). All these figures are complicated by changes in territory and the structure of the working population. Undoubtedly the war and the inflation had destroyed capital in Germany to a great extent and this accounted for the high dependence on capital imports that developed up to 1929.

From all this an argument was insistently advanced by employers in these middle years of Weimar, particularly by the coal and steel barons of the Ruhr, that the German economy was overstretched, that too much of the national cake was taken up by wages and by social payments and not enough by investment. Coal and steel belonged everywhere in Europe to the slow-growth, stagnant sector of the economy. The dependence of Germany on maximisation of coal production in the immediate postwar years and under the pressure of reparations had given the mine owners much political clout. They continued to enjoy greater weight than the real importance of their industry warranted in the middle years. In the coal industry wages do not seem to have outstripped productivity, which improved by over one-third between 1925 and 1929. In spite of this mine workers' wages dropped back in relation to wage rates in other industries. In the iron and steel industries wages may have risen somewhat as a proportion of costs between 1925 and 1929.

If there was a lack of investment in the German economy in those years high wage costs and social payments were at most one of many causes. Misdirection of investment during the inflation years and restrictive credit policies by the Reichsbank may have been others. Among industrialists the coal and steel barons were least benevolently disposed towards the political social and economic system represented by the republic. To some extent they and employers generally had succeeded in undoing much of the social compromise symbolised by the *Zentralarbeitsgemeinschaft* and the eight-hour day established in 1919.

In January 1924 it was in fact the unions which took the initiative in leaving the ZAG. It was largely a psychologically conditioned move, for with the stabilisation the labour movement felt a final sense of defeat. The unions in the ADGB, about 85 per cent of organised German workers, were rapidly losing members, from 7.7 million in the middle of 1923 to less than four million by the end of 1924, though by 1929 the figures had recovered to nearly five million in 1929. The two other trade union organisations, the Christian unions linked to the Centre Party and the much smaller liberal Hirsch-Duncker unions, known for short as *Christen* and *Hirsche* (stags), had also lost a lot of their members.

The election results of May 1924 showed that the bourgeoisie were once more in the ascendant. Yet the social aspirations of the German people, reaching much beyond the confines of the organised working class, were still alive and all but the least enlightened of employers knew it. It was part of the balance painfully established in the middle 1920s that some of these aspirations should be satisfied, even if this did impose a burden on the economy. Compulsory arbitration, unemployment provision and housing were three areas of social policy of particular importance during the golden years.[10]

Arbitration of industrial disputes had been brought in during the First World War and continued in the demobilisation procedures after the war. The unions were normally suspicious of arbitration and particularly of binding arbitration, since it tampered with the freedom of collective bargaining. In the disturbed conditions of the post-war years there was a tendency to use compulsory and binding arbitration in cases where strikes, often 'wild' strikes, threatened vital supplies. In November 1920 a 'wild' strike among Berlin electricity workers caused Ebert to issue an order under article 48 imposing arbitration and a cooling-off period of three days after publication of the arbitration award. In spite of protests from the unions this order remained in force for the remainder of the republican period.

Attempts at formal legislation on arbitration never succeeded; the system in force after 1923 was based on the enabling act passed in October 1923. It can therefore be argued this major example of state intervention shows the failure of the Weimar state to function on the basis of parliamentary pluralism and its resort to executive, even authoritarian, methods of government to enforce social harmony. The relevant order, of 29 December 1923, gave a very broad definition of the reasons for which an arbitration award could be made binding: 'if its execution is for economic and social reasons required'. A social purpose was thus expressly acknowledged. In the exceptionally severe economic conditions in the transition from hyperinflation to stabilisation this could only mean some protection for wage earners from extreme hardship. In the period between 1924 and 1932 over 77 000 arbitration procedures were undertaken, of which nearly 4000 were made binding. On the eve of the great depression about two-thirds of all wage earners covered by pay agreements were affected by arbitration and about a third by binding arbitration.

Only about one-third were therefore covered by agreements reached by free collective bargaining.

The free trade unions gradually became more favourably disposed towards binding arbitration and to what came to be called 'the political wage'. In September 1925 the deputy chairman of the ADGB had still argued that compulsory arbitration encouraged workers to stay out of unions, because they could reap the benefits without becoming members. Two years later Hilferding, as the leading socialist theoretician of the day, said at the Kiel party congress of the SPD: 'We must hammer it into the brain of every worker that his weekly wage is a political wage, that it depends on the parliamentary representation of the working class, on the strength of its organization and the social balance of power, what the pay at the end of the week is.'

By the same token the employers, initially ambivalent in their attitude to binding arbitration, became gradually more hostile. They came to see it as the most flagrant example of the lack of evenhandedness of the republican political system and a major element of the high social costs imposed upon industry. In fact the industries where binding arbitration was most frequently applied, such as coal mining, show an increase of wages below average, while for example the construction industry, where wages rose rapidly between 1925 and 1929, binding arbitration was only rarely resorted to. The relative high proportion of lockouts to strikes, one to ten in the period 1919–23 but six to five from 1924 to 1929, shows neither greater social harmony nor a tilt of the power balance against employers. The great lockout in the Ruhr iron industry in November 1928, in defiance of a binding award, is, however, clear evidence how determined employers in heavy industry had become to break this aspect of the Weimar social compact, if necessary by defying the state itself.[11]

The arbitration system was most significant in industries and sectors where unionisation was weak and where in the absence of imposed awards there would have been no general wage agreements at all. This was particularly the case in agriculture and among white-collar employees, yet both these groups were especially prone to be anti-republican and to support nationalist and extreme right-wing parties. The system itself had become a part of state corporatism, a stage beyond the corporatism based on the relationships between organised interests. It can also be regarded as an aspect of organised capitalism, a concept invoked by theoreticians both from right and left. Conflicts were politicised and a great burden placed on the state, which came under attack from both sides. The arbitration system may have contributed to the rigidity of the German economy before the great depression and thereby made the response to the depression more difficult. It seems more doubtful if the employers' claim that it caused an excessive rise of wages in relation to productivity can be substantiated. The binding awards had to take into account economic as well as social considerations. The German ministry of labour, in operating the system, paid at least as much attention to the former as to the latter.[12]

Housing was an area in which public policy rather than the market had been the determining factor since the war. Even before 1914 inadequate housing for Germany's rapidly increasing industrial working class had had a powerful influence on the configuration of politics. Workers herded together in bleak tenement blocks in the burgeoning industrial centres had fuelled the astonishing upsurge of the SPD. The physical as well as spiritual alienation of this mass army had created the ghettoes in which the socialist subculture flourished. The war had further aggravated the situation by spawning new industrial concentrations at breakneck speed while cutting the building of even the most rudimentary accommodation. The control of rents was therefore inevitable and had to be continued in the post-war period and into the era of hyperinflation.

However much many house owners may have benefited from the inflation by getting rid of their mortgage debt, the income from rent virtually vanished. The corollary was that the market and private house building could not be expected to meet the demand for dwellings, as no realistic return on capital was possible. The provision and above all financing of housing therefore became a predominantly public responsibility, to be discharged by Reich, *Länder* and communities.

Before 1914 the net annual increase in the housing stock was calculated at 200 000 units. In the post-war years up to 1925 only half that figure was reached in many years and even at the peak in 1922 was less than 150 000. From 1925 to 1930 the number of units built climbed rapidly, reaching over 300 000, only to fall back again between 1930 and 1934. Nearly half this building programme was financed from public sources between 1924 and 1931. Around 30 per cent came from a tax (*Hauszinssteuer*) levied, beginning in 1924, on the permitted increase of fixed rents, which by 1927 had been allowed to rise to a level of 120 per cent of the pre-war or peacetime rent. In addition many cities and communities raised loans, often in the United States market, to finance housing.

In some cities widely admired housing projects were undertaken, influenced by the ideas of the Bauhaus and Le Corbusier. There was, however, also criticism that not enough cheap housing was being provided. The importance of Weimar's housing programme may be gauged from the fact that it accounted for around a fifth of all investment and for around a sixth of industrial and artisan employment. Therein lay a difficulty for the economy as a whole when the depression came. As public revenues collapsed the building programme declined precipitately. Whereas over two million workers were employed in the construction industry in 1929, by 1932 the number had dropped to 775 000 and the industry had one of the highest rates of unemployment.

Housing therefore had a strongly pro-cyclical effect, when it could have acted as a stabiliser. The reasons were partly political rather than economic. The large public housing programme financed out of taxation had often been criticised as a misapplication of scarce resources. Such views came to be in the ascendant in the deflationary climate of the Brüning government, which preferred to cut taxes and trust to the regenerative power of the market.[13]

The adoption of a scheme of unemployment insurance in July 1927 was a high-water mark of Weimar social policy. It supplied the missing link in Germany's welfare system established by Bismarck. Provision for the unemployed had assumed importance at the beginning of the war, when unemployment had temporarily risen very high. It then became of major importance again in the demobilisation phase. An ordinance on care for the unemployed (*Erwerbslosenfürsorge*) was one of the early social achievements of the revolution.

At this stage responsibility was still left with local communities, where it had always rested. The Reich now contributed half the cost and the *Länder* another third. The central government imposed some limits, such as a period of 26 weeks as the maximum entitlement to benefit. Attempts were soon made to achieve a permanent settlement on the basis of the insurance principle, which some other countries, notably Britain, were already operating.

The long-serving Reich minister of labour from the Centre Party, Heinrich Brauns, who held the office from 1920 to 1928, played a leading role in putting forward legislative proposals for unemployment insurance, as he did on the question of arbitration. The Centre Party's commitment to social policy was part of a delicate balancing act between its working-class and middle-class followers, between its adherence to market principles and the imperatives of social conscience. The Centre Party was essential to all governmental coalitions and its presence in government was one more reason why the political ascendancy of the bourgeois parties had to be counterbalanced by attention to social questions.

Unemployment receded as a problem during the inflationary boom of the early 1920s and the various insurance proposals then under discussion were never enacted. The upsurge of unemployment in 1923 led to important changes. The financing of unemployment was linked to the contributions paid by employers and employees to sickness insurance, thus taking some of the burden off the public revenue. This brought a fully-fledged insurance scheme even nearer. The scheme eventually adopted in 1927 was based on a broad consensus between trade unions and employers' organisations. In the Reichstag only communists, Nazis and a few members of the DNVP voted against it and it passed with 356 votes against 47, with 16 abstentions. This shows that one should not underestimate the integrative power of the Weimar political system, admittedly at the moment of its highest economic prosperity.

The administration of the insurance scheme was entrusted to an independent institute of the Reich. A new network of local labour exchanges was established. There was an entitlement of 26 weeks' benefit on the basis of employment for 26 weeks in the previous twelve months. Whereas the German sickness insurance and pension system had always distinguished between manual and white collar workers (*Angestellte*) and still continued to do so, this scheme to a large extent covered both categories. There were equal contributions from employers and employees and the scheme was calculated as viable on the basis of a maximum of 800 000 unemployed. Within two years this maximum was to be much exceeded and the scheme's loss of viability was to become a major factor in bringing the governability of the republic to an end.[14]

ORGANISED CAPITALISM: INDUSTRY,
AGRICULTURE, *MITTELSTAND* AND
REVALUATION

The notion that German capitalism in the middle years of
Weimar was moving away from the market and turning into
organised capitalism received much impetus from the evidence of
rationalisation, concentration and cartelisation in German industry. American models of mass production, moving belt
methods and economies of scale were closely observed in
Germany, part of an American 'wave' which became even more
marked after the Second World War. Words like 'Fordism' and
'Taylorism' entered the language. Concentration and cartelisation were also the consequence of excess capacity, particularly in
the older basic industries like coal and steel, but even in an
industry like machine tools, which between 1925 and 1929 could
scarcely utilise three-quarters of its capacity.

Over-investment in the older industries during the inflationary
boom may have been due to the mistaken view that they would
recover their prewar importance and to the exceptional political
influence of heavy industry in the immediate postwar years. An
inquiry instituted by the Reichstag produced the information that
in October 1926 nearly two-thirds of the nominal capital of public
companies was attributable to about 15 per cent of these
companies. The two best known examples of concentration were
IG Farben and *Vereinigte Stahlwerke* (Vestag), both formed at the
end of 1925. The former controlled 35 per cent of the capital and
employed about a third of the workers in the chemical industry.
The Vestag was built on the ruins of the vertically integrated
Stinnes concern. It produced 50 per cent of German crude iron,
43 per cent of crude steel and 40 per cent of of rolled steel.

Added to concentration there was cartelisation, which was not
effectively inhibited by any legislation. In 1925 the German
government estimated that there were about 3 000 cartel arrangements in operation. In the coal and steel industries about 90 per
cent of products were affected by such arrangements.[15] Far from
reducing cartelisation, the government got involved in these
arrangements through subventions and through its policies on
tariffs. In January 1925 Germany had regained full control over
its tariffs, which had been limited by the Versailles treaty for five
years.

Much of the policy-making in these areas was the result of collaboration between the relevant government departments, such as the economics ministry, and interest and industrial organisations, such as the Central Association of German Industry (*Reichsverband der Deutschen Industrie*). When and where necessary parties, cabinets and the Reichstag had to give their final endorsement. The weakness of the political as opposed to the bureaucratic part of this process illustrates the advance of state corporatism. One of the reasons why the DNVP had to give up its stance of outright opposition to the republic was that the interest groups linked to it needed to be involved in this area of decision-making.

Cartels and tariffs were also an important aspect of foreign policy, where it was Stresemann's declared intention to use to the full the one remaining feature of Germany's former status as a great power, namely her economic weight. In German history the state, particularly the Prussian state, had always been interventionist. Economic liberalism, what in Germany was often called Manchesterism, was never as predominant in the development of German capitalism and industrialism as it was in the Anglo-Saxon countries. The German relationship with the economic free market was almost as ambivalent as it was with political pluralism.

The concept of organised capitalism was much discussed in Germany in the 1920s. A Marxist theoretician like Hilferding professed to see in it a progression away from the chaos of the free market. He hoped that the workers would begin to reap some benefits from this phase of declining capitalism. Economic liberals were more critical and diagnosed misallocation of resources and arteriosclerosis. M.J. Bonn, member of the DDP, adviser to governments and later an exile in Britain, wrote: 'It is the capitalism of tinkers, who are determined to kill the vital forces of the capitalist order . . .' When the depression came this arteriosclerosis may well have made it more difficult for the self-corrective forces of a market economy to take effect.[16]

There was a consensus that agriculture was in even more dire straits than industry. A worldwide agricultural depression started in the middle 1920s and played a major part in aggravating the great depression. The war had produced an over-expansion of agricultural capacity, which now caused prices to tumble. The world price of wheat doubled between 1913 and 1920 and then fell back to a third of the 1913 level by 1931. German agriculture was particularly vulnerable, for it produced less of the more marketable refined products, such as dairy products. Experts have calculated that the return on capital in German agriculture was negative in most years after 1925. The problem was also a regional one, because the areas most obviously affected were the Prussian provinces east of the Elbe, Pomerania, East and West Prussia, Upper Silesia. These were also the border provinces threatened by Poland.

The political consequences were very adverse. The Land Association (*Reichslandbund*) was closely linked to the DNVP and exerted pressure for protective tariffs and direct subventions. The failure to institute any kind of land reform now came home to roost. Heavy industry, which also had its begging bowl out, often made common cause with right-wing agrarians. There was a continuation of the tradition of solidarity between agrarian and industrial big producers begun under Bismarck. Small peasant farmers still followed in the wake of the great landowners, as they had done in the imperial era, even though their interests by no means coincided. In agricultural areas in parts of Germany, for example Schleswig-Holstein, where small farmers were predominant in agriculture, there was political radicalisation. As early as 1927 the Nazi Party, with its blood and soil ideology, began to make headway in this province, like East Elbian Prussia also a border province curtailed by Versailles. When it was a case of protecting German soil and those who tilled it against foreign threats, particularly from the encroaching Slavs, even the republic could hardly withhold its support. *Osthilfe* (eastern aid) became a recurring feature of Weimar politics.[17]

Other groups in the *Mittelstand* felt their position to be unsatisfactory as inflation gave way to stabilisation. Among them were small shopkeepers and independent artisans. Developments during and after the war had pressed them hard and left them with a sense of isolation. They were excluded from the armistice between capital and labour enshrined in the *Zentralarbeitsgemein-schaft*. They had always been opposed to the labour movement and to socialism and taken their position on the right of German politics. It was hard for them to accept certain features of the post-revolutionary constitutional settlement, such as article 165 of the constitution guaranteeing the right of codetermination and representation. They found it difficult to live with even the very watered-down form this constitutional right was given in the works council law of 1920. The whole social security apparatus of the republic and the taxation required to finance it was not to their liking.

In the retail trade and among small shopkeepers there was strong antagonism to the great department stores and this feeling was always markedly tinged with anti-Semitism. In the 1920s department store chains, like Tietz and Wertheim, mostly Jewish-owned, assumed a higher profile, while the small retailer felt a loss of protection and status. Initially such voters may well have turned to the DDP as the most obvious bulwark against the left, but they quickly turned to other parties like the DVP and the DNVP. Even here they gradually experienced disappointment, because these parties were too much swayed by the bigger battalions of industry and commerce.

The obvious power of big business in the DVP and the consequent disillusionment of middle-class voters accounts to some extent for the heavy losses suffered by the party in May 1924 and for the gains of the DNVP. Just at this point some of the DVP's big business supporters were, however, switching to the DNVP. Thus small shopkeepers and independent artisans turned increasingly to splinter parties like the Economics Party (*Wirtschaftspartei*, also known as *Reichspartei des deutschen Mittelstandes*). In May 1924 this party obtained over half a million votes and by December 1924 its support had risen to 700 000, 1.8 and 2.3 per cent respectively. By 1928 the Economics Party ran close to the DDP with 4.5 against 4.9 per cent; it could still muster nearly 4 per cent in 1930 before rapidly losing its voters to the Nazis. The party made a particular issue of the grievances of house owners, of low rents and then of the special tax on rents (*Hauszinssteuer*). Like other political formations of this period catering for special interest groups and their grievances, the Economics Party lacked one of the fundamental characteristics that distinguish a political party from a mere lobby, namely the ability to integrate a variety of social groups. It tried to counter this by propagating an ideology, a *Mittelstandsideologie*, which itself reflected the widespread hostility to parliamentarism and political pluralism among its followers. In May 1924, when the Economics Party first contested a national election and was still mainly appealing to house owners, it issued this appeal: 'Leave the morass of political parties, if you value your house, your property . . . Be German, honest and united!'[18]

Another group which felt itself marginalised after 1918 were white-collar workers. These had always cherished their separate status superior to that of the blue-collar proletariat. Their sickness insurance and pensions were administered by a separate institution; before 1914 they may well have enjoyed a standard of living somewhat above that of manual workers, with better security and other benefits. The term 'private civil servant' (*Privatbeamter*) was used by many who worked in larger enterprises. Many of these status and economic advantages disappeared during the war and the revolution. The number of white-collar workers of all types, clerical and technical, increased, but they suffered a degree of proletarianisation. Consequently there was for a time a turn to the left and a disposition to resort to the collective action familiar to manual workers.

In 1920 nearly half of the white-collar employees that were organised in professional associations belonged to the *Allgemeiner freier Angestelltenbund* (AfA). This body then had nearly 700 000 members, was linked to the ADGB and the SPD and was, if anything, on their left wing. In the middle 1920s the AfA was overtaken in numbers by the more right-wing *Gesamtverband Deutscher Angestelltengewerkschaften* (Gedag), a sign that the republican allegiance of white-collar employees was weakening again. Their political position remained ambivalent, for many of them, particularly the increasing number of women, came from and remained linked to a working-class background.[19]

Revaluation of debts was an issue which kept most of the *mittelständisch* and agrarian groups, however disparate their real interests, in a state of excitement and resentment during the stabilisation phase. For a long time the time-honoured maxim 'mark equals mark' had prevailed in law, but as the inflation proceeded the courts became aware that this offended against another basic legal principle 'equity and good faith' (*Treu und Glauben*). Immediately after the introduction of the *Rentenmark* a sensational judgment by the Supreme Court (*Reichsgericht*) laid it down that the discharge of a debt on the basis of its nominal value ran counter to *Treu und Glauben* when the currency had ceased to keep its value. The association of judges at the Supreme Court later issued a statement that legislation at variance with this judgment could not be expected to be upheld by the courts. The opinion was widely expressed that the judges had taken so strong and unusual a position because they were themselves among those hit by inflation.

Government action became inevitable but was severely circumscribed by the overriding necessity to ensure the success of the new currency. A revaluation of public debts would immediately place a burden upon finances of the Reich dangerous to the stability of the *Rentenmark*. A decree of 14 February 1924 issued under the enabling act recognised the principle of revaluation and implemented a basic rate of 15 per cent on the gold mark value of various forms of private debts and mortgages. The revaluation of public debts was postponed till after the end of reparations. The effective rate of revaluation was lower than 15 per cent because of the way interest payments were treated. The decree also imposed new taxes on the inflation gains of debtors of which the *Hauszinssteuer* proved the most productive.

The decree therefore left creditors dissatisfied while opening up new means of taxing debtors. While this may have been necessary to protect the new currency it satisfied no one and kept the revaluation issue at the forefront of the two Reichstag election campaigns in May and December 1924. It was ruthlessly exploited by the nationalist anti-republican parties. Two laws of 25 July 1925 recognised a revaluation of 25 per cent for some purposes, but left the moratorium on payments, 1 January 1932, in force. The revaluation of private debts was bound to cause hardship either to creditors or debtors and generally to both. The main result of the legislation was to keep the issue and the resentments surrounding it alive. There was now also some compensation for holders of the public debt. They managed to retrieve somewhere between one-fifth and one-seventh of their original holdings, not unreasonable in comparison with other countries like France and Belgium, where there had also been inflation but no hyperinflation. None of this could end the resentment caused by the capricious reallotment of wealth by the inflation.[20]

PARTIES, COALITIONS AND THE ELECTION OF HINDENBURG

The uneasy balance between a sense of stability nurtured by returning prosperity and continuing resentments harboured by broad sections of the population was reflected in election results in the Reichstag elections of December 1924 and the presidential ballots of March and April 1925. These elections set the political framework for the middle years of the republican period. A second dissolution of the Reichstag within seven months was precipitated by the failure to broaden the second minority government headed by Wilhelm Marx.

The DVP attributed its heavy losses in the May election to the fact that the DNVP had been able to syphon off its support by enjoying the luxury of opposition. Although the inclusion of the DNVP in the coalition might well make the conduct of foreign policy even more difficult for Stresemann, his reliance on SPD support was unpopular with the nationalist, middle-class and industrial members of the DVP. The split in the DNVP over the Dawes Plan had raised hopes that a learning process was at work in the party which might move it away from nationalist demagoguery. The DNVP preferred, however, to continue to cultivate the resentment of anti-republican voters in the freedom of opposition.

At the same time the possibility of bringing the SPD back into government was explored, for in Prussia the great coalition including both SPD and DVP had remained in office. Moreover, the DDP, which was in the Marx government, was disinclined to see the cabinet's centre of gravity shifted further to the right. The leftward extension also proved impossible, for both DVP and much of the Centre Party were against it. The SPD was not willing to take responsibility for any policies detrimental to the interests of its working-class voters, such as the new protective tariffs under heated discussion at this moment and for the time being blocked by the SPD *Fraktion*. New elections, it was hoped, would offer a way out of this deadlock.

In order to prevent too frequent dissolutions of the Reichstag the Weimar constitution laid it down that a dissolution could be granted only once for the same reason. There was therefore an element of unconstitutionality in this second dissolution within a year and it set a dangerous precedent. The underlying reasons for it, the absence of a majority in the Reichstag for a combined package of domestic and foreign policies, was the same in the autumn as it had been in the spring.

The December elections did nothing to resolve it. In spite of its internal divisions revealed by the votes on the Dawes Plan, the

DNVP campaigned unashamedly on a nationalist, stab-in-the-back-myth ticket. The SPD's campaign held out to its proletarian supporters the imminent prospect of a collapsing bourgeois republic and its replacement by a socialist republic. Both the DNVP and the SPD were being pulled away from the centre by the competition from the extremes of right and left, the combined *Völkische* list and the KPD. Even the parties in the centre were affected by this pull from the wings, the DVP and Centre Party to the right, the DDP to the left. Yet as the results of these second elections in 1924 were to show, only as broad as possible a coalition of the centre could provide stable government.

There was in fact a diminution in the strength of the extremes in December as against May 1924, as one would expect in the improving economic climate. There was also a perceptible move to the left. The radical right, officially called National Socialist Freedom Movement (*Nationalsozialistische Freiheitsbewegung*), was reduced from 6.5 to 3 per cent. The DNVP slightly improved its position, from 19.5 to 20.5 per cent, but had failed to pick up all that the radical right had lost. On the left the SPD was clearly the largest party again, with 26 against 20.5 per cent. The KPD dropped from 12.6 to 9 per cent. The two left-wing parties together therefore increased their share of the vote from 33.1 to 35 per cent, while the combined nationalist right-wing vote dropped from 26 to 23.5 per cent. The two liberal parties achieved some recovery from the losses suffered in May: the DVP rose from 9.2 to 10.1 per cent, the DDP from 5.7 to 6.3 per cent. The Centre Party recovered slightly, from 13.4 to 13.6 per cent; the BVP, badly damaged in May by its dubious role in the beer hall putsch, recovered more substantially, from 3.2 to 3.8 per cent. The Reichstag thus elected served for nearly three and a half years and therefore formed the basis for the operation of the political system for most of the republic's middle period.

Simultaneously there were elections to the Prussian Landtag. The results here were similar to those in the Reich, but the comparison is with the previous Prussian elections in February 1921 (and November 1922 in Upper Silesia). In this comparison the three Weimar coalition parties, the SPD, the Centre Party and the DDP, had a reduced share of the vote but came within an ace of a majority in December 1924. The existing great coalition in Prussia was, however, brought to an end, because, as in the Reich, the DVP wanted the inclusion of the DNVP in the government and therefore the formation of a centre–right coalition.

It was just such a coalition that was now formed in the Reich. In spite of its strident election campaign against Stresemann's foreign policy the DNVP now agreed to enter the government for the first time. Hans Luther, previously finance minister, was the new chancellor. In a formal sense this claimed to be a cabinet of personalities rather than parties and Luther himself did not belong to any party, though he was close to the DVP. The new cabinet did not seek a vote of confidence, but only the approval of the Reichstag. In practice this was a majority government further to the right than any previous republican government. Not only the SPD but also the DDP remained outside it, although Gessler, still formally a member of the DDP but no longer a member of the Reichstag, carried on as minister of defence.

The complexity of the Weimar parliamentary system was again fully in evidence. Governments such as this one rested on agreements over some areas of policy, but not over others. The DNVP's support for the government's foreign policy was much more tenuous, and open to attack inside the party, than the SPD's support. Yet over wide areas of domestic policy the SPD was in total opposition to the Luther government. By refusing to join a great coalition the SPD had in fact brought this right-wing government into existence, but it was forced to do so by the pressure of its own followers and the electoral competition of the KPD. Fortunately for the viability of the system there were now only 45 communist and 14 Nazi deputies, 59 out of 493, completely opposed to the system itself.[21]

It was of even greater long-term importance that not only the cabinet but the presidency moved decisively to the right in the spring of 1925. In the closing months of 1924 a financial scandal with anti-Semitic overtones, the Barmat affair, had given the enemies of the republic a convenient handle in their campaign to discredit 'the system'. Ebert had been marginally involved and the Marx government had been weakened in its closing stages. Ebert himself had brought a libel action against a *völkisch* journalist who had accused him of high treason because of his participation in the strikes of January 1918. Such accusations had been constantly levied from the right in their unrelenting campaign against the republic and its personalities. Ebert had had to bring some 170 libel actions, even though he was loath to do so, unlike Bismarck, who kept a supply of forms ready for the purpose and used the procedure to terrorise his opponents. On this occasion the court condemned the journalist to three months' imprisonment, but also declared that in a strictly legal sense Ebert might be held guilty of treason. The president was deeply wounded, in spite of declarations of support from all of the cabinet and from many other public personalities. He may have delayed treatment of appendicitis in order to give evidence in court. He died, aged 54, on 28 February 1925. His term of office was due to run out on 30 June 1925.

Whatever the criticism of Ebert's policy during the revolution, he had discharged his office with great distinction, yet had never struck much of a chord with the mass of the people. It was only to be expected that the far left regarded him as a traitor to the working class while the unreconstructed right considered him a traitor to the fatherland. Yet even many of those less prejudiced wanted a more resplendent symbol as head of state than this modest, ordinary man, who occasionally had to appear in a top hat.

The procedure for electing the president now went into operation for the first time. If no candidate received an absolute majority, there had to be a second ballot. This was not a run-off between the two leading candidates on the first ballot. New candidates could be brought forward and a simple majority was now sufficient. At first there was a chance that Gessler would become the agreed candidate of the non-socialist parties. His defence of the Reichswehr in difficult situations had made him acceptable on the right. Gessler's candidature was prevented by Stresemann, who voiced his concern that Gessler's close connection with the Reichswehr would complicate the delicate diplomatic negotiations then in progress, which would in the autumn lead to the signature of the Locarno treaties.

In the absence of any broadly supported candidate most of the party groupings put up candidates. Jarres, minister of the interior under Stresemann and Marx and on the right wing of the DVP, became the candidate of the right and polled the highest number of votes, 38.8 per cent. His strongholds were the Prussian provinces east of the Elbe, Pomerania in particular, and Protestant areas in general. Otto Braun, about to return as Prussian prime minister, was the SPD's candidate and polled 29 per cent. He did best in the left-wing strongholds of central

Germany, Magdeburg, Leipzig, Dresden and Brunswick. Marx, the Centre Party candidate, obtained 14.5 per cent and did best in the Catholic Rhineland. There was a separate BVP candidate, the Bavarian prime minister Heinrich Held, who polled no less than 66.4 per cent in Lower Bavaria and a respectable 43.8 per cent in Upper Bavaria; but in the country as a whole he got only 3.7 per cent. Thälmann, the KPD candidate, got 7 per cent, with the best results again in Merseburg and Düsseldorf East. Hellpach was the DDP candidate, with 5.8 per cent, and particularly good results in Baden and around Berlin. Ludendorff, the *Völkisch* candidate, received only 1.1 per cent, with considerable support only in Bavaria and even there below 5 per cent. These results give a useful insight into the political configuration of Weimar electoral politics. They also give evidence of a further improvement in the general atmosphere since the Reichstag elections of December 1924. Support for the extremists of left and right had been considerably reduced, perhaps partly through abstentions, for participation had dropped below 69 per cent.

What followed could make one believe that a jinx beset the Weimar Republic. It was essential for the Weimar coalition parties that they should now find an agreed candidate. Wilhelm Marx quickly emerged as that candidate. He had twice failed to win an absolute majority for the Weimar coalition government he had formed in Prussia after the resignation of Otto Braun. A deal was made that he should become the Weimar coalition candidate for the presidency, while Braun was re-elected as Prussian prime minister, an office which he held continuously until 1932. If the results of the first presidential ballot were any guide, Marx could count on nearly 50 per cent of the vote. If the right was to trump this it had to find a more attractive candidate than Jarres.

Thus they turned to Hindenburg, who had already been talked about as a potenial president five years earlier. Stresemann voiced the same objections against him as he had brought forward against Gessler, but had in the end to put a brave face on the imperial field marshal's political resurrection at the age of 77. Significantly it was Tirpitz who was sent to persuade the reluctant field marshal to submit himself for election. It was in many ways an act of desperation, for some nationalists had never forgiven Hindenburg his 'betrayal' of the Emperor in November 1918. The Hindenburg candidature was indeed unsympathetically received in the Western press.

Two factors contributed to Hindenburg's election. The first was the decision of the BVP to support him rather than the Catholic Marx. In Bavaria a nationalist Protestant was still preferable to a Catholic supported by the SPD. The results of the second ballot in the predominantly Catholic parts of Bavaria showed that this view was shared by most of the BVP voters. The second factor making Hindenburg's election possible was the decision of the KPD to run Thälmann again in the second ballot. 'It is not a task for the proletariat to select the smartest representative of the interests of the bourgeoisie, to choose the lesser evil between the civilian dictator Marx and the military dictator Hindenburg.' The SPD warned that a vote for Thälmann was a vote for Hindenburg and most of its voters heeded this warning, yet the KPD candidate still obtained 6.4 per cent of the vote. The percentage for Hindenburg was 48.3 and for Marx 45.3.

Many convinced republicans tried to make the best of this result. It was argued that the election of this *Ersatzkaiser* would reconcile many Germans to the republic and many anti-republicans feared that there was force in this argument. Hindenburg himself made it clear that he would respect the constitution. Otto Meissner, the state secretary in the presidential office and a supporter of the DDP, retained his office. Nobody could then foresee that he would also retain it under Hitler. Hindenburg's election was a defeat for the republic at least comparable to the defeat of the Weimar coalition in 1920. Hindenburg was the man who had put the stab in the back myth into general circulation. He was a figure total alien to the parliamentary democratic system in which he now had to play a key role. From the beginning he had advisers in the Reichswehr, for whom the preservation of a parliamentary democracy was not a high priority. One of the commanding heights of the republic was now in all but hostile hands.

For the moment the old field marshal had every intention of keeping the solemn oath to the constitution which he took upon entering his high office and there was disappointment among anti-republicans at his strictly correct conduct. Already in his early years as president there were, however, many important occasions when his sympathies and prejudices were clearly evident in his actions, even though no violation of the constitution was involved.[22]

LOCARNO AND ENTRY INTO THE LEAGUE OF NATIONS

Hindenburg's election fell in the middle of the prolonged manoeuvres at home and abroad that finally produced the Locarno treaties in October 1925. It had long been discerned that the missing link in the achievement of genuine European stability was the satisfaction of French security needs. In the wake of the Dawes settlement there was much public discussion of this problem. The Geneva protocols put forward by France in October 1924 would have gone a long way towards strengthening international security by reinforcing the obligations imposed by membership of the League of Nations through compulsory arbitration and sanctions. In line with the interests of France, the status quo would also have been strengthened.

This initiative failed because the new British Conservative government elected in October 1924 was unlikely to take on these obligations. On 29 December 1924 the British ambassador in Berlin, Lord D'Abernon, who was close to many leading Weimar politicians, especially Stresemann, had a conversation with Carl von Schubert. He had just become state secretary of the German foreign office and had long been the most influential advocate inside the German foreign policy establishment of a policy of western-orientated reconciliation. D'Abernon suggested that the time might be ripe for a German initiative leading to a security pact, already unsuccessfully attempted by the Cuno government.[23]

Stresemann had good reason to take up this suggestion at this moment. A threatening situation was brewing up over the problem of German disarmament and the general inspection carried out by the Inter-Allied Military Control Commission (IMCC). This matter had been a constant irritant during the Dawes Plan negotiations. The German foreign office had had to fight hard to force the Reichswehr, stubbornly committed to a policy of evasion, to allow the inspection to proceed. It was becoming clear that France, backed by the other powers, would use a somewhat unsatisfactory report by IMCC to postpone the evacuation of the Cologne zone of occupation, due on 10 January 1925. The German public's reaction to this postponement could well mean the end of Stresemann's whole rapprochement policy started by the Dawes Plan. There was also a danger that the

Western powers might themselves put a security pact in place of the abortive Geneva protocols, a pact in which Germany would not be a partner. She would thus revert to being an object of international arrangements rather than an equal partner, as she had been in the Dawes Plan negotiations. Consequently Stresemann reacted in muted fashion to the delay in the evacuation.

Immediately after the formation of the Luther government, and with the knowledge of the new chancellor, he dispatched a memorandum to London and subsequently to Paris which became the basis of the negotiations leading up to Locarno in October 1925. The essential ingredients of the German offer were a recognition of Germany's western borders as final. This acceptance of finality did not include Germany's eastern borders. In the east Germany offered a renunciation of force in the pursuit of her revisionist aims, this renunciation to be buttressed by arbitration treaties. Concurrently there was to be a settlement of outstanding commercial problems both west and east. Germany's place as a trading nation had already been a major factor in the Dawes Plan; trade questions were also raised by the expiry, on 10 January 1925, of the requirement in the Versailles treaty that Germany should grant most-favoured-nation treatment to her former enemies without reciprocity.

For Germany the recognition of her western frontiers meant giving up any claim to Alsace-Lorraine and also to the lesser adjustment of the German–Belgian frontier around Eupen and Malmedy. The proposed pacts meant a clear western orientation of German foreign policy. In any case most of the major powers were now recognising the USSR, so that Germany could not long maintain the special position vis-à-vis Russia obtained at Rapallo. On the other hand the link with Moscow still lent some extra strength to the German position, nor did it come to an end as a result of Locarno. The treaties under negotiation in 1925 were, however, a further long step away from the essentially unrealistic notions still cherished by German nationalists and supported by Seeckt and the Reichswehr, defiance of Versailles, pursuit of economic self-sufficiency, the dissolution of Poland in alliance with the Soviet Union.[24]

The journey to Locarno therefore involved fierce clashes of opinion in Germany, which became enmeshed with the highly complex negotiations required to produce agreement between the powers involved in the treaties. The fact that the DNVP had entered the government just as the process began and that Hindenburg became president before many months had passed made the position of Stresemann and the German foreign office even more difficult, but in some respects also reinforced it. Initially the German memorandum was kept secret but by March it was out in the open. Stresemann had to make the most of the advantages which would accrue to Germany: beginning of the evacuation of the Rhineland, in many ways even more important than the end of the Ruhr occupation, the hope of earlier evacuation of further occupation zones, developments favourable to German interests in the Saar, the continuation of foreign credits for the German economy, the possibility of better treatment of German minorities in the East and ultimately of frontier revisions.

Only some of these aims were realised at Locarno and some never in Stresemann's lifetime. The political necessity which forced Stresemann to emphasise the revisionist aims of his policy for public consumption have made some historians argue that he was never anything but a German power-politician biding his time. This is probably a misreading of his aims. While he believed in the continued existence of the nation state as the ultimate reality, he was also strongly convinced of the interdependence of nation states in the conditions of modern industrialism. In Europe this interdependence required institutionalised cooperation and it would also have to include the United States. Germany's economic potential would be the means of restoring her status as a great power.[25]

The move towards Locarno placed the DNVP as a member of the governing coalition under great strain. The party's leaders, now headed by Martin Schiele, the minister of the interior, gave muffled agreement to Stresemann's policy. They quickly ran into opposition from their followers and from the party press, already dominated by Hugenberg, and by their provincial organisations. For many German nationalists the Dawes Plan and Locarno were traumatic events: they undermined the psychological defences painfully built up by the non-recognition of defeat, the stab in the back myth, the hope of a new dominant Reich. The strategy of the DNVP leaders in the face of these pressures was to make it appear that the security pact ideas were Stresemann's own and not the cabinet's, to isolate the foreign minister and drive a wedge between him and Luther. A restraining influence on the DNVP was the fact that it had to remain in the coalition for the reasons it had joined it: to press the interests of its affiliated agrarian and industrial lobbies.

Once the new tariff law was passed on 17 August 1925 it became easier for the DNVP to leave the cabinet and it did so over the ratification of the Locarno treaties. Even an outspoken German note on the war guilt question could not mollify the DNVP. Although this spelt the end of the Luther coalition as a majority government it did not impede the ratification of the treaties. The SPD had strongly supported all the developments that led to Locarno and it was unthinkable that it would allow the treaties to fail. The only question was whether the SPD would force another dissolution of the Reichstag, but for this current electoral prospects were too uncertain. The DDP also supported the treaties from outside the government. It was always anxious to emphasise its nationalist credentials and never retreated from the principle that all Germans, wherever they were, had the democratic right to return to a Greater Germany. In contrast to views in the DNVP and further to the right, the DDP stressed that the return to great-power status had to be peaceful and by agreement. The DDP's nationalism was in no way anti-republican.

The Reichstag approved the Locarno settlement as a whole by a vote of 292 to 174 and three abstentions. The noes came from the DNVP, the *Völkische*, the Economics Party and the KPD. For the increasingly Stalinised Communist Party Locarno was a capitalist conspiracy against the Soviet Union, led by Britain, in which the German working class was forced to take part by the betrayals practised upon it by Stresemann and the SPD.[26]

The acceptance of the Locarno treaties once more precipitated a governmental crisis in Germany. In some quarters there was still the hope that it would become a crisis of 'the system', although this was now less likely than it had been two years earlier. In parliamentary terms the choice was between a great coalition including the SPD or a bourgeois minority government. The SPD was no more in the mood to take on the responsibilities of government than it had been previously. The moment was particularly unpropitious, for in the winter 1925–6 a renewed economic downturn had driven the unemployment figures well above the two million mark. It was the result of the Reichsbank's tight credit policies and of the wave of 'rationalisation' in industry. The SPD's insistence that there should be a legal reinstatement of the eight-hour day became the official reason for the failure to form a great coalition. The price the SPD had to pay for its determination to stay in opposition was the return of Luther as chancellor, who in domestic affairs had never made a secret of his right-wing sympathies.

Those who had nothing but contempt for the Weimar 'system' were strengthened in their convictions by this governmental crisis lasting some six weeks. The influence of the president, the other constitutional pole of the system, was also enhanced by this crisis. While no unconstitutional conduct can be imputed to Hindenburg it became clear that he was reluctant to have the SPD back in government and keen to have a government which left open the possibility that the DNVP might return to it. On the other hand the DNVP's efforts, abetted by Hindenburg, failed to limit the government's freedom of manoeuvre in foreign affairs. The policy of Locarno would be continued and Stresemann retained his office.

One central feature of this policy, Germany's entry into the League of Nations, remained to be accomplished. For Germany the allocation of one of the permanent seats on the League council would seal her return to the circle of great powers. On the other hand the obligation under article 16 of the covenant to take part in sanctions created difficulties for Germany as a disarmed country and in her relations with Russia. This special situation was dealt with in an annex (F) to the Locarno treaties.

Considerable difficulties emerged in the course of 1926 in actually bringing Germany to Geneva and these threatened at times the whole spirit of Locarno. The problem arose from the desire of other countries, particularly Poland, to have their great-power status recognised by a permanent seat. For Poland Locarno meant a deterioration of her international position. For German nationalists the League symbolised the dominance of the victorious enemy powers and the campaign against Germany's entry became the focus of the DNVP's opposition to the government, of which it was no longer a member. Germany finally took her seat in the League in September 1926, a high point in the hopes of reconciliation and peace entertained during this period.

A week after the German delegation had appeared at the Palais des Nations, Stresemann and the French foreign minister Briand met at the small Jura village of Thoiry to discuss further progress and closer German–French collaboration and European unity. The deal envisaged was that in return for German economic help the outstanding issues in Franco–German relations, notably the evacuation of the Rhineland ahead of the date laid down in the treaty, would be comprehensively cleared up. The more distant goals envisaged at Thoiry were soon lost sight of. The main reason was the return to office of Poincaré and his success in solving French economic problems and strengthening the franc without German help. Yet at least until the onset of the world economic crisis the Locarno process did not go into reverse and some further progress was made.

Although German policy remained firmly Western-orientated it had never been Stresemann's intention to disregard the advantages accruing to Germany from continued good relations with Russia. What was considered unrealistic was that the Soviet Union could ever be a substitute for the West in German calculations or the means of an open defiance of the Versailles system, as Seeckt and others hoped. The Germans therefore resisted all Soviet overtures designed to deflect them from the path to Locarno. Just before the German delegation left for Locarno a trade treaty was signed with Russia. In April 1926 this was followed by the Berlin treaty, a reaffirmation of Rapallo, including an undertaking of neutrality in so far as it was compatible with the obligations Germany was about to incur under the League covenant. The secret military arrangements with Russia continued, but eventually became a matter of political controversy in Germany. Stresemann was always conscious of the fact that no distinction between the Soviet Union as a power and her role as the centre of a revolutionary movement was possible and that in no country was it less appropriate to ignore this second aspect of Soviet policy than in Germany.[27]

DOMESTIC POLITICS: REFERENDUM ON DYNASTIC PROPERTY, THE FLAG CONTROVERSY, THE FALL OF SEECKT

The government crisis over Locarno had erupted at the very moment when the question of the return of the property of Germany's former ruling houses had become a major domestic issue. It was difficult to distinguish between the public and private property of the dynasties overthrown by the revolution. The problem was dealt with at the level of the *Länder*, but there was always the possibility of legal action being brought under the Reich constitution. To counter the likelihood of endless litigation, in which the courts would always take a view very favourable to the property rights of the dynasties, legislation was necessary.

This gave the KPD a chance, in November 1925, to introduce a proposal in the Reichstag which amounted to confiscation without compensation of former dynastic property. The beneficiaries were to be small peasant owners, the homeless and recipients of war pensions. It was a plan cleverly designed to appeal to those who were at this moment suffering from the rigours of the stabilisation policy and were aggrieved over revaluation. It became the first occasion when the constitution's provisions for a people's request (*Volksbegehren*) and a referendum (*Volksentscheid*) were actually put into operation.

The only way in which the SPD could counter the KPD's blatant reversion to the tactic of 'unity from below' was to campaign, though separately from the communists, for the proposal to dispossess the former ruling houses without compensation 'for the benefit of all'. The SPD's decision was also a consequence of the party's refusal to join a great coalition in January 1926, for it felt itself unable to support the new cabinet's compromise plan judged to be too favourable to the former princes. The broad coalition campaigning for dispossession also included a number of prominent intellectuals with liberal, left-wing and pacifist sympathies, for example Albert Einstein and Kurt Tucholsky. Arrayed against dispossession were the bourgeois parties, but with different degrees of emphasis and reasoning. The DDP had put forward compromise proposals designed to combine regard for the rights of property with the 'natural sentiments' of the German people for equality of sacrifice in a time of general distress. This was also the line officially taken by the Centre Party. The right, including the DVP, the DNVP, industry, the agrarians, Stahlhelm and most of the *Völkische*, campaigned strongly against the referendum when it became clear that the left supported it. In the recently resurrected NSDAP, now separated from the *Völkische*, the left-wing, for example the brothers Strasser and the young Goebbels, wanted to back dispossession, but Hitler called it 'a Jewish swindle'. Hitler was just about to impose his control over the movement and this issue confronted him with an early test of his reclaimed leadership. The campaign over the expropriation of the princes thus provides a good insight into the deep fissures in German society and their impact right across the political spectrum.

The first stage of the procedure, the collection of signatures in favour of the KPD's proposals, took place from 4 to 17 March 1926. About four million signatures, 10 per cent of those entitled to vote, were required to enable a referendum to take place. In fact over 12.5 million voters signed, a remarkable success, exceeding by about two million votes the combined SPD–KPD vote in December 1924. The referendum itself took place on 20 June 1926. Since the proposal was considered a change in the constitution, the requirement was that a majority of those entitled to vote should support it. This made it in practice impossible for the expropriation law to succeed, but the support it generated, nearly 14.5 million, about 39 per cent of the electorate, was again remarkable. This time the combined SPD–KPD vote of December 1924 was exceeded by nearly four million.

A more detailed analysis of the results of both *Volksbegehren* and *Volksentscheid* in 1926 shows that a considerable number of previous voters of the Centre Party and of the right-wing parties, particularly in large cities, had supported expropriation. In the strongholds of the DNVP in East Elbian Prussia many previous DNVP voters supported expropriation in the referendum, having been unable to do so in the people's request, because of the formidable social pressures brought to bear, including that of the Lutheran churches. Even a letter by Hindenburg to the anti-expropriation committee, all but supporting their point of view, made no difference, but it was a risky move by a president meant to be above party. The supporters of the right who voted for expropriation had not permanently shifted their allegiance to the left, which remained as deeply divided as ever. These results give an insight into the depths of resentment felt by many Germans at this time, their volatility as voters and the potentialities of a demagogic, populist appeal. It was not the left that would eventually launch such an appeal.[28]

While the campaign over the expropriation of the princes was still going on, the second cabinet formed by Hans Luther fell over an issue that had a good deal in common with the dispossession of the former ruling houses. The issue was the republic's flag, black, red and gold, as opposed to the imperial colours, black, white and red, a question that had always aroused great emotion. Somewhat gratuitously, perhaps to please Hindenburg, an order had been issued to German diplomatic and consular offices in major ports round the world that they should in future show not only the republican flag but also the flag of the merchant marine, which, under a previous compromise, was black, white and red, with black, red and gold as a jack. The order caused a furious outcry among the committed supporters of the republic and it was on a motion of the DDP that Luther was defeated in May 1926. Again a government crisis nearly became a state crisis, because of the strong support of Hindenburg for Luther over this issue. The nervous state of the moment may be gauged from the fact that a police raid authorised by Severing, the Prussian minister of the interior, on the home of Class, the leader of the Pan-German League, unearthed incriminating material about a planned putsch.

The time for coups was over for the moment, but the government crisis was no easier to resolve than it had been five months earlier, the blow to confidence in 'the system' equally great. Among those who briefly attempted to form a new cabinet was the mayor of Cologne, Konrad Adenauer. The government he wanted to form, a great coalition including the SPD, was hardly on the cards at that moment, when the SPD was associated, however distantly, with the KPD in the referendum campaign. In the SPD itself there was more awareness about the losses and risks suffered by remaining in opposition, but nothing could be done until the referendum was out of the way. The DNVP, on the other hand, was still not willing to support Stresemann's policy unequivocally, for the question of entering the League was still not resolved. Thus there was no alternative to a continuation of the existing minority government, but with a new chancellor. He was not new either, for it was again Wilhelm Marx, who had been minister of justice in the Luther cabinet. It was becoming increasingly part of the Weimar style of coalition formation that transience was built into the process. This third cabinet formed by Marx was envisaged to last until the referendum on dynastic property was out of the way, or alternatively until Germany had taken her seat at Geneva. After the referendum the coalition might be extended leftwards to include the SPD. After entry into the League the return of the DNVP might become a possibility.[29]

The nervousness in republican circles, which had been evident in the controversy over the flags, flared up again in the autumn of 1926, first over the position of Seeckt and then over the secret military links with the Soviet Union, which he had done more than anybody to cultivate. The Chief of the Army had allowed the eldest son of the German Crown Prince to participate in army manoeuvres in uniform. When this was revealed in the German press a storm broke. On this occasion Gessler refused to be, as he himself put it, the fall guy for the army, which he had been so often before. The defence minister was already under attack from the left wing of his own party, the DDP, for his lenient attitude to anti-republican manifestations in the Reichswehr. The DDP was at this time again feeling the stresses which German left liberalism had experienced throughout its history, the tug-of-war between a leftward orientation, alliance with the SPD and the proletariat, and the competition of the parties and interest groups arrayed on the right. It was part of the process of liberal disintegration and of the fragmentation of the centre that was a marked feature of these middle years of Weimar. Gessler demanded Seeckt's resignation and the army chief found no support from Hindenburg. The old field marshal and the intellectual general had never been bosom friends. Some in Seeckt's entourage, including Colonel von Fritsch, himself ousted by Hitler eleven years later, were inclined to press for a putsch. This had never been Seeckt's way and it would have had little chance of success now, particularly when Hindenburg was providing an alternative figurehead.

The end of the *Ära Seeckt* was ambivalent in its meaning. The general had turned the Reichswehr into a state within a state, a task made easier for him by the restrictions on its size imposed by Versailles. He had not felt justified by circumstances to push his distant relationship with the republic over the edge into disloyalty. Since the beginning of stabilisation he had not fully succeeded in redefining the relationship between his force and the republic. He had always been a strong opponent of Stresemann's policies and had voiced his views in the many cabinet meetings he attended. In the army he had followed an old-fashioned line in many respects. He was reluctant to recognise fully the revolutionary consequences of total war fought with rapidly changing technologies.

Seeckt's departure meant that there was now less direct political influence from the Reichswehr, particularly in foreign policy, and a greater readiness to acknowledge the supremacy of the civil power in these spheres. Some of the younger officers who now came to the fore were, however, more aware than Seeckt of the army's need for greater resources and of its dependence on the willingness of the population as a whole to support military preparedness. The relationship between the army and the civilian population in the later stages of the war had been too negative and repressive and many officers knew this. However much most officers might dislike the republic, they had a vested interest in its stability if they wanted to achieve greater military preparedness and a more favourable allocation of resources. The relative stabilisation of the international order in the Stresemann years meant that the Reichswehr could no longer think of overthrowing that order, but had to see itself as the military back-stop to Germany's regained but limited great power status. It remained difficult to establish a more appropriate niche for the army when many sections of the German people remained hostile to the military. Such problems brought the Reichswehr back into politics by a different route, however hard it might try to slough off the reputation of a counter-revolutionary force. It was left to Seeckt's successors, above all to Groener, who succeeded Gessler in 1928, and to his protégé Kurt von Schleicher to manage this problem. The new Chief of the Army, Paul von Heye, was a less significant figure.[30]

Within weeks of Seeckt's departure the left's suspicions about the Reichswehr received fresh impetus. An article in the *Manchester Guardian* revealed details of weapons produced for Germany in the Soviet Union and of links between the German and Soviet armed forces. This was the moment when Stresemann was about to achieve a major success, the final withdrawal of the Inter-Allied Military Control Commission (IMCC) on 31 January 1927. On 16 December 1926 Scheidemann made a speech in the Reichstag, in which unfolded a catalogue of accusations against the Reichswehr, not only the secret armaments in Russia, but also the long and ongoing links between the Reichswehr and right-wing paramilitary organisations. The speech showed how difficult it was going to be, even with Seeckt gone, to normalise relations between the armed forces and the largest German political party. It also had the effect of finally ending any chance of a great coalition being formed within the existing Reichstag.

A vote of no confidence moved by the SPD was supported by the DNVP, another example of the negative union of opposites that was such a feature of Weimar politics. The minority government of Marx was defeated by a vote of 249, the SPD, the DNVP, the KPD, NSDAP, to 171, the DVP, the DDP, the Centre Party and some minor groups. In the resultant government crisis Hindenburg pushed even more vigorously than earlier for a right-wing government including the DNVP. Schleicher played a role in the negotiations and already the possibility of a presidential government, using article 48 and relying on the president's willingness to grant a dissolution, was being discussed.

The fourth government formed by Marx was a bourgeois coalition, which through the inclusion of the DNVP came close to a majority. The Centre Party had for electoral reasons been initially reluctant to see such an outcome. Although the party had become steadily more conservative it had to pay regard to its working-class trade union wing. In Prussia there was a close relationship between the Centre Party and the SPD which neither side wished to give up. There was, however, also a whole range of cultural, educational and denominational issues on which the Centre Party could find a common conservative ground with the DNVP. It was precisely this cultural, educational conservatism, particularly the possibility of a new law on denominational education, that now forced the DDP into opposition. The bargaining power of this internally riven party was in any case diminished. Gessler gave up his membership of it in order to retain his defence portfolio.

The price of the DNVP's return to government was, however, the acceptance by the party of Locarno and of Stresemann's continued tenure of the foreign office. It also agreed to the opening statement of the new coalition which affirmed 'the legal validity' of the republican nature of the state founded by the constitution of Weimar. It was not exactly a resounding profession of republicanism by the DNVP, but nevertheless a further shift towards the acceptance of the republic by the party.[31]

CULTURAL ISSUES: ANTI-PORNOGRAPHY LAW, *NEUE
SACHLICHKEIT*, DENOMINATIONAL SCHOOLS

The emergence of cultural conservatism as a divisive issue but also
as the means of a new alignment had been signalled just before the
fragile Marx minority government fell. The signal was the anti-
pornography legislation which had been under discussion for a
long time. A proposal finally emerged under the title 'law for the
protection of youth against literary rubbish and dirt' and was
accepted by the Reichstag on 3 December 1926 by 248 votes
against 158 with three abstentions. It provided for the establishment of representative committees, as well as a central examining
office, charged with the compilation of an index of offensive
publications. The opponents of the bill saw in this the imposition
of a cultural and political censorship. The SPD, KPD and fifteen
members of the DDP formed the opposition, while the DNVP, the
Centre Party and the BVP, the DVP, twelve members of the DDP
and the national socialists supported the law.

Unbridgeable ideological differences inflamed by raw sensitivi-
ties and suspicions were again revealed. Within the DDP the
battle was particularly fierce and the split total. Some respected
members of the party, Theodor Heuss, later the first and widely
revered president of the Federal Republic after the war, and
Gertrud Bäumer, one of the few prominent women in politics,
argued for the law on pragmatic grounds. Heuss said in his
speech, perhaps addressing those members of his own party who
did not agree with him, that social policy was implicit not only in
wage agreements, but there was also 'a social policy of the soul'.
Vulnerable youth had to be protected against the dissemination of
false values.

Such laudable objectives were shared by many opponents of the
bill, but they could not forget the habit of demonising and
repressing dissent prevalent before the revolution. The speeches of
the leading DNVP and Centre Party supporters of the bill could
only remind them that these habits were still alive. The Lutheran
pastor Mumm, for the DNVP, cited a catalogue of depravities
that went on in Berlin, for so many conservative Germans the
Sodom and Gomorrah of the day. For good measure Mumm
blamed it on foreign influences and sounded the anti-Semitic note:
'. . . those in whose veins runs other, not German blood, and who

cannot empathize with Christian sensibilities'. The Centre Party's speaker pontificated with great pathos about the unity of art and *Volksgemeinschaft*, a word on many lips well before 1933. The ambivalence of Catholic attitudes to the republic was only too apparent. The Centre Party might be one of the main stays of 'the system', but the Catholic doctrine remained anti-pluralist, anti-liberal and anti-modern.

The great liberal newspapers and the progressive literary and artistic establishment fought passionately against the *Schund und Schmutz* legislation. Theodor Wolff, the editor of the *Berliner Tageblatt*, resigned from the DDP, of which he had been a founder member. Kurt Tucholsky wrote in the *Weltbühne*, the crusading journal of the left-wing intelligentsia: 'This state in its present form has neither the ability or legitimacy to legislate for culture; the deep gulf that splits this nation is not reflected in it; it pretends to deal with a united nation. That is not true . . . . It is far less important to preserve youth, in any case alienated and economically powerless, from aesthetic rubbish than to conserve the little bit of intellectual freedom that still exists . . .' The *Schund und Schmutz* law of 1926 soon dropped out of view and the fears it aroused proved exaggerated. The clash of cultures which it highlighted continued to reverberate.[32]

In Weimar's middle years the progressives were at any rate fighting their corner strongly. The mood among them had changed from the heady days of the revolution when a new era in human affairs seemed to be dawning and Utopianism ruled. The disillusion which set in accounts for the sour tone of writers like Tucholsky in their attitude to republican reality. Not all was negative, however, for the new modernity, much of it American-inspired, based on technical progress, mass entertainment through film and radio, sexual liberation, was viewed positively by many intellectuals and artists. The term *Neue Sachlichkeit*, best translated as a new down-to-earth, sober attitude, a deliberate avoidance of high-flown romanticism, enjoyed wide currency. It was originally applied to a post-expressionist trend in the visual arts and especially architecture. It meant turning away from ornate and ornamental styles in building and towards the rational use of new materials and techniques. The modernity and experimentalism in all the arts, for which Weimar is still remembered, never gained general acceptance. It was dismissed as 'cultural bolshevism' or 'asphalt literature'. Such cultural antagonisms are to be found in many places other than Weimar Germany, but as the controversy over the *Schund und Schmutz* law shows, they were here politicised to an unusual degree.[33]

From January 1927, with the fourth cabinet formed by Marx, the centre of gravity in Reich politics had moved more clearly to the right than ever before. Four ministries were headed by members of the DNVP. Keudell, the minister of the interior, had supported the Kapp Putsch and now replaced social democrats with more politically congenial civil servants whenever he could; 1927 and most of 1928 were also the years when the economic situation was at its most favourable from the point of view of wage and salary earners. Unemployment was fairly low, in the five to six per cent range in the summer months. Real weekly earnings rose quite rapidly.

Germany's emergence from the depression of 1925–6 owed something to mildly counter-cyclical policies pursued by the government. Peter Reinhold, the finance minster from the DDP, who held office for most of 1926, was a believer in spending as close as possible to a deficit. Later he was blamed for the problems affecting Germany's public finances. At the time he was popular with industry and German industrialists were never more favourably disposed towards the republic. Much attention was aroused by a speech given at the Dresden meeting of the RDI in September 1926 by Paul Silverberg, the head of the leading German lignite company and a man of influence in many industrial organisations. He expressed an unequivocal acceptance of the republic and admitted that industry had in the past failed to develop a satisfactory relationship with the SPD and the trade unions. 'It has been said that you cannot govern against the workers. This is wrong, it should read "you cannot govern without the workers".' He also demanded that industry should be allowed to get on with its job without too much interference from the state. He claimed that in the recent slump of 1925–6, the so-called rationalisation crisis, industry had found its own remedy through cartel arrangements and amalgamations. He complained again about the heavy social payments with which industry was burdened. Silverberg's call for a more positive attitude to trade unions and SPD did not command wide support in industry, but was a sign of the times. The new-found stability of the republic, in which all but the extremists of left and right had a vested interest, was based on a social compromise accepted by industrialists as well as politicians.[34]

It was thus the centre-right cabinet of Marx that was responsible for the most notable social achievement of this period, the unemployment insurance scheme. There was also a new law regulating hours of work which, while not restoring the eight-hour day across the board, provided for overtime arrangements favourable to wage earners. The minister most concerned with this legislation was the long-serving Heinrich Brauns from the Centre Party. For this party it was now more essential than ever to have something to show its working-class wing, having acquiesced in a centre–right rather than a great coalition.

The DNVP for its part insisted on further favours to agriculture, the continuation of the tariffs imposed in 1925 and now due for renewal. Agriculture and particularly small farmers had not shared in the general prosperity and by 1927 the situation had become critical. The debt burden carried by agriculture, which the inflation had drastically reduced, had risen again. Rising debt and falling profitability was a lethal combination and in due course affected both small farmers and large landowners. Schleswig-Holstein was an area where the problems in agriculture had reached crisis proportions even in 1927, with a rising number of forced sales. The small farmers in this province, traditionally liberal, were becoming radicalised and even resorting to violence. Protective tariffs could only alleviate not cure this problem.[35] Within the Marx government Martin Schiele, the minister of agriculture from the DNVP, was a strong representative of the agrarian lobby.

Another group which received favourable treatment from this government in the cause of social stability were civil servants. Collectively they had not yet made good the reduction in their financial status suffered since the war. By 1926 the professional association of civil servants linked to the free trade unions had lost well over half its members; the *Deutscher Beamtenbund* (German Civil Servants' League), theoretically non-party, but increasingly right-wing, was approaching the million mark. Civil service salaries were now raised by about one-sixth and this had a knock-on effect in the *Länder* and the communities, and probably on the level of wages generally. Although the number of civil service grades was increased so as to restore some of the diminished differentials, in general the gap between the lower and higher grades remained smaller than it had been in the past. This enabled the SPD to vote for the law, which might otherwise not have passed.[36]

The minister of finance, Köhler, responsible for the higher civil service salaries, became the recipient of a memorandum from the reparations agent, Parker Gilbert, in which he expressed concern about the state of German public finances. *Länder* and communal authorities were borrowing heavily abroad and overspending. They were often taking up short-term credits to finance long-term projects, some of which were luxuries rather than necessities. Part of the problem was the distribution of revenues between the Reich and subordinate authorities. The proportions originally fixed in the Erzberger reforms had never been adequately adjusted. Payments under the Dawes Plan were being financed not by an export surplus, but through the inflow of foreign loans. Gilbert's concern was to prepare the ground for a new permanent reparations settlement and to draw attention to the need to maintain the confidence of American investors. His strictures were avidly seized upon by German employers and also by Schacht, the president of the Reichsbank. Even at this high-point of inter-war prosperity, it could be argued, the republic was purchasing acceptance and social peace by overstraining the economy and making itself vulnerable if the economic future should prove less favourable.[37]

The fourth Marx cabinet had been constructed to pass a school law compatible with the denominational aspirations of the Centre Party and the DNVP. When the attempts to pass such a law failed the end of this cabinet was in sight and fresh elections to the Reichstag, in any case due by the end of 1928, had to be envisaged. Under the Weimar constitution the Reich for the first time claimed responsibilities in the area of education which had previously been entirely a matter for the *Länder*. Paragraph 146 of the constitution was a painfully contrived compromise which proclaimed a common elementary school as the norm, but left open the possibility of denominational schools where a majority of parents desired them. There was also a blocking paragraph 174, which maintained the status quo in the *Länder* until such time as the Reich would legislate to give effect to paragraph 146. Since up to 1927 the Reich had been unable to legislate, this meant that, contrary to what the constitution envisaged, the vast majority of schools were denominational. In some *Länder*, however, notably Saxony, Thuringia, Baden, Hesse, some smaller *Länder* and some areas of Prussia the common elementary school (*Simultanschule*) prevailed. The proposals put forward by Keudell in 1927 would have established the principle of parity and would thus have allowed denominational schools to be introduced on demand in places where the *Simultanschule* was the norm.

The two ministers in the cabinet from the DVP, Stresemann and the economics minister Curtius, made it clear from the beginning that they could not bind their *Fraktion*. On this issue many in the DVP, whose liberalism was otherwise increasingly threadbare, wanted to live up to the tradition of Bismarck's *Kulturkampf*. Curiously enough there had been a disposition in the SPD to sacrifice their traditional support for secular education for the sake of the great coalition and in Prussia compromise with the Centre Party over education had always been accepted. On the other hand there were some on the left of the Centre Party, including former chancellor Joseph Wirth, who also preferred a great coalition to insistence on the denominational school. For the majority in all parties, however, this was another ideological issue on which purity of principle could not be sacrificed. It was this long-standing habit of preferring ideological consistency to compromise which was at the root of the governmental instability of Weimar. The failure of the proposed school law was increasingly likely in the autumn of 1927 and became final in February 1928. Progressively political energies became focused on the Reichstag elections which would then become inevitable.[38]

THE LEFT: THE SPD, THE *REICHSBANNER* AND THE KPD IN A POST-REVOLUTIONARY SITUATION

On the eve of these elections the SPD, since December 1924 again the largest party, had been in a posture of qualified opposition for well over four years and for the whole of two legislative periods. Many of the leading men of the party, particularly those who did shoulder governmental responsibilities in Prussia, kept reminding their followers of the disadvantages of this position. Even in opposition the party could never escape its basic identification with the republic in the eyes of the nation. The identification was

constantly reinforced by the need to support the foreign policy of
Dawes, Locarno and Stresemann. After the death of Ebert only
one of the three commanding heights of the constitution, namely
the government of Prussia, remained partially in the hands of the
party. Yet throughout this period democracy, parliamentarism
and the republic, while no longer under immediate threat from a
coup, remained constantly under attack.

For the majority of party activists, including the rank and file of
the Reichstag *Fraktion*, other considerations proved more important. In competing for working-class votes against the KPD it was
more important to attack the bourgeois republic and fatal to be
seen in the company of bourgeois parties. Beyond tactical and
electoral considerations there was the fundamental question what
kind of party the SPD was to be in this post-revolutionary era.
Circumstances were forcing the party strongly in the direction of
becoming a left-wing mass party, recruiting members and voters
from as broad a social background as possible, capable of entering
into partnership with other republican parties to form the
coalitions inevitable in a multi-party system.

There were equally powerful circumstantial forces that ensured
that the party could not move rapidly from what it had been for
all of its existence, an oppositional proletarian class party. In the
Görlitz programme of 1921 there had been an attempt to take
into account the post-revolutionary situation and broaden the
party's appeal. The Heidelberg programme of 1925 represented a
reversion to traditionalism. It was largely the work of Hilferding,
who based himself on a draft prepared by Kautsky. The rhetoric
of class war and common ownership was more cautiously
employed than at Erfurt in 1891, there was positive support for
the republic, but the continuity of Marxist modes of thought was
evident and inevitable. Some of the powerful Marxist theoreticians who had come back into the party as a result of unification
with the USPD criticised even these limited modifications of the
full Marxist panoply. Paul Levi, former leader of the KPD, who
had found his way back to the SPD through the USPD, published
a news sheet consistently critical of the Heidelberg line and
advocating unrelenting class war. His view of parliamentarism
was that parliament should form the arena for an all-out struggle.

At the Kiel party congress in May 1927 there was renewed
debate about widening the appeal of the party. Especially the
small farmer, under economic pressure at that moment, was to be

addressed and this meant playing down any suggestion that the SPD was planning to attack private property. It fell again to Hilferding to put an ideological figleaf over the differences in the party. He did so by highlighting his concept of organised capitalism, which he portrayed as a state of affairs that could be made into a stepping stone to socialism if the party used all the opportunities of seizing political power that were available to it under the parliamentary system.

These discussions about ideologies and programmes at party congresses were not treated as a high priority by the party leaders. They knew that the realities of the party's social composition and habits of thought could not be rapidly changed. Membership statistics indicate that it was still overwhelmingly made up of male manual workers, nearly three-quarters of the total. Nevertheless party activists were well aware of the benefits to be reaped from wielding government office, for the advantages were constantly being demonstrated in Prussia.

Albert Grzesinski, who became Prussian minister of the interior in October 1926, when Severing had to retire for health reasons, was even more assiduous than his predecessor in appointing officials loyal to the republic, frequently members of the SPD. By early 1928 a third of *Oberpräsidenten* and, even more significantly, half the big city police chiefs were members of the SPD. As long as the SPD retained its hold on power in Prussia it was always possible to argue that participation in Reich coalitions was not necessary for the safety of the republic and of democracy, since they were already sufficiently guaranteed by the Prussian bastion.[39]

There was also a right wing in the SPD that advocated, not merely on short-term tactical grounds, that the party should dilute some of its traditional Marxism. The *Reichsbanner Schwarz-Rot-Gold*, the party's paramilitary formation, was a major location of such revisionism. For a long time the SPD leaders had been reluctant to allow such an organisation to come into existence. The persistence and virulence of paramilitarism on the right, even after the crisis of 1923, changed these attitudes. The *Reichsbanner* was intended to be a republican rather than an SPD organisation. Leaders of the DDP and of the Centre Party were members and these parties were represented in the governing body. Lower down the membership, probably around a million in 1925, was drawn mainly from the SPD. The *Reichsbanner* had to stand for a united defence of the republic in comradeship with those bourgeois parties whose republicanism was beyond dispute. It also had to strike a patriotic note, distinctly *grossdeutsch*, to match the patrioteering from the right. The colours black, red and gold were used to purvey a conscious *grossdeutsch* republicanism harking back to 1848.

Increasingly there was emphasis on military training to match the militancy of the right-wing paramilitaries. In military terms the *Reichsbanner* was never the equal of its right-wing opponents, but its numbers were impressive and on parade occasions it could give the impression that the republic had solid force behind it.

Among the founders of the organisation was Friedrich Otto Hörsing, who as *Oberpräsident* of the Prussian province of Saxony had shown great resolution in putting down violence from right and left. Another leading personality, the SPD journalist Karl Höltermann, was much concerned to break the hold of the right on patriotic rhetoric. There was an effort to modify the negative view of German history prevalent among left-wing Germans. Words like *Vaterland* and *Volksgemeinschaft* were as fervently invoked as they were on the right. In the early 1930s the *Reichsbanner* began to use terms like 'Führer' and 'Gau'.[40]

Another group in the SPD that was concerned to break out of the Marxist mould and to match the national appeal of the right was the Hofgeismar circle. It arose from a small section of the socialist youth movement, the Young Socialists, which catered for the 18–25 age group, many of them from middle-class academic backgrounds. Here the task was to find an answer to the nationalist and romantic solidarity ethos with which the right was appealing to the young. Socialist intellectuals from this group, for example Carlo Mierendorff, later executed for his part in the 20 July 1944 plot against Hitler, were responsible for some forward-looking and unorthodox analyses of the SPD's predicament. In the short run they were not able to make much headway against the Marxist traditionalism of most SPD functionaries and activists, but as the party's situation grew more desperate in the last years of the republic their views stood out amid the general dearth of fresh ideas.

None of these groups could effectively counteract the lack of national sentiment that tainted the SPD in the eyes of many Germans. The party could never convince millions of patriotic Germans, deeply wounded by defeat and apparent national dishonour, that its support for fulfilment did not stem from congenital disregard for legitimate national interest. Since the SPD was in the eyes of the very same Germans identical with the republic, this proved to be a dangerous psychological weakness for the Weimar state.[41]

History did not grant the SPD the time to resolve the dilemma between remaining a proletarian Marxist party and becoming a reformist mass party. In whichever way this dilemma might have been resolved it was probably inevitable that for the time being the German labour movement would remain divided between a moderate and a radical wing. It was a tragedy that the radical wing, the KPD, should have its policies so strongly influenced by the exigencies of the Soviet state and by the consequences of the struggle between the factions within the Russian Communist Party.

Ruth Fischer, the de facto leader in 1924 and 1925 and a revolutionary activist in 1923, came to the natural conclusion that for the time being there was no chance of a German October. When this conclusion did not suit Zinoviev, the General Secretary of the Comintern, in his desperate struggle with Stalin, Ruth Fischer and others like her were excluded from the party. The leadership fell into the hands of men like Thälmann and Walter Ulbricht, who were prepared to follow the Moscow line slavishly. By 1928 this was Stalin's line, dictated in large part by his paranoid suspicion of what remained of the opposition. The hard core of the KPD was by this time simply an extension of the Soviet state and there was no longer any possibility that discussions or votes at party congresses could shift it.

All these twists and turns had surprisingly little effect on the strength of the KPD, which remained more or less static between 1924 and 1930. Membership fluctuated between about 95 000 and 145 000, well below the peak of 1923. There was a great turnover of members: those with revolutionary expectations and in search of radical certainties joined and turned away again in disappointment. Electorally the party performed above average in the strongholds it had inherited from the USPD. The KPD was a male working-class party even more overwhelmingly than the SPD, but there is little evidence that its members and voters came from a lower stratum than those of the SPD. The party had a stronger appeal to the unemployed than the SPD, not surprisingly since it was untainted by any connection with the existing state.

The unemployed were sometimes skilled workers fallen victim to rationalisation. This appeal to the unemployed became a factor of real importance in the great depression. Stalinisation did not lessen the party's appeal to intellectuals. Willi Münzenberg, the editor and organiser of many newspapers and rallies, worked with great skill in this field and attracted many fellow travellers.

Changes in the party line laid down from Moscow did not affect the image of the party as a radical anti-systemic organisation and there was room for such a party irrespective of the balance between left and right within the SPD. It is instructive to look at the example of Brunswick, admittedly a small *Land* of only half a million inhabitants surrounded by Prussia. Here the USPD had always been stronger than the MSPD and when the parties were reunited the Brunswick SPD was strongly influenced by the USPD tradition and was markedly left-wing. Consequently the KPD was relatively marginal in the 1920s, polling between 4–5 per cent of the vote. In 1927 the SPD, after a period in opposition, won over 46 per cent of the vote and formed a single-party government. All this could not prevent the NSDAP from scoring well above the national average in Brunswick from 1930.[42]

THE RIGHT: THE DNVP BETWEEN GOVERNMENT AND OPPOSITION; HITLER RE-ESTABLISHES HIS PARTY; STAHLHELM AND CONSERVATIVE REVOLUTION

Whatever the difficulties on the left, in the run-up to the 1928 Reichstag elections the right was in an even worse position. The DNVP's return to government had aggravated the divisions among its supporters. It was fortunate for the party that foreign policy did not have the high profile it had had in previous years. The sense of anticlimax after Thoiry, the fact that no further zone of occupation was evacuated, helped the party to bridge the gap between its traditional anti-fulfilment rhetoric and its collaboration in a cabinet with Stresemann. In fact the party was able to impose some limits on the foreign minister's freedom of manoeuvre. It compelled him and the government in general to use language which made it difficult to claim the full credit for the remarkable successes achieved by the Locarno policy. This in turn meant that foreign opinion, particularly French opinion, was given the impression that the Germans would pocket any concession with an ill grace and immediately ask for more. Nevertheless the hostility to Versailles, fulfilment and the republic was so deep and ineradicable among the DNVP's followers that nothing could overcome the constantly erupting tensions in the party and its affiliated organisations.

The position was aggravated in 1927 by the onset of the agrarian crisis. Many of those who had supported the party's participation in government to secure the interests of agriculture now found that even a protectionist policy forced on the cabinet by the DNVP could not solve their economic problems. The role of the DNVP and of the East Elbian landowners as the spokesmen for agriculture began to be called in question. This showed itself not only in the early inroads made by the radical right in the shape of the NSDAP in small-farming areas like Schleswig-Holstein. In February 1928 a new party called the Christian National Farmers and Rural Volk party (*Christlich-nationale Bauern-und Landvolkpartei*, for short *Landvolk*) was founded. One of the joint presidents of the *Reichslandbund*, Karl Hepp, joined it, as did many influential personalities in regional *Landbünde*. The CNBL was not opposed to the DNVP and its programme and ideology were similar, except for the greater emphasis on the needs of the small farmer as a *Stand* (estate). The rise of this party, with nearly 600 000 votes and 10 deputies in 1928 and over 1.1 million votes and 19 deputies in 1930, was a major factor in the decline of the DNVP. Not only had the DNVP never succeeded in becoming a broad-based conservative party, it was now also losing its standing as representative of the agricultural interest.[43]

On the radical right Hitler had made the best of the fiasco of the beer hall putsch at his trial in the spring of 1924. The court was a Bavarian special court, a *Volksgericht*, an aspect of Weimar justice that more than any other deserves the opprobrium heaped upon it. It was a Bavarian *Volksgericht* that had, in 1922, imposed upon Eisner's secretary, Felix Fechenbach, a sentence of seven years' penal servitude for his part in publishing, in 1918, the diplomatic documents showing the role played by the German government in the events of 1914. This flagrant case of partisan justice was only rescinded in 1926, but Fechenbach was murdered by the Nazis in 1933.[44] The trial of those implicated in the beer hall putsch took place in front of a similarly constituted court under Bavarian emergency legislation. The Bavarian minister of justice, Franz Gürtner, later Reich minister of justice from 1932 till his death in 1941, was a member of the DNVP. The dubious role played by the Bavarian government in the putsch made the whole procedure something of a farce.

Hitler was given a platform that commanded national attention. He portrayed himself as a martyr of the national cause and asked how one could commit treason against the revolution of 1918, which was itself an act of treason. His performance at the trial enhanced his reputation in *Völkische* circles in comparison with other leaders and greatly helped him to reestablish his position after coming out of prison. Hitler was given a sentence of five years' honourable confinement, which meant his release after a short period of probation. While in prison until December 1924 he was given every facility to communicate with the outside world and he was able to dictate *Mein Kampf*, a turgid piece of self-justification. He adamantly refused to be drawn into the disputes among his followers.

In the two Reichstag elections of 1924 the NSDAP campaigned in conjunction with the *Deutsche-Völkische Freiheitspartei*, the group split off from the DNVP in 1922. The latter fought mainly in the north, what remained of the Nazis in the south. Ludendorff was the most prominent figure in the *Völkische* block. In the Bavarian Landtag elections immediately after the end of the trial the *Völkische* received over 17 per cent of the vote; in the Reichstag election a month later a similar result was achieved in Upper Bavaria and nearly 21 per cent in Franconia. By December these proportions had dropped to 4.8 and 7.5 per cent respectively.

Hitler was therefore faced with an uphill task when he came out of prison. His greatest asset, his power as a demagogue, was limited by the fact that he was barred from addressing public meetings, in Bavaria until 1927 and in Prussia until 1928. He could, however, address closed party meetings. That he managed to impose total control over his movement in these circumstances might be regarded as greater evidence of his remarkable power to dominate than his later unchallenged control of the Third Reich. In both cases his bohemian life-style and disinclination for regular work did not prove an obstacle to domination.

In 1925 there were three major aspects to Hitler's reassertion of control: getting a grip on what was left of the movement, distinguishing it from other groups in the *Völkische* spectrum, and deciding on a strategy. An initial step was to take the NSDAP out of the *Völkische* block within in which it had fought elections in 1924. Here Hitler made the most of the fact that the NSDAP could be regarded as a revolutionary force, while so many others in the *Völkische* movement had their roots in old-style conservatism. It also involved demolishing Ludendorff's claim to any political role. Hitler backed Ludendorff's separate candidature on the first presidential ballot in March 1925. His derisory showing, 1.1 per cent of the vote, proved conclusively that Ludendorff had no future in politics. On the second ballot Hitler switched his support to Hindenburg, in spite of the doubts that existed in *Völkische* circles about the field marshal's candidature.

Hitler was thus determined to play his own hand, deliberately disregarding all other *Völkische* groups and with complete ideological flexibility. In order to do this he had to build the party entirely around his own myth as the Führer who had suffered martyrdom in 1923 but would eventually lead all Germans to their glorious destiny. In 1925 only people whose relationship with reality was in any case disturbed would be likely to swallow such a claim. Hitler was therefore concerned to build up a following of total and fanatically dedicated believers, even if it was small. He imposed tight bureaucratic and financial control from party headquarters in Munich. Here a number of grey bureaucrats, men like Franz Schwarz, the treasurer, Philipp Bouhler, the chief administrator, and Max Amann, the publisher, ran the party on Hitler's behalf and relieved him from the day-to-day drudgery. The system of *Gauleiters*, regional satraps, linked by ties of personal loyalty to Hitler, was established, but it was not clear in all cases whether they also enjoyed a status in their own right.

The Munich headquarters milked the movement as best they could for financial resources. These came mainly from membership dues, entry fees to meetings and the sale of party papers and literature. A few wealthy supporters, like the Bechstein family in Munich, still made contributions. In the middle 1920s there was probably a membership of some 35 000, but Munich found it difficult to tap this financial potential to the full.[45]

It was an important coup for Hitler that in 1926 he managed to bring the northern, Strasser wing of the movement under his control. A key event was the Bamberg meeting in February of that year, when Hitler won the day in a long charismatic harangue, which in essence amounted to no more than a claim that his own unquestioned leadership was the party's best and only hope. It had intitially looked as if the northern *Völkische* movement would remain in the loose association with Bavaria that had previously prevailed, but Hitler's exclusive claims made this impossible. It thus became necessary to resolve the position of a number of prominent figures whose associations, both organisationally and ideologically, had been with the NSDAP rather than the *Deutsch-Völkische*.

Among these the brothers Gregor and Otto Strasser and the young Joseph Goebbels were the best known. Their distinguishing mark was that they took revolutionary socialism seriously and saw themselves replacing the false prophets of Marxist socialism with a truly German socialism among the working class. Such a synthesis of political opposites permeated much of German right-wing theorising. The Strassers despised the low, shady demagogues, the men like Julius Streicher and Hermann Esser, whom Hitler was happy to use in the Bavarian Nazi movement. They had no intention of subordinating themselves to the Munich party bureaucracy. On the other hand they felt closer to Hitler, the revolutionary, than to the older ex-conservatives who abounded in the *Völkische* movement. Hitler won them over by staking everything on his leadership while leaving all ideological options open. He gave no clear lead on the two most important policy issues of the moment, whether the party should participate in parliamentary elections and to what extent it should concentrate its efforts on the urban proletariat. Most northern Nazis were against getting involved with parliamentary politics, but for the proletarian socialist orientation. The Strasser brothers never completely swallowed the Hitler myth and both eventually parted company with him. Goebbels, a young foot-loose intellectual, remained captive to the myth to the end. Given his undoubted propagandist and organising talents it turned out to be Hitler's most important conquest at Bamberg and Goebbels soon found himself as the Gauleiter of Red Berlin. The appointment indicated that Hitler himself felt that the urban proletariat offered for the moment the most fertile field for increasing Nazi support. In fact this strategy proved a disappointment and it was the agrarian crisis of 1927–8 that first enabled the Nazis to make a significant break-out from their political ghetto.

The meteoric rise of the NSDAP a few years later should not obscure the fact that for the time being they were in a ghetto and that Hitler's tactics in many respects reinforced the barriers around them. In north Germany the *Deutsch-Völkische*, who now called themselves a *Bewegung* (movement), rather than a party, could still do better in elections in some regions in 1926 and 1927 than the NSDAP. Even in the Reichstag elections of 1928 their vote was still about a third of that of the Nazis, in spite of some of their Reichstag deputies having joined the Nazis in 1927. The Nazis were a stagnant movement, the dedicated followers often reliving the past rather than looking forward to the future. The dividing line between fanatical, selfless devotion to the movement and inbred sectarianism was thin. Much of the following was made up of insignificant, unsuccessful and unappealing members of the *petit bourgeoisie*, whose ability to influence others was less than their capacity to repel them.

Hitler's deliberate vagueness on strategy, leaving all options open, could turn out to be a strength, but for the time being his emphasis on his personal myth turned his followers into a sect. Hitler concealed the strategic vacuum by providing a diet of unrelenting anti-Semitic diatribes which were effective in rallying his immediate supporters, but even he knew that something more positive would be needed to appeal to a wider following. In one of his rare appearances outside his normal milieu, in a speech to Hamburg businessmen in 1926, Hitler completely avoided the anti-Semitic theme. In retrospect the party might look like a tightly-controlled, lean organisation ready to pounce upon any political opportunity. At the time it was more often seen as a marooned dinosaur.[46]

A problem for which Hitler found no entirely satisfactory solution at this stage was the relationship between the party and the right-wing paramilitaries, particularly the party's own SA. He was determined to enforce the supremacy of political control and not to have his course circumscribed again by the paramilitary subsidiary. Even though he did not spell it out too clearly, he was convinced that for the time being the path of legality had to be followed. No excuse should be given to the authorities to tighten the prohibitions on the party and on himself.

In April 1925 Hitler parted company with Röhm, who resigned all his party posts, went to South America as a military instructor in 1928, but was recalled in 1930 to head the then much enlarged SA. Röhm never gave up his idea that the *Völkische* paramilitary formation should be the core of the movement and eventually the

militant army of the new Reich. In pursuit of this he tried to
revive his force under the name *Frontbann*. This was too dangerous
for Hitler, nor could Röhm any longer be of use to him as a
linkman to the Reichswehr and other organisations of the radical
right.

Hitler had to mark time in harnessing what was a vital, but
unruly, element of potential support for his movement. It was
over a year before he could find a new SA leader, Franz Pfeffer
von Salomon, a Prussian ex-Freikorps officer. Strict limits were
put on what the SA could do, so as not to invite retribution from
the authorities. Nothing could change the fact that the SA
attracted denizens of the former Freikorps subculture, men who
gloried in brutality, despised bourgeois society and aspired to
relentless nihilistic activism. They saw themselves as the heart and
soul of the movement and conflict with the party and its chain of
command, the Gauleiters, was in the air. For the moment it was
not on a sufficiently large scale to cause major upset nor was
Hitler's overall control in danger.[47]

Hitler's movement was thus a tightly organised strand within a
broad stream of anti-republican nationalism. Its deliberate
separateness was a weakness, but could also become an opportunity. The Stahlhelm was the biggest nationalist organisation
outside the strictly party-political field and many of the members
of the diverse, often now illegal, combatant leagues had joined it.
By the middle 1920s it was increasingly trying to make its
influence felt in politics. Hindenburg was an honorary member
and felt particularly close to it. 'Into the state' was a current
Stahlhelm slogan, which for some meant a more accommodating
attitude to the republic, but for most expressed the desire to work
through the existing system in order to transcend it.

The aims of the Stahlhelm comprised all the stereotypical
demands and opinions of the nationalist right: non-recognition of
the extorted Versailles *Diktat* and repudiation of the dishonourable war guilt confession and all obligations stemming from it;
readoption of the glorious black, red and white, the colours under
which the German people fought their heroic fight; expansion of
German territory to include all ethnic Germans and provide for
the economic needs of the nation; strengthening of authority at
home by transferring power from the divided parliament and its
parties to a stronger presidency; strident opposition to the forces of
Marxism and internationalism and the divisiveness of class war;

cultivation of the healthy farming elements in the nation and reduction of foreign influences in German life.

All these clichés of the nationalist right were permeated with the front-line ideology of struggle, discipline and solidarity. War was the great majestic, mystical experience that had unified the nation. For a time the Stahlhelm published a journal, *Die Standarte*, in which conservative nationalist intellectuals like Ernst Jünger adumbrated this front-line ideology.[48] It was part of what became known as the conservative revolution, an anti-enlightenment, anti-rational, anti-liberal intellectual fashion that traced its ancestry to Nietzsche. It was partly a generational symptom, for among the roots of these attitudes was also the anti-bourgeois youth protest movement of Wilhelmine Germany.

There was much harking back to the meeting on the Hohen Meissner near Kassel in October 1913, when the need for German youth to cultivate its inner freedom was asserted. The same generation then went out 'in a shower of roses and blood', as Ernst Jünger put it, to fight. The battle of Langemarck in the winter of 1914 was invoked, where large numbers of student volunteers went heroically to their deaths. Other contributors to the mood of conservative revolution were Oswald Spengler and Moeller van den Bruck. Spengler contributed cultural pessimism and the idea of Prussian socialism. Prussia, with its highly developed ethos of service to the state and the common good, represented a higher form of socialism than the class socialism of Marx. Moeller van den Bruck also proclaimed socialism, a specifically German synthesis of Western individualism and Eastern collectivism. The new society was to be realised in the mystical Third Reich, a revived medieval term. He met Hitler in 1922 but was not impressed. The socialism of Moeller van den Bruck and Spengler was an aspiration for national solidarity rather than a plan for concrete action.[49]

The fact that organisations like the Stahlhelm were willing to promote the ideas of the conservative revolution shows the depth and seriousness of the repugnance felt in nationalist circles to the existing system. This world of ideas, nebulous when it came to the concrete situation of the moment, could, however, not do much to resolve the political dilemma of nationalist right. The Stahlhelm, like the DNVP, was divided between those who were for the time being prepared to play within the existing system and those who opposed it outright. One of the two leaders, Franz Seldte, later

Hitler's minister of labour, was of the former, Theodor Duester-berg, the other leader, more of the latter persuasion. At one time Stresemann hoped that Seldte would swing his movement into support of his policies and thus give them a broader popular base. By 1927, as anti-republicanism came to be in the ascendant in the Stahlhelm, Seldte distanced himself from Stresemann.

In preparation for the 1928 Reichstag elections the Stahlhelm hoped to use its political potential to promote a more united right wing including DNVP, DVP as well as the smaller interest parties. Nothing could disguise the fact that as the election drew nearer such efforts were not succeeding, for the gulf between moderates and radicals within the right was far too wide.[50]

LIBERAL DECLINE AND THE ELECTIONS OF 1928

The elections were to produce a further weakening of the two liberal parties and this was not unexpected. Liberalism had long ceased to be an ideology sufficiently specific to sustain a party and integrate a substantial body of voters. As an ideology it was severely out of fashion. Its one fleeting reappearance in the politics of the moment had been the campaign against the denomina-tional school law by the DDP and the rearguard action against the law from within the coalition by the two DVP ministers. This rearguard action merely showed how difficult closer union of the two liberal parties would prove to be in practice, for a main motive for the DVP was that the DDP, out of government, would steal a march on it in areas like Baden, where non-denominational education was important to liberal Protestants. There was a body to promote liberal unity, *Liberale Vereinigung*, of which Stresemann became an honorary president, but many on the left of the DDP were strongly opposed to such initiatives. For them the DVP was far too closely identified with big business. The DVP still had one major asset, the charismatic figure of Stresemann.

Even though the highest hopes after Thoiry had not been realised, much progress had been made in economic cooperation. In September 1926 an industrial agreement between France, Germany, Belgium and Luxembourg covering the market in raw steel went into operation. Following the withdrawal of the Inter-Allied Military Control Commission and further troop reductions in the Rhineland long negotiations led to the conclusion of a

Franco–German trade agreement in August 1927 based on most favoured nation treatment. There was renewed hope of a long peaceful development in European affairs, with a Franco–German customs union as a potential goal. Germany was now playing a leading role in the League of Nations and her influence in eastern and south-eastern Europe, mainly based on economic factors, was growing. All these developments were linked with the personality of Stresemann. That section of the German public that placed its faith in international collaboration, and at this point it was probably the majority, was persuaded that he had achieved much and that there was more to come. The foreign minister's prestige enabled him to keep in check the pressures from the strong industrial lobby in his party.[51]

Elections in various regions in late 1927 and early 1928 had raised expectations on the left and caused apprehension on the right. In Brunswick in late November 1927 the SPD vote risen by a quarter and the DNVP fallen by nearly a half compared with 1924. A less spectacular improvement of SPD fortunes had taken place in Bremen. In Hesse the DNVP had lost, but the gains on the left had gone to the KPD. The DDP was buoyed up by a good result in Hamburg in February 1928, but this was an exceptional dissolution of the town parliament and one of the party's leading figures, Carl Petersen, was mayor of the city.

When the Reichstag elections took place on 20 May 1928 the resurgence of the left and the decline of the DNVP were confirmed. Nationally the SPD had its best result since 1919 with nearly 30 per cent of the vote. The KPD also pulled in an extra half million votes and boosted its share from 9 to 10.6 per cent, but it did not go back to the level obtained in May 1924. The DNVP lost nearly a third of its vote of December 1924 and its share dropped from 20.5 to 14.2 per cent. The split-off Landvolk party accounted only partly for this loss. Commentators have stressed the fragmentation of the middle of the political spectrum which occurred in this election. The DDP and DVP between them lost 800 000 voters and their combined percentage slipped from 16.4 to 13.6 per cent. The Centre Party and BVP together also lost about half a million voters and dropped 2.2 per cent. The various interest and agrarian parties, some of them newly established, increased their share of the vote from 7.5 to 13.9 per cent. The NSDAP got slightly over 800 000 votes and obtained twelve seats. If the 266 000 votes for the *Deutsch-*

Völkische are added, the extreme right-wing vote was slightly larger than it had been in December 1924.

The NSDAP retained some of its strongholds in Franconia and made headway in the small farming communities of the Geest, the poor, sandy land bordering the North Sea in Schleswig-Holstein and Lower Saxony. In rural communities of less than 2000 inhabitants in the Geest region of Schleswig-Holstein the Nazi share of the vote rose from 2.4 to 15.9 per cent between December 1924 and May 1928. The Kreis with the second highest Nazi vote in 1928 was Wittmund in Ostfriesland, where the share was 34 per cent against 30 per cent in December 1924.

From all this it could not have been anticipated that the NSDAP would within a short time become the main beneficiary of the fragmentation in the centre of German politics. In May 1928 electoral participation was 75.6 per cent, the lowest for the whole Weimar period. The SPD probably owed some of its success to its ability to mobilise its voters more effectively than its opponents. The SPD's strong showing was confirmed in the Landtag elections which took place simultaneously. In Prussia its share of the vote rose by over 4 per cent to 29 per cent and the Weimar coalition government of Otto Braun now had a narrow majority, 229 out of 450 seats. In Bavaria the SPD share rose from 17.2 to 24.2 per cent, in Württemberg from 16 to 23.8 per cent and in Oldenburg, where the previous elections had been held in May 1925, from 22.5 to 28.9 per cent. These elections could not and did not cure some of the endemic problems of the Weimar political system, but they gave no indication that this system was about to enter a terminal crisis.[52]

4 Crisis, Collapse and the Coming of Hitler

THE GREAT COALITION

The SPD was the most obvious winner in the elections of May 1928 and its return to government, so often discussed in the previous four years, now became almost inevitable. In turn this meant that there was little alternative to the establishment of another great coalition stretching from SPD to DVP. A Weimar coalition would have been scarcely viable: the Centre Party and the DDP, both licking their wounds after election losses, were not keen to go into coalition with an enlarged SPD without the counterweight of the DVP on the right. The election had been a clear verdict against the bourgeois government of Marx and, if now reconstituted, it would have been in an even more marked minority. Nevertheless the negotiations to establish a great coalition proved very difficult and took five weeks.

At first Otto Braun, the Prussian prime minister who had won a resounding victory in the Landtag elections, was under consideration as the new SPD chancellor. If he had combined the two offices it would have revived a practice going back to Bismarck. A reform of the federal structure of the Reich had only recently been discussed in a constitutional conference and a committee of Reich and *Länder* representatives had been set up to work out proposals. The illogical structure of the Reich had remained a matter of debate, even though the earlier great clashes between Bavaria and the Reich were now being carefully avoided. There was continuing difficulty about the allocation of tax revenues and concern about the duplication and waste of resources. There were still a number of scarcely viable dwarf states. An association for the promotion of constitutional reform, known as the Lutherbund after its chairman, ex-chancellor Hans Luther, was the respectable face of the broad and many-faceted dissatisfaction with parliamentary democracy Weimar style. A central feature of any changes would always have had to be a new relationship between Prussia and the Reich, towards which a combination of the offices of Reich chancellor and Prussian prime minister could have formed a step.

Braun did not have sufficient support in the Reichstag *Fraktion* of the SPD to become chancellor candidate and the position went to Hermann Müller, the long-serving co-chairman of the party, who had held the offices of foreign minister and chancellor in 1919 and 1920. He was an accommodating, popular personality of high integrity, but neither forceful nor charismatic. His cabinet was initially not a party coalition but merely a collaboration of personalities from the different parties. There was no commitment by the parties, specifically not by the DVP, to support the government on all issues. The Centre Party distanced itself by providing only the minister of transport. Although the parties represented in this cabinet commanded 301 out of 491 seats in the Reichstag, the chancellor did not ask for a vote of confidence at the outset, but only for approval of the government's declaration of policy. The weaknesses of the Weimar political system were again strikingly demonstrated.[1]

The building of *Panzerkreuzer A* had also made cabinet formation difficult.[2] In January 1928 Otto Gessler, minister of defence since 1920, had finally been forced to resign. Staunch republicans held him responsible for the Reichswehr's semi-detachment from the republic and virtual freedom from political control. His position had been undermined by his involvement in the continuing row over the national flag. The equal display of the black, white and red alongside the black, red and gold colours at the opening of the memorial to the Tannenberg victory in September 1927 had caused offence to republicans and the Prussian government had boycotted the ceremony. The final straw was the revelation that secret financing of naval armaments had been carried on for many years by an officer in the defence ministry.[3]

Gessler's successor was General Wilhelm Groener, who retained his post until May 1932. Groener's closest adviser was his protégé Colonel Kurt von Schleicher, who had already been influential under Seeckt through his links with the political world. Schleicher's central role as a policy-maker was further formalised in 1929, when he became chief of the specially created *Ministeramt* (ministerial office) in the rank of major-general. Groener and Schleicher were concerned to build a strong non-political position for the Reichswehr. They tried to promote an image of the Reichswehr as a reliable force, which no longer harboured any illegal anti-republican elements, but which was entitled to have its concerns for national defence fully respected by the political establishment.

The SPD's electoral campaign against *Panzerkreuzer A* had naturally alarmed them because it had revealed the continuing strength of anti-militarism in the German working class. They were anxious to encourage those elements in the labour movement and in the SPD and trade union leadership who saw the need for adequate military defence. Groener and Schleicher had the full support of Hindenburg and this powerful trio viewed an SPD-led government with little enthusiasm, yet were continually attacked as compromisers from the nationalist right.[4] The Müller government could not have been formed if the question of the funding of *Panzerkreuzer A* had not simply been left unresolved in the inter-party negotiations; it would almost immediately have broken up again if the tentative decision of the previous government to authorise the funds had not been adhered to. The KPD's request for a referendum on the question had the purpose of exacerbating the SPD's discomfiture.[5] The small number of inscriptions for the *Volksbegehren* showed that the SPD leaders were right to avoid the impression that their party was neglectful of the defence of the fatherland. The German worker remained anti-militarist and suspicious of the political orientation of the armed forces, but he was also patriotic.

THE RUHR LOCKOUT AND THE YOUNG PLAN

The controversy over the *Panzerkreuzer A* was overshadowed by the great lockout in the Ruhr iron and steel industry in November 1928. In spite of cartelisation and marketing agreements between German and French producers the industry was already affected by lack of economic buoyancy. At the same time it was faced by considerable wage demands from the powerful German metal workers union (*Deutscher Metallarbeiterverband*, DMV). This was a moment when wages were pushing ahead of productivity, possibly as a result of the knock-on effect of the big civil service pay rises of the previous year.[6] The employers decided to use the occasion to mount a direct challenge to the system of compulsory arbitration by refusing to accept a binding award from an official arbitrator.

It soon became apparent that they had miscalculated, for there was broad public sympathy with the workers. Locked-out workers had no right to unemployment pay under the law of the previous year, but the Reichstag now voted to provide funds to local authorities for the support of these workers and their families. All parties supported this step and the vote was 267 to 59, but 15 DVP deputies absented themselves from the vote. In view of the potentially disastrous economic consequences the Reich government decided to intervene by appointing Severing as a special arbitrator. He managed to compose the differences by awarding wage increases lower than the original award, but also a reduction of hours. The lockout was ended, but the complex legal situation was not resolved until January 1929 by a verdict from the Reich court of labour. This declared the original award invalid and amounted to a considerable setback for the arbitration system and for the Reich ministry of labour. Although the acceptance of the Severing award did not find favour with the more extreme employers, the final outcome meant that the employers had to some extent achieved their aim of rolling back the interventionist state and restoring the primacy of the market.[7]

This episode can be interpreted as part of a capitalist offensive against the Weimar social compromise or as the imposition by the employers of a veto on the state's freedom of manoeuvre in social policy. It was, however, not a conclusive victory for at the height of the depression the Brüning government once more strengthened the capacity of the arbitration system to impose compulsory awards.

The attitude of the unions to arbitration never ceased to be ambivalent and uncertain, for they feared any diminution of the freedom of collective bargaining. On the whole they still put their trust in a state in which their party colleagues, Wissell, minister of labour, Severing, minister of the interior, and others, wielded power, but soon this state ceased to be a democracy.

The Ruhr conflict showed again the extent to which economic disputes were politicised under the Weimar dispensation. Ernst Fraenkel, a legal adviser to the metal workers union, wrote nearly forty years after the event that in this conflict a ghostly presence, the future Nazi trustee of labour, could already be seen.[8]

The fate of the Weimar social compromise and of German democracy was still as closely as ever tied up with Germany's external situation and great problems were coming up in this area. The Dawes Plan as an interim solution was reaching the end of its useful life. In 1928–9 German reparations obligations under this plan would reach the stipulated maximum of two and a half billion marks. The provisions in the Dawes Plan for protecting the external value of the mark in the transfer of reparations payments were not in practice worth very much. In view of the German trade deficit reparations payments depended on the inflow of foreign, mainly American, loans. A new settlement would, however, involve the acceptance by Germany of long-term, even if scaled-down obligations. The military evacuation of the Rhineland was the irreducible German demand in return for such a final reparations settlement. Since the evacuation of the Rhineland was in any case due in two stages in 1930 and 1935 under the Versailles treaty, the time during which a premature evacuation would be regarded as a worthwhile concession by German nationalist opinion was rapidly running out.

On the other hand the dependence of the German economy and of reparations payments on the inflow of foreign loans made the German economy desperately vulnerable. The mere suggestion that the Dawes system would run down without anything to replace it would drastically reduce German creditworthiness and have devastating consequences. In a cabinet meeting on 1 May 1929, when a deadlock in the negotiations had just caused a run on the mark and a raising of German interest rates, Wirth said that a Dawes crisis could not be mastered with normal parliamentary methods and Stresemann added that few could imagine the horrendous dimensions of a Dawes crisis.

Fortunately the international atmosphere was quite favourable for the negotiation of a new cooperative international settlement. Parker Gilbert, the American reparations agent, was pushing for a replacement of the Dawes Plan by a permanent settlement. His posititon was not entirely disinterested, for the United States as the ultimate creditor would benefit from a final settlement. The elections of May 1928 had created a positive impression abroad, especially in France, and had calmed fears of the 'other' revanchist Germany. The signature of the Kellogg Pact in August 1928, in which the great powers renounced war as a means of settling disputes, was another high-water mark for the policy of reconciliation. Chancellor Müller himself attended the League meeting in Geneva in September 1928 at which the agreement in principle was announced that there would be negotiations about an early evacuation of the Rhineland and a final settlement of the reparations problem.

After much haggling it was decided to leave the solution of the reparations problem to a committee of experts chaired by Owen D. Young, the chairman of the American General Electric Company. By the time this committee met in February 1929 the German domestic situation had already deteriorated. Official statistics put unemployment at 2.85 million in February 1929, 14 per cent of the labour force. There was growing impatience with the Locarno policy right across the political spectrum. Even within the German foreign office there were voices advocating a more robust, less cooperative stance.

Two members of the German delegation to the Young committee shared the scepticism about the continuing conciliatory course of the cabinet, of Stresemann, increasingly incapacitated by ill-health, and of his state secretary Schubert. One of the sceptics was Schacht, who was moving closer to the nationalist opposition and preparing the ground for an attack on whatever might be the outcome of the negotiations. Schacht had always harboured ambitious schemes for the revision of Versailles and he now tried to push these forward during the deliberations of the Young committee. He claimed that the German economy, especially its agrarian sector, could only be put on a sound basis if the Polish corridor and the former German colonies were returned to Germany. The other sceptic was Albert Vögler, a director of the Vestag. He had been chosen as a delegate by Stresemann to tie German heavy industry into the settlement, but resigned in protest at the size of the payments imposed on Germany. It was another example of the influence heavy industry could exert on the German political situation. The Müller government could not afford to let the Young negotiations fail and even Schacht realised in the end that failure would have immediate grave economic consequences for Germany.

Under the Young Plan Germany accepted annual reparation payments averaging two billion marks for 59 years, that is until 1988. The first payment for 1929–30 was, however, considerably lower at less than 750 million marks. This immediate reduction was crucial for the solution of Germany's domestic budgetary crisis. The supervisory arrangements and mortgages imposed by the Dawes Plan were to be ended and there was thus a restoration of German sovereignty, but this was hotly disputed by nationalist opponents of the plan. In future the imposition of sanctions for non-payment would require a reference to the International

Court of Justice at the Hague and the Bank for International Settlements was established as a supervisory organ.

The details of the Rhineland evacuation were painfully negotiated at the two Hague conferences, in August 1929 and January 1930. By this time the nationalist opposition, led by Hugenberg and Hitler, was already in full cry in the referendum campaign against the Young Plan. On 3 October 1929 Stresemann died. The date finally decided for the evacuation of the Rhineland was 30 June 1930, a last triumph for the dying foreign minister. It proved to be too late to save the policy of conciliation initiated at Locarno.

Whatever immediate advantages Germany gained from the Young Plan they were overshadowed by the psychological incubus of a debt that was to continue for another sixty years. This was exploited to the full by the nationalist opposition. The Western powers, particularly France, were in fact chasing shadows in these negotiations. Within two years reparations were suspended and a year later ended. It would have been wiser if France, Britain and the United States had made the saving of the precarious German democracy their first priority, but they were themselves restrained by inescapable domestic exigencies. Stresemann's death had symbolic as well as immediate impact. Without him the thrust of German foreign policy quickly changed towards greater assertiveness and independent action. This underlines how deeply and genuinely Stresemann and the officials he had selected as his advisers were committed to international collaboration. There was no contradiction between this commitment and the aim of revising Versailles and restoring Germany as a great power by peaceful means. Stresemann was a realistic nationalist fighting a constant no-holds-barred battle against a national opposition steeped in myth and lacking his own realism. In domestic policy the removal of his influence was swiftly followed by a much harsher climate.[9]

RADICALISATION ON THE RIGHT AND THE LEFT: THE REFERENDUM ON THE YOUNG PLAN; THE STALINISATION OF THE KPD

The most obvious signs of political radicalisation that had in the meantime occurred were on the right. The defeat of the DNVP in the Reichstag elections had caused deep frustration and the question of the monarchy once more became the focus for the tensions in the party. The policy of participating in republican coalitions had led the party in 1927 to vote for a watered-down version of the law for the protection of the republic, originally passed after the murder of Rathenau in 1922. It still included a clause giving the government the right to prevent members of the former ruling dynasties from entering Germany, the so-called 'emperor clause'. Monarchists attacked this as a particularly dishonourable surrender of principle and attributed the defeat of 1928 to such compromises. Even Hindenburg was now blamed for his trimming conduct and for having lent respectability to the hated republic. There was a strong counterblast from another wing of the DNVP. Walther Lambach, a DNVP Reichstag deputy and secretary of the *Deutschnationaler Handlungsgehilfenverband*, the white-collar union, published an article in June 1928 in which he argued that monarchist sentiment had declined. He cited the position of Hindenburg and the plebiscite on dynastic property as evidence. He called for a more popular kind of conservatism.

The many-sided divisions in the DNVP, between the advocates of a pragmatic mass party and the adherents of an uncompromising anti-republicanism, came to a head at a party congress in October 1928. Count Westarp, who had struggled to keep the party from splitting, was forced to resign the leadership, though he remained chairman of the parliamentary *Fraktion*.

His successor, Alfred Hugenberg, was to exercise an important and malign influence on German politics till 1933. He had become chairman of the Krupp board of directors in 1909, had become influential in West German heavy industry and was ideologically closely linked to the Pan-German League. In the course of channelling the funds of heavy industry into annexationist propaganda during the war he had built up a great media empire. It included Berlin as well as provincial newspapers, news agencies and also the new medium of film. The Hugenberg concern was built round the Scherl publishing company and the Ufa (Universum Film A.G.) film company. It formed a counterpoise to what nationalist right-wing circles regarded as the liberal, internationalist domination of the media especially through the Jewish publishing houses of Ullstein and Mosse.

Hugenberg was an abrasive, stubborn, difficult personality, opinionated and confrontational. His emergence into a central position in right-wing politics had a very divisive effect which in the end benefited only Hitler. Many on the right, from Hindenburg downwards, including members of the *Ruhrlade*, the inner cabinet of the Western coal and steel industry, found him increasingly wrong-headed and impossible to work with. When Hugenberg began to attract the political limelight his character-istic slogan was 'solid or mash' (*Block oder Brei*). Those who wanted a broad conservative party able to influence republican politics were the mash, his prescription was dynamic force through principled confrontation.

In due course the result was that bourgeois spectrum of politics became even more fragmented than it already was in the elections of 1928. The radicalisation on the right could also be perceived in the Stahlhelm. A message of hate for the republic proclaimed by one of its provincial leaders was widely supported and raised the question whether Hindenburg could remain an honorary member. In a meeting between the president and the two Stahlhelm leaders Seldte and Duesterberg this matter was glossed over by some patently dubious assurances. There was also much support in the Stahlhelm for an amnesty for the *Feme* murderers, men who had killed informers for reporting infringements of the disarmament provisions of the peace treaties. It was significant that Hitler was exploiting the *Feme* affair demagogically and thus finding common ground with respectable nationalism.[10]

For the moment the effect of Hugenberg's leadership of the DNVP was that the Müller government had to face increasingly ferocious opposition from the right. Müller tried to strengthen his government in the winter of 1928–9 against these challenges. They came not only from the radicalised nationalist opposition, but were also due to the difficult financial situation of the Reich. Narrow party egotism was again seen at its worst. The parties were still refusing to shoulder their responsibilities for the executive government of the country. The DVP could not join the Prussian government, because the Centre Party thought this might endanger the negotiations in progress for a Prussian concordat. The Centre Party temporarily withdrew its one representative in the Reich government in February 1929, in order to emphasise the party's claims, and only in April, after a tenuous compromise over the budget had been agreed, did three members of the party rejoin the cabinet. It was increasingly realised that the break-up of this cabinet would not merely precipitate a government crisis, but a crisis of the state.

The difficulties the chancellor experienced with the Centre Party were a reflection of the poor showing of the party in 1928. Marx resigned the leadership, but the determined drive of Stegerwald, from the trade union wing of the party, to succeed him failed. Kaas was a compromise candidate and for the first time the party was led by a priest. Stegerwald became chairman of the *Fraktion*, but was succeeded in December 1929 by Heinrich Brüning, who had also come up through the Christian union movement. All this did not amount to a straightforward swing to the right in the party, but signified some disillusion with the parliamentary system and a quest for strong leadership. Brüning was increasingly talked of as the coming man, with whom the generation that fought in the trenches would take over. He was a financial specialist, strongly patriotic and conservative, his trade union connections notwithstanding.[11]

There was also radicalisation on the left. The sixth world congress of the Comintern, meeting from 17 July to 1 September 1928, had signalled a swing to the left for the world communist movement. This was partly due to the desire of Stalin, having overcome the left-wing opposition of Trotsky, to subdue the right wing of the party, of which Bukharin was the most prominent representative. Stalin was preparing for the end of the New Economic Policy and the switch to enforced collectivisation and industrialisation through extreme depression of consumer demands. The risks these policies posed to the survival of the Soviet regime were so great that Stalin could only feel safe if all opposition was suppressed. The swing to the left would also mean the use of the international communist movement as a protective screen for the Soviet Union, at a time when Stalin again feared an attack from the capitalist world.

Thus the thesis of social fascism, that reformist socialist parties were objectively fascist and represented the most immediate threat to the proletariat, was revived. The SPD was the classical case of social fascism: its pro-Western foreign policy made it plausible to portray it as an agent of an international imperialist conspiracy against the Soviet Union. Within the KPD the predominance of the Moscow faction led by Thälmann was already so complete that opponents of the social fascist thesis, dubbed right-wing deviationists and conciliationists, were easily marginalised and for the most part expelled from the party. The end of any tenuous moves towards common action with the SPD, either from above or below, and the attack on the SPD as the spearhead of bourgeois treason within the proletariat was not too difficult to sell to the KPD rank-and-file. It fitted into the long history of struggle between the two parts of the labour movement since the war; it was reinforced by the rivalry and by the sociological and regional differences between the two parties.

The events of 'bloody May', the clashes in Berlin during the May day demonstrations of 1929, came conveniently for the KPD leadership to reinforce the image of the SPD as the total enemy. The growing tendency to violent confrontations between communists, social democrats and Nazis, deliberately fostered by the two extremist parties, had compelled the SPD police chief of Berlin, Friedrich Zörgiebel, to impose a ban on open-air demonstrations. This was reinforced in March 1929 by a declaration of the Prussian minister of the interior Grzesinski that strong action would be taken against the excesses of radical organisations. Perhaps unwisely and provocatively Zörgiebel decided to maintain the ban on demonstrations even for the traditional May Day celebrations. Inevitably the KPD decided to defy the ban. As result there were violent clashes between the police and crowds in some of the working-class districts of Berlin that were also KPD strongholds, especially Wedding, Neukölln and Friedrichshain. There were around thirty dead and two hundred wounded. There was little sign of elaborate communist preparations, let alone moves towards a putsch, and much of the aggression against the police came from unemployed youths.

Nevertheless the martyrs served a convenient purpose for the KPD leadership in its fight against the SPD and in its efforts to gain sympathy. For example Carl von Ossietzky, later himself martyred by the Nazis and the recipient of the Nobel peace prize, attacked Zörgiebel in the *Weltbühne*, the left-wing intellectual journal. For Weimar's liberal and left-wing intelligentsia the apparently genuine communist proletarianism had more appeal than the grey petit-bourgeois bureaucracy of the SPD. An immediate consequence was the prohibition of the *Rote Frontkämpferbund* (Red Front Fighters League), the communist paramilitary organisation, in Prussia and later in the Reich. The

German labour movement entered its terminal struggle totally divided and the division was not only from the top downwards, but from the grass roots upwards.[12]

In the meantime Hugenberg, the new leader of the DNVP, embarked upon an attempt to rally the whole of the nationalist, anti-republican opposition against the Young Plan. The Stahlhelm had already made plans to use the referendum procedure provided by the constitution to promote a far-reaching plan of constitutional reform. Hugenberg had no difficulty in convincing leading figures in a potential right-wing coalition that an attack on the Young Plan offered a much better prospect. In July 1929 he established a committee to prepare a proposal against the Young Plan, which would be carried into effect by means of a *Volksbegehren* and if necessary a *Volksentscheid*. The DNVP leader rated it a great success that he was able to marshal a broad range of support in this committee, including the Stahlhelm, the Pan-German League, the *Reichslandbund*, the Landvolk Party, important industrialists like Fritz Thyssen, and Hitler. The adhesion of the NSDAP, in retrospect seen as the most important by-product of this initiative, received less publicity at the time.

After his relative failure in the Reichstag elections in May 1928 Hitler had put much greater emphasis on courting the middle-class and the farming vote and had toned down the revolutionary and the socialist note in his propaganda. He was not averse now to contacts with other elements in the nationalist opposition, but always without compromising the independence and separate identity of his organisations. A few Freikorps revolutionaries left the Nazi Party and a few national bolsheviks joined the KPD, but Hitler's gains far outweighed his losses. In pursuance of his policy of radical and total opposition Hugenberg and his associates made public, in September 1929, a so-called 'Freedom Law'. It repudiated the war guilt clause of the Versailles treaty, instructed the Reich government to seek the unconditional end of the Rhineland occupation and it prohibited all German authorities from accepting any obligations arising from the war guilt clause, including those just agreed at the first Hague conference.

Most controversial was paragraph four of the Freedom Law, which deemed the chancellor, Reich ministers and their plenipotentiaries guilty of high treason if they accepted such obligations and therefore liable to a sentence of penal servitude. This paragraph caused a storm of indignation in all the republican parties, but it split the nationalist opposition. While extremists like the NSDAP insisted on retention of paragraph four, moderates in the DNVP, among agrarians and industrialists and even in the Stahlhelm, wanted it deleted. Hugenberg went ahead, determined to achieve his rally of all radical anti-republicans, and the collection of signatures for the law took place between 16 and 29 October 1929. The Reich government mounted a strong campaign against the law, but Hindenburg typically refused to take sides, on the ground that any constitutional step he might have to take to give effect to the Young Plan provisions had not yet arisen. The result of this people's request was that just over 10 per cent of the electorate, the required minimum, supported the proposed law. It then went before the Reichstag, where the controversial paragraph four was rejected by 311 to 60 votes.

What was most significant about this vote was that after great tensions within the DNVP, centring around the moderate Gottfried Treviranus, fourteen deputies of the DNVP and seven of the *Landvolkpartei* voted against the penal servitude clause. Hugenberg, in his eagerness to keep the Nazi extremists in his campaign, had deepened the split in his own party. In the referendum itself, held on 22 December 1929, the Freedom Law was supported by an unimpressive 13.8 per cent of the electorate and therefore failed.[13]

Even before the referendum was held there were indications that the NSDAP was achieving spectacular gains in Landtag, provincial and communal elections. In May 1929 the Nazis raised their share of the vote in Saxony to 5 per cent, compared with 1.6 per cent in October 1926. In Baden in October 1929 their share was 7 per cent, compared with 1.2 per cent in October 1925. In Thuringia they obtained 11.8 per cent in December 1929, against 3.5 per cent in January 1927. This led to the first Nazi participation in a *Land* government. Wilhelm Frick became Thuringian minister of the interior and education. In the Prussian provincial and communal elections in November and December 1929 the Nazis made big gains in some areas. Overall they obtained about 5 per cent of the votes compared with 1.8 per cent in May 1928. In Berlin, where the *Völkische* had got only 1.5 per cent in October 1925, the NSDAP now got 5.8 per cent, almost entirely from middle-class districts. Other big gains took place in Schleswig-Holstein, Hanover, Kassel and Wiesbaden.

Hitler's strategy of playing on agrarian distress and middle-class fears was paying off in the uncertain economic climate. The national publicity and respectability gained in the referendum campaign also helped.

THE REICH'S FINANCES AND THE FALL OF MÜLLER

The financial difficulties of the Reich were one of the main reasons why the government wanted to see the Young Plan in operation as soon as possible. In the autumn of 1929 the growth of the floating debt was making immediate action necessary and casting a shadow over the budget for the year 1930. The size of the deficit had been much aggravated by the high level of unemployment experienced in the exceptionally harsh winter of 1928–9. The figures were rising again in the more normal winter of 1929–30 and by February 1930 reached approximately three and a quarter million, about a sixth of the employed population and above the level of 1929. The unemployment scheme established in 1927 had not been able to accumulate the reserves necessary to cope with such a level of unemployment and had to be subsidised by the Reich. This burden was superimposed upon a deficit inherited by the Müller government and a lack of buoyancy in the revenue due to the slackening of economic growth in 1929.

The calls from German industry for a lowering of its tax burdens became more insistent and the demand was made that any reductions in expenditure resulting from the Young Plan should be used for that purpose. The *Langnamverein* (Longname association, the short title for the association for the preservation of common entrepreneurial interests in the Rhineland and Westphalia, which went back to imperial days) was demanding fundamental political changes – 'at last a rally of all forces which are, let us say, not consciously socialist in Germany into a united and purposeful front, such as the opposite side has always formed in the last few years with great "success"'. This was how Paul Reusch, chairman of the coal and steel concern *Gutehoffnungshütte* and one of the inner circle of German industrialists, put it. Like most of the more pragmatic leaders of industry Reusch had nevertheless opposed what he considered the 'foolish' referendum campaign mounted by Hugenberg. The RDI, while still reluctant to make open demands for political changes, published in

December 1929 a memorandum entitled 'Rise or Fall ?', claiming that the German economy was at a turning point and would not survive without lower taxes and less social spending and state interference.

The most sensational challenge to the Müller coalition came again from Schacht as Reichsbankpresident. In November 1929 he warned foreign banks against subscribing to a loan which Hilferding, the SPD minister of finance, hoped to raise to meet the deficit in the Reich revenues. Shortly afterwards Schacht issued a declaration that the Young proposals, to which he had put his signature, had been 'falsified' not only by further Allied demands, but by the failure of the Reich government to put its financial house in order. For the moment a final showdown was avoided. On 14 December the Müller government received a vote of confidence in the Reichstag by 222 to 156 votes, but this could not disguise the fact that the coalition was near disintegration. The BVP deputies abstained to warn against the future imposition of a beer tax. More significantly only 24 of the 45 DVP deputies voted for, and 14, all the industrial representatives, voted against the government. Stresemann was no longer there to restrain the industrial wing of the party. At the opposite end of the political spectrum 28 left-wing SPD deputies abstained.

In the SPD and the trade unions there was once again a yearning for opposition and a growing reluctance to accept compromises which favoured the class enemy. Hilferding resigned and so did his state secretary Popitz. Both men eventually became victims of the Nazis in very different circumstances: Hilferding was caught in his French exile in 1941 and Popitz, after holding high office in the Third Reich, was executed after the July 1944 plot against Hitler. Moldenhauer from the DVP was appointed minister of finance and Schäffer, who was soon to take a leading part in carrying out the financial policies of Brüning, became his state secretary. Only one factor kept the great coalition alive for a few more weeks, the need to enact the proposals of the Young Plan. Even on the right only the more extreme sections, such as Hugenberg and his followers in the DNVP, were prepared to plunge Germany into the crisis which the rejection of the plan would have entailed.[14]

The idea that the end of the Müller government might signal a more fundamental change in German politics had been in the air for some time and had wide ramifications. Hindenburg said once that Müller was his best chancellor, only a pity that he was a socialist. He hoped that sooner or later the opportunity would arise to govern again without the SPD, though he remained determined to proceed constitutionally. By the end of 1929 more specific ideas were being entertained in the ministry of defence by Groener and Schleicher. If the great coalition broke up, Müller might not to be allowed to dissolve the Reichstag, but a more right-wing government might be given the use of article 48 to deal with the economic emergency and already Brüning was envisaged as the possible head of such a government.

The leading academic constitutional lawyer Carl Schmitt was putting forward highly refined critiques of the Weimar constitution and proposing the president as the guardian of the constitution, who through modifications could realise its true intentions. In earlier publications Schmitt had already analysed the decay of classical liberal parliamentarism; he had also put forward the strongly anti-liberal concept of the friend–foe principle, namely that the recognition of this distinction constituted the essence of political as opposed to other types of action.[15] Schmitt's acute observations on what he called 'the fragile multi-party state' supplied a perfect rationale for what Hindenburg, Schleicher and the moderates in the political and industrial right wing wanted: a more authoritarian, anti-Marxist mode of governing developed out of the reserve constitution which according to Schmitt was implicit in the document adopted in August 1919. There would be no sudden, overt breach of the constitution, but a gradual transformation. The legal positivism inherent in the Weimar constitution, namely that it provided rules but no norms, would be exploited to the full. The letter of the law would not be broken even if the spirit was and no offence would be given to the deep-seated German attachment to legality. Hindenburg, Groener and Schleicher had often been the targets of attacks from the more rigoristic and hot-headed among the national opposition. They had no desire to go too far in the direction prescribed by such radicals nor to invite more confrontation with the SPD than was strictly necessary.

The early weeks of 1930 until the fall of the coalition on 27 March did not add any fundamentally new element to the situation. During the second Hague conference in January, which finalised the Young Plan, Schacht continued to highlight his differences with the Reich government, warning of a deflationary crisis as well as claiming that the Young Plan would make the imposition of sanctions on Germany in case of non-payment easier than the Dawes arrangements. The former warning was borne out by events, the latter was unnecessary scaremongering. In the SPD Schacht was seen as a dangerous backseat driver and his resignation on 7 March was the last occasion when the party had something to celebrate before it left office. His place was taken by Hans Luther, who was shortly to prove a willing ally for Brüning's deflationary policy.

For most of the bourgeois spectrum of parties and interests, however, the passage of the Young Plan legislation remained a priority, but it became linked with the determination to achieve a settlement of the Reich's financial problem. The nub of the problem was still the sensitive question how to ensure the solvency of the unemployment scheme. The SPD wanted the contributions raised from the 3 per cent level fixed in 1927. The attempt to increase them in the spring of 1929 had failed, but in December 1929, with unemployment rising steeply, they were raised to 3.5 per cent till 30 June 1930. The question was whether they should be further raised, possibly to 4 per cent. This was strongly opposed by the DVP, whose deputies wanted the accounts of the Reich Institute for Unemployment Insurance balanced by reducing benefits. The parties in the coalition, other than the SPD, tended increasingly towards the DVP's view. Many other tax and financial compromises were explored during the prolonged negotiations between the parties. For the SDP the touchstone always was that the burden on the working masses and on the unemployed should be limited; for the DVP and the other coalition parties the aim was to lighten the tax burden on industry and maintain the inflow of foreign credits. The BVP kept up its opposition to the raising of the beer tax.

Once the Young Plan legislation had passed the Reichstag on 12 March the cement holding the coalition together had gone and the participation of the SPD in government could be dispensed with. The moderates on the right were in sight of their long-desired goal. Before the Young Plan legislation was complete Hindenburg had given the impression that he might allow the Müller government powers under article 48 to enact the finance package by the beginning of the financial year on 1 April. Thus the linkage between Young Plan and a balanced budget would be maintained. As soon as the Young Plan laws had been accepted, however, it was made clear that the president was not likely to grant Müller the use of article 48 nor was he prepared to dissolve the Reichstag at the SDP chancellor's request. At the DVP's Party congress on 21 and 22 March the powerful heavy industry wing of the party was in no mood to go back on its demand that the unemployment scheme should be made solvent without outside assistance. Attempts at compromise continued till the eleventh hour, but on 27 March it emerged that the SPD *Fraktion*, driven into a corner and in spite of warnings from some of its leaders, was not prepared to retreat any further. In the absence of an agreed financial package Müller resigned and the last cabinet of the Weimar republic to govern with the support of the Reichstag disappeared.

Whose fault was it? The question has been debated ever since. Was German democracy really allowed to founder over half a per cent on the unemployment insurance contributions? There can be no doubt about the widespread desire on the right, from Hindenburg downwards, to govern without the SPD. The president and his advisers were willing to grant a bourgeois government what had just been refused to Müller, the use of article 48 and the right to dissolve the Reichstag. More far-reaching constitutional changes were envisaged but were still in the realm of speculation. The SDP's reaction to being thus cornered was understandable, but with hindsight can be seen to have been a mistake of historic proportions. The party, still by far the largest in the Reichstag, did not recover its position through a spell in opposition, as on previous occasions, and soon its options were to become desperately narrow. Only three years later it had been all but extinguished, many members were in exile or in concentration camps and some had been horribly murdered. Weimar politics could not function without a degree of collaboration between the SPD and the bulk of the bourgeois parties. This collaboration had now broken down.[16]

BRÜNING TAKES OVER

Brüning became the central figure in German politics for the next two years. The hope was that he would prove a sufficiently effective leader to satisfy the widespread craving for strong government while preserving the rule of law and a healthier form of parliamentary government. He would be the Führer who would keep out that other Führer who was becoming the preferred alternative for an ever-growing number of Germans. The contrast between the personalities of Hitler and Brüning could hardly have been greater. The chairman of the Centre Party *Fraktion* kept a deliberately low profile, appropriate to a civil servant rather than to a politician. The qualities in which he excelled were administrative: competence, realism and *Sachlichkeit*, inadequately translated as objectivity. His undoubted integrity, self-discipline and asceticism were not without appeal, but for the increasingly desperate masses he lacked charisma.

Brüning could not escape from the circumstances that had brought him to office, even had he wanted to. He was dependent on Hindenburg, it was expected of him that he would reorient German politics towards the right and that he would use the crisis to pull the country out of the parliamentary and financial morass. Brüning himself belonged to the generation of politically active Catholics who wanted to forget the long period of second-class citizenship their fathers had suffered and to prove themselves second to none in their devotion to the fatherland. Brüning's relationship with Hindenburg, the devoted junior officer to the imperial field marshal, was shaped by these emotions.

It came naturally to Brüning to appeal to his countrymen's self-discipline and to ask them to endure hardship in order to free Germany from the humiliation of Versailles. The pursuit of national redemption through financial rectitude was a goal above politics that must, in Brüning's view, command the broadest support. The catastrophic rise of national socialism was therefore almost a sideshow, a phantom that would vanish as soon as the eternal needs of the German nation were seen to have been vindicated. In the meantime there were sound patriotic elements in the NSDAP who could be persuaded into supporting the true national interest. Brüning's failure, to the extent that it was rooted in his own outmoded concept of politics, had all the elements of high tragedy.

Brüning was able to present his cabinet within three days of Müller's resignation, which confirmed the impression that it had been planned for some time. It was a coalition not of parties but of personalities, as Müller's had initially been. It did not mark a clean break with the past, for no less than eight of its members had belonged to the previous cabinet. It did not represent as clear a turn to the right as many had hoped: Wirth, at the ministry of the interior, and Stegerwald, at the ministry of labour, represented the left wing of the Centre Party, which Brüning could in no way afford to ignore. His own party's collaboration with the SPD in the Weimar coalition cabinet in Prussia was as much a fact of life for Brüning as was his dependence on Hindenburg.

On the other hand the composition of the cabinet signalled the hope that it might find broad support on the right. Treviranus had after leaving the DNVP founded the *Volkskonservative Vereinigung* (Popular Conservative Association), soon to come before the electorate as a separate party. He was close to Schleicher and his presence in the cabinet was evidence of the general's concept that this cabinet, largely his brainchild, might base itself on a new and stable alignment on the right. Even more significant was the presence of Martin Schiele as minister of food, as the agricultural portfolio was called. He had opposed Hugenberg's leadership of the DNVP and was about to leave the party. He was a major figure in the Green Front (*Grüne Front*), a loose cooperation of *Reichslandbund* and the mainly Catholic *Bauernvereine* formed in the spring of 1929 to strengthen the agricultural lobby across the political parties. The Green Front had fought for continued protection during the negotiations for a Polish–German trade agreement, one of Stresemann's last achievements in an effort to improve relations with Poland in 1929. In the Brüning government the agrarians were so strong that the Polish–German agreement was not submitted to the Reichstag for ratification and lapsed.[17] Hindenburg had been especially concerned that the claims of agriculture, and particularly of the hard-pressed East Elbian landowners, should be strongly represented in the new government. *Osthilfe* was to have a large impact on the course of events leading to 30 January 1933 and flagrantly contradicted the rigid cost-cutting pursued in all other areas.

The third minister, whose presence in the Brüning cabinet indicated a greater solicitude for right-wing groups, was Professor Bredt of the Economics Party, who took over the ministry of justice. Hugenberg was, however, still the most important political leader on the right and his attitude to Brüning was hostile from the beginning. The chancellor could not possibly concede his demand that the Centre Party should cease to be in coalition with the SPD in Prussia and should bring the Braun government down. Nevertheless Hugenberg found himself under great pressure, especially from the agrarian interest in the DNVP, not to oppose the Brüning cabinet straight away. When the SPD brought a no confidence motion against the new government Hugenberg reluctantly agreed with the majority of his *Fraktion* not to support it. When Brüning's financial programme, with its large hand-outs and additional protective tariffs for agriculture, came before the Reichstag the DNVP was once again split. Only about two-fifths of the party's deputies followed Hugenberg's uncompromising line. This encouraged the hope that Brüning might after all be able to govern with a Reichstag majority and would not have to resort to article 48, as he had threatened to do. Brüning's assumption of office on 30 March 1930 does not therefore mark the conclusive end of parliamentary government. This was only brought about by the further deepening of the financial crisis during the next few weeks.[18]

This crisis was still mainly seen in terms of the impact an obstinately high level of unemployment made upon the budget of the Reich. The collapse of the New York stock market in October 1929 had given a signal that the international economy, led by the United States, might be entering upon a period of weakness. The stock market collapse had itself given the American economy a downward kick. In the spring of 1930 there had, however, been some recovery in the American stock market and the economic downturn seemed no different from previous cyclical movements of this kind.

This was also the prevailing view in Germany. In order to allow the self-correcting forces of the market to operate it seemed essential to bring order into the public finances. The numbers of those officially registered as unemployed fell after the winter of 1929–30 to over 2.6 million in May 1930, but this was still over a million more than in the same month of 1929. From then the numbers rose steadily when seasonal factors should have reduced them. The Brüning cabinet discussed the sluggish state of the labour market and the desirability of stimulating it, but any major fiscal stimulation was out of the question.

An agreement about balancing the budget even among the parties represented in the Brüning cabinet proved very difficult and by 18 June the finance minister, Moldenhauer, was forced by the pressure of his own DVP *Fraktion* to resign. On 16 July the government's proposals were put before the Reichstag, but were withdrawn when part of them were voted down by a combination of the SPD, most of the DNVP, the NSDAP and the KPD. Brüning now made good the threat that had long been in the background: the proposals were enacted as emergency decrees under article 48. The SPD immediately tabled a motion under paragraph 3 of article 48, that the emergency decrees be declared invalid. This motion was carried by 236 to 222 votes. The affirmative votes came from the SPD, the KPD, the NSDAP and from 32 deputies of the Hugenberg wing of the DNVP. Some 25 DNVP deputies voted with the government. The threat to dissolve the Reichstag, also in the background since March, was carried out and elections were fixed for 14 September. The emergency decrees were re-enacted under article 48 on 26 July, the first of four major emergency packages put into operation by the Brüning government.

Unemployment insurance contributions now went up by a full per cent to 4.5 per cent. Only weeks had passed since the great coalition split over half a per cent. A limit was imposed on the liability of the state to keep the scheme in balance, something strongly demanded by the DVP, and the contributions went up to 6.5 per cent in the autumn. Local communities were empowered to impose additional drink taxes, including a beer tax. They could also impose a poll or head tax, which the SPD had strongly opposed because of its impact on the poor. Permanently employed public servants had to pay an emergency contribution (*Notopfer*) and higher incomes had to bear additional income tax. These two measures had been opposed by the DVP. The *Osthilfe*, aid to agriculture in the eastern provinces, was also part of this package.[19]

THE SEPTEMBER 1930 ELECTIONS: THE NAZI BREAKTHROUGH

Brüning had not been able to escape from the circumstances which had given birth to his government, the desire of Hindenburg and those around him to govern without the SPD and with a strong commitment to the agrarian interest. It was doubtful if it was constitutional to dissolve a Reichstag which had used its right to declare article 48 emergency decrees inoperative.

Brüning had in the early days of his chancellorship obtained confirmation from the state secretaries in the ministries of interior and of justice that a government defeated in the Reichstag could still ask for a dissolution. The state secretaries had also given it as their opinion that a caretaker government holding office until the election of a new Reichstag could still use article 48.

Brüning had thus anticipated at the beginning of his term of office that he might find himself in the position that had now arisen. It was unlikely, however, that the founders of the constitution had ever envisaged that the president would use his emergency powers in conjunction with his power to dissolve the Reichstag. In Ebert's day article 48 had been used with the aim of dealing with an emergency in order to re-establish constitutional government. Now it was being used to achieve a permanent modification of the constitution.

The dissolution of the Reichstag lay in the logic of the policies that had been followed at least since March, but politically it had catastrophic consequences. The Nazi breakthrough in September 1930 made the ostensible aim of Brüning's policy, the resuscitation of German public finances and the improvement of the economic position, immeasurably more difficult. Germany's foreign creditors were only too well aware what the Nazi threat meant and withdrew their money. The economic crisis reached a new level of gravity.

Brüning himself had been doubtful of the wisdom of holding new elections in the closing days of the Müller government. In the meantime there had been unmistakable signs that Nazi support was rising alarmingly. In the Saxon Landtag elections, where there was an electorate of over three and a half million, the NSDAP obtained 14.4 per cent of the votes on 22 June 1930 and became the second largest party in the Landtag. This compared with 5 per cent in May 1929. The Nazi success was largely due to the decline of the bourgeois parties, a process soon to be re-enacted at national level. The combined vote of DVP and DNVP fell from 21.4 per cent in 1929 to 13.5 per cent in 1930. The KPD got 13.6 per cent compared with 12.8 per cent a year earlier.

The violent militancy of national socialism and its capacity to penetrate into many aspects of the nation's life was strikingly illustrated by Frick's activities in Thuringia, by Nazi infiltration into the Reichswehr and into the students' associations in the universities. Frick had appointed a number of Nazi police officials, which had caused the Reich minister of the interior, first Severing, then Wirth, to refuse to pay the Reich contribution to the Thuringian police force. He had appointed a professor of race science at the University of Jena, against the opposition of this university. This had earned him congratulations from the students of the *Technische Hochschule* in Munich, where in 1929 the Nazis had obtained 20 per cent of the votes to the student committee. At Erlangen in Franconia and Greifswald in Pomerania the Nazi vote in the ASTA (*Allgemeine Studentenausschüsse*, general student committees) had already reached over 50 per cent in 1929 and would climb to 76 and 60 per cent for the academic year 1930–1.

Nowhere was anti-republican resentment and romanticised chauvinism more rampant than in the universities, among professors as well as among the mainly middle-class students. Avowed democrats and liberals had great difficulty in getting university appointments. The minority of republican university teachers had to run a gauntlet of attacks from nationalist students.

Economic pressures were severe for many German students, even before the depression deprived them of job prospects. They often came from homes where the inflation had wiped out the savings used in the past to finance higher education fees. A national socialist student association had been founded as early as 1926 and Baldur von Schirach, given the grandiose title of Reich Youth Leader after 1933, became its organiser. Between 1928 and 1929 its membership doubled and a year later it had trebled again.[20]

The appeal of Nazism to nationalist, middle-class youth, disillusioned and radicalised, could be seen working even more dangerously in the Reichswehr. In spite of appeals from Groener and Schleicher against association with Nazi extremism sympathy with the national-revolutionary thrust of the Nazi ideology was widespread among junior officers. In March 1929 Hitler had attacked the party political neutrality of the Reichswehr, which in his view made the army into an instrument of the democratic Marxist republican politicians. He saw the Reichswehr's future as the core for a new people's army that would be the spearhead for a German national and racial renaissance.

This speech was widely distributed in the army. It made a great impression on three young officers of the Ulm garrison, whose disillusion with the current Reichswehr leadership was compounded when they were ordered not to go out in uniform in order to avoid clashing with a KPD demonstration. In November 1929 they made contact with NSDAP headquarters in Munich and proposed to set up Nazi cells in the Reichswehr to prepare for a 'German freedom rising'. Although in accordance with the prevailing party line their Nazi interlocutors warned them against illegality, they expressed sympathy with the officers' aims. The three officers were eventually arrested, but their trial did not take place until after the elections of September 1930. The appearance of Hitler as a witness at this trial made it into a *cause célèbre*.[21]

These and many other signals indicating the breadth and depth of the national socialist assault on the republic could leave no doubt that Hitler would make massive gains in any elections, though the full extent of his triumph could not be foreseen. Brüning hoped that the moderates who had split off from the DNVP and were already organising themselves would make a strong showing at the polls and broaden the basis of his government. If the fiasco that Hugenberg's policy was expected to produce for the DNVP would also lead to some increase of support for the NSDAP, such a result would not be entirely unwelcome to Brüning. He shared the widespread belief on the right that a degree of crisis would clear the air. It was significant that on 30 June 1930 the last Allied troops would leave the Rhineland, as agreed at the Hague conferences.

The next stage in casting off the shackles of Versailles would be to demonstrate that the long-term obligations imposed by the Young Plan would not be capable of fulfilment. The rise of extremism in Germany would show the world that in due course the extraction of reparations would have to come to an end. Hindenburg had refused to attend the celebrations to mark the end of the Rhineland occupation until a ban on the Stahlhelm in the western provinces, imposed by the Prussian government, was lifted. It was an explosive issue which Brüning, dependent upon Hindenburg, had to handle with extreme caution.[22]

The continued existence of the Weimar coalition government in Prussia was still anathema to all on the right wing of politics, including the president. Brüning headed a 'Hindenburg' cabinet, but the political transformation still fell well short of what those around the president, particularly Groener and Schleicher, really wanted. Hindenburg was as ambivalent as ever, unwilling to lend his full prestige to Brüning, reluctant to incur the disapproval of his traditional friends on the right. Foreign opinion could only note that there would be no gratitude in Germany for concessions made, only the demand for more.

The announcement of the September elections precipitated frantic political manoeuvres. The consolidation of political groupings to the right of the Centre Party and to the left of Hugenberg's followers was now an immediate necessity, yet had proved elusive for months if not years. Even now all efforts failed to consolidate the groups that had progressively split off from the DNVP and they fought the election as three separate parties, though there was some junction of lists at constituency and Reich level.

The *Konservative Volkspartei* (Conservative People's Party), started by Treviranus, now also included the former DNVP leader Count Westarp. It had the ambitious aim of providing a German version of tory democracy, popular conservatism prepared to participate constructively in affairs of state, albeit a state that would transcend the weak parliamentarism of the present. The *Konservative Volkspartei* was unable to achieve a fusion with the *Landvolkpartei*, whose leading personality, Schiele, remained, like Treviranus, a member of the Brüning cabinet. There was yet a third conservative party, the *Christlich-Soziale Volksdienst* (Christian Social People's Service), which harked back to ideas of the imperial court preacher Stoecker, who had attempted to wean the workers from their socialist loyalties. Its leaders were some former DNVP deputies with close links to the Lutheran churches.[23]

Attempts at a fusion of the two liberal parties had run into the sand after Stresemann's death. Koch-Weser, the DDP leader who had taken part in the earlier fusion talks, now embarked upon the desperate gamble of combining with the *Jungdeutscher Orden*. At one time second only to the Stahlhelm as an organisation of right-wing militancy, Arthur Mahraun's order had in recent years been more inclined towards constructive participation in republican politics. It had supported the western orientation of Stresemann's foreign policy. The aura of a romantic nationalist youth movement that clung to the *Jungdo* raised the hope that the fusion would bring some rejuvenation to the DDP. Mahraun hurriedly disclaimed the ingrained anti-Semitism of his organisation in order not to scare off the DDP's Jewish voters. It was a measure of the desperation of the moment that this ill-assorted marriage produced only one major defection from the DDP, Anton

Erkelenz, a representative of the liberal Hirsch-Duncker trade unions. Erkelenz had always been a staunch republican and had seen it as central to the DDP's role that it should form a link between middle and working class. He now joined the SPD.[24]

The fusions and attempted fusions in this central spectrum of German politics were marked by a desire to present a counter to the tarnished image of traditional party politics and parliamentarism. There was much talk of *Sammlung*, leadership, transcendence of class divisions, support for the new Hindenburg authoritarian government. The impact on the voters was slight and could not compete with the dynamic form of *Sammlung* offered by national socialism. The proportional representation system put little pressure on small parties to amalgamate, for any group, however small, could make some showing and perhaps elect a deputy by combining with another list. It could even be argued that voters were in this way given the opportunity of supporting exactly the mixture they wanted, when otherwise they might drift elsewhere. This fragmentation, already so marked in 1928, might, however, induce the voter to put his vote where he thought it would really count. The 'wasted vote' argument, familiar in first-past-the-post systems like the British, worked powerfully for the Nazis in 1930.

The Nazi breakthrough was not only sensational, it finally destroyed a party system that had proved remarkably stable through the traumatic events of defeat and revolution. The percentage of NSDAP votes increased from 2.6 per cent in 1928 to 18.3 per cent, the absolute number of voters from 812 000 to 6.4 million, an eightfold increase.

The highly sophisticated effort that has gone into analysing the Nazi triumph and its subsequent further extension cannot overcome the fact that it is no longer possible to reach definitive conclusions about the motivations of men and women most of whom are now dead. Some of the immediate conclusions reached by contemporaries still sound plausible, but do not fare too well in the light of modern statistical analysis. Commentators pointed to the sharp rise in electoral participation compared with 1928. Over four million more votes were cast, even though the electorate had increased by only about 1.7 million. The percentage of those voting increased from 75.6 to 82 per cent. It was concluded that a lot of these new voters turned to the Nazis, that the previously apathetic and unpoliticised had been bamboozled by sheer demagogy. It was 'an uprising of stupidity'. This argument only partially survives recent analysis: the rise of the Nazi vote was not much more marked in districts where electoral participation increased strongly than in those where it was less strong.

Another conclusion that seemed obvious to contemporaries was that the Nazis had been the main beneficiaries from the precipitate decline of the DNVP, a loss of nearly two million votes and a percentage drop from 14.2 to 7.0. This conclusion fares slightly better in modern statistical analysis, but has to be held against the fact that the correlation between the decline of the DVP and, surprisingly, the SPD votes and the rise of the Nazi vote between 1928 and 1930 is not much less strong. In addition about a quarter of the losses suffered by the DNVP in 1930 are accounted for by defections to the *Landvolkpartei*.

This raises the question of how far the Nazi vote of 1930 was mainly a middle-class vote and to what extent the NSDAP, having largely failed in its urban strategy up to 1928, was now attractive to workers. There seems to have been little impact on the urban, largely unionised industrial proletariat, which remained loyal to the left-wing parties, though registering a shift from SPD to KPD. The Nazis did, however, make progress among blue-collar workers in smaller urban centres, where one can assume a lesser degree of unionisation and employment in smaller firms. A consensus about the degree of working-class support for the NSDAP remains elusive, particularly for the election of 1930, when the vote was still more widely dispersed between parties than came to be the case by 1932. In the first election of 1932, the peak of the pre-1933 Nazi support, at least 30 per cent of the Nazi vote came from workers and their dependants, while some authorities put the percentage as high as 40. Even this would still underrepresent the working class among Nazi voters, compared with their proportion in the population as a whole, about 45 per cent.

Nevertheless, a large proportion of Nazi support therefore came from workers and the party's claim that it was a national movement cutting across classes cannot be denied. It is generally agreed that the Nazis were not the party of the unemployed and that it was the KPD that benefited disproportionately from the votes of the unemployed. The KPD vote rose from 10.6 per cent in 1928 to 13.1 per cent in 1930, the number of voters from 3.26 to 4.59 million.

The common generalisation that the Nazi Party was a movement of the Protestant middle class is only an approximation to the truth. There is a consensus, however, that the Centre Party and BVP voters proved the most resistant to the Nazi appeal, though the resistance weakened by the final election of March 1933. The connection between white-collar employment and Nazi voting, often assumed in the older literature, does not seem firmly established. Such employees, many of them female, came in fact from a wide variety of social backgrounds and could be socially mobile both upwards and downwards. Although the decline of the AfA showed that fewer were linked to the free trade unions, they were still in a dependent status.

Civil servants, on the other hand, seem to have shown an above average propensity to vote Nazi even in 1930. They had already been affected by the cuts of the first Brüning emergency package. Small farmers in Protestant areas, who in regions like the Geest of Schleswig-Holstein had already started to turn to the Nazis in 1928, gave them some of their largest gains, mainly at the expense of the DNVP and the Landvolk. Other middle class groups whose contribution to the Nazi upsurge was above average were small traders and rentiers.

Some recent studies have emphasised the strength of the Nazi appeal to the upper echelons of the middle class, the academically educated, the higher professions and the entrepreneurial class. Information about Nazi Party membership, defective as it is, shows this group to be strongly overrepresented in the party from the beginning. Owing to the small size of the samples, and the difficulty of precisely identifying the components of this group, this is statistically treacherous territory, particularly when applied to elections. The electoral breakthrough of 1930 did, however, weaken the lower-middle class character of the Nazi Party.[25]

Contemporaries were aware of the unscrupulous, no-holds-barred propaganda techniques employed by the Nazis. In 1929 Goebbels had taken over from the young Himmler as the party's propaganda chief. One aspect of this propaganda drive was that it was carefully calculated to address the disparate and often incompatible interests of the many groups that were now potential Nazi supporters. Certain overarching themes, the Hitler cult, total opposition to the system and all its domestic and foreign political associations, parties, parliaments, Versailles, the Young Plan, violent nationalism and anti-Semitism, these

could all serve to hide the contradictions and incompatibilities of
what the Nazis were offering to all and sundry.

Hitler had engaged Walther Darré as his agricultural adviser
and in May 1930 a policy statement on the rural population and
agriculture had been issued. It talked the language of 'blood and
soil' (*Blut und Boden*) and proclaimed the importance of the
farming community to racial health. Much was made of an
earlier statement of Hitler that 'expropriation' did not apply to
the legitimate property of farmers, but only to speculative anti-
social Jewish property.

It was not, however, immediately obvious how extravagant
attention to the rural community could be squared with equally
unrestrained praise for the small shopkeeper, a group also
particularly vulnerable to the Nazis, but not likely to be helped
by artificially high agricultural producer prices. With the small
retailer a strong pitch was made by attacking Jewish department
stores and socialist consumer associations. The multiple contradictions of the Nazi propaganda assault raised hopes among many
observers, accustomed to applying rational criteria to politics,
that the movement could not possibly retain its unity.[26]

The long-running and unresolved tensions between Hitler and
the national socialist left around the Strasser brothers was in fact
surfacing again. The Nazi participation in the Thuringian
government in coalition with the arch-capitalist DVP, the
association with Hugenberg and finally Hitler's outright condemnation of a metal workers' strike in Saxony, just ahead of the
Landtag elections there, had made the position of 'left' Nazis
increasingly uncomfortable. In May 1930 Hitler had a long
confrontation with Otto Strasser, the younger of the two
brothers, in Berlin. Within a few weeks he and his group, as
well as other 'national revolutionaries', were out of the party.[27]

All this caused scarcely a ripple in the dynamic upsurge of
Hitlerism. There was much about the nature and tactics of
national socialism that should have led to a splintering and
sectarianisation of the movement. It did not happen because of
the personality of Hitler and the cult that was successfully built
around him. At a moment when the many groups in the central
spectrum of German politics were unable to achieve even minimal
collaboration the NSDAP forged ahead as the great catch-all
party.

Most contemporary and later observers of the stunning Nazi breakthrough of 1930 have sensed that detailed explanations of it, however well-founded and sophisticated, do not do full justice to the magnitude and horror of what happened. Sheer irrationality induced by panic, a profound social psychological disorientation, an existential *Angst* came into play. Many sections of the German population had suffered such disorientation ever since 1918, but now one more bout of disillusionment made it possible to form a great army of the disorientated. It was a tragedy that the grotesque figure of Hitler offered itself as the medium through whom and around whom it could be rallied, while there was no one to oppose him adequately.[28]

The German political establishment had no first-hand knowledge of Hitler, who was not a member of the Reichstag and did not live in Berlin. Many leading political figures, from Brüning downwards, now made a point of meeting the Nazi leader. A factor came into play which has often been regarded as crucial in the rise of Hitler, the common tendency to underestimate him. This only increased the Führer's own gruesome determination to get his own back, if necessary violently when the time came, an essential feature of his monstrous will to power. Few even remotely gauged his sheer extremism and destructiveness. In 1930 or even 1933, however, it would have required exceptional insight to foresee that this man would become Germany's fate. To most of those accustomed to move in the political world it was inconceivable that an oddball like Hitler might engulf Germany in an even greater catastrophe than that of 1918 and put an end to Bismarck's Reich.

BRÜNING GOVERNS BY DECREE

Brüning's ability to shape the course of events was now more than ever circumscribed. The parties represented in his government commanded only about a third of the new Reichstag. Out of its 577 members, 107 Nazis and 77 Communists, nearly another third, formed an 'anti-systemic' opposition. To this could be added the 41 DNVP deputies led by Hugenberg. The Brüning cabinet was therefore more than ever dependent on Hindenburg. Yet the president remained as reluctant as he had been during the election campaign to lend his prestige to 'his' cabinet and Brüning did all he could to preserve Hindenburg's non-political image. The president's entourage, Otto Meissner, his state secretary, and his son Oskar von Hindenburg, 'the son not provided for in the constitution', were mainly concerned to shield the old man from the attacks of his right-wing friends. No one could be sure whether at the age of 83 the president would able to serve out the eighteen months that remained of his term of office.

Yet Hindenburg had set policy objectives for the Brüning government which severely limited its freedom of action. There had to be continued support for agriculture and particularly for the hard-pressed big landowners in the East Elbian Prussian provinces, who had the president's ear. Even more important were the requirements of the Reichswehr constantly brought to Hindenburg's attention by Schleicher and Groener: it had to have its proper share of resources, however great the pressure on the national budget; it needed the support of Stahlhelm and even the SA, especially in the eastern border provinces, and must on no account be driven into a confrontation with them. In foreign policy the more revisionist tone adopted since the death of Stresemann, particularly in relations with France, had to be maintained. Above all there must be no return of the SPD to government. Yet without the toleration of the SPD in the Reichstag the government could not survive. This factor, together with the Weimar coalition in Prussia, formed the only substantial counterweights to Brüning's dependence on the president.

The overwhelming immediate problem was still the deficit in the Reich budget. The circumstances in which this had to be handled were now even more adverse. In the three weeks following the elections some 800 million marks of foreign deposits were withdrawn from German banks. The government stood in urgent need of a dollar loan, the issue that had precipitated the resignation of Hilferding and the break-up of the Müller government. On the morrow of the election views of the future ranged from a return to the great coalition to the inclusion of the NSDAP in the government. Otto Braun called for 'a union of all reasonable men', but it was a vain hope. With the backing of Hindenburg Brüning quickly reached the decision to remain in office with his existing cabinet, for no reconstruction of it seemed either possible or necessary. The pretence was kept up that the realities had not changed and that the chancellor would face them with his accustomed objectivity – *Sachlichkeit*.

Continued use of article 48, let alone an enabling act, were only possible with the help of the SPD. The election had had a sobering effect on all wings of the party, for the result had demonstrated the extent to which it had got out of touch with the real mood of the people. The accusations so often levied against the party, that its superannuated functionaries were blinkered by organisational fetishism and had become privileged *Bonzen* (bosses), seemed uncomfortably close to the truth. The SPD was not only faced by the obvious threat of fascism, it had also to come to terms with the fact that the KPD had shown itself to be more in tune with the most underprivileged, the unemployed, the ghetto proletariat of big cities and highly industrialised areas.

Awareness of danger produced no real consensus in the SPD on tactics. The left still drew the conclusion that the lesson to be learnt from the fiasco was to revert to unrelenting class warfare and to withdraw from all cooperation with an ever more reactionary state. Symptomatic of this view was a speech by Siegfried Aufhäuser, the chairman of AfA, the white-collar union: 'We are too much a state party, too little a workers' party . . . . Like a flirtatious girl we offer the bourgeoisie the charms of the SPD, instead of showing them the fist.'

The opponents of toleration had, however, no plausible alternative. If Brüning fell, a right-wing government of Hugenberg and Hitler would follow, which would abolish the last vestiges of democracy and the rule of law. It was argued, not only in the SPD, that it might be the best tactic to let such a government come to power and run itself into the grave. Variants of this argument were heard right up to 30 January 1933. In the autumn of 1930 it seemed to the principal leaders of the SPD a high-risk strategy they could not possibly contemplate. Amongst other things it would entail the surrender of the one remaining SPD bastion, the Prussian government with its control of the Prussian police. Toleration of the Brüning government until its fall at the end of May 1932 now became the SPD's consistent policy. In the end it could only demonstrate that the party was in a 'no-win' position.

The price Brüning was able and willing to pay for the SPD's support was minimal, for his dependence on Hindenburg and other right-wing groups was greater and he knew that for the SPD there was no alternative. For the next twenty months the SPD had to condone measures that imposed ever-increasing hardships on its followers. In the spring of 1930 the SPD and the free trade unions had still strained at a gnat, now they were having to swallow a succession of camels. Even the Prussian coalition of Otto Braun could not, in the end, be saved. The tragic impotence, even irrelevance of the left in the face of the Nazi upsurge was not only a result of its deep division, but of the fact that after September 1930 there was no longer a genuinely parliamentary system within which it could operate.[29]

When the newly elected Reichstag met on 16 October 1930 a series of votes on various measures proposed by the Brüning government showed clearly the alignment of forces: the SPD provided nearly half of the over three hundred deputies that voted for the government measures, while over two hundred deputies from the NSDAP, the DNVP and the KPD voted in opposition. Even the *Landvolkpartei*, represented by Schiele in the cabinet, voted against Brüning, in spite of all the measures he had taken to support agriculture. Schiele was voted out of his position as chairman of the *Reichslandbund*, which was increasingly infiltrated by Nazis, though he remained in the government. A few weeks later Bredt, the justice minister and representative of the Economics Party, was forced by his party to resign. Brüning's earlier hope, that a right-centre majority might emerge to sustain him, had vanished.

Among the measures the SPD now had to swallow in return for their support was a further rise of unemployment insurance contributions from 4.5 to 6.5 per cent. There was to be no further support for the unemployment insurance scheme from the Reich in future. While the conditions under which local authorities could grant income support were mostly tightened, there were reductions in commercial and land taxes. All public employees had their salaries and pensions reduced by 6 per cent. The measures to help agriculture and raise agricultural prices were maintained. The financial settlement (*Finanzausgleich*) between Reich and *Länder* was adjusted to the disadvantage of the latter. This was a step towards constitutional reform, the *Reichsreform* that had proved so elusive, by the back door.

Subsequent emergency decrees progressively eroded the autonomy of *Länder* and communities by way of the financial lever. Of particular constitutional importance was the presidential emergency order of 24 August 1931 (called *Dietramszeller Verordnung*, after the president's holiday retreat in Bavaria), which empowered the *Länder* to intervene to balance the budgets of local authorities even if this conflicted with the constitutional position in the *Land*. The Brüning regime of ruling by decree therefore had highly centralising implications, the full political force of which were not realised until Hitler came to power.

For the moment it was again the relationship between Prussia and the Reich that was particularly affected by these financial problems. They increased the pressure towards some kind of amalgamation of the Prussian with the Reich government. The mutual interdependence of the Brüning and Braun governments also pointed towards such an amalgamation, but it would have meant the return of the SPD to the Reich government. In the final consolidated emergency decree promulgated by the president on 1 December 1930 some concessions to the SPD were incorporated, but it was nevertheless a programme which ran counter to the equitable spreading of the burden to which the party was committed.

When the emergency decrees were laid before the Reichstag Brüning managed to avoid the direct vote of no confidence which the Nazis wanted to force. The motion to declare the emergency decrees invalid was again supported by NSDAP, KPD, DNVP, *Landvolk* and even most of the Economics Party. The SPD voted against the motion, but eight left-wingers absented themselves. The Nazi deputies in the Reichstag appeared in SA uniforms and turned the proceedings into a bear garden. In the streets of central Berlin they took part in attacks on Jewish shops and Jewish-looking passers-by. It was with a sense of relief that the Reichstag was adjourned for nearly two months until the beginning of February. Long parliamentary holidays became an unavoidable feature of the Brüning regime.[30]

Germany had thus reached, by gradual stages, a halfway house between a parliamentary and an authoritarian system. Long after these events Brüning claimed in his memoirs that his own aim was to restore the monarchy and establish a system similar to the British.[31] There is, however, little sign that such plans affected the immediate evolution of policy.

Historical debate has focused on the question of whether Brüning's deflationary policies were unavoidable and whether they had any chance of success. A distinction has to be made between the periods before and after the banking crisis in the summer of 1931. Until the summer of 1931 there was hardly any expectation that this phase of the business cycle would turn out any different from what had been experienced in the past. The severe but temporary downturn of 1925–6 was a recent memory and it was widely expected that the self-correcting tendencies, postulated in classical economic theory, which had asserted themselves five years earlier would do so again.

The course of the economy until the late spring of 1931 seemed to bear out these expectations. Unemployment, as measured by the official statistics of those registered as unemployed at labour offices, reached a peak of nearly five million in February 1931, compared with 3.7 million a year earlier. By May the numbers had dropped by nearly a million, compared with a drop of about 700 000 in 1930.

There was a broad consensus behind the policies Brüning was pursuing and agreement with the extra-parliamentary measures he was using. Since the fall of the Müller government, a high water mark of industrial influence in politics, there had been at least two serious attempts by the RDI and the ADGB to reach an understanding. Both sides had reason to dislike the increased influence of the agrarians in the Brüning government. Among industrialists views were divided. Some moderates thought a return to a great coalition was to be preferred, as it would bind the SPD into necessary but unpopular measures. This view was not shared by the leaders of heavy industry, who were glad to see the end of the SPD in government. Only a small minority supported the Hugenberg national opposition before and after the elections of September 1930 and even after these elections the NSDAP was the preferred option of only a few mavericks among major industrialists.

The free trade unions had helped to push the SPD into opposition in March 1930, but soon had reason to regret the course of events even more than the party. The decline of the economy weakened the unions inexorably and reduced their bargaining power. From a peak close to five million members in 1929, itself much below the nearly eight million of the early 1920s, membership was dropping to an average of 3.8 million in 1931. There was in fact no renewed alliance of employers and unions in 1930 and the days of the *Zentralarbeitsgemeinschaft* were far away.

Attempts by Brüning's minister of labour Stegerwald in November 1930 to produce an agreement between employers and unions about a simultaneous wage and price reduction ran into the sand. The more intransigent employers saw in the crisis a chance to end national wage bargaining and the influence of the unions altogether. The *Vereinigte Stahlwerke*, for example, made determined attempts by early 1931 to operate on the basis of plant wage agreements. The unions clung to such protection as the established corporatism of the state still offered them. There was also a perceptible loosening of the bonds between SPD and the ADGB, for the party in its impotence was of decreasing use to the the unions. Neither employers nor unions had, however, in the winter of 1930–1 any alternative to offer to Brüning's austerity programme and accepted it, though without much enthusiasm.[32]

A MORE ASSERTIVE FOREIGN POLICY: DISENGAGEMENT FROM THE STRESEMANN ERA; RADICALISATION AT HOME: THE RISE OF THE STORMTROOPERS AND OF POLITICAL VIOLENCE

In the apparent absence of an alternative Brüning used the crisis not only to achieve a restructuring of the economy and the constitution, but also to make progress in eliminating the remaining features of the Versailles system. Once Allied forces had left the Rhineland it became clear that the Brüning government was moving away from the policies of Stresemann and the spirit of Locarno. It had been an objective of Hindenburg and Schleicher in appointing Brüning that such a shift should occur. Their aims were fully shared by the chancellor, though here, as in his move towards presidential government, caution was his watchword. There could be no question of an immediate abandonment of the Young Plan, the focus of the national opposition's demagogic campaign, for this would have destroyed Germany's international credit. The Brüning government, however, never tired of telling their western interlocutors that the radicalisation of German politics was the consequence of insufficient concessions made to Germany over the years. Immediately after the results of the September 1930 election became known Brüning instructed his foreign minister Curtius,

who was at Geneva, to stress that ten years of fulfilment policy
had remained inadequately rewarded and was marked 'by the
gravestones of some of our best leaders, like Erzberger and
Rathenau' and that 'a nation's capacity for suffering had limits'.

In May 1930 Briand presented a major new initiative for the
development of institutionalised political and economic collaboration in Europe within the framework of the League of Nations.
The German government gave it the cold shoulder and merely
put the emphasis on the obstacles it would present to German
revisionist aims. Much more emphasis was put on Germany's
right to equal treatment in the on-going negotiations about
disarmament. Under Brüning less interest was taken in relations
with the West and Germany's eastern concerns received more
attention. The one area in which government credits became
more freely available in 1931 was for the purpose of financing
exports to the Soviet Union.

An even more important initiative was the promotion of a
German–Austrian customs union, first mooted during a visit by
the Austrian chancellor to Berlin in February 1930. The project
had the support of Curtius and of Bülow, who succeeded
Schubert, Stresemann's right-hand man, as state secretary in
June 1930. When news of the German–Austrian customs union
leaked out prematurely in March, it was a bombshell which
seriously damaged Franco–German relations.

As the internal situation in Germany became more intractable
in the winter of 1930–1 the achievement of a spectacular success in
the demolition of Versailles loomed larger in Brüning's calculations. If his policies were driving ever larger numbers of Germans
into the arms of the extremists and especially of the Nazis, then
something positive might yet emerge if it could be demonstrated
to the world that the maintenance of the Versailles system was no
longer possible.[33]

Whatever Brüning's long-term aspirations may have been for
constitutional reform at home and an end to Versailles and
reparations abroad, his immediate room for manoeuvre remained
painfully restricted. This was particularly evident in the circum-
spect way he dealt with Nazi violence. Severing, who had
returned as Prussian minister of the interior in October 1930,
and Wirth, the Reich minister of the interior, had between them
accumulated massive evidence that would have enabled action to
be taken against the NSDAP as an organisation hostile to the

republic. Yet action of this kind was sidetracked and Brüning preferred to take at face value Hitler's oath of legality given in late September 1930 at the trial of the three young Reichswehr officers from Ulm.[34] This oath was a major factor in establishing Hitler's personal status as a legitimate political figure and potential coalition partner.

It was on this basis that Brüning was able to include Hitler in his consultations following the elections of September 1930. At this interview the chancellor encouraged Hitler to continue his nationalist agitation as it would help the government in its long-term aim of achieving a final resolution of the reparations problem. Brüning's suggestion may have been mainly designed to impart a positive note to a first meeting that was otherwise mainly negative. Hitler's offer to despatch three members of his party into the cabinet was scarcely realistic. Nevertheless the chancellor kept his lines of communication to the Nazi leadership open and on the whole threw his weight against any rigorous measures designed to curtail Nazi agitation and violence. For example when Brunswick acquired a Nazi minister of the interior after September 1930 Brüning prevented a repetition of the action taken in the Thuringian case and the contributions to police costs in Brunswick were not blocked.[35]

In the meantime Groener and Schleicher had begun to modify the strong stand taken against Nazi infiltration in the Reichswehr which had led to the Ulm prosecutions. The Nazi movement and its paramilitary arm, the SA, were now so large that they constituted a sizeable element in that 'national' part of the population on which the Reichswehr had ultimately to rely. At the end of 1930 Hitler had still imposed a ban on stormtroopers taking part in officially sponsored military exercises. An SA man was a political fighter, according to Hitler, and should give no comfort of any kind to the political system he was aiming to destroy.

Relations between SA and party, both increasing dramatically in size, were, however, already becoming a problem and in January 1931 Hitler recalled Ernst Röhm to become the SA's Chief of Staff. Hitler's former protector was never likely to become a mere instrument of the Führer and the seeds were sown that led to the Night of Long Knives on 30 June 1934. For the moment, however, Hitler needed Röhm to control what was undoubtedly the most difficult element in his mass following. Yet the new SA leader was still an ex-army officer and it was natural that he should seek contact with the Reichswehr. In March 1931 he paid his first visit to Schleicher. With Brüning's agreement individual members of the SA began to be accepted into the *Grenzschutz*, the border guard in the eastern provinces.[36]

There were other straws in the wind that showed how difficult it was for the Brüning government to get away from the orientation to the right that had led to its establishment. In December 1930 Goebbels as Gauleiter of Berlin unleashed a campaign against the film of Remarque's book *All Quiet on the Western Front*, which was reviled as a calumny on the German soldier. The Nazi campaign culminated in the throwing of tear gas and stink bombs and the release of white mice into the cinema audience. Severing had appointed the redoubtable Grzesinski as Berlin police chief in succession to Zörgiebel. His deputy was Bernhard Weiss, a Jew, and these two men became prime targets of Nazi hatred during the next two years. Grzesinski mounted a police operation to enable the film to be screened without disturbance. Hindenburg was besieged with protests from the national opposition and the Brüning government threw its weight behind a move by the censorship authorities banning the film.[37] There is no indication that the chancellor personally disagreed with the ban, which had also been demanded by the Centre Party. This sequence of pressure, from the national opposition on the president and from him on the chancellor, was a persistent feature of the Brüning regime. To counterbalance such pressure the chancellor was also in frequent and friendly consultations with the Prussian government and the SPD leadership, but ultimately he was neither inclined nor able to concede much to them.[38]

In the spring of 1931 there was a sense, not merely that the economic slump might itself be bottoming out, but that in the arena of high politics matters were not going too badly for Brüning. The adjourned Reichstag reassembled on 3 February 1931 for what turned out to be its last session of any length. The government managed to pass some important changes in the procedures of the assembly, which would in future curtail the ability of the anti-parliamentary parties to play havoc with the proceedings. In future proposals for expenditure had to be linked to measures to raise the appropriate revenue. Fictitious motions of confidence, such as the NSDAP had brought to flush out the SPD, could no longer be moved and there had to be a direct motion of no confidence. The right to interpellate was curtailed, so was the right to call for a vote by name, devices which had been misused to stall the progress of business. The president's power to stop a speaker was enhanced.[39] The members of the NSDAP and the DNVP thereupon declared a boycott of the Reichstag. Hypocritically the Nazi speaker accused the government of breaking the constitution and declared that his party would only return to prevent 'an especially cowardly measure by a majority hostile to the Volk'.

The exodus of the anti-parliamentary right eased the government's problems but also exacerbated the SPD's quandary. Groener, Schleicher and Hindenburg insisted that initial expenditure for a further battleship, *Panzerkreuzer B*, should be included in the 1931–2 budget. This item could only pass if the SPD abstained, for the right-wing parties were no longer present to provide a majority. Thus the SPD was again confronted with an agonising decision, either to cause the fall of Brüning or to vote for something which in the climate of constant spending cuts was even more difficult to justify to their followers than the expenditure on the previous battleship. The dilemma was further aggravated by more *Osthilfe* measures to help agriculture, which meant more spending on big estates as well as the higher food prices already resulting from the high agricultural tariffs. The concessions offered by Brüning in private discussions with SPD leaders were very limited and some, like the removal of tariffs on quotas of imported frozen meat, were subsequently defeated by the agricultural lobby.

After the passage of these measures by the end of March 1931 the SPD had also to agree to a further adjournment of the Reichstag until October. By this time the mood in the SPD was already so defensive that the revolt against these instalments of the toleration policy remained very limited. Nine SPD deputies disobeyed the party whip and some later formed a separate party, the Socialist German Workers Party (SAP). Like the splinter movements on the right its impact remained minimal. The KPD made the most of the SPD's uncomfortable position. When the Reichstag took its prolonged holiday there was, however, a feeling that the Brüning government had shown considerable powers of survival.[40]

Immediately after the departure of the Reichstag an emergency decree was promulgated by the president under article 48 to deal with political excesses. Notification had to be given of political meetings and these could be prohibited if there was a threat of civil disobedience or the likelihood of the state, its institutions or of religious communities (this was a response to the Nazi's anti-Semitic and the KPD's atheist propaganda) being held in contempt. There were further provisions against the carrying of weapons and the wearing of uniforms. This decree was the result of pressure from Severing and the Prussian government.[41]

An immediate consequence of its promulgation was that the smouldering tensions within the Hitler movement between the party and the SA came to a head. Röhm's appointment as SA chief had not resolved the divergencies of view about the SA's role. As both organisations mushroomed in size the sociological differences between their memberships became more marked. This was the time when the party had a great influx of middle-class members, who were climbing on to the bandwagon but whose stay as members, though not necessarily as voters, was often brief. The SA had a greater tendency to attract working-class recruits, especially among the young and the unemployed. Among its leaders there were many from the opposite end of the social scale, former Freikorps officers and even one of the Kaiser's sons, Prince August Wilhelm, known as Auwi. Among the educated and even among intellectuals the 'new barbarians' appealed to the *nostalgie de la boue*.

In the SA the revolutionary element in Nazism, the nihilistic activism and the ideology of struggle for its own sake was most highly developed. By the same token there was discontent with Hitler's policy of legality and his courtship of the middle classes and even the élites. The role of the SA in the promotion of violence and terror as a means of compelling attention, loyalty and submission could be seen most clearly in large cities. In Berlin a battle had developed in the depressed working-class districts like Neukölln and Friedrichshain between the KPD and its now illegal *Rote Frontkämpferbund* and the SA for control of streets and taverns. Here the majority of youths and men were unemployed and spent most of their time in their 'fortress', with rival gangs of communists and Nazis fighting for control. Popular parlance had it that there were many 'beefsteaks', brown on the outside, red on the inside, or that there were many floaters between the street gangs of extreme right and left. It was in this ambience that a particularly brutal SA leader, Horst Wessel, who lived with a prostitute, was murdered in January 1930. Goebbels promoted him into a major martyr and the Horst Wessel song became one of the two national anthems of the Third Reich.[42]

When the Brüning government at last took notice of the endemic street violence with its decree of March 1931, Hitler, in pursuit of his legality tactics, had to tread warily, even though he unleashed a ferocious propaganda onslaught against the alleged violation of the constitution. Walter Stennes, the SA leader in Berlin and the eastern provinces, for long dissatisfied with the drift of Hitler's policy, broke into open defiance and for the moment it looked as if there was a serious revolt in the SA. As so often before and after, Hitler managed to quell the rebellion with his personal prestige and charisma. Stennes was excluded from the party. The incident gave hope, however, to all those who felt the Nazi movement could not possibly maintain its cohesion. These hopes were reinforced when almost simultaneously with the Stennes revolt Frick was forced to resign from his post as Thuringian minister of the interior and education by a vote of the DVP. Hitler seemed to be in difficulties as a revolutionary as well as in his pretence of legality. This pretence was, however, given more credibility by Hitler's apparent resolute squashing of the Stennes revolt.[43]

THE BANKING CRISIS OF 1931: FROM RECESSION INTO SLUMP; THE POLITICAL CONSEQUENCES

The momentary sense of relief which the Brüning government experienced in the spring of 1931 proved very short-lived. The catastrophic outcome of the elections of September 1930 had not changed the chancellor's strategy. He would continue to repair Germany's public finances through deflation and sit out the rise of political extremism. For the moment he would adhere to the Young Plan, but he was already looking towards ending reparations altogether. Success abroad would enable him to ride out political turmoil at home and the rising violence at home could be used to extract more concessions abroad. It was hardly a strategy beyond making the best of a bad job, whatever Brüning may have claimed in his memoirs.

Events were about to make his balancing act even more precarious. In part the growing difficulties were themselves the consequence of misjudgments by the German government. The proposal for the Austrian–German customs union, becoming public in late March 1931, quickly proved to be one such misjudgment. The Austrian *Creditanstalt*, the largest Austrian bank, collapsed on 11 May 1931. There may have been a link between this crash and the publication of the customs union proposal. The resulting row made it difficult to deal with the collapse and with the subsequent banking crisis in Germany. France was the one country in a position to alleviate the banking crisis, but French opinion was now thoroughly disenchanted with the conciliatory policy championed by Briand. French help in the Austrian crisis and later in the German banking crisis became conditional on the abandonment of the customs union, on the suspension of plans for *Panzerkreuzer B* and on an end to German revisionist demands. These were demands which the Brüning government could scarcely concede, given its dependence on Hindenburg, Groener and Schleicher. The reaction from the national opposition would have been violent.[44]

In the meantime the German budgetary position had deteriorated so much that another bout of emergency measures appeared to be imperative. Throughout May 1931 the cabinet and officials were working on measures which were promulgated over the president's signature on 5 June. They were devastating in their severity. There was a further reduction of 10–12 per cent in unemployment insurance benefit, coupled with a reduction of the period during which benefit was available. This also entailed a reduction in the payment to those who had run out of insurance benefit and were relying on so-called crisis payments. The third line of support for the destitute was payment from local authorities, but these were now also subject to rigorous control. In early 1931 over two and a half million unemployed had been in receipt of insurance benefit, but by the summer this number had been more than halved. On the other hand those in receipt of crisis payments and local authority welfare payments had risen from around 1.6 million in the winter of 1930–1 to over 2.6 million by October 1931. By the summer of 1932 insurance benefit recipients numbered less than a million, while the two other categories had risen to about 3.7 million. These figure give some impression of the enormous pressure of destitution to which the growing army of unemployed were now subjected.

The emergency orders also provided for another reduction of 4–8 per cent in the salaries of public employees. There was further assistance to agriculture, some measures for price reductions and some modest proposals to increase employment.[45] In order to make these draconian decrees slightly more palatable the government coupled them with a strong attack on the 'tribute payments' which had been undertaken on assumptions not borne out by events. This proved to be as ill-advised a step as the Austrian customs union. Rumours about such an initiative, coupled with the Austrian collapse, led to an outflow of foreign funds from German banks amounting to about 600 million marks in two weeks. The crisis coincided with a much-heralded visit by Brüning and foreign minister Curtius to Chequers for conversations with MacDonald and Henderson. Invitations for this visit had gone out in March and were a signal that the British government was eager to show its support for the German chancellor. Brüning had allowed the Franco–German relationship to cool, but he was anxious to maintain the good will of the Anglo–Saxon powers. Neither the Austrian customs union, about which Britain, like France, had not been consulted, nor the demand for a further revision of reparations had been enthusiastically received by British ministers. There was, however, some understanding for Brüning's difficulties, highlighted by hostile demonstrations from dockworkers when he embarked for his British trip at Cuxhaven.[46]

On Brüning's return journey the Nazis orchestrated attacks on the chancellor all the way back to Berlin, where the survival of his government was now in doubt. Neither the support of the DVP nor the SPD could any longer be taken for granted and the recall of the Reichstag was being demanded. The council of elders (*Ältestenrat*), made up of representatives of the parties and headed by the President of the Reichstag, had the power to recall the plenary session. In the next eighteen months of adjournments and dissolutions it assumed a crucial importance. Brüning had to fight hard with the political parties to prevent the recall, by making it clear that it would entail his resignation. The possibility that the government might fall accelerated the withdrawal of funds from the German banking system.

As so often before and after during his chancellorship, Brüning turned the severity of the crisis to his advantage. It became something of a habit with him to claim that this very severity was not unwelcome to him. The leaders of the SPD had no alternative than to continue to back him. In conversations with Kaas, the Centre Party leader, Dingeldey, the new leader of the much diminished but still crucial DVP, and Vögler, the director of the *Vestag*, he showed a far-reaching willingness to move further to the right, in ending reparation payments, in reconstructing the cabinet and in changing the system of compulsory arbitration. Kaas and Vögler expressed doubts as to whether the crisis could be mastered without dictatorial methods, but on this Brüning did not commit himself.[47]

Although an immediate governmental crisis was avoided the economic crisis moved on relentlessly. The Reichsbank had to raise its discount rate from 5 to 7 per cent, a destructive move at a time of deep recession. There was some alleviation when it became apparent that Brüning would survive and even more so when on 20 June the President of the United States declared a reparations moratorium. Tense negotiations with the French government about the moratorium produced a renewed acceleration in the outflow of foreign money from German banks. Within days of the final agreement on the moratorium there followed the collapse of the Danatbank, Germany's largest private bank, on 13 July. Another major bank, the Dresdner, was also in difficulties. These problems were due not only to the collapse of industrial undertakings such as *Nordwolle*, a big textile firm, but also to the financial difficulties which had engulfed local and municipal authorities. Germany's chronic capital shortage, the difficulties in balancing the Reich budget and the reliance on short-term foreign credits were coming home to roost. There had to be a banking holdiday, a further rise in the discount rate, exchange control and a standstill on foreign credits. The future of the capitalist system was in doubt as never before.[48]

The crisis in the summer of 1931 represented another drastic diminution in Brüning's freedom of action. It only became apparent now that this economic slump was of unprecedented severity and that the self-correction in which it was possible to believe in the spring was not happening. It was therefore only from this point on that the alternative of a countercyclical policy could come under serious consideration. The cards were heavily stacked against such a policy, either in the form of more credit creation by the Reichsbank, or through a devaluation of the mark, or through fiscal stimulation.

Job creation, other than of a minimal or self-financing kind, was only possible through more credit or higher budget deficits, which required more credit. Credit creation by the Reichsbank was severely limited by international agreements dating back to the Dawes Plan and continued under the Young Plan. The international community had eliminated by law the possibility of the German government escaping from its obligations as it had done during the great inflation. Domestic fear of inflation was only reinforcing these limits on the Reichsbank's freedom of manoeuvre.

There was in fact greater flexibility in the Reichsbank after the banking crisis of July 1931: for instance the coverage for bank notes by gold or hard foreign currency was fixed at 40 per cent, but dropped to 25 per cent. The discounting of bills became more flexible and by 1932 several low-key credit creation schemes were in operation, for example an *Akzept & Garantiebank* to support the banks, and credits to finance exports to the Soviet Union.

Some of the techniques used by Schacht in the early years of the Nazi regime have their origins in the Brüning period. Until reparations were positively ended in 1932 great care had to be taken in such matters, otherwise another crisis such as occurred in the summer of 1931 might recur and the negotiations to end reparations might founder. The improvement of the German export performance by means of the general downward pressure on prices was a further aspect of Brüning's economic strategy. The chancellor kept emphasising that reparations were no longer being paid for out of foreign loans, but through the German export surplus. He hoped that the reluctance of the depressed foreign markets to accept more German goods would generate further pressure on the western governments to put an end to the reparations tangle. This part of Brüning's strategy was dealt a body blow when the British pound was devalued in September 1931 and other currencies followed suit. It was politically and psychologically almost impossible for the German government to devalue the mark. The result was that German exports, other than those to Russia, collapsed in the winter of 1931–2. At 1928 prices exports dropped from nearly 13 billion marks in 1931 to 8.1 billion in 1932.[49]

Without domestic credit expansion job-creation schemes were narrowly circumscribed and this was recognised in the various plans put forward. The Brüning government had itself appointed a commission under the former long-serving minister of labour Heinrich Brauns to investigate employment creation. The commission's suggestions, published in the spring of 1931, comprised a shortening of hours, some public works at artificially pegged wages and a form of labour service.

After the July banking crisis there was an increasing interest in reflationary measures, both within the government and bureaucracy, in industry and in the trade unions. It remains true that Brüning himself was very reluctant to take any risks with reflation and preferred to wait until reparations were finally out of the way. Some have ascribed this rigidity to his austere personality, but the objective pressures to stick to financial stringency were substantial enough.

In Brüning's view the budgetary problems he had inherited from the Müller government had themselves been caused by the spending policies adopted in 1926 by Reinhold, the finance minister, to pull out of the recession of 1925–6. They had been aggravated by Köhler's policy of raising civil service pay in 1927. Schäffer, as state secretary in the finance ministry involved in the discussions about reflation and work creation, shared the chancellor's view that extreme caution was required and that the lack of balance in the Reich finances could spark another banking crisis. In any case modest anti-cyclical measures taken in the autumn of 1931 or later could not possibly become effective until well into 1932. The countervailing downward pressures remained strong: for example the government's own massive support for agriculture was inhibiting the downward pressure on consumer prices, while the credit squeeze on local authorities was keeping the construction industry in deep depression. The economic argument thus shifts back to the political.

Counter-cyclical measures, however slight, might have had a psychological and political impact, but Brüning was temperamentally opposed to anything he considered purely cosmetic. For his strategy to be successful he needed time and it was running out. Two crucial dates were known all along, the end of Hindenburg's term of office and the Prussian Landtag elections, both due in April 1932. Brüning hoped that the premature Reichstag elections of 1930, which turned out to be so disastrous, would yet have the silver lining that the next elections could be postponed till 1934.

In the meantime the one big political and psychological coup within his reach, the end of reparations, loomed ever larger in his calculations. This potential success was, however, losing its capacity to assuage the profound bitterness of the people. For the man in the street the priority was now instant relief from economic hardship and the national opposition was looking for foreign victories greater than the end of reparations. Against such expectations any success in foreign policy Brüning was likely to offer would avail little.

Even before the economic situation had become critical in the summer of 1931 ominous political developments were being hatched. As early as February the Stahlhelm had initiated the procedure for a people's request proposing changes in the Prussian constitution that would lead to a premature dissolution of the Prussian Landtag and the end of the hated 'Marxist' government. At this stage the Stahlhelm was not on a course of outright hostility to Brüning and moderates like Seldte did not want a frontal assault on the 'Hindenburg' chancellor. The Stahlhelm was, however, trying to play a leading role in the national opposition and promoted huge patriotic rallies, at Coblence in October 1930, at Breslau on 31 May 1931, at which not only the external foe, France and Poland, but also the enemy within, the Marxist parties and the Prussian government, came under strong attack.[50]

The Prussian referendum campaign was another such enterprise and Hugenberg and the DVP felt compelled to support it. So did Hitler, but with characteristic independence and scant regard for his allies. By June over six million signatures had been collected for the Stahlhelm proposals, but this was well below the vote of the three supporting parties in September 1930. Since it could hardly be expected that the Prussian Landtag would commit suicide in accepting them the prospect of a referendum rolled on inexorably. It took place on 9 August 1931 and was therefore in full swing during the banking crisis. Almost at the last minute the KPD, prompted by Stalin and Molotov, decided to support the referendum, thereby making common cause with the NSDAP. Braun and Severing were attacked by the KPD as tools of Brüning and trailblazers for fascism.

The Communist rank-and-file in the working-class districts of Berlin and other big cities did not solidly follow the suicide tactics of their leaders and communist support of the referendum may well have scared off some right-wing voters. 37.1 per cent of those entitled to vote, 9.8 million voters, voted yes. The combined DVP, DNVP and NSDAP vote in September 1930 had been about 30 per cent. It was not sufficient to turn the Stahlhelm proposals into law and force an immediate election in Prussia, but it was hardly a ringing endorsement of the Braun government, which had pulled out all the stops to get a high abstention rate.[51]

There was other evidence for a further rapid advance by the Nazis since the previous September. At the beginning of May 1931 they obtained 27 per cent of the vote in Schaumburg-Lippe, the smallest of the German states with an electorate of less than 35 000. It was, however, significant, that in a state where the combined left-wing vote remained at over 50 per cent, the NSDAP at a stroke had become much the largest party of the right. In Oldenburg a fortnight later the Nazis got 37.2 per cent of the 272 000 valid votes, compared with 7.5 per cent in 1928. Here they had an early following among poor farmers, as in Schleswig-Holstein, but a five-fold increase was dramatic.

Even more threatening for Brüning in the summer and autumn of 1931 were the signs that his standing with Hindenburg was declining. In the early part of the year Groener, Schleicher and Brüning had been in close harmony. Schleicher had usually used his influence with Hindenburg on behalf of Brüning when the president was under a barrage of attacks from quarters such as East Elbian landowners or the Stahlhelm because the policies pursued by 'his' chancellor annoyed them. Hindenburg and his entourage were, however, above all concerned not to get too exposed and the more isolated Brüning became the more difficult they found it to sustain him. Schleicher and to a lesser extent Groener increasingly convinced themselves that there was much that was positive in the Nazis and even in Hitler personally. They thought that Hitler's professions of legality could be taken at face value and that, for example in squashing the Stennes revolt, he had shown that he could stand up to the revolutionaries in the Nazi movement.

Particularly in East Prussia collaboration with the SA in the *Grenzschutz* was developing well. The commander of the East Prussian Military District was General von Blomberg, previously chief of the *Truppenamt*, the disguised general staff, in the ministry of defence. His chief of staff was Colonel von Reichenau, a man unusual in his unorthodoxy and political cynicism among traditional army officers, and his chaplain was Ludwig Müller, an outright Nazi sympathiser. Here an anti-Schleicher faction was forming that was to play a crucial role in ensuring Reichswehr acquiescence in the Nazi take-over in 1933.

Schleicher himself was developing a view about the management of Germany's crisis that hinged on 'taming' the Nazi movement, a *Zähmungskonzept*. Hitler and his party were to be brought into government, so that they would have to share in the responsibility for unpopular measures. There would be a gradual transition to a permanent authoritarian regime built round the presidency, backed by the army and dedicated to a final rehabilitation of Germany from the Versailles system. In the autumn of 1931 Schleicher was still committed to Brüning, who, because of his standing abroad and his successes in the reparations problem, remained indispensable. Schleicher was, however, looking forward to early changes in the Brüning government, in particular to the departure of Wirth and Curtius, that would give it a more rightward orientation. Dependence on the SPD would be reduced and the Prussian government, long a thorn in the flesh of the Reichswehr and with its days in any case numbered, would eventually be eliminated through constitutional reform.

Schleicher's ideas were regarded with sympathy by Hindenburg and his circle, with whom the general was in constant contact through the field marshal's son Oskar. Groener was probably slightly more concerned to observe the constitutional niceties than Schleicher, but at this stage their relationship was still untroubled. From time to time Schleicher saw his patron Groener as Brüning's successor and as the man round whom the new system would be built. An estrangement had, however, arisen between Hindenburg and Groener when in 1930 the latter, a widower, contracted a second marriage considered unsuitable for an officer. The early arrival of a baby, maliciously nicknamed Nurmi after the Finnish long-distance runner, the sight of the general pushing a pram in the streets of Berlin, all this damaged Groener's image and also weakened Brüning's position.[52]

The industrialists were another element whose support for Brüning was wavering and through the DVP they could directly affect the future of the government. There had for some time been a faction within the RDI and DIHT (*Deutscher Industrie-und Handelstag*) who had favoured making common cause with the national opposition and calling for an immediate end to all transfer payments and reparations. Such views had most support in heavy industry, but even in the *Langnamverein* and the *Ruhrlade*, the inner cabinet of major industrialists, a deliberate rush into catastrophe did not have a majority. Neither Hugenberg nor Hitler was attractive to the leading industrialists but Brüning was also regarded as having failed to deliver the goods. He had not decisively ended the social burdens of Weimar and was still too dependent on the SPD.

In September 1931 feelings among employers in the Ruhr coal industry were once more exacerbated by the way in which Stegerwald, the minister of labour, handled the compulsory arbitration procedure. On 30 September the RDI issued a strong declaration putting the blame for the crisis on the way economic and social policy throughout the Weimar period had undermined the proper operation of the capitalist system. Not capitalism was at fault, but the uneasy compromise between socialism and capitalism that had prevailed since 1918.[53] At this moment the economic position was heavily overshadowed by the British devaluation of the pound. Three days later the industrial wing of the DVP forced a decision on the party to leave the government and to support a motion of no confidence in the Reichstag, about to reconvene.

The position of Curtius, the foreign minister from the DVP, had already become untenable. He was largely held to blame for the ignominious failure of the Austrian customs union, declared incompatible with the treaties by the International Court of Justice. Brüning used the occasion to carry out the long anticipated reconstruction of his cabinet and to get rid of men like Wirth, regarded as too left wing. The chancellor himself took over the foreign ministry and Groener added the interior to the defence portfolio. A number of industrialists, among them Vögler and Silverberg, refused an offer to join the cabinet, but Warmbold, a member of the I.G.Farben board, became economics minister.[54]

The move to the right did not conflict with the chancellor's underlying convictions, but he knew that without the counter-weight provided by the SPD and the Prussian government he himself would become dispensable. Otto Braun and his finance minister Höpker-Aschoff had earlier put forward a proposal for the long-discussed merger between the Prussian and the Reich government, the two sides of the Wilhelmstrasse, which would also alleviate the critical financial situation in Prussia. Braun would join the cabinet as vice-chancellor and Severing as minister of the interior. This proposal would have pre-empted the likely end of the Braun–Severing government after the Prussian Land-tag elections in April 1932. There was much support for this solution among the upper echelons of the Reich and Prussian bureaucracy and it was often ascribed to Hermann Pünder, Brüning's faithful state secretary in the chancellery.

Opposition by Schleicher and Hindenburg scuppered this attempt to balance the imminent rightward reconstruction of the Brüning cabinet by additions from the left. The future of the Prussian government and with it the control of the police in three-fifths of Germany was vital in a situation increasingly drifting towards civil war. The efforts of Severing to put some damper on Nazi violence were weakened by pressure from Hindenburg and Schleicher, often supported by Brüning, to proceed with even-handed severity against the KPD. On the day of the Prussian referendum, 9 August 1931, two police officers were killed by Communists. One of the killers was the later security chief of the DDR, Erich Mielke. A ban on the KPD came under serious discussion at this point, for Groener and Schleicher felt that the KPD's threat of revolution was a real one. In fact neither in resources nor organisation could the KPD come anywhere near to mounting a revolutionary rising. Much of its strength was among the weakest section of the working class, the unemployed, and KPD membership was in constant flux. Communist verbal violence served the authorities as an alibi for not taking action against the more real danger from the Nazis. For large numbers of voters the communist threat was a plausible reason for supporting Hitler. As the Nazi tide rose there were rumours that the police in Berlin and other cities were being infiltrated by Nazis and were no longer reliable.[55]

Brüning's reluctance to back strong action against the Nazis by Severing and others was also due to the need, within a few months, of prolonging the Hindenburg presidency if possible without an election. Brüning hoped to enlist the support of Hugenberg and Hitler to that end and immediately after the cabinet changes had a further meeting with Hitler. Even at this late stage the chancellor felt that he could treat the Nazi leader as a potentially useful element in his own strategy of survival. In the longer run he expected the irrational national socialist upsurge to subside again.

Brüning had also helped to arrange on 10 October 1931 an audience for Hitler and Göring with Hindenburg, the first meeting between the field marshal and his eventual successor. This proved to be counterproductive, for the president, now aged 84, took a dislike to the Bohemian corporal, as he habitually called him. It was a mixture of Prussian Protestant hauteur and deep-seated instinct. Hindenburg's reluctance to install Hitler in the chair of Bismarck was to impose at least some delay on the Nazi arrival in power.

Hindenburg's personal aversion was not shared by some of his fellow generals. A month earlier the chief of the Reichswehr, von Hammerstein-Equord, had had a meeting with Hitler. Hammerstein was every inch a laid-back grand seigneur and never gave up his strong distaste for the brown movement. Nevertheless, after four hours with Hitler his conclusion was that that he wanted really the same things as the Reichswehr, only at a different pace. In January 1932 Groener was reported in the minutes of a meeting with senior officers as giving this description of Hitler: 'Sympathetic impression, modest, decent individual, with best intentions. In appearance the keen self-taught type . . . . Intentions and aims of Hitler are good, but he is an enthusiast, ardent, diffuse. Minister has entirely agreed with him to support his aims for the good of the Reich. Minister has expressed very strongly to the *Länder* that Nazis have to be justly treated, only excesses to be fought not the movement as such . . .'[56]

THE HARZBURG FRONT: BRÜNING'S BELT TIGHTENING

The formation of the second Brüning government on 9 October 1931 was seen by the national opposition as a great victory and it was undoubtedly a further stage in Brüning's decline. Two days later there took place at Bad Harzburg a great rally of the national opposition, the outcome of many weeks of careful planning by Hugenberg. In spite of all evidence to the contrary, stretching from the referendum on the Young Plan to that on the Prussian constitution, the obstinate DNVP leader believed that he could achieve a *Sammlung* of all the national groups opposed to the moderate course of Brüning and in favour of an all-out attack on Marxism and parliamentarism at home and on Versailles abroad. With irredeemable arrogance Hugenberg believed in his own capacity to control such a coalition.

Bad Harzburg in the *Land* Brunswick was chosen as the venue for the rally because a coalition of the DNVP and the NSDAP was in power here. A broad spectrum of the national opposition was represented ranging from members of former ruling houses, including the Hohenzollerns, through senior military figures, including Seeckt, now a Reichstag deputy for the DVP, the leaders of the Stahlhelm, the agrarians led by the chairman of the *Reichslandbund* Count Kalckreuth, Pan-Germans like Heinrich Class, some prominent industrialists to the Nazi leaders headed by Hitler. It was, however, noticeable that some well-known industrialists and DVP politicians were absent.

Even more noticeable was the fact that Hitler played his own game, ostentatiously snubbing all others, for example by leaving the reviewing stand after the SA formations had finished marching past. The strength of Hitler's position was indisputable: election after election had shown that his following had increased dramatically from its already strong showing in September 1930. Only he among those gathered at Harzburg commanded the big battalions and he was now also seen as a serious negotiating partner by Hindenburg and Brüning. Thus the Harzburg front was no more real than all previous attempts to achieve a *Sammlung* on the right.

The most immediate threat to Brüning from the Harzburg meeting came from a speech made by Schacht. During his remarks the former president of the Reichsbank referred to the mark as 'a currency which no longer serves the normal exchange of goods, but has the sole purpose of hiding the illiquidity of our financial institutions and of the public purse'. This blatant attempt to undermine the fragile German credit evoked a strong rebuttal from Dietrich, the finance minister. Schacht was by this time clearly banking on a takeover by Hitler and he was soon to set up a bureau to act as liaison between industry and the Nazi movement. The incompetence displayed by Luther in dealing with the banking crisis had produced a demand that he be replaced by Schacht. The latter's recall would, however, have entailed a fundamental shift in policy: a right-wing government with Hitler, an end to reparations and a reliance on autarky. At this moment Brüning regarded Schacht as more dangerous than Hitler.[57]

The chancellor was able to survive the meeting of the Reichstag from 13 to 16 October with a narrow majority, almost entirely supplied by the Economics Party, while most of the DVP now voted against him. The SPD stuck to its toleration policy, for Harzburg had made it only too clear what the alternative would be. The Reichstag was then adjourned till 23 February 1932. As Germany entered what everybody knew would be a very hard winter the situation was dominated by two pairs of major factors: the deteriorating economy and rising unemployment, accompanied by the further growth of the extremist parties, particularly the NSDAP. The political framework within which these explosive developments had to be dealt with was about to be affected by the other pair of factors, the end of the Hindenburg presidency and the Prussian Landtag elections, both due in April 1932.

Brüning continued to stick to his deflationary strategy and to justifying it by making a virtue of necessity. He still hoped that there was enough time for his strategy to show results. He continued to believe that the Nazi mass movement was a temporary phenomenon and that for the time being Hitler was a man with whom he could do business. He was therefore disinclined to use the full rigour of the law against the Nazis. This would have been difficult in any case, given the increasing tendency of the Reichswehr and Schleicher to avoid confrontation with the SA and the determination of the president to appear even-handed. As for Hindenburg's term of office, Brüning hoped to prolong it by a two-thirds vote in the Reichstag, mainly supplied by the right, but the support of the SPD would also be essential. If this should prove impossible, he hoped that Hindenburg could at least become the agreed candidate of the right in an election by the people.

As for the SPD, Brüning believed it had no alternative to toleration and that its one remaining bastion, the Braun coalition in Prussia, would come to an end with the Landtag elections. His own party, the Centre Party, would then be released from its alliance with the SPD. Already the possibility of forming a Centre–NSDAP coalition was under discussion in various *Länder*. Brüning was fully aware of the dangers of handing unrestricted power to Hitler, a situation that might well arise if, in the absence of Hindenburg, Hitler was elected president. This is broadly the essence of Brüning's views which emerges from his memoirs.

One may well be sceptical that his more far-reaching plans for a constitutional monarchy affected his immediate strategy. It also seems unlikely that the SPD leadership secretly agreed with his strategy to the extent he claims. The overriding weakness of Brüning's policy continued to be that the first pair of factors, economic catastrophe accompanied by the revolutionary dynamism of Hitler, were not recognised as an overwhelming threat, to be dealt with as an absolute priority.[58]

In the autumn of 1931 there could be no doubt about the massive support Hitler was attracting. A week before Brüning reconstructed his cabinet there had been elections in Hamburg, a bastion of the left. In 1928 the SPD and the KPD together had over 50 per cent of the vote, but now the SPD dropped from 35.9 per cent to 27.8 per cent, while the KPD rose from 16.6 per cent to 21.9 per cent. At the other extreme the NSDAP rose from 2.2 per cent to 26.2 per cent, while the bourgeois parties from the DDP to the DNVP were decimated. The Centre Party was never a force in Protestant Hamburg. On 15 November 1931 in the Hesse Landtag elections, which the Nazis had not contested in 1927, there was a vote of 37.1 per cent for them. The SPD dropped from 32.6 per cent to 21.4 per cent, the Centre Party from 17.7 per cent to 14.3 per cent, while the KPD rose from 8.6 per cent to 13.6 per cent. A Centre–NSDAP coalition became a real possibility and this had repercussions for Brüning's tactics at this point.

Ten days after these elections a Nazi defector handed to the Frankfurt police the so-called Boxheim document, which contained detailed plans for a Nazi seizure of power, including the instant death penalty for all breaches of 'discipline', draconian powers for local SA leaders, rationing of food and commandeering of property. The author was Werner Best, a young Nazi lawyer in Hesse and later a Gestapo chief and governor of Denmark. Officials in the Reich ministry of justice dealt with this matter with conspicuous caution and delay. It was another instance of the policy under which, aided and abetted by the Brüning government, the courts maintained the fiction of Nazi legality.[59]

A fortnight later the Berlin police chief Grzesinski wanted to arrest and deport Hitler during a press conference the Nazi leader had called at his Berlin headquarters near the chancellery, the

Hotel Kaiserhof. Brüning and his state secretary Pünder dissuaded Braun and Severing from taking any action. It was becoming evident that in the higher ranks of the bureaucracy a growing number of officials were now influenced by the possibility of an eventual Nazi takeover.[60] The judiciary was more than ever inclined to mete out much harsher treatment to the left than to the right.

In September 1931 members of the Berlin SA unleashed what came to be known as the Kurfürstendamm pogrom, when Jewish or Jewish-looking passers-by and restaurant-goers were brutally attacked. The trial of the SA men was obstructed by constant objections to the Jewish connections of the judge and of members of the jury. It took courage to stand up to the intimidation that was now widespread. The leader of the Berlin SA Count Helldorf, who became the capital's police chief in 1933, but was eventually executed for his part in the plot of July 1944, got off with a fine after a prolonged delay. Against this the editor of the *Weltbühne*, Carl von Ossietzky, was given an eighteen months' prison sentence for revealing military secrets, when he had merely written about the well-known military links with the Soviet Union. The anti-republican prejudices of many German judges were aggravated by the economic pressure they, like other public servants, experienced from successive salary cuts. They were also aggrieved by having to adjudicate in so many cases that were basically political. Those who were openly identified with the republic were already in a dangerous position.[61]

By early December 1931 the Brüning government was once more compelled by the deteriorating financial situation to consider a further package of emergency decrees, the fourth major batch. The third package in early October had received less attention and did at least contain some sweeteners, such as easier access to unemployment benefits for the young unemployed. There was now less of a consensus about the continuation of the deflationary course. In the discussions on credit creation Schäffer, the state secretary in the finance ministry, had postulated something like a Keynesian multiplier effect. Wilhelm Lautenbach, a senior official in the economics ministry and sometimes called the German Keynes, gave a lecture on job creation on 1 December 1931, but his approach to the expansion of credit was cautious. At least three ministers, Dietrich (finance), Stegerwald (labour) and the newly appointed Warmbold (economics), were now interested in job creation and counter-cyclical moves. Warmbold even threatened resignation over the unrelievedly deflationary nature of the December package. There was an economics advisory council, which Brüning had appointed partly to produce some consensus about measures to deal with the crisis, partly to help in prolonging Hindenburg's term as president. Here Silverberg, the deputy chairman of the RDI, presented a detailed plan involving a credit creation of one to two billion marks. The trade unions' plan for anti-cyclical work creation, known as WTB Plan after its three authors Woytinski, Tarnow and Baade, was about to be launched, but did not become a subject of debate until the new year.[62]

It was still relatively easy for Brüning to stick to his rigid course of holding out (*durchhalten*) in strict economy until the reparations problem was solved. The subject could so easily be politicised: here irresponsibility, as in Schacht's speech at Harzburg, inflation, autarky, defiance of all international ties; there Brüning's sober realism and honesty.

At the centre of the fourth package of emergency decrees of 8 December 1931 there was a lowering of wages, public salaries and of prices and rents. All wage and salary settlements were reduced to the level of January 1927. If they exceeded the 1927 level by more than 10 per cent they were reduced by 10 per cent; if they had not been reduced since July 1931 they were reduced by 15 per cent. A large range of public salaries, pensions and benefits were reduced by 9 per cent. There was to be a similar reduction of prices and rents and a reduction from 8 to 6 per cent of most interest rates.

It was a most far-reaching interference with the operation of the market, but it was doubtful whether the overall effect would not amount to a further reduction of consumer purchasing power. In fact no expansion of German exports could be achieved by this attempt to reduce German costs even further, given the actual rise of the external value of the mark following Britain's abandonment of the gold standard in September. There was still an almost complete consensus that there could be no devaluation of the mark until the reparations problem was finally solved. The room for manoeuvre may have been very limited, but there was in this package and its presentation not a whiff of a psychological counterblast to the massive onslaught on the increasingly fragile Brüning regime that came from the national opposition and particularly from Hitler. The chancellor was simply piling on the misery.[63]

And what misery it now was. At the end of February 1932 the number of unemployed was officially put at 6.128 million. It was estimated that nearly another million and a half were unemployed but not covered by the official statistics. In all three systems of relieving poverty, the unemployment insurance, crisis subvention (*Krisenunterstützung*) and welfare payments by local authorities entitlements and level of payments had been constantly reduced by successive emergency decrees. As a higher proportion of the unemployed fell into the third net, local authorities tried to shunt them back into the two other nets by arranging short periods of employment, sufficient to recover some entitlement from the insurance institute or the crisis subvention. The Reich Unemployment Institute reduced its expenditure between 1931 and 1932 by nearly 50 per cent, a particularly bizarre by-product of the emergency decrees. Its surplus of 372.8 million marks in 1932 could have supported three-quarters of a million unemployed.

Yet somewhere around a third of the unemployed received no support at all. Among the great mass of unemployed industrial workers, who were normally the breadwinners for their families, this produced all the familiar symptoms of apathy, withdrawal, despair, loss of self-respect and skill. The depth of the German depression also produced some strange and alarming by-products, hundreds of thousands wandering with their families through the country, looking for work or support. There were gangs of young urban unemployed, with leaders, insignia and molls. Their politicisation, by the KPD or the NSDAP, was only marginally successful.

The cuts in welfare benefits had a levelling effect on the unemployed, but there was still a considerable difference between those in work and the unemployed. It was one of the factors feeding the struggle between the KPD and the SPD. Yet even those in employment suffered severe reductions in their standard of living, partly through the reductions imposed by the emergency decrees, even more through short-time working. The reduction in the cost of living only partially compensated for the reduction in nominal income. If nominal hourly wage rates, nominal weekly wages and real wages are taken as 100 in 1928, then the first had dropped to 80, the second to 69 and the third to 86 in 1932. In the same period industrial production dropped from 100 to 58.7. The trade unions reported nearly a quarter of their members on short-time in 1932, with compensating wage adjustments. White-collar employees, independent artisans, shopkeepers and similar groups were sometimes as much affected by the fear of unemployment and of proletarianisation as by the actual experience of it, but their situation was bad enough. The annual turnover of the footwear trade dropped by 39.8 per cent, of the textile trade by 41.3 per cent and of furniture retailing by 48.4 per cent between 1929 and 1932. Germany headed the suicide league in 1932: there were 260 suicides per million inhabitants, against 155 in France, 133 in the United States and 85 in Britain.[64]

HINDENBURG'S RE-ELECTION

The evidence of social catastrophe inexorably undermined Brüning's position in early 1932 and made his efforts seem increasingly irrelevant. He used all his skill and energy to prolong the Hindenburg presidency only to find that in the end the eighty-four-year-old president abandoned him. In a series of meetings with Hitler and Hugenberg he hoped to get their agreement to a prolongation of Hindenburg's term by a two-thirds majority in the Reichstag. In conversations with the SPD leaders he asked them not only for their support, but also to keep it secret until he had persuaded the national opposition to give their support. The SPD's position was by now so weak that they had to swallow almost anything to avoid a Hitler presidency. Brüning found that Hitler's and Hugenberg's price for agreeing to prolong Hindenburg's term was his own resignation and the immediate dissolution of the Reichstag and the Prussian Landtag. Brüning even offered his resignation, so as not to stand in the way of Hindenburg's continuation in office, but the president refused it with the words: 'My dear, good friend, don't do this to me!' In the course of these exchanges Hitler, with typical hypocrisy and effrontery, mounted the high horse of defending the constitution against Brüning's alleged plan of circumventing it.[65] There was thus no alternative to promoting Hindenburg's candidacy for election by the voters. Given the president's sensitivity about being separated from his friends and normal supporters among nationally minded Germans this became a very delicate operation. Brüning tried hard to promote a broad coalition of support for Hindenburg but there was never any chance that either Hugenberg or Hitler could be persuaded to endorse the field marshal.

A few days after Hindenburg's candidature had been confirmed, Hitler's own was announced to a jubilant crowd by Goebbels in the Berlin Sportpalast. For a time many had hoped that Hitler might be prevented from contesting the presidency by the fact that he did not possess German nationality. This obstacle was removed by his appointment to an official position in the Brunswick legation in Berlin by the Nazi minister of the interior of that *Land*. Such an appointment entailed the conferment of German nationality and by this subterfuge Hitler was, in the nick of time, able to contest the presidency. His candidature destroyed any hope of a joint candidate being promoted by the deeply divided Harzburg front.

The Stahlhelm and DNVP now put up their own candidate, Duesterberg, the second leader of the Stahlhelm. Hindenburg was thus the candidate of the left and centre and it was for the same reason easier for the SPD to instruct its voters to support him. In spite of Brüning's best efforts the field marshal had become the candidate of those who had in 1925 opposed him. Hindenburg sent a long letter of justification to von Berg, the former chief of the emperor's civil cabinet. Berg had supported Hindenburg's candidacy and had been attacked for it in the newspaper of the German nobility. In his letter Hindenburg justified his continuing support for Brüning, denied that he was opposed to the formation of a right-wing government or that he was the candidate of the left or of a 'black–red' coalition. It is not difficult to discern in this letter the deep discomfort Hindenburg felt at having been pushed into a battle against those with whom he had politically most in common.[66]

The first presidential ballot was fixed for 13 March 1932 and the beginning of the campaign coincided with a another brief meeting of the Reichstag. The speeches showed the confusion and the shift of fronts which the imminent battle for the presidency was producing. Goebbels launched a bitter attack on Hindenburg: 'Tell me who sings your praises and I will tell you who you are! Praised by the Berlin asphalt press, by the party of deserters . . .' and here he was drowned by cries of protest. The most effective reply came from the young SPD deputy Kurt

Schumacher: 'The whole national socialist agitation is one long appeal to the inner beast [*der innere Schweinehund*] in man. If we respect anything in national socialism, it is only that for the first time in German politics it has succeeded in the total mobilisation of human stupidity . . .' Ulbricht for the KPD called to the German worker: 'never again Hindenburg, and not only: down with Hindenburg politics, but down with Hindenburg-social democracy . . .' Groener in his speech tried to justify his order issued at the end of January which virtually rescinded his orders of 1929 and 1930 barring Nazis from the Reichswehr and associated organisations. Again it amounted to an acceptance of the legality of national socialism and put the SA on a par with the *Reichsbanner*.

The Brüning government escaped from this sitting with a majority of 24, obtained mostly from the Weimar coalition parties. While the Economics Party, which was in any case rapidly losing its following to the Nazis, supported the chancellor, the Landvolk and the DVP opposed him. The latter were now hopelessly split. In response to the growing disenchantment of the heavy industry wing with Brüning, the chairman, Dingeldey, had frantically tried to remain linked with the Harzburg front, but in the end supported the Hindenburg candidature.[67]

The election campaign showed the desperate confusion into which the German political scene was plunged at a moment of deep social crisis. The moderate left and the Centre Party had at least only one candidate to campaign for, but in the only broadcast Hindenburg delivered on the eve of polling he again emphasised that he was not the candidate of the left and expressed regret that he was being misunderstood by some of his former voters and old comrades. Brüning campaigned vigorously on behalf of the president whose support for his chancellor was beginning to waver. Only when praising Hindenburg did Brüning command any emotion, otherwise his message of salvation through economy and realism could offer little hope. Joint campaigning by the parties backing Hindenburg was difficult. Often it was emphasised that support for the field marshal did not mean support for Brüning, let alone for the 'Marxist' SPD.

For Hitler this was the first of six great national election campaigns during the next twelve months (two presidential ballots, the Prussian Landtag and three Reichstag elections) which he fought with a huge mass movement behind him and as a clear candidate for total power. He had entered the presidential race with considerable hesitation the more it became obvious that Hindenburg would be his principal opponent. Against the field marshal and in the prevailing confusion of camps he was far from certain that he could win. Nevertheless the two presidential campaigns showed all the typical characteristics of Nazi electioneering: saturation coverage, limitless verbal violence, a combination of pretended legality and massive threat that has never been surpassed in cynicism. There was injured innocence when opponents expressed outrage at Nazi violence; there was open glorification of SA barbarism as marking the end of effete democracy and of the whole of decadent bourgeois civilisation. Particularly in the short campaign preceding the second ballot Hitler himself used an aeroplane to give an impression of irresistibly modern dynamism and to enhance his own image as the messiah coming down from a higher sphere.

The two minor candidates, Thälmann for the KPD and Duesterberg for Stahlhelm and DNVP, could not realistically hope to win, but they aimed to reduce the vote for Hindenburg. For Thälmann this had the purpose of showing his ability to draw voters away from the SPD. For Duesterberg the object was to bring about a second ballot, when the less extreme conservative-nationalist camp might yet be able to influence the choice of candidate.

On the first ballot Hindenburg missed by only 173 000 votes out of nearly 38 million cast the 50 per cent necessary to secure election. The voters of the Centre Party and the BVP had shown remarkable discipline in voting for the Protestant Prussian field marshal, but then he appeared to be still linked with their leader Brüning. Even more remarkable was the way the SPD constituency had swallowed their doubts and followed the party line. Thälmann, with 13.2 per cent of the vote, had done better than the KPD in 1930, but not as well as the communists had done at some of the intervening Landtag elections. He did well in the party's traditional strongholds like Berlin, Düsseldorf East and Saxony and central Germany.

It could hardly please Hindenburg that Hitler had run him so close on his own home ground of East Prussia, where the vote divided 43.8 per cent to 34.5 per cent. Hitler's showing of 30.1 per cent was a disappointment to many Nazis, but it hardly justified the complacency expressed in some republican quarters. The

NSDAP had scored a much higher proportion of the vote than in September 1930, but not as high as in some recent regional elections. It is interesting to compare the result with the predictions made by Pünder in his diary a week before polling. He estimated Hindenburg's total very accurately, underestimated Hitler by some two million votes and overestimated Thälmann by about the same amount.[68]

Duesterberg, the DNVP Stahlhelm candidate, had scored a disappointing 6.8 per cent, just over two and a half million votes, and now withdrew. A united right-wing candidature proved as elusive as ever. For a moment it looked as if the Crown Prince might assume that role, a prospect that might have induced Hindenburg to withdraw. The proposal was vetoed by the ex-Kaiser and the last chance of a Hohenzollern restoration disappeared. Thus the contest was between the imperial field marshal and the Bohemian corporal and it caused much comment that the Crown Prince declared openly for the latter. It was symptomatic of the extent to which the traditional, conservative opposition to the 'system' was now prepared to throw in its lot with Hitler. The *Reichslandbund* declared for Hitler, because, in spite of all the costly help it had been given, agriculture in the non-Catholic regions was now strongly opposed to Brüning.

Hugenberg gave his followers no instructions for the second ballot. The consequences of his courtship of Hitler had been devastating, but he could still not bring himself either to admit his mistake or to give up his total opposition to Brüning and to what remained of the republic. Industrialists were still divided in their attitudes. Nazi supporters, particularly Fritz Thyssen, were working hard to convert disillusionment with Brüning into positive support for Hitler. Thyssen had been the organiser of the famous meeting of the Düsseldorf Industry Club on 26 January 1932, which was addressed by Hitler. Most of the industrial leaders were, however, not yet prepared to support a Nazi take-over and officially the RDI, as represented by its chairman Carl Duisberg, had backed Hindenburg. It was significant that soon after the first presidential ballot Paul Reusch, the director of the *Gutehoffnungshütte*, had a meeting with Hitler and offered him the benevolent neutrality of newspapers under his control for the second ballot. Other industrial leaders in the *Ruhrlade* and *Langnamverein* were coming to the view that the replacement of Brüning by a right-wing government no longer

dependent on SPD toleration could only be accomplished in
cooperation with Hitler. Schleicher's *Zähmungskonzept* was thus
shared by many industrialists.[69]

The second presidential ballot on 10 April 1932 saw a drop in
electoral participation of over a million votes, but at 83.5 per cent
it was still very high. Hindenburg obtained 53 per cent and had
700 000 more votes than on the first ballot. Hitler's vote was 36.8
per cent, 6.7 per cent and two million more than four weeks
earlier. Thälmann's vote dropped by 1.3 million to 10.2 per cent.
For Hindenburg personally this result was a disappointment, for it
strengthened the feeling that many of his former friends had
deserted him. A detailed analysis shows that many former
Duesterberg supporters and probable members of the Stahlhelm
switched to Hitler, even though Duesterberg had urged them to
back Hindenburg. On the first ballot Hitler had done better than
Hindenburg only in Pomerania, Schleswig-Holstein and Chem-
nitz-Zwickau. In the latter case this result was due to the high
vote for Thälmann of nearly 20 per cent. On the second ballot
Hitler added East-Hanover, Merseburg and Thuringia to the
constituencies where he beat Hindenburg. There is evidence that
some Thälmann voters also switched to Hitler, an indication that
there was a pure protest vote which could be very volatile.[70]

The result caused much satisfaction among committed republicans. The Centre Party and the BVP were heartened by the
steadiness of their supporters. In staunchly Catholic Lower
Bavaria, for example, Hindenburg got over 70 per cent and
Hitler less than 30 per cent of the vote. In Catholic areas
Hindenburg had an even more marked preponderance among
women voters. Commitment to the Catholic church remained
stronger among women than among men. For the SPD it was
claimed that the two presidential ballots showed signs of
rejuvenation.

At the end of 1931 the Reichbanner had taken the initiative in
the formation of the Iron Front (*Eiserne Front*), an attempt to beat
Nazi demagoguery at its own game. Hitler's psychological
warfare and assault on the emotions was to be matched by
similar methods. The Reichsbanner was already tending to adopt
uniforms, a khaki shirt, and its formations could be used to convey
an impression of strength and dynamism. A countersymbol to the
swastika, three parallel arrows, denoting the trinity of SPD, trade
unions and Reichsbanner, the political, economic and physical

power of the working class, was introduced. It could be used very effectively to disfigure swastikas. Höltermann, now de facto leader of the Reichsbanner, proved himself an inspirational speaker at mass rallies.

It was originally intended that the Iron Front should, like the Reichsbanner, be a cross-party enterprise, but in fact it became simply an arm of the SPD. The party took over the political direction of the campaign, for, as always, the party bureaucrats were intensely suspicious of any rival movement and anything that might take on a life of its own among the rank and file. It was this bureaucratic conservatism, paired with an unreflecting residual faith in the Marxist predictions, that had made it so difficult for the SPD to react to the crisis and to arrive at an adequate assessment of the Nazi danger. Nevertheless the Iron Front and the rallies promoted under its slogans during the presidential campaign gave rise to some renewed optimism.[71]

It was an illusion. Hindenburg did not regard himself as the candidate of the Weimar coalition and neither did many of those who voted for him. At best his re-election could be seen as some barrier to political extremism and some guarantee for the rule of law, and even this hope proved illusory within a year. Although Hitler had failed to win he had shown his capacity to mobilise an enormous and exceedingly diverse constituency. More than ever he had managed to promote simultaneously two fundamentally incompatible images, the conservative and the revolutionary. Ever larger numbers among the respectable sections of the population had seen in him their only option. At the same time he had appealed to the eschatological expectation among the dispossessed masses of a violent settling of accounts with the existing system and a totally new beginning. Even as the second presidential ballot was being held the chain of events had started to roll that was to bring the Brüning regime to an end within seven weeks.

THE BAN ON THE SA: BRÜNING'S FALL

During the presidential campaign Groener, in his capacity as Reich minister of the interior, had come under increasing pressure from several *Länder* governments to take action against the SA. On 17 March, four days after the first presidential ballot, Severing had ordered a search of Nazi buildings in response to persistent rumours that the SA was being held ready for a coup. The search did in fact confirm that the SA had been put into a state of alarm on the day of the vote. Other *Land* governments also wanted action, particularly the Bavarian, which, like the Prussian, was facing Landtag elections on 24 April. This pressure did not fit in with Groener's and Schleicher's policy of maintaining links with the SA and using it for national defence requirements. Nevertheless the evidence that the Nazis were planning to seize weapons allocated to the *Grenzschutz* and were spying on the police caused even Schleicher to feel that the pressure to strike against the SA could no longer be resisted.

The decision to take action was made at a meeting with Brüning on the day of the second presidential ballot. By then it had, however, become clear that many Reichswehr commanders were opposed to drastic action and as a result Schleicher had shifted his ground. He would have preferred to give the Nazi leadership preliminary warning that they should control and possibly dissolve the recalcitrant sections of the SA. Hindenburg also showed reluctance to take action that would subject him to fresh accusations from the right. Nevertheless he signed the decree dissolving the SA and its ancillary organisations on 13 April. Within two days the president wrote to Groener that evidence had reached him that organisations belonging to other parties might require the same treatment as the SA. He passed on material about the *Reichsbanner*, which had been sent to him, behind Groener's back, by Hammerstein, the commander of the Reichswehr. This correspondence was immediately handed to the press in order to demonstrate the president's concern for even treatment for left and right. It was becoming clear that even a slight move to the left by the Brüning cabinet was at once endangering the very basis of its existence, the support of Hindenburg and the Reichswehr.[72]

The Landtag election campaigns, which had been one of the reasons for the ban on the SA, took place on 24 April and produced the expected upsurge of the Nazi vote. In Prussia the NSDAP, which in 1928 had obtained 1.8 per cent and six deputies, now got 36.3 per cent and 162 deputies. The SPD dropped from 29 per cent to 21.2 per cent and their representation from 137 to 94. In Bavaria the Nazi vote rose from 6.1 per cent to 32.5 per cent, the SPD fell from 24.2 per cent to 15.4 per cent, but the BVP slightly improved its position and remained the largest party by a whisker. In Württemberg the Nazi vote rose from 1.8 per cent to 26.4 per cent, the SPD fell from 23.8 per cent to 16.6 per cent. In Hamburg, where only seven months had elapsed since the previous election, the NSDAP rose further from 26.2 per cent to 31.2 per cent, but the SPD vote rose from 27.8 per cent to 30.2 per cent, while the KPD dropped from 21.9 per cent to 16 per cent. Contrary to the national trend the DDP also rose from 8.7 per cent to 11.2 per cent. In Anhalt, with an electorate of just under a quarter of a million, the Nazis leapt from 2.1 per cent in 1928 to 40.9 per cent and formed the government.

In general these results confirmed that the Nazis had just about doubled their support since September 1930. They had done so mainly at the expense of the bourgeois parties, but there was also some drift from the SPD to the NSDAP. Apart from this most of the SPD losses had benefited the KPD. The Centre Party and the BVP had again shown themselves most resistant to the radicalisation of German politics. The mopping up of the smaller interest parties by the Nazis continued: the Economics Party, for example, dropped from 4.5 per cent in the Prussian Landtag elections of 1928 to 0.9 per cent in 1932. Even more striking was the decline of the DVP: in the Reichstag elections of 1930 it had still been able to obtain 5 or 6 per cent and even more in the Protestant areas of Prussia. Its total vote was now down to 1.5 per cent. The party had backed the Prussian referendum and the Harzburg front in 1931, Hindenburg in 1932. No wonder its voters were confused.

Brüning's calculation that his disastrous dissolution of the Reichstag in 1930 had at least given more time for his policies to achieve results was largely proved illusory by these elections. They rammed it home that his government no longer represented the will of the people. They could only confirm Hindenburg, Schleicher and others in their view that it was high time to replace Brüning with a more right-wing government, which must include the Nazis. Immediately following these elections there were meetings between Schleicher and Hitler and a whole web of secret contacts and negotiations. It became clear that Hitler's price was a revocation of the SA ban and new Reichstag elections. What he was prepared to give in return was much less precise: possibly the toleration of a right-wing government, similar to the toleration hitherto given by the SPD to Brüning.

In Prussia the Landtag elections did not lead to an immediate change of government. Before the old Landtag was adjourned it had adopted an important change of procedure, by which an absolute instead of a relative majority was required for the choice of a prime minister, if a first ballot had voted the incumbent out. This change made it impossible for the newly elected Landtag to choose a new chief minister, unless the KPD had been willing to bear the odium of installing a Nazi in that office by voting to reverse the procedural change.

Thus the Braun government was able to stay in office as caretaker government. The only alternative would have been a NSDAP-Centre Party coalition, but attempts to bring it about proved as elusive as they had done in Hesse six months earlier and as they were to prove in the Reich later. The mere fact that a black–brown coalition was now constantly on the agenda showed how Janus-faced political Catholicism had become. Its hostility to godless Marxism, a label indiscriminately applied to the SPD and the KPD, could be as significant as its condemnation of the racial doctrines of national socialism.

The Prussian government's hold on power was in any case now tenuous. Otto Braun's health was breaking down, his wife had been an invalid for years and a mood of resignation overtook him. He was a democrat and once the people had voted against him he could not go on. The SPD had already lost two of the positions of power it had once controlled, the presidency and a place in the Reich cabinet. Now a third position, a share in the control of Prussia, was about to be surrendered.

In Bavaria the situation remained more stable: the BVP minority government of Heinrich Held was able to carry on and was indeed one of the last bastions to fall to the Nazis in March 1933. It was a reversal of the situation in the early 1920s when Bavaria was the scourge of the republic and Prussia its mainstay.[73]

Only one factor now kept the Brüning government going, foreign policy. Reparations and disarmament were the two salient issues. Brüning's rigid persistence with deflation had been based on the assumption that he could convert the Hoover moratorium into the final end of reparations. Informed international opinion was gradually moving in that direction. The seven powers involved in the reparations question had set up a committee following the banking crisis of July 1931 to investigate Germany's immediate and long-term credit needs. Its report, published in

August 1931 and largely written by Sir Walter Layton, the editor of *The Economist*, analysed the whole international trade and debt problem and diagnosed that Germany needed and deserved long-term credits.[74] The implication was that these would only be forthcoming if the reparations problem was finally out of the way.

This gave the German government something to build on, but the path towards final cancellation was long and tortuous. At a cabinet meeting on 16 December 1931, in the middle of long and complicated negotiations and manoeuvres, Brüning said wrily and with considerable prescience that first Hindenburg's term would have to be prolonged and then the French and the Prussian elections in April or May would have to be awaited and 'after that I'll be pensioned off to Basle'.[75]

Attempts to call a meeting at Lausanne to decide a settlement in January 1932 were postponed, not least because the German government was in the middle of the attempt to prolong Hindenburg's term. Under the pressure of his domestic situation Brüning was already demanding a final suspension of reparations and a statement to that effect to the British ambassador in Berlin, Sir Horace Rumbold, was leaked to the press on 9 January 1932. The demand for total cancellation was at the centre of Brüning's last Reichstag speech as chancellor on 11 May. When the Lausanne meeting eventually did take place in June 1932 Brüning had fallen.

Disarmament was also becoming a key issue at this time in the relations between the major powers. The beginning of a disarmament conference in Geneva in February 1932 was the culmination of many years of international discussion. The more robust assertion of the German demand for the revision of Versailles under Brüning meant that Germany now took her stand on full equality of treatment in armaments. By implication this would involve a revision of Part V of the Versailles treaty. In 1932 Germany was not in a financial position to rearm to any major extent and equality of treatment would therefore mean the disarmament of others to the German level. In principle it might, however, mean that in the future there would no longer be any limits on German armaments.

Brüning's last trip abroad as chancellor and foreign minister at the end of April 1932 was concerned with the interlocking questions of reparations and disarmament. He did not return with the immediate success that he so badly needed and the result of the Prussian elections on 24 April may well have aroused scepticism abroad about his chances of survival and as well as fears about what would come after him. Brüning's tactics of using internal radicalisation to extract concessions from the entente powers was beginning to backfire. Nevertheless he still enjoyed great prestige abroad and this was undoubtedly a restraining a factor on those like Schleicher who were visualising the future without him. Brüning's survival at least as foreign minister seemed a possible way out.[76]

By the beginning of May 1932 the signs were multiplying that his position as chancellor was seriously undermined. Warmbold, the economics minister, resigned. He had opposed aspects of the fourth package of emergency decrees in December and advocated, though not with any great consistency, work and credit creation. Since he was a director of I.G. Farben, his departure was seen as another sign that industry was losing confidence in Brüning.

In mid-April a congress of the ADGB had pinned its colours to work and credit creation by adopting the essentials of the WTB Plan, which had been under discussion for several months. It was named after its three authors Woytinski, head of the statistical office of the ADGB, Tarnow, chairman of the woodworkers union, and Baade, a SPD Reichstag deputy and economist. It envisaged the creation of work by public bodies such as railways, post and local authorities, for about one million workers by the creation of about two thousand million marks of credit, ultimately through discounting by the Reichsbank. As there would be a considerable saving on unemployment pay the real creation of credit would amount to only 1200 million marks. The WTB Plan was not supported by the SPD, because leaders like Hilferding had reservations. The SPD was still afraid to back anything that looked inflationary. The Marxist diagnosis of the crisis also stood in the way. The WTB Plan, like the prescriptions of Keynes later, were attempts to cure a capitalist crisis, while in the SPD there was still a strong feeling that the crisis should be used to transcend capitalism.

Disagreements about work creation were only one sign that SPD and ADGB were less close than they had been: the ADGB was now demanding the end of reparations more stridently than the SPD, which was still committed to the policy of international collaboration. ADGB support for Brüning on reparations and SPD support on deflation could no longer help the chancellor much. The ADGB was increasingly weakened by unemployment, the SPD by its electoral decline, demonstrated most clearly in the Prussian elections. It is arguable that its failure to come out with a work creation plan aggravated the SPD's loss of votes, at a time when conquest of unemployment figured prominently, if unspecifically, in Nazi propaganda.

In a speech in the Reichstag on 10 May Gregor Strasser exploited the differences between the SPD and the ADGB on credit creation, supported it cautiously on behalf of the NSDAP and advocated a clutch of other work creation schemes, such as labour service and rural resettlement. He spoke of 'the anticapitalist yearning of the masses', a phrase which became famous. He followed this up by distributing 600 000 copies of a *Sofortprogramm* (immediate programme) with more specific proposals for work creation.[77]

The May meeting of the Reichstag precipitated Groener's fall. It fell to him to defend in the chamber the ban on the SA and the refusal to extend it to the *Reichsbanner*. He was ill and could not override the noisy barracking from the Nazi benches. In the Reichstag record Groener's speech reads well, but it seemed to be the universal impression afterwards that it had made the minister's position untenable. Schleicher indicated that he and other generals would resign if Groener stayed on as defence minister. With a second and even more important minister gone within a week there could be little doubt that the Brüning government must be nearing its end.

In an atmosphere of intrigue and in a situation dependent on the day to day reactions of individuals the exact course of events and the reasons for it will always remain somewhat obscure. Schleicher was the key figure and his perception that there had to be a right-wing government tolerated by Hitler rather than the present government tolerated by the SPD was being pushed to the point of implementation by the course of events. The ban on the SA had turned out to be a step that ran counter to this perception and Schleicher's talks with Hitler had convinced him that the ban had to be revoked if there was to be any deal with the Nazi leader. All this fitted in with the mood in the presidential palace where there was growing reluctance to cover the Brüning regime by signing more emergency decrees.

Schleicher's relations with the Hindenburgs, father and son, were close at this time and there is evidence that the son was influencing his father's mood of irritation over the false position in which he had been put and was continuing to be put by Brüning. The Hindenburgs may have feared that they would encounter social ostracism from their fellow Junker landowners. Hindenburg made it clear that he did not wish to work with Groener any longer. This put in question Groener's intention to stay on as interior minister, while giving up the defence ministry. Significantly Schleicher played for time when Brüning offered him the defence portfolio in succession to Groener.

For the moment the political situation was put into cold storage as the president departed for a Whitsun holiday on his East Prussian estate Neudeck. During his absence a further batch of emergency decrees were under discussion in the cabinet. Schlange-Schöningen, the Reich Commissioner for Eastern Aid and himself a Pomeranian landowner, had worked out proposals for the sale by auction, compulsory if necessary, of heavily indebted estates to the Reich. This land could then be used for resettlement, particularly of urban unemployed and their families. The idea of such agrarian resettlement of an urban population that could no longer find industrial employment was widely favoured as an antidote to the economic crisis. It had the support of Stegerwald and the ministry of labour.

When news of this proposed resettlement decree became public on 21 May it created a storm of indignation in agrarian circles. The Brüning government was accused of 'agrarian bolshevism'. Among letters of protest addressed to Hindenburg were one from Count Kalckreuth, president of the *Reichslandbund*, and from Baron von Gayl, the director of the East Prussian Land Society and about to become minister of the interior in the Papen government. When Hindenburg returned to Berlin he was determined not to sign the resettlement decree, but this would have entailed the resignation of Schlange-Schöningen, who had the backing of Brüning.

This clash provided the immediate occasion and opportunity for Brüning's dismissal. When Hindenburg received the chancellor on the morning of Sunday, 29 May, he drew a piece of paper from his pocket from which he read: '1. The government, because it is unpopular, no longer has my permission to issue emergency decrees. 2. The government no longer has my permission to make changes of personnel.' When Brüning returned the following morning to deliver the resignation of his government, his audience was delayed until 11.55 a.m. so that it could only last five minutes – at noon the president was in the habit of attending the changing of the guard. Brüning, already physically exhausted, took to his bed for several days, so great was his shock and bitterness at the treatment he had received. He felt that he had been brought down 'a hundred metres before reaching the goal'.[78]

The shock reverberated round the world, for even contemporaries could see that it was a fateful moment and might spell the end of the republic. Brüning was the last chancellor to govern with any kind of constitutional legitimacy. His personal integrity, intelligence and devotion to duty have never been doubted by men of good will. He was also secretive and sometimes paranoid. The debate about his place in history is focused on two main issues. The first question is whether his method of government by decree can be regarded as a last attempt to preserve a non-dictatorial political system or should be seen as a stepping stone to dictatorship. The second question is whether there were any realistic alternatives to Brüning's policies.

As to the first question, the crisis which occurred in the parliamentary system in 1930 cannot be laid at Brüning's door, nor did he display any indecent haste in resorting to presidential decrees. He did, however, take office on the clear understanding that the powers of the president under article 48 of the constitution would be at his disposal. This method of government was also in harmony with his most fundamental convictions and remained so throughout his life, even during his American exile. He believed that good government was the product of experts guided by objective considerations, while the crudities of mass politics could be only a regrettable distraction. In practice this made him dependent on Hindenburg and his unofficial advisers on terms which were never clearly spelt out. Ironically Hindenburg, Schleicher and others were in the end more sensitive than Brüning to the need for popular support and this was one of the main reasons why they abandoned him. In his memoirs Brüning gave so much prominence to his plans for constitutional reform culminating in a restoration of the monarchy, because without this aim his chancellorship looks even in retrospect like a series of ever more desperate improvisations. The only part of Brüning's constitutional plans that in fact had any immediate relevance were those concerned with changes in the federal structure of the Reich and especially with the relationship between Prussia and the Reich. Brüning did not pursue with any vigour the plans in the summer of 1931 to join the Reich and the Prussian governments, which would have amounted to something like a return to coalition with the SPD.[79]

The question about possible alternatives to Brüning's policies has usually been looked at mainly from the economic point of view. The argument is strong that before the spring of 1931 alternatives to deflation and balanced budgets were hardly on the agenda, while after the banking crisis of the summer of 1931 the room for manoeuvre was very limited. Economic alternatives cannot, however, be separated from political choices. An alleviation of the German economic crisis would have required a great deal of international collaboration. From the start Brüning headed in the opposite direction, away from the concept of international economic and political interdependence that had dominated the Stresemann era. The impractibility of the Young Plan was to be demonstrated, agricultural protectionism would not only meet the wishes of Hindenburg and the agrarians, it would also give Germany new weapons in rebuilding its influence in eastern and south-eastern Europe. The maintenance of intimate relations with Paris was no longer a priority: Briand's plan for Europe was spurned, the Austrian customs union pursued in a ham-fisted way. Better relations with France might have helped in dealing with the banking crisis of 1931. In January 1932 Brüning still gave priority to ending reparations even if it meant further delay in adopting reflationary measures. The more nationalist foreign policy pursued by Brüning was, however, built into the basis of his government and was part of the orientation to the right which had brought him to office.

Thus Brüning was caught in a series of vicious circles: he could not be too conciliatory abroad, because this was not acceptable to Hindenburg and the Reichswehr. But no matter how assertive he was, he could never satisfy the national opposition. As the crisis deepened, no foreign policy success could stop the political radicalisation at home. The policy of instrumentalising this radicalisation to achieve further concessions abroad became counterproductive, for foreign opinion feared that Brüning would fall and would be succeeded by an extreme nationalist government.

It seems unlikely that Brüning's vision of a return to semi-constitutional government in the imperial mode could have been successful, particularly when it had to be pursued in collaboration with a president like Hindenburg. But as the nominee and faithful servant of Hindenburg and those around him Brüning neither could nor would return to genuine parliamentarism. Weimar-style parliamentarism may have been too deeply discredited to survive, but without some form of popular imprimatur it was difficult to save even the rule of law, as Brüning aimed to do. His dependence on Hindenburg ensured that his attempt to do so was abruptly cut short.

THE PAPEN GOVERNMENT: THE PRUSSIAN COUP OF 20 JULY 1932

The shock with which Brüning's fall was greeted by the parties and the press shows how inadequately the pitfalls of the presidential regime were appreciated among those sections of the public that retained some loyalty to the republic and the rule of law. Berlin was full of rumours of intrigues, but it was nevertheless assumed that the chancellor would survive. He appeared to have the authority of a newly re-elected president behind him and the toleration of the Reichstag was again demonstrated in the votes of 12 May. In accounting for his fall much importance was therefore attached to the backstairs influences brought to bear upon the president by his landowning neighbours during his holiday at Neudeck. In particular the influence on Hindenburg of his old friend Elard von Oldenburg-Januschau was blamed. The presidential office was at pains to deny that he or some others frequently named had anything to do with the events leading to the fall of Brüning.[80]

The principal wire-puller was undoubtedly Schleicher. A week before the event Groener had commented perceptively to a friend: 'Schleicher is undoubtedly the *spiritus rector* . . . . Since I did not stick with him over the Nazi question, I spoilt his finely calculated game . . . . It is not the Nazis, whom he wants to help into power, but himself and that through Hindenburg, on whom he has through his close friend the son of Hindenburg the greatest influence . . . . But the old man has become difficult, as could be seen over the SA ban. He, the old man, dropped me without shame . . . and will do the same to Brüning, if he can only find a chancellor for the Hindenburg line – latest invention against

Schicklgruber [Hitler]. Schleicher trusts in his skill to lead the Nazis by the nose . . . . He takes a lot upon himself, but dares to do so because he has Hindenburg in his pocket . . . . Schleicher has long had the idea of ruling with the help of the Reichswehr and without the Reichstag. But his plans, which of course he now no longer reveals to me, are pretty obscure, and perhaps the Nazis are his superiors in cunning and duplicity'.[81] It was a clear-sighted view of the position on 22 May and predicts much of what would prove the undoing of Schleicher's strategy in the next eight months.

Schleicher's role as principal wire-puller was clearly revealed when the name of the next chancellor burst upon an unsuspecting public. Franz von Papen had sat upon the back benches of the Prussian Landtag as a Centre Party deputy, but his links with that party had been tenuous since he had refused, in 1925, to back his party colleague Wilhelm Marx for the Prussian premiership. Insofar as Papen could be said to belong to the Centre Party he was on the extreme right of it, but he had some influence through his control of the party newspaper *Germania*.

He belonged to the Westphalian Catholic aristocracy and through his wife was connected with Saar industry, which gave him a link with French industrial circles. It was widely remarked that he was a member of the exclusive Herrenklub and also a gentleman rider, a *Herrenreiter*. When someone said to Schleicher that Papen had nothing in his head, Schleicher replied 'he is no head, but a hat'.

The object of the unlikely choice was that with Papen a purely presidential cabinet would be formed, free of party ties, in which Schleicher himself as defence minister would wield the main influence. As soon as Papen was approached on behalf of the president, Kaas, the chairman of the Centre Party, made it clear to him that acceptance would mean exclusion from the party. Outrage at Brüning's treatment was running high in the party and governed its attitude during the next few months rather more than was wise. If Schleicher hoped that by picking Papen he would get support from the Centre Party he could not have been more mistaken.

Papen, however, obeyed the personal appeal of Hindenburg to take office. The cabinet he formed immediately became known as 'the cabinet of barons', but more relevant was the fact that none of its members were members of the Reichstag. Some were members of the DNVP, which they demonstratively left to emphasise their non-party position, even more never had any party ties. Four ministers – Neurath (foreign affairs), Gürtner (justice) Schwerin-Krosigk (finance) and Eltz-Rübenach (post and transport) – continued to hold the same office under Hitler. Since this cabinet could not count even on the toleration of the present Reichstag, it had to be dissolved immediately. The explanation, that it no longer corresponded with the will of the people, sounded implausible coming from a government with virtually no popular base. The elections were postponed to the latest permissible date, 31 July.

The first of Hitler's demands was thus met, the second, the lifting of the SA ban, would follow within ten days. The toleration offered in return meant virtually nothing, for it had no longer to be given in Reichstag votes.

The lifting of the SA ban meant that the capacity to terrorise the streets was fully restored to the Nazis. They treated it as a triumph and as proof that their drive to power was now unstoppable. Some of the *Länder* governments, such as Bavaria, which had taken the initiative in calling for the ban in April, tried to keep some restraint on Nazi violence by prohibiting the wearing of uniforms. Even this was revoked by another emergency decree from the Reich government. The *Länder* governments tamely accepted the position and the Prussian government, already aware of plans to send in a Reich commissioner, had never taken a strong position. It was clear that the policy of avoiding confrontation with the Nazis, long practised under Brüning, was now carried a step further. Gayl, the minister of the interior, declared in a cabinet discussion: 'In the longer run it will be impossible for the police to fight on two fronts, against the KPD and the NSDAP. From this point of view the lifting of the ban on uniforms and the total integration of the national socialists into the state was essential.'[82]

There was a big gulf between what the Papen government could do in practice on the basis of its slender support and the large claims it made as a new form of presidial government. Even in his first speech on the radio the new chancellor had uttered phrases which could only sound ominous to the republican parties and carry a challenge to the left. He accused all postwar governments of having promoted state socialism and a welfare state which had sapped the moral forces of the nation. He vowed

to put a stop to the moral disintegration of the people, which had
been aggravated by class war and cultural bolshevism. He talked
about the subversion of all cultural life by atheistic Marxist
thought.

Around the Herrenklub there had been much talk of a 'New
State', no longer based on the ballot box, parliaments and parties,
but vaguely corporatist, aristocratic-élitist, an authoritarian third
force between democracy and totalitarianism. Edgar J. Jung, one
of Papen's close collaborators, who was murdered on 30 June
1934, had written a book which categorised democracy as the rule
of the inferior and diagnosed its decay and replacement by a 'New
Reich'. The periodical *Die Tat* proclaimed similar ideas. The so-
called *Tatkreis* was close to Schleicher and generally seen as the
ideological inspiration of the Papen regime. Hans Zehrer, the
editor of *Die Tat*, had written in the May issue, when Brüning was
still in office, that 'the present government is in its inner meaning
so much in harmony with the German character, that the
enduring features of the future authoritatively based state are
already preponderant. The path will not be back to the old
parties and parliaments . . . . It will lead further in the direction
in which Brüning has already been forced. Germany is on the way
to a non-liberal, authoritarian form of government, which is
removed from the western and Roman principles of parliamentarism or dictatorship.' Carl Schmitt remained the most intellectu-
ally powerful protagonist of these visions.[83]

It was never likely that the Papen government, deprived from
the moment of its inception of almost any vestige of support, could
fulfil such ambitious, confused and insubstantial aims. Coherence
was lacking from the beginning, for Schleicher's main concern was
the military aspect of neutralising or absorbing the Nazis, while
Papen's priority was constitutional reform. The reality was that
the government had to go ahead with the emergency decrees
already prepared by Brüning. Because of the time lost the
measures were even more severe than planned by Brüning: the
period of entitlement to unemployment benefit was cut from
twenty weeks to six instead of thirteen. The level of support given
by all forms of income subvention was limited to the level of 1927.
In spite of Hindenburg's protest already made to Brüning, cuts in
support for war widows and orphans and for the war disabled
were implemented. The eastern settlement proposals were
suspended, but the new government professed its adherence to

the principle of resettling the unemployed. There were minor work creation schemes. The decrees reinforced the feeling on the left that this was a reactionary government intent on declaring war on the workers.[84]

On reparations and foreign policy generally Papen was able to reap where Brüning had sown, but the domestic benefits he derived from this were no more tangible than they had been for his predecessor. The reparations conference met at Lausanne on 16 June. Papen went to it with plans to offer the French a military alliance with an anti-bolshevik flavour in return for cancellation of reparations, recognition of Germany's right to equality of treatment in military and security matters, and abrogation of article 231 of the Versailles treaty, the war guilt clause. Papen's pro-French orientation, influenced by his industrial connections, was one of the reasons for the reserve even conservative elements in the national opposition displayed towards him.

Edouard Herriot was now back as French prime minister, after elections at the beginning of May, which had shown a swing to the left. This gave the Lausanne conference a better chance of success, but Papen did not get anywhere with his more ambitious schemes. There was, however, a final settlement of the reparations problem. After an interval of three years Germany would become liable to a last payment of three thousand million marks, to be discharged by the issue of bonds, but this sum was never paid.

Even this end of reparations aroused criticism in the German nationalist press, but mild approval in liberal and left-wing papers. Thereafter a much harder line was taken at the disarmament negotiations in Geneva, partly because Schleicher now demanded it on behalf of the Reichswehr in the cabinet, partly because such posturing helped in the imminent Reichstag elections. Just a week before the elections the German delegation withdrew from the negotiations. It was a tactic which eventually paid off, for in a declaration dated 11 December 1932 the British, French and Italian governments affirmed the principle that Germany should have equality of treatment within a system which offered security to all nations. By this time Schleicher was chancellor, but the real beneficiary was Hitler.[85]

The end of reparations impinged only marginally on the bitter and violent German electoral campaign. Schleicher had suggested that the cabinet should carry on with its tasks as if there was no election on 31 July, but the contest which he had light-heartedly precipitated showed up the dangerous isolation of the government he had sponsored.

On the left the 'cabinet of barons' was opposed with the utmost vehemence. For the SPD the release from the policy of toleration raised hopes of electoral advantage. Among the rank and file there was a strong feeling that this was the moment for a 'unity front'. This never had any realistic chance given the entrenched positions of both the KPD and the SPD. There were some contacts at local level, some calls for unity from intellectuals like Albert Einstein and Käthe Kollwitz, some initiatives from the ADGB. The KPD could not depart from its 'social-fascist' line and would not have been allowed to do so by Moscow. Unless this line had been dropped the SPD could hardly soften its anti-communist stance. The SPD was also constrained by its continuing determination to uphold what remained of its Prussian bastion. Both parties had to be concerned to restrain those among its followers who were too eager to cooperate with the other left-wing Party. The divided left thus remained condemned to near-impotence. This did not stop the Papen government from professing, even in its internal discussions, to see the KPD as a threat greater than the Nazis.

The government received only minimal support from the bourgeois parties. The Centre Party and BVP remained strongly hostile, although there were some, including Adenauer, who would have liked a more positive attitude towards Papen. Efforts to bring about a union of bourgeois parties continued and they were backed by industrialists like Reusch. The big obstacle was still Hugenberg, who controlled the only party of any consequence left in this part of the political spectrum. Concentration of what were by now small splinter parties, the DVP, the Economics Party and the *Staatspartei*, the former DDP, also proved as elusive as ever and the only concrete result was a junction of lists between the DNVP and the DVP. Hugenberg had not been consulted when members of his party joined the Papen government and the support he gave to the government in the election campaign was lukewarm. He criticised aspects of the Papen emergency decrees but approved of the removal of the Prussian government on 20 July.[86]

All these manoeuvres mattered much less than the attitude of the Nazis. Hitler had no intention of being associated with the Papen government and its unpopular emergency decrees and the withdrawal of the ban on the SA did not soften his attitude towards Papen. Inside the Nazi Party there were differences of emphasis, not too obvious to the public. This was the period when Gregor Strasser was at the height of his influence and was undertaking a far-reaching reorganisation of the party's structure. He was preparing the NSDAP for a gradual takeover of state power by turning the party's structure into a microcosm paralleling the state's macrocosm.

A more logical intermeshing of the party's regional structure, the Gauleiters, with its functional affiliates, for example Darré's agricultural apparatus or the NSBO (*Betriebszellenorganisation*, works cells intended to infiltrate the unionised workers), was created. Strasser's idea of a gradual takeover of power was somewhat along the lines practised by communist parties in Eastern Europe after the Second World War. Strasser was widely regarded as the second man after Hitler and had many links with industry, the *Tatkreis*, the trade unions and Schleicher. Many considered him the most constructive of the Nazi leaders, in contrast to a sheer demagogue like Hitler, but to others he retained a vaguely left-wing profile. Hopes of taming the Nazis came to be largely based on Strasser.

In fact Hitler always remained fully in control and could allow Strasser to improve Nazi organisation without surrendering any of his authority as Führer. He and most Nazi leaders, particularly Goebbels, were convinced that events were not pointing to a gradual approach to power, but that a campaign of relentless dynamic propaganda would bring the party to power by winning a majority. Hitler's own role was still focused on a propaganda crusade with no holds barred. Maximum verbal aggression was combined with minimal substance. Everything was devoted to obtaining the greatest emotional response; so that, for example, a normal staple of Hitler's rhetoric such as anti-Semitism was now less prominent, for the 'Jewish question' was not the main concern of the moment for the mass audiences he was addressing.

Two regional elections in June 1932 may well have confirmed him in the view that he could take Germany by storm. On 5 June the Nazis won 49 per cent of the vote in Mecklenburg-Schwerin, where they had obtained 4.1 per cent three years earlier. There was an electorate of just over 450 000 in this state. In Hesse, with an electorate of nearly a million, the Nazis had 44 per cent of the vote on 19 June, when seven months before they had had 37.1 per cent. Thus the ferocity of the Nazi drive for power continued unabated in the election campaign, unrestrained by any undertakings of toleration that Schleicher and Papen thought they might have received from the Nazi leader.[87]

The Papen government had itself given a powerful impetus to the near-revolutionary violence that accompanied the election campaign by rescinding the ban on the SA. It was, however, this violence that gave the government the pretext for the coup against the Prussian government on 20 July. It came hardly as a surprise, for ever since Papen's accession there had been rumours that a Reich commissioner would be sent in. Since it had lost its majority in April the Braun–Severing government had shown signs of being resigned to its eventual demise. The possibility that it might be replaced by a NSDAP–Centre Party coalition, which might give the Nazis control over the Prussian police, had already led Brüning to prepare plans for a takeover.

Such plans were yet another version of the long-running projects for a reform of the Reich–*Länder* relationship or of the even broader aim of changing the Weimar settlement in its entirety. The thrust of such projects varied widely. A change in the Reich–Prussia relationship could have been a way of strengthening the Brüning government from the left and finding a way back to something like a great coalition. It could equally well have been a way of clinching the more rightward orientation of the Reich government and getting rid of the hated Weimar coalition government in Prussia. In the hands of Papen it was the latter rather than the former and some saw it as a reassertion of the hegemony of a Junker-dominated Prussia.

The Papen cabinet's approach to what would in effect be a major breach of the constitution was marked by a reluctance to risk a formal breach of legality that was characteristic of these final months of Weimar. There was always the fear that anything that was not legally watertight might lay the government open to a serious reverse in the courts. Gayl, the minister of the interior, managed to overcome the hesitations of his colleagues by reporting an incident involving Severing's state secretary in the Prussian ministry of the interior, Wilhelm Abegg. It was reported that Abegg had received two leading Communists and had appealed to them to restrain KPD violence in order to prevent a Nazi takeover or the sending of a Reich commissioner to Prussia. News of this interview was carried to Gayl through Rudolf Diels, an official of the Prussian interior ministry, who was to become the first head of the Gestapo the following year. The use Gayl made of this intelligence in the cabinet shows how exclusively the real danger to the state was now perceived as coming from the KPD, even though its paramilitary formation, the *Rote Frontkämpferbund*, had been illegal since 1929. The spying activities of Diels showed how far the loyalty of the Prussian bureaucracy had become undermined.[88] Many officials were preparing to leave the sinking ship of the Braun–Severing regime.

The final excuse for putting the plans for the Prussian take-over into action was provided by 'bloody Sunday' at Altona, a part of Hamburg, on 17 July. It was caused by a provocative march of SA and SS through working-class districts where the KPD was the mainstay of local self-defence. The Altona troop of the SA was notorious for its violence and its capacity to provoke was reinforced by the fact that some of its members were former KPD supporters. Eighteen civilians were killed, but only three policemen were injured.

Since the lifting of the ban on the SA 99 people had been killed and 1125 had been wounded in Germany, most of them in Prussia. All this could by no means be laid at the door of the Prussian government and the Prussian police. In fact if the warnings of Severing and others had been heeded over the years the battle for the streets might never have assumed the importance it had by 1932. For the immediate aggravation of the situation the Papen government itself must bear the main responsibility.[89]

The question of whether Papen's Prussian coup could or should have been resisted has been hotly debated. In retrospect it looks like the last occasion when a show of force on behalf of the republic and of democracy might have been possible. The main weapon would have had to have been a general strike, which had helped to defeat the Kapp Putsch in 1920. Twelve years later, with a third of the German labour force unemployed, this was a blunt weapon. The word to use it, also the command to activate the *Reichsbanner*, was never given from the top. There can be no doubt that the decision to give in without resistance was another blow to the morale of the republican forces. By the day of the coup it was almost too late to do anything. Broadly based defensive measures also involving the South German governments would need to have been prepared.

The one concrete countermove, an action brought in the *Staatsgerichtshof*, the highest German court, was in fact supported by the South German governments. When it returned its verdict on 25 October it to some extent vindicated the Braun government. The Reich government could temporarily take over functions of the Prussian government, but that government was still entitled to represent Prussia in the Reichstag, the Landtag, the Reichsrat and in the other *Länder*. The concrete consequences of this verdict were minimal, for in the meantime the real republican defenders, for example Grzesinski and Weiss, the chief and deputy chief of the Berlin police, as well as many other republican police chiefs and officials had long been removed. A state of siege had been imposed in Berlin and Brandenburg on 20 July and power had been vested in the local Reichswehrcommander, von Rundstedt. When they refused to vacate their offices, Gresinski and Weiss were briefly taken into custody. It is difficult to disagree with Severing, who believed that resistance by the police against the Reichswehr was hopeless and that in most places, other than Berlin and a few big cities, would not have been supported by the police.

The only decision that was left to the leaders of the SPD and the trade unions on 20 July 1932 was whether to give the signal for a civil war they would almost certainly have lost. Since 1930 their position had been so eroded that it was not a signal they could realistically give. Even now the position had something of the ambivalence that had justified the SPD's policy of toleration. The Papen government's move was overtly and avowedly against a remaining bastion of the republic and the left, but it also erected a potential barrier to a Nazi takeover. The KPD's offer to participate in a general strike against the coup was for the SPD a poisoned chalice. It seemed wiser to concentrate one's forces for the election due ten days later.[90]

On 31 July the Nazis reached their pre-1933 peak in a national election, with 13.8 million votes and 37.4 per cent, against 6.4 million and 18.3 per cent in September 1930. Their triumph was somewhat marred by the fact that their expectations had been even higher and that the result merely confirmed what the second presidential ballot and the Prussian Landtag elections had foreshadowed three months earlier. The Nazis had clearly reached the limits of the voter potential they could exploit.

The only other parties that could still command substantial support were the SPD, the Centre Party and BVP, the KPD and the DNVP. The rest of the parties, including the once important DVP and DDP (now *Staatspartei*), were together reduced to less than 5 per cent, when in 1930 they had still accounted for over 22 per cent. The DNVP was further reduced from 7 per cent to 5.9 per cent, but at least it still had a presence.

Hitler had managed to keep his vast and heterogeneous collecting basin in being, even if he could not extend it any further. It reached from unemployed members of the Lumpenproletariat, intent upon revolution, to the upper classes, who saw in him their bulwark against Marxism.

On the left the SPD lost another 600 000 voters while the KPD gained 800 000, though as a result of even higher participation, up from 82 per cent to 84 per cent, the combined left-wing total slipped by about 1.5 per cent. Given the political impasse into which the SPD had been driven and its avowed refusal to support any programme of reflation or job-creation it was perhaps surprising that it did no worse. The KPD's accession of strength was diverse: some straight switching from SPD, some increase of strength in previously weak rural or Catholic areas. The chief effect of the Communist success now and in the next election was not to increase the real threat of a revolutionary coup, but to increase the fear of it and the exploitation of that fear. The SPD's immobility was also aggravated by such signs of success from its left-wing rival.

PAPEN FAILS TO FIND SUPPORT: THE SECOND REICHSTAG DISSOLUTION

As for the overall political situation, it was more than ever deadlocked. The Papen government remained suspended in a political vacuum, its only support the president. It had constantly claimed to be above parties and in the final stages of the campaign had used the Prussian coup to reinforce that claim, yet the very reason for calling the elections had been to bring the Reichstag more in line with the popular will. Even Papen and Schleicher realised that without popular support no government could carry on for long. In the new Reichstag, out of a total of 608 deputies, there was a block of of 222 SPD and KPD deputies on the left and 230 NSDAP deputies on the right. The only other substantial block were the 97 Centre Party and BVP deputies.

Theoretically a brown–black coalition was now possible in the Reich, as it had been in Prussia since 24 April. Such a coalition contradicted the clear line on the incompatibility of Catholic doctrine and Nazi ideology taken by the Catholic bishops and clergy, which had helped the Centre Party/BVP vote to remain solid. Against this it was now argued by the leaders of the Centre Party that they could tame the Nazis as effectively as they had tamed the godless SPD. Even in the Vatican there was now a feeling that it might be better to end the no longer viable collaboration with the SPD in Prussia and replace it by an opportunistic anti-bolshevik alliance with the NSDAP. The Cardinal state secretary in the Vatican Pacelli, previously papal nuncio in Munich and Berlin and later Pius XII, may have encouraged this attitude.

A black–brown coalition was no more likely to be formed in the Reich than in Prussia, for the Nazis would not be satisfied with the limited power the Centre Party could offer and were probably negotiating only to increase the pressure on Papen. Nevertheless the Papen government had to take the threat of a black–brown coalition seriously.[91] The preferred option for Papen and his colleagues would have been to bolster their position by taking a few Nazis into the government. Schleicher had a long a talk with Hitler, probably on 5 August, during which it became clear that the Nazi leader would only agree to the participation of his party in a government of which he was the head and which would be likely to ask the Reichstag for an enabling act.

Although Schleicher was for a time prepared to advocate Hitler's appointment as chancellor, neither he nor Papen were ready to hand him total power. It was even more important that Hindenburg, on his return to Berlin from East Prussia on 10 August, was not prepared to offer the chancellorship to Hitler. The refusal was rammed home at an interview between Hindenburg and Hitler, in the presence of Papen, Frick, Röhm and Meissner on 13 August. A communique issued immediately afterwards by the president's office stated that Hindenburg had refused Hitler's demand 'that he and his party be handed the conduct of state affairs in their entirety'. The president had stated that 'it was not compatible with his responsibility before God, his conscience and the Fatherland to hand over total governing power to the national socialist Party, which wanted to use this power in a one-sided way'. At the end of the interview Hindenburg was supposed to have shaken his finger at Hitler and said 'Herr Hitler, no putsches'.[92]

This interview and the way it was made public proved to be a severe tactical setback for the Führer. It also exposed, however, the flimsy foundations of the policy of taming the Nazis or enlisting their toleration, the linchpin of Schleicher's efforts for many months. None of the components of his policy were falling into place. A dynamic mass movement with strongly revolutionary elements could hardly be tamed in this way. Even a man less ruthless than Hitler would hardly have put himself in a position of responsibility without power.

The view that Nazism was not a monolithic movement and that specific leaders and sections could be detached continued to be held by Schleicher and others. At a cabinet meeting on 10 August, in the discussions about the inclusion of Nazi ministers in the government, Schleicher said that there would be clashes between such Nazi ministers and the SA and SS. The general similarly deluded himself that personalities would play their allotted roles in his schemes: that Hitler would be persuaded by more amenable Nazi leaders like Gregor Strasser, that Hindenburg would always accept his advice and that Papen would act as his mouthpiece. On 13 August Schleicher had already experienced, as he was later ruefully to admit, that Hindenburg had the unpredictable self-will of a very old man. For the moment this self-will helped to keep Hitler away from the levers of power.[93]

However dubious the taming concept now was, Hitler's strategy of legality was also in trouble. In the Nazi movement the brusque rebuff by Hindenburg had aggravated the crisis of disappointed expectations in the aftermath of the Reichstag elections. The SA expected the takeover to begin and when it failed to do so immediately unleashed a wave of terror, which was particulary severe in East Prussia and Silesia. The incident which received most publicity was the murder, on 10 August, of a young Communist sympathiser at Potempa, not far from the Polish border in Upper Silesia. He was dragged from his sleep and trampled to death in front of his mother by drunken members of the SA.

On the day of the murder a new emergency decree against the growing violence had been put into operation by the Papen government. This enabled politically motivated crimes to be brought to trial very swiftly and on 22 August four of the perpetrators of the Potempa murder were sentenced to death and a local leader of the NSDAP also received the death sentence for incitement to murder. Hitler used these sentences as the occasion for a strident declaration of all-out war against the Papen government. He sent a telegram to the convicted men assuring them of 'of his boundless loyalty in face of this monstrous blood sentence'.[94] It was an indication of the extreme tension that now existed between the revolutionary and the respectable elements of his movement and his strategy. It should also have been a warning to all of what to expect if he ever came to power. The Papen government, by virtue of its commissarial authority in Prussia, commuted the death sentences to life, on the grounds that the perpetrators could not have been aware of the new emergency decree when the crime was committed. Although the liberal press was also in favour of commutation, the Papen government had still not given up all hope that the Nazi movement could be tamed in some fashion.

For the moment Papen and his colleagues had no alternative but to go on governing while guarding their political flank as best they could. The economic crisis had shown little seasonal improvement over the summer months. Officially measured unemployment had dropped from just over six million in February to just under 5.4 million in August, the estimated overall total from 7.62 million to 7.16 million, equivalent to 38 per cent and 35.4 per cent of the employed population respectively.

There were, however, some indications that internationally the economic slump was bottoming out. The reparations restraint on the German government's freedom of manoeuvre in financial matters was now removed. The Papen government could therefore contemplate a change from the priorities that had still marked its first set of emergency decrees in June, inherited from the Brüning government. The decrees promulgated on 4 September provided for a postponement of taxes on industry, such as turnover tax, through the issue of certificates. Tax rebate certificates were also to be given to employers for each additional worker they took on. These certificates were negotiable. There was a further programme of job creation through public works.

Long-standing demands of industry were met through the suspension of compulsory arbitration, already initiated administratively, and by a general relaxation of the system of wage agreements. The government also declared itself sympathetic to a further reduction of quotas for agricultural imports and undertook to enter into negotiations with the countries concerned.

This programme ushered in a period during which industry became very well disposed towards the Papen government. The only part of the programme about which many sections of industry had reservations was the plan for agricultural import quotas. It was feared that these would invite retaliation and thus further reduce German exports. The politically weak Papen government could not come to a clear decision between the industrial and agricultural pressures to which it was exposed, but on the whole it came down in favour of the former.

In public the reaction to these proposals by the left-wing parties and the trade unions was unequivocally hostile. These policies seemed to bear out that it was a reactionary 'cabinet of barons'. In private the ADGB was not nearly so negative and maintained contact with the government. Schleicher's ideas about a *Querfront*, a cross-bench alliance, from Strasser to the free trade unions, remained politically alive, but nebulous and ultimately impracticable.

The economic measures of the Papen government marked a real change of course towards an active anti-cyclical policy and most of them continued to be effective until well into the following year, by which time Hitler was in power. They formed the starting point for the steps taken by Schacht when he was put in charge of economic policy by Hitler. The employment premium was, however, not widely taken up and was discontinued early in 1933.[95]

The promulgation of the economic measures was an indication that the Papen government meant to carry on in spite of its lack of political support following the breach with Hitler on 13 August. Throughout the second half of August negotiations continued between the Nazis and the Centre Party about the formation of a coalition in the Reich and Prussia. For the Centre Party this was a way of asserting its traditional key role in the new party situation produced by the elections of 31 July. It was also a way of binding the NSDAP into responsibility without handing it an irrevocable hold on power. For Hitler it was a way of putting pressure on Papen, but Strasser may well have seen in what was sometimes referred to as a Schleicher–Hitler–Stegerwald government a way for national socialism to come to power. In the NSDAP men like Göring and Frick were inclined towards the Strasser course, while Goebbels on the whole supported Hitler's all-or-nothing strategy. Brüning became involved in the negotiations on behalf of the Centre Party.

On 30 August the new Reichstag met and elected Göring as its president. The Reichstag president was always chosen from the largest party. Papen made a serious mistake in not attending this meeting with an order for a renewed dissolution at the ready. Instead he was at Hindenburg's East Prussian estate, in the company of Schleicher and interior minister Gayl. At this meeting it was decided to dissolve the Reichstag and risk a breach of the constitution by postponing new elections, on the grounds that in the present emergency the president was entitled to take such an extra-constitutional course by virtue of his general responsibility for the well-being of the nation. Had this strategy been adhered to, Hitler might have been forced off his legality course and into a coup attempt which might well have failed. It was, however, a high-risk strategy particularly for the Reichswehr and even at this meeting Schleicher did not fully commit himself to it. He clung to some kind of non-confrontational *Zähmungskonzept*, even though its current version built around Papen had clearly failed. In the meantime the Reichstag had adjourned and left the date of the next meeting to the new president, Göring. The Nazis were no keener than Schleicher on an immediate confrontation and they knew fresh elections would be more likely to bring them losses than gains. In the following few days there were further attempts to explore the NSDAP–Centre Party coalition, but Hitler clung to the demand that he should be chancellor.

On 12 September the Reichstag met again, a meeting that has become famous for its farcical proceedings. Göring deliberately ignored Papen's request to speak and deprived him of the chance to dissolve the Reichstag before it could vote on a KPD motion of no confidence in the government. This motion was passed by 512 to 42 votes, with five abstentions. Its legal validity was in doubt, because the chancellor's overriding right to be heard and present the dissolution order had been flouted. Nevertheless this was a devastating moral blow to the Papen government. If there was ever a chance that Papen would simply go on governing, with new elections indefinitely postponed, it rapidly vanished.

Schleicher was now in favour of delaying new elections and had fortified himself with the views of three legal experts, including Carl Schmitt, that a postponement was constitutionally justifiable because of the emergency. The cabinet, however, considered a delay beyond the statutory sixty days too risky. They were aware that the Centre Party and the Nazis might bring a prosecution against Hindenburg for breaking the constitution. Legalism prevailed once more, even though the substance of the constitution had been almost completely eroded, and the election was fixed for 6 November, the fifth major election in Germany that year. Although Papen's authority and reputation for competence had received a body blow, the dissolution and the new elections were also aggravating the dilemma of the Nazis. The strategy of legality looked increasingly like a cul-de-sac. In his diary Goebbels confessed his fear that 'they would win themselves to death'.[96]

There was even less chance that Papen could strengthen his position in this second electoral contest than there had been in the first. The one party of any size that now unequivocally supported him was the DNVP, but it was still led by Hugenberg. All attempts to produce a united bourgeois block were no more successful now than before. In the meantime Papen continued to peddle his ideology of the 'New State', but could make little concrete progress with his much-touted constitutional reforms. There was talk of a new chamber, which would guarantee the government greater independence from unstable party combinations; the raising of the voting age and additional votes for heads of families and veterans were mentioned; and the permanent removal of the division between the Reich and Prussia remained a prominent aim.

For most of the month of October the court case about the coup of 20 July made headlines. While this case was pending Papen could hardly take steps towards constitutional reform that would have entailed an overt breach of the constitution. After the verdict of the court, which did not in practice reverse the actions taken since 20 July, Papen went further in combining the Prussian with the Reich government. Bracht, the Commissioner for Prussia, became a member of the Papen government and so did Popitz, who had been put in charge of the Prussian finance ministry.[97]

In the meantime Schleicher was developing the plans, reaching back into the Groener era, to bring the various paramilitary organisations into a scheme that would in practice turn them into a national military reserve for the Reichswehr. The formation of a Reich Trust for Youth Training was announced. There was also to be further development of the voluntary labour service. The problem with these initiatives was that they were wide open to infiltration by the SA and other Nazi organisations, although the attempt was also made to secure the cooperation of the Stahlhelm and even the *Reichsbanner*. The SA sent large numbers to the training courses organised by the Reich Trust. In these moves Schleicher was not only pursuing his *Zähmungskonzept*, but they have also to be seen in the context of the efforts to secure equality of treatment for Germany in the disarmament negotiations then in progress.[98]

In the economic field the Papen government continued to veer between the pursuit of agricultural protection through quotas and heeding the warnings of industry about provoking retaliation against German exports. Braun, the agriculture minister, made public statements in support of the former and Warmbold, the economics minister, in support of the latter.

None of this could disguise the isolation of the Papen government in the electoral contest. For the moment it was outright confrontation with the Nazis. In a speech on 12 October Papen denied that he or Hindenburg had kept Hitler out of office. What had been rejected was his claim to total power. Papen had this to say about Nazi doctrine: 'Its principle of exclusivity, of all or nothing, its mystical messianic faith in the Führer, with his violent eloquence, as solely ordained to guide the national destiny gives it the character of a religion.'[99] Hitler replied with violent attacks on the reactionary Papen cabinet. Circumstances were forcing Nazi propaganda to put greater stress on anti-capitalist, anti-establishment slogans. Big rallies were mounted to give the impression that the party had lost none of its dynamism. The day of youth at Potsdam on 2 October, for example, had up to 100 000 Hitler Youth parading in front of the Führer.

The bitter, though to the close observer by no means terminal, hostility between Papen and Hitler did not lessen the more fundamental clash between the government and the left. It was given added impetus by the consequences of the government's demolition of wage agreements. There was a wave of strikes, for example among Hamburg transport workers.[100] Bitterness was increased when compulsory arbitration was used to enforce wage reductions. The unions had in such circumstances little alternative but to give way. This gave added scope to the KPD and its revolutionary trade union opposition (*Revolutionäre Gewerkschafts-opposition*) to levy its customary accusations of class treason against the union and SPD leadership. In this they were now sometimes joined by the NSBO.

Within the moderate labour movement further strains were appearing. The obvious weakening of the SPD made it seem advisable to some leading figures in the ADGB to put greater distance between themselves and the party. The contacts with Schleicher and Strasser, slight though they were, told the same tale. Höltermann, the leader of the *Reichsbanner*, now took the view that only the Reichswehr could prevent a Nazi takeover. The mirror image of labour's hostility to Papen was the generally favourable view still taken by industry. Some leading figures like Reusch, who had earlier set much store by bringing the Nazis into government, were now somewhat disillusioned with the Brown Shirts. It was realised within the RDI that the prospects of the Papen government receiving greater popular backing were slight, but the talk of reducing parliamentarism and increasing executive authority was well received among industrialists.[101]

The final stages of the election campaign were overshadowed by a strike of transport workers in Berlin. It was notable for the fact that it was called against the advice of the the official trade union representation and that the communist RGO and Nazi NSBO collaborated in promoting it. For the KPD this was another form of the 'unity front from below'. For the Nazis and particularly for its Berlin Gau led by Goebbels it posed a dilemma. Collaboration with the Communists would scare off middle class voters, but in its current hostile posture towards Papen the party could not afford to give up its anti-capitalist appeal and working-class support. Particularly in Berlin the election results were to show a below average decline of the Nazi vote in working-class districts and an above average decline in middle-class areas.

Even more important were the longer-term perspectives that could be deduced from the Nazi–Communist collaboration in the transport strike, incidental though it was. The example could be used in support of alarmist arguments about the dangers of a simultaneous uprising from the extremes of right and left. It could also be used to support the contention that a decline of the Nazis would principally benefit the Communists and that it had therefore become urgent to bring about the long-delayed 'taming' and inclusion of Hitler in the government.[102]

The result of the Reichstag elections on 6 November reinforced such arguments. The most obvious feature of the results was the decline in the Nazi vote of over two million, from 37.4 per cent to 33.1 per cent. At the other extreme the KPD obtained over 600 000 more votes and increased its share from 14.5 per cent to 16.9 per cent. The SPD lost another 700 000 votes and its share of the vote dropped from 21.6 per cent to 20.4 per cent, just below its previous lowest percentage in May 1924. The parties supporting Papen could record a moderate success: the DNVP pulled in nearly another 950 000 votes and rose from 5.9 per cent to 8.9 per cent and what was left of the DVP had a slight renaissance, 225 000 more votes and a rise from 1.2 per cent to 1.9 per cent. Not surprisingly there was voter fatigue and the participation rate dropped from 84.1 per cent to 80.6 per cent, a loss of about 1.4 million votes.

Just as the Nazis had benefited more than other parties from the increase in participation since 1930, they now lost dispro-portionately. The Nazi decline was seen, particularly in republi-can and left-wing circles, as a sign that the Nazi 'spectre', widely regarded as insubstantial all along, was about to disappear as rapidly as it had appeared. What such comment failed to perceive was the fact that the precise level of support commanded by Hitler might no longer be so significant; that in fact in his weakened position he was more suitable to play his part in some form of 'taming'.

As with the Berlin transport strike, a direct correlation was thought to be at work between the performance of the two extremes. The rise in the KPD vote was simplistically and falsely seen to be related to the drop in the NSDAP vote and it was feared that this process might go much further. In fact most of the rise in the KPD vote was at the expense of the SPD and more than a quarter of the rise took place in and around Berlin, obviously as a result of the transport strike. There may have been a small migration from NSDAP to KPD in these areas, but the main losses of the NSDAP were in middle-class areas. Such voters were clearly scared off by the radical and proletarian stance of the Nazis, particularly in connection with the transport strike. The KPD made some further small gains in rural areas, sometimes at the expense of the NSDAP, but sometimes also from the Centre Party and the BVP. The Catholic parties lost over 450 000 votes, about 0.7 per cent. Catholic voters were confused when the sinfulness of Nazi doctrine was preached from the pulpit while the clerical leaders of the Centre Party were engaged in coalition talks with the Nazis.

In the new Reichstag the 286 deputies of the NSDAP, the Centre Party and the BVP, the black–brown block, no longer had a majority of the 584 seats, another minor source of satisfaction for the Papen government. As for the KPD, it was confirmed in its proletarian triumphalism by the election results. The ultimate victory of the revolution was more certain than ever and even a period of fascist dictatorship would merely be a brief interlude before the inevitable triumph of the proletariat. In the SPD there was a degree of perplexity and consolation was being sought in the fact that the 'Marxists', whom the opposition was always lumping together, were once again stronger than the fascists by a million and a half votes. Some of the younger SPD intellectuals, whose sensibilities had not been blunted by Marxist orthodoxy, men like Carlo Mierendorff of the Hofgeismar circle, pointed to the need to replace the totally eroded Weimar democracy by a new vision. Their demands for a more authoritative government able to embody the true will of the people were not too far removed from the nebulous corporatism of the *Tatkreis* and other right-wing reformers.[103]

FROM SCHLEICHER TO HITLER: THE NAZI TAKEOVER

The immediate crisis of the state was no nearer solution after these November elections than it had been fourteen weeks earlier. Papen could attempt to stay in office, but sooner or later this would require a formal breach of the constitution and, more seriously, might turn the latent civil war into an open one. The problem would not be substantially different if the Hindenburg presidential regime was continued with another chancellor. Hitler could again be approached to bring his mass movement into government and one could try to hedge him in with appropriate safeguards. He still controlled the largest party and more than half the deputies outside the 'Marxist' left. A government which included the Nazis could either be a presidential one or could attempt to gather a majority in the Reichstag.

It was one of the paradoxes of the situation that the election result and the distribution of seats in the Reichstag was still important, when the Reichstag had for months been unable to function and when there was almost a consensus that the Weimar parliamentary regime was past recall. All the philosophising about a 'New State' could not get round the fact that in 1932 a modern industrial society could not be governed without popular consent. If a government under Papen or someone else was really to govern without the Reichstag, then it had first to be demonstrated that the formation of a government on the basis of the newly elected Reichstag was impossible.

This was the main purpose of the prolonged negotiations with Hitler conducted first by Papen and then by Hindenburg. Hitler for his part was determined not to be caught again as he had been on 13 August. In one of his meetings with Hindenburg he used the argument that decline in his movement would cause a surge of Marxism: 'If this movement collapses, then Germany will be in the greatest danger, then there will be 18 millions Marxists and among them perhaps 14 or 15 million Communists. It is therefore entirely in the national interest that my movement should survive and this presupposes that my movement will have the lead.'

Hitler thus stuck to his all or nothing attitude, founded on his 'unshakeable' conviction that his was a revolutionary mission of 'world historical' importance in the pursuit of which he was prepared to gamble everything. In spite of the risk that his refusal of a partial share in government would plunge his movement into an acute crisis, he would would not budge from this position. Schleicher and Papen were therefore once more frustrated in their long-standing aim to 'tame' the Nazi movement. This left them only with the alternative to carry on with the presidential government and risk a breach of the constitution at some point.[104]

An important incident in these negotiations was the present-ation of a petition to Hindenburg, signed by some leading industrialists, asking him to entrust Hitler with the chancellor-ship in a presidential cabinet. This document has often been used, particularly in the historiography of the DDR, to prove that industry wanted Hitler as chancellor and even that he was therefore the tool of capitalists. The petition argued that only through the direction of affairs by the leader of the biggest national party could the necessary confidence for economic recovery be created. It does not, however, bear the weight that Marxist historians have tried to put on it.

Many of the leading figures did not sign, though three of these, Vögler, Reusch and Springorum, indicated that they were broadly in sympathy, but were not prepared to put their names to it. The petition did not therefore express a clear majority view. It was true that some major industrialists, notably Thyssen, had remained sympathetic to the Nazi movement during the autumn, in spite of the radical anti-capitalist propaganda that Goebbels and others were putting out. Schacht was still busy trying to bring industry and national socialism together. Hitler for his part wanted to maintain these contacts and to get as much support and money as possible from industry. Schacht's bureau had little success and Schacht himself turned more to the Keppler Circle, built up by Hitler's economic adviser Wilhelm Keppler. It did not recruit many industrialists of the first rank, apart from Vögler and the Cologne banker Kurt von Schröder. Walther Funk was in charge of the economic department in the Brown House. With his clear commitment to private enterprise he gave no offence to industry. There were also Strasser's many links with industry.

None of this meant, however, that there was any consistent support for national socialism among major industrialists. Even heavy industry in the Ruhr, often regarded as the sector most sympathetic to Hitler, was at this stage still committed to Papen, if possible reinforced by Nazi mass support in an innocuous manner. When Schacht was collecting signatures for the petition to Hindenburg he had to tell Hitler that 'with heavy industry it was heavy going'. The meeting of the *Langnamverein* on 23 November was still entirely supportive of Papen's policies and his constitutional reform plans. The *Ruhrlade* was virtually out of action at this time, because personal animosities had arisen among these leading industrialists over the attempts to rescue the Flick empire through the purchase of shares by the Reich.[105]

It is not entirely clear at what point Schleicher finally came to the conclusion that Papen was no longer the man for the task and that he had to take it on himself. There was by this time no doubt that Papen was a red rag to many sections of opinion, to all of the left, to the Centre Party as well as to the Nazis. Schleicher had been more successful in deflecting hostility from his own person and through his *Querfront* links he was still keeping many balls in the air at the same time. Hindenburg still clung to Papen and was prepared to risk a breach of the constitution, possibly involving the use of force, in his company.

At a cabinet meeting on 2 December it finally became clear that hardly any of Papen's colleagues were prepared to follow him in such an adventurist course. The defence minister called in his assistant Lieutenant-Colonel Ott who reported on a war game held within the last few days at the defence ministry. The object was to find out if there were enough security resources available to safeguard public order against Communists and Nazis, especially in case of a general strike supported by both sides, while still maintaining a minimal border guard. It was reported that the Reichswehr would find itself in a very difficult position, especially in East Prussia, where many of the younger border guard members were Nazis.

Papen now saw that his time was up and returned his commission to the president. Hindenburg accepted Papen's resignation with great reluctance and gave him a photograph of himself with the first line of the soldier's song 'I once had a comrade . . .' (*Ich hatt' einen Kameraden*) inscribed in his own handwriting. The president accepted the inevitable and appointed Schleicher to succeed Papen, but he now harboured resentment against the man who had separated him from his favourite chancellor. Schleicher, whose advice he had so often followed during the last three years, was no longer 'his dear young friend' and it was unlikely that he would risk for him what he had just been willing to risk for Papen. It was ominous that Hindenburg turned down Schleicher's plan to send Papen as ambassador to Paris. The president wanted the ex-chancellor to be kept close at hand for advice.[106]

Schleicher's game plan was more pragmatic than that of Papen. He hoped to rally enough support across the parties to gain toleration from the Reichstag to carry on and win a breathing space. His many contacts over the years and even during the last few days before Papen's fall had convinced him that there was now sufficient disposition among the leading Nazis to take a more cooperative line and to force Hitler into the same path. Even if this should fail, Schleicher saw the possibility of splitting the Nazi movement, given its current state of crisis. At the same time his contacts with leading trade unionists like Leipart, the chairman of the ADGB, made him feel hopeful that he could count on a more cooperative attitude from the right wing of the SPD.

During his first week of office Schleicher experienced both success and failure. The Reichstag met, but in contrast to what had happened to Papen in September, there was no outright confrontation with the government. The Nazis were desperate to avoid another immediate dissolution and even the SPD, in spite of its public display of hostility to Schleicher, did not want to face another election. Some of Papen's emergency decrees, those dealing with social policy and wage agreements, were revoked. This was an attempt on Schleicher's part to move away from the reactionary image that had dogged his predecessor. The Reichstag adjourned and it was left to the assembly's president, Göring, and the council of elders to call the next meeting.[107]

Matters developed less auspiciously for Schleicher in his efforts to get Nazi support. On 4 December the NSDAP suffered heavy losses in the communal elections in Thuringia. In some places, for example Weimar, the Nazi vote dropped by 35 per cent compared with the Reichstag elections only four weeks earlier. The average loss was nearly a quarter and about 40 per cent compared with the July elections. In Saxony there had been losses of around 20 per cent only a week after 6 November.

This was the background to Strasser's final confrontation with Hitler. Everything seemed to point to the conclusion that Strasser's strategy of taking power gradually now offered the only hope for the Nazi Party, but Hitler had resisted with messianic fervour. One of Schleicher's first moves as chancellor was to make a secret offer to Strasser of the post of vice-chancellor, to be held in conjunction with the premiership of Prussia. After a long and acrimonious meeting at the Kaiserhof, Hitler's Berlin headquarters, Strasser suddenly resigned all his party posts, though not his party membership. The gap between Hitler's push for total domination and Strasser's wish to play a constructive role in the national interest was unbridgeable.

Strasser had, however, never wanted to be disloyal to Hitler and he did not have any real base in the party from which he could effectively challenge Hitler. Withdrawal seemed to him the only way out and immediately after sending his resignation letter he left for a holiday in Italy. For a brief moment Hitler was alarmed and talked of suicide. He told Goebbels: 'if the party disintegrates, I'll put an end to it all in three minutes with a bullet'. He could hardly believe his luck when he realised that Strasser had planned no serious challenge. Hitler moved rapidly to keep control of the party and personally assumed the post of Reich Organisation Leader which Strasser had vacated. He largely dismantled the structure built up by Strasser.

It was not quite the end of Schleicher's attempt to split the Nazi Party through Strasser or to find some other way of bringing the party to support his government, but in fact one of the main assumptions on which he had taken power had collapsed.[108]

Schleicher was no more fortunate in his overtures to the left. His attempts to present himself as a 'social general', backed by the repeal of some of the Papen edicts, cut little ice. He continued his contacts with the leadership of the ADGB, but when news and rumours about these contacts became public, Leipart and others found themselves under attack in the SPD. They had to step very warily, for any evidence that party and unions were drifting apart was eagerly seized upon by the right-wing press. With hindsight it is easy to argue that the SPD would have done better to adopt a less hostile attitude to the Schleicher government, in view of what was shortly to befall the party. The argument of avoiding a worse alternative had, however, governed SPD policy for most of the Brüning era and there was no inclination to go down the same path again in the even less attractive circumstances surrounding Schleicher.[109]

The tentative and as it turned out largely unsuccessful efforts of Schleicher to improve the atmosphere with the unions and with the left caused uneasiness in industrial circles. The revocation of the Papen measures of September were seen as a retrograde step and the general tone of the Schleicher government's economic ideas, as they emerged from the general's radio address on 15 December, were regarded as amateurish and interventionist. There was disappointment that Schleicher did not develop Papen's constitutional reform plans and fears that he was aiming to return to a more parliamentary, party-based regime comparable to that of Brüning. Such reservations about Schleicher's policy were expressed by some of the politically influential industrialists like Reusch and Silverberg. The official policy of the RDI, as expressed by the president Krupp and the executive director Kastl, remained in support of the Schleicher government. The *Reichslandbund*, already Nazi dominated, moved quickly into a much more forthright condemnation of the Schleicher government. It disliked the general's emphasis on agricultural resettlement as a cure for unemployment and regarded the policy on quotas, a source of conflict throughout the Papen period, as totally inadequate. By January the *Reichslandbund* was attacking Schleicher in the most unbridled terms and in language that owed much to its Nazi affiliations: 'The plundering of agriculture in favour of the omnipotent moneyed interests of the internationally orientated export industries persists.'[110]

The Christmas holidays gave Schleicher a much needed breathing space, but soon thereafter it became clear that he was carrying on in a power vacuum. Unless he could break out of it before the Reichstag was due to reassemble on 24 January he would have to risk the same extra-constitutional course that he himself had regarded as impossible in the final hours of Papen.

Now the fact that Schleicher no longer had the full confidence of the president, coupled with the continued influence enjoyed by his disappointed predecessor in the presidential palace, came to be an important factor in his downfall. Arrangements had been made for a meeting between Papen and Hitler, to be held on 4 January 1933 at the house of the Cologne banker Schröder, a member of the Keppler circle and Nazi sympathiser. The main object of the meeting was to explore once more the possibility of Hitler entering the government, either as chancellor or in the form of some kind of duumvirate with Papen. Since it was known that Papen still had access to Hindenburg it was felt that he might be able to pave the way for something that in one form or another had been on the agenda for at least the last six months. The meeting was supposed to be secret, but the participants were in fact photographed entering the Schröder flat. It was this attempted secrecy that added to the perception that this was a plot against Schleicher. Papen immediately worked overtime to dissipate this impression and five days later had an apparently amicable meeting with Schleicher.

Immediately after seeing Schleicher Papen saw Hindenburg and received the president's approval for his attempts to clarify the political situation further. He apparently gave Hindenburg the impression that Hitler might be induced to drop his hitherto irreducible demand for the chancellorship. Between the Cologne meeting and his return to Berlin Papen had also met some of the leaders of western heavy industry, including Vögler and Springorum. Their dislike of the 'state socialism' of Schleicher led them to support the idea of a new government, which would include both NSDAP and DNVP, and of which Papen would be the central figure. The approval of influential industrialists for Papen's efforts was one of the reasons why Hindenburg now hoped that the former chancellor might advance matters, given the fact that Schleicher seemed to have drifted into an impasse and in any case no longer enjoyed the president's full confidence. The president in fact entrusted Papen as a private individual to explore the formation of a new government behind the back of the incumbent chancellor. Even in the media there was now a general feeling that Schleicher was slipping and this lent added weight to Papen's comings and goings.

Against this loss of confidence the chancellor seemed unable to make any telling countermoves. At a meeting between Schleicher and Hugenberg it was suggested that the DNVP leader should enter the government and be put in charge of the ministries concerned with economic policy. Schleicher turned this down, for it would have meant giving up the 'social' dimension of his policy. Further attempts to enlist Strasser, after his return from Italy, came to nothing and in any case could no longer bring any significant Nazi support to the government. By mid-January Hitler had turned the full blast of his fury on Strasser, branded him a traitor and excluded him from the party.

Another line that Schleicher was pursuing in December and January was contacts with Otto Braun, who still legally held the office of Prussian prime minister. Braun suggested that Schleicher should revoke the order of 20 July 1932, that he should dissolve the Reichstag and defer new elections, while he, Braun, would dissolve the Prussian Landtag and also defer elections. When the elections would eventually be held, in the late spring or even later, the Nazi spectre would disintegrate and they would have operating parliaments in the Reich and Prussia. In practice the obstacles to such a plan were insuperable: Hindenburg would never have agreed and Braun for his part would have found it difficult to get the SPD to support him. He would have been branded a class traitor. Nevertheless these discussion show that Braun at any rate, and possibly Schleicher, were aware of the extreme danger that threatened Germany and were prepared to consider unorthodox means to counter it.[111]

The weakening of Schleicher's position had brought the Nazis fully into play again, but it was also important for Hitler to show that his own mass support was not ebbing further. Hence he threw all his resources into the Landtag elections in the small state of Lippe-Detmold scheduled for Sunday 15 January. The electorate numbered less than 120 000, of which 82.2 per cent had voted in the November Reichstag elections, a proportion which now rose to 85.1 per cent as a result of intensive campaigning by all parties. The Nazi share of the vote rose from 34.7 per cent in November to 39.5 per cent, still below the nearly 41 per cent of July 1932. Nazi propaganda made the most of this result to show that in spite of the electoral setbacks of November and December Hitler was still the leader with the overwhelming support of the 'national' part of the population.

The rise of the Nazi vote was largely achieved at the expense of the DNVP. Lippe was the state where Hugenberg had his private estate and where he controlled one of the main newspapers. He took a conciliatory stance towards Hitler in this election, in spite of the bitter hostility that had raged between the DNVP and the NSDAP throughout the autumn, the former supporting, the latter opposing Papen. Already Hugenberg was keeping his options open for the role which he might hope to play in a cabinet of national concentration that might arise if Schleicher should fail. Other parties might equally well have made something of the Lippe result: the SPD vote rose from 27 per cent to 30 per cent, the KPD vote fell by more than four percentage points; the DVP and the *Staatspartei* (formerly DDP) increased their votes considerably from a low base. It was, however, Hitler's hand that was strengthened in the byzantine intrigues that went on in anticipation of Schleicher's downfall.[112]

Papen, equipped with Hindenburg's commission to clarify the political situation, had several more meetings with Hitler. They took place at the villa in Berlin-Dahlem of Joachim von Ribbentrop, a champagne salesman who had married into the family owning Germany's biggest champagne firm. Hitler still wanted the chancellorship in a new government of national concentration and Papen could still not be sure that Hindenburg could be persuaded to appoint the Bohemian corporal. At one of these meetings, on 22 January, Oskar von Hindenburg and Meissner were present. They had first shown themselves at the opera and then slipped quietly away in the interval and taken a taxi to Ribbentrop's villa. Hindenburg's son had a long face-to-face talk with Hitler and according to Meissner said on the way home that he no longer saw any alternative to Hitler's chancellorship, especially as Papen agreed to it.

The strong front now taken by the *Reichslandbund* against Schleicher had also had its effect on the president. On 21 January the DNVP, hitherto regarded as broadly supportive of Schleicher, issued a sharp attack on him and his economic policies. Moreover it was rumoured that on the reassembly of the Reichstag the misappropriation of *Osthilfe* funds, for the purchase of racehorses and other luxuries, would be raised. Accusations of scandal might reach the Hindenburg family in connection with the Neudeck estate. It was a fact that when this estate was given to Hindenburg in 1927 it had been made over to Oskar for the avoidance of death duties. By the last week of January 1933 there were thus many reasons for the immediate entourage of Hindenburg to persuade the old man to drop his objection to a Hitler chancellorship.[113]

Schleicher had remained hesitant and inactive amid all the machinations conspiring towards his fall. On the day of the Lippe elections he told Schuschnigg, the visiting Austrian minister of justice: 'Herr Hitler is no longer a problem. His movement has ceased to be a political danger. The whole question is solved and is a concern of the past.' On 16 January there was agreement in principle in the cabinet that the plan to breach the constitution by dissolving the Reichstag again before it could deliberate and pass a vote of no confidence should be reactivated. New elections should then be postponed beyond the constitutional sixty days on the grounds that a state of emergency existed. It was only on Monday, 23 January that Schleicher sought audience with Hindenburg to ask for his cooperation in these plans. Now the president refused to commit himself and rumours of this soon became public, although Schleicher issued vigorous denials. The death knell of the Schleicher government had sounded.

It was not surprising that Hindenburg now refused to grant to Schleicher what seven weeks earlier he had been prepared to grant Papen. It was after all Schleicher who had brought Papen down by indicating the Reichswehr's refusal to risk such a confrontation. Hindenburg may well have feared that any formal breach of the constitution would create a presidential crisis, just at a moment when the Hindenburg dynasty was already threatened by scandal. Meissner and Oskar von Hindenburg, under the impact of the conversations with Hitler on the previous evening, must have helped the president to reach this decision not to expose himself personally by going along with Schleicher's plans for a formal coup d'état.[114]

When the reassembly of the adjourned Reichstag was finally fixed for 31 January, this became the deadline by which the crisis had to be resolved one way or another. Hindenburg had not finally dismissed Schleicher nor had his reluctance to make Hitler chancellor been totally overcome. Kaas and Brüning as leaders of the Centre Party were still insisting that the constitutional rights of the Reichstag must be respected. If a majority government was now to be formed it could only be with their assistance, but in fact a coalition of the Centre Party, the NSDAP and the DNVP, whether under Schleicher, Papen or Hitler was in practice impossible. The renewal of the Harzburg front, which would not have produced a majority government, but merely a more broadly based presidential cabinet, still presented difficulties.

Hugenberg remained highly suspicious of Hitler and made his entry into a Papen–Hitler cabinet dependent upon stringent conditions: control of economic policy by himself and no further dissolution of the Reichstag. The entry of the Stahlhelm into the combination was also desired, but by no means easy. Seldte was prepared to take office in the new cabinet of national concentration, but Duesterberg, the second leader, had been too badly bruised in his encounters with the Nazis.

The position of the Reichswehr, in Hindenburg's eyes the most crucial question of all, remained doubtful. Even after his resignation as chancellor on 28 January Schleicher still assumed that he would remain minister of defence in the next government. His position had, however, become weaker even within the army. Many senior officers wanted to put an end to the high-profile involvement in politics that Schleicher, the archetypal desk general, had forced on them. Hindenburg's qualms about the position of the Reichswehr under a Hitler cabinet were put at rest by the recommendation that Werner von Blomberg, the commander of the East Prussian district and currently at the Geneva disarmament negotiations, should become minister of defence in the new government. The fact that Blomberg and his chief of staff Reichenau were Nazi sympathisers was not known to the president.

On 28 January, a Saturday, Schleicher finally handed in his resignation. The weekend was filled with frantic negotiations and rumours of coups. To the last it remained uncertain whether a government of national concentration with Hitler as chancellor, but with most of the portfolios in the hands of the DNVP, Stahlhelm and non-party ministers, would actually be formed. Schleicher and other generals felt that this was now the only way out, for a Papen–Hugenberg government might pitch the Reichswehr into the confrontation with the SA which had so long been feared.

On Sunday, 29 January, rumours were put into circulation that Schleicher and Hammerstein would move troops from Potsdam to arrest Hindenburg. False as these rumours were, they removed any lingering reluctance on the part of Hindenburg to appoint Hitler. It was true that at an earlier stage plans were under consideration in the defence ministry that Hindenburg would be removed on grounds of incapacity. Until the Reichstag changed the law during its December sitting this would have meant that the chancellor took over the presidential duties. Schleicher would thus have had a free run for his plans. To the last Schleicher seems to have deceived himself that he would remain defence minister in the new government. When on the morning of 30 January Blomberg arrived back from Geneva Oskar von Hindenburg met him at the station and took him straight to his father, to be sworn in as minister of defence ahead of the rest of the cabinet. The vital acceptance by the Reichswehr of the Hitler cabinet was thus ensured.

In the new cabinet there were three Nazis, Hitler himself, Frick as minister of the interior, and Göring as minister of aviation, a ministry yet to be created. Hitler had wanted to hold the position of Reich Commissioner for Prussia along with the chancellorship, but had to leave this to Papen. Göring was, however, the commissarial minister of the interior for Prussia and thus had control over the Prussian police. Papen was vice-chancellor and had the right to be present during the chancellor's audiences with the president. Hugenberg was minister of economics and food and agriculture. Seldte was minister of labour. Four ministers were taken over from the Papen and Schleicher cabinets, Neurath (foreign affairs), Gürtner (justice), Schwerin von Krosigk (finance), and Eltz-Rübenach (post and transport). It looked therefore as if the concept of taming had at last been put into action.

It was still a minority government that might have to use the president's emergency powers under article 48, but it had a much broader base than those of Papen or Schleicher. In the existing Reichstag it commanded 42.5 per cent of the seats. Through an arrangement with the Centre Party it might be able to carry on without fresh elections and this constituted another element in the taming concept. Even as the new cabinet assembled to be sworn in by the president, this major safeguard against the drift to one-party dictatorship was immediately knocked aside. Hitler demanded that he should be given the right to dissolve the Reichstag. Hugenberg strenuously resisted, but finally gave way. The decision was confirmed at the first cabinet meeting on the afternoon of 30 January. One alternative was to prohibit the KPD and declare its mandates invalid. This overt breach of the constitution was considered too risky by a majority of the ministers, as it might precipitate a general strike. The other possibility, an accommodation with the Centre Party, had already proved elusive during the previous days and Hitler had no difficulty in demonstrating by the following day that it remained indeed impracticable. The stage was therefore set for another Reichstag election within five weeks. It would be held under conditions vastly more favourable to the NSDAP than those of 1932.[115]

Hitler's appointment as chancellor on 30 January 1933 proved to be the decisive step in the establishment of the Nazi dictatorship. It has remained a black day in world history, arguably the most fateful moment in the twentieth century, the beginning of vast horrors and barbarities, the prelude to unmitigated catastrophe. Many contemporaries were aware that an epoch-making event had taken place, which they had either feared or hoped for, though even the most pessimistic could not foresee the depth of the disaster about to engulf them. Among Hitler's own following there was an almost instantaneous change of mood, from the atmosphere of crisis and disintegration that had threatened the movement in the previous few weeks to a mood of triumph. For many hours that Monday evening the SA marched past Hitler, standing at an open window of the chancellery. To him and them it was clear who were the masters now and that a revolution was about to commence.

Unfortunately it was much less clear to the opponents, soon to be the victims, of the new regime. In the Centre Party, in the SPD, even more in the ADGB, there was a widespread belief that a Hitler cabinet, seeking a Reichstag majority which it might later lose again, was a better alternative than a Schleicher military dictatorship or, even worse, a reactionary Papen–Hugenberg cabinet. From this grew the increasingly desperate and abject attitude of propitiating the new regime, which led the Centre Party to vote for the Enabling Act on 23 March and which made the trade unions seek a niche in the new order by making a show of their 'national' reliability. The SPD, to its credit, was quicker to shed such illusions. It voted against the Enabling Act and Otto Wels announced its decision in a brave and defiant speech. When he made it in the Reichstag's temporary home after the fire, the Kroll Oper, the building was surrounded by stormtroopers baying for blood and he could not be sure whether he or his colleagues would escape with their lives.[116]

The fact that the events of 30 January appear with historical hindsight to be the point of no return has led to a particularly minute examination of the final intrigues that jockeyed Hitler into office. The underlying, counterfactual assumption is that if only Hitler and the NSDAP had been kept out of office at this juncture, they would never again have had the opportunity. Critical as the state of the Nazi movement had become, Hitler still had many cards to play, even if at the last minute Hindenburg, Papen, Hugenberg and others had managed to do without him once again. A reversion to the Strasser strategy of collaboration was still open to him. He could have backed this with the threat of his huge paramilitary forces. The course of events would then not have been vastly different from that which actually did occur. Ever since the days of Brüning Hindenburg, Schleicher, the Reichswehr and many others had been unwilling to confront this threat in open battle. Such a battle would have been too much like the one that Seeckt refused to face at the time of the Kapp Putsch, when he said that Reichswehr did not shoot on Reichswehr. Had Hitler's appointment on 30 January been aborted, as seemed possible right up to the last moment, the threat would not have simply disappeared.

Another common view of the 30 January 1933 is that of an alliance between the German élites, industrial, agrarian and military, and the Hitler mass movement. Many elements in these élites had undoubtedly seen the Nazis as possible allies and partners for a long time. Once Hitler was seen to be wielding real power they for the most part accepted the situation with alacrity. Élite behaviour can, however, only explain the course of events to a limited extent. By 1932 the power vacuum at the centre of German affairs was such that the conduct of individuals had become more important than the thrust of social groups. The whims of the octogenarian president, the moods of Schleicher, the vanity of Papen, mattered more than the views of *Reichslandbund* or RDI. The élites as well as the small circle of decision-making individuals were conscious of their weakness in face of the radicalised and politicised masses. This made them pay an almost exaggerated respect to the apparently successful mass mobilisation achieved by Hitler. If the German élites had retained more of their self-confidence they might have managed this crisis more successfully. As it was, the erosion of power had progressed so far that Hitler's ruthless penetration into the vacuum after 30 January met with no resistance. Only accommodation, *Gleichschaltung*, was possible and even Hitler himself was astonished at the ease of his take-over.[117]

The decision to hold Reichstag elections on 5 March 1933 had already knocked away a vital prop to the framing or taming of Hitler. A few days later Papen himself made possible the strictly illegal dissolution of the Prussian Landtag, so that elections could be held simultaneously with the Reichstag elections on 5 March. A presidential decree of 4 February made possible the suppression of newspapers and the prohibition of meetings. This order was used comprehensively against the KPD during the election campaign. Many SPD and Centre Party newspapers had publication bans imposed on them, but court orders declared some of these invalid.

Göring instructed the Prussian police not to act impartially but to refrain 'from hindering those parts of the population that supported the government of national concentration in their welcome and necessary collaboration with the lofty aims of the government'. On 17 February Göring issued his notorious order declaring that any policeman who used his weapon against communist terror had his full support and on 22 February he enlisted 50 000 auxiliary police, mostly from the SA Under the constitution of the German broadcasting authority the government had privileged access to the radio. Hitler and Goebbels now made use of this facility in the election to an extent undreamt-of by previous governments.

At a secret meeting with leading industrialists on 20 February Hitler and Göring declared that these elections would be the last for the next ten, perhaps hundred years. Schacht then asked them to take out their cheque books and they did so to the tune of three million marks. The NSDAP's financial worries were thus over.

On 27 February occurred what turned out to be the most important event of the election campaign, the Reichstag fire. It came so conveniently for the Nazis that it was for a long time assumed that the fire must have been started by them, but this now seems on balance unlikely. On the day after the fire Hindenburg was induced to sign another emergency decree which temporarily declared inoperative some of the basic constitutional rights, such as the freedom of the person, of assembly and of opinion. This decree remained until 1945 one of the pillars on which the Nazi dictatorship rested.

A wave of detentions, particularly of KPD functionaries and members, and dismissals of dissenting officials swept the country just ahead of the elections. In spite of this the Hitler cabinet only had an absolute majority by combining the NSDAP's 43.9 per cent with the DNVP's 8 per cent of the vote.

After 5 March the revolution from below gathered momentum, particularly in those *Länder* and communities where the Nazis were not yet in power. The most dramatic events took place in Bavaria, where the government of Heinrich Held, the leader of the BVP, struggled in vain to avoid obliteration. Last-minute appeals to Hindenburg, plans to proclaim a Bavarian monarchy, it all availed nothing.

On 21 March the meeting of the new Reichstag began with a solemn ceremony at the garrison church in Potsdam, one of the first propaganda coups staged by Goebbels, recently appointed minister for culture and 'popular enlightenment'. In his diary and with the utmost cynicism he called the day of Potsdam a comic tear-jerker (*Rührkomödie*). In fact the ceremony was part of the Nazi's successful creation of a mood: that this brutal seizure of power was a national uprising, a great lifting of the national spirit after fourteen years of treason and ignominy. Many patriotic Germans found it impossible to resist this mood.

The passage of the Enabling Act followed two days later. Hitler had talked of the need for such an act ever since in the previous year the formation of a government under his leadership had moved into the realm of possibility. By the time it became law the Nazi takeover had long passed the point of no return. If the Enabling Act had failed it would have been no more than an inconvenience. Another way of confirming the spurious legality of the Nazi takeover would no doubt have been found. Violence, pseudo-legality and deception were thus the main elements in the establishment of Hitler's totalitarian state.[118]

5 Epilogue: Why did the Weimar Republic Fail?

In Weimar's closing years it seemed increasingly likely that only far-reaching reforms of the constitution could save the essentials of democracy and the rule of law. Nevertheless right up to the last moment it remained possible, though not probable, that Hitler's accession to power might be avoided. Even after it had occurred it was by no means certain that the attempts to tame and frame him would fail so swiftly and completely. Thus outcomes always remained open, even if in the final stages options had greatly narrowed.

The most pervasive cause of Weimar's failure was that too many Germans did not regard it as a legitimate regime. There was a brief interlude between the armistice and the publication of the Versailles terms when a large majority of the population was willing to give the new order a chance. This 'dreamland' episode ended abruptly when it became clear that the adoption of democracy had not saved Germany from a harsh peace settlement. Thereafter the republic was always opposed by a large part of the population, which saw itself as the genuinely 'national' section. The size of this section and the degree of radicalism with which it fought the republic fluctuated over the years. In the final years there was a virtual consensus that the specific political arrangements of the Weimar constitution had become unworkable. The difference was between those who wanted to preserve the rule of law and those who supported a totalitarian replacement and by 1932 the latter were in a small majority. It is difficult to see what the politicians who were catapulted into power in 1918 by Germany's military collapse could have done about this lack of legitimacy. They could have affirmed more clearly the responsiblity of Germany's former rulers for her post-war plight, but it seems unlikely that this would have reconciled those who were unwilling to acknowledge the German defeat in the war and accept the republic.

Other failures are laid at the door of the SPD leaders who came to power in November 1918: the failure to make use of the

316

democratic potential of the council movement, the lukewarm approach to the socialisation of basic industries, particularly the coal mines, the reluctance to tackle the problem of land reform. It is argued that more fundamental reforms of this kind would have given the republic a firmer socio-economic underpinning, but it is not certain that they would have made a vital difference to the republic's chances of survival. The councils were very diverse in their composition and for the most part regarded their task as strictly limited and temporary. It is not easy to see what role, other than a fairly peripheral one, they could have played once a democratic parliamentary political system was in place. The nationalisation of some basic industries like coalmining might have reduced the influence of the strongly anti-democratic sections of heavy industry. The existence of a few nationalised industries in predominantly market-based economies has, however, often proved to be of marginal significance. As for land reform, the peasantry in Weimar Germany was no less markedly anti-democratic than the big landowners.

The military problem was of greater salience. Two strongly detrimental legacies survived from the revolutionary period, the militarisation of political life and the segregated position of the Reichswehr. The former was due to the unwillingness of large numbers of front-line soldiers to reintegrate into civilian life. Many of them found employment in the Freikorps and became the promoters of a counter-revolutionary, ultra-nationalist, nihilist activism. In the stable middle years this threat receded or was channelled into organisations like the Stahlhelm, legal in their activities but nonetheless anti-republican in sentiment. After 1929 the paramilitary threat re-emerged in even more politicised form, above all in the SA. Political conflict assumed a form akin to civil war and vitiated the democratic process.

As to the Reichswehr, the limitation on its size under the Versailles treaty turned it into a segregated professional army with an officer corps drawn almost entirely from the traditional military caste. After the resignation of Noske in March 1920 the republican parties, particularly the SPD, failed to subject it to effective political control. Gessler and Groener as defence ministers saw it as their task to shield the Reichswehr from prying political eyes. An attempt was made after the departure of Seeckt in October 1926 to create a more confident relationship between the army and the political world. The roles were reversed again when the power vacuum created by the failure of the Reichstag to function effectively pushed the Reichswehr into the position of a political arbitrator after 1929. Through the personal link between Hindenburg and Schleicher the Reichswehr first helped to create the power vacuum, then sought to fill it, until in the end it could not prevent Hitler from filling it with his revolutionary mass movement. Thus the republic was saddled with a damaging legacy by the armaments limitations in the Versailles treaty and by the failure of the SPD leadership, anti-militarist as they were, to gauge correctly the politico–military problem.

Another heavy burden imposed upon the republic was the reparations question. By keeping the wounds of defeat and national humiliation open it made it virtually impossible to end the virulent nationalist agitation against the republic at any time during its existence. A lethal cocktail of anti-democratic, anti-liberal, anti-modernist sentiment contained ingredients which had been present in Germany long before 1918, but was rendered more poisonous by the repeated reminders of national humiliation. The reparations problem kept the psychological consequences of Versailles alive. In many German minds their economic sufferings became directly linked with the foreign oppression imposed upon the nation. Yet Versailles was not the carthaginian peace it seemed. It was a compromise between French and Anglo-Saxon aims and left Germany's strategic potential for the future intact. If anything it enhanced that potential because of the situation in Eastern Europe, partly created at Versailles. The Soviet Union was weakened and for this reason, and also because it was an ideological pariah, could no longer play the role in the European concert of powers that it had done before 1914. The states of the *cordon sanitaire* set up in eastern Europe, led by Poland, would turn to Germany if forced to choose between Moscow and Berlin.

All this meant that Germans, psychologically wounded by defeat and its consequences, could yet pin their hopes on revising the outcome. The main difference was between those on the right who from the beginning saw revision in terms of outright defiance and those in the centre and on the left who saw gradualism, fulfilment and negotiated change as the only realistic means of revision. For virtually all sections of opinion the restoration of Germany's great power position was common ground. The primacy of foreign policy, a doctrine which had for long convinced many German that only a political system strong on authority was suitable to their circumstances, was still widely accepted. It was another potent addition to the anti-democratic cocktail. In view of this the pursuit of a policy based on international interdependence, linked with the name of Stresemann, must be considered all the more creditable. It was destroyed by the renewed rise of national egotism and demands for autarky as a result of the economic crisis after 1929. The primacy of foreign policy took on new meaning when, on the one hand, the extreme right blamed the economic crisis on Germany's continued enslavement by her foreign enemies, most recently through the Young Plan; while on the other hand the Brüning government sought to use the crisis to end reparations, recover Germany's freedom of action in south-east Europe and her right to equality of treatment in armaments. If the policy of developing the European framework through agreement, particularly with France, had been continued after Stresemann's death, the economic slump need not have become as severe as it did in Germany.

The Weimar constitution and the way it functioned did not in the end ensure its survival. It did, however, weather the deep crisis of the early 1920s and had a capacity for coping with difficulties which should not be underestimated. The fundamental compromises on which the republic was based endured at least until 1930 and their total failure was not then, as we have seen, a foregone conclusion. One fundamental compromise was the collaboration between majority socialism and the bourgeois–capitalist parties. Politically it took the form of the Weimar coalitions in the Reich or Prussia, the great coalition of 1923 or 1928 to 1930, or the broad but not always formalised consensus on foreign and economic policy of the middle 1920s. It survived in a limited form in the toleration granted by the SPD to Brüning till May 1932. Economically the Weimar Republic's basic compromise was initially enshrined in the *Zentralarbeitsgemeinschaft* and later in a consensus on social and economic policy. The shrinkage of the economic base after 1929 endangered this compromise, but political leadership designed to preserve rather than destroy it would have had a chance even in the depression. The political influence of German industry was at its height when, through the DVP, it helped to undermine the compromise in March 1930, but industry, like many other élite groups, found it easier to destroy than to put something in its place. In the end nothing could take its place but the dangerous pact with Hitler.

There were undoubtedly specific weaknesses in the Weimar political system. The proportional representation system, which relied so much on party lists and virtually excluded the element of personal representation, had few friends. Vested interests with financial clout could secure representation on the lists of the weaker parties out of proportion to their electoral strength. The existence of splinter parties was constantly complained of and made it easier for the NSDAP to achieve a breakthrough after 1928. The inability of the smaller bourgeois parties to unite was, however, as much a failure of political leadership as it was a consequence of electoral mechanics. The way in which a strong presidency enabled the parties in the Reichstag to evade their responsibilities for providing an effective executive proved unhelpful. The parties were confirmed in the habits they carried over from the imperial period: addiction to ideological purity, commitment to affiliated interest groups, preference for opposition over assuming the burdens of government.

The complications of the federal system and the dualism of Reich and Prussia were always under attack and became objects of reform proposals. Nevertheless it is impressive how this system, with its complex diffusion of power and its thriving municipalities inherited from imperial Germany, could operate effectively and master crises of great severity. For this it needed men like Ebert and Stresemann, committed to preserving a liberal democracy. Most of the leading figures in the final crisis, Hindenburg, Schleicher, even Brüning, had no such commitment. Their aim was to transcend the Weimar system, no longer regarded as legitimate by the majority of the population.

The presidential cabinets after 1930 facilitated a seamless development from semi-authoritarian to totalitarian rule. This trend was helped by two major factors. One was the prevailing legal positivism of the Weimar period, which enabled the observation of legal norms to be used as a cover for fundamental constitutional change. The other was the reliance on a powerful bureaucracy, which had a long tradition of claiming to be above politics. Yet its senior members had always been politically appointed. In the Brüning cabinets two ministries, economics and justice, were for much of the time headed by civil servants,

Trendelenburg and Joel, who had previously been their respective state secretaries.

The Weimar Republic needed economic elbow room to function successfully. In the middle 1920s there was a pent-up demand for the prosperity lost in war and defeat and this put a strain on the economy. More specifically the rise in wages, salaries and purchasing power in the most properous years of 1927 and 1928 may have pre-empted some future growth and aggravated distributional pressures. The economy had moved a long way towards corporatism and economic conflicts had become highly politicised, through mechanisms like the compulsory arbitration system. None of this need have deprived the governments after 1929 of all their freedom of action. The Brüning government was established with the intention of combining a more assertive foreign policy with rehabilitation of the Reich's finances through deflation. It was a course which went both politically and economically out of control. A more cooperative international climate might have resulted in a less depressed German economy, which in turn might have helped the international economy as a whole to overcome the slump more successfully.

The perils and pains of modernity had already played a major role in shaping the atmosphere and consciousness of imperial Germany. The First World War had greatly accelerated the modernisation process. After 1918 everything from economic innovation to popular culture and sexual morality was in a state of flux and experimentation. This was not peculiar to Weimar Germany, but defeat and upheaval enhanced unease and disorientation. It lends fascination to what now in retrospect appears characteristic of the Weimar social and cultural scene. At the time it did little to help the republic to consolidate itself. The liberal intelligentsia did not warm to what they saw as the greyness of Weimar politics. The national opposition and a large part of the population saw their contempt for the republic confirmed by the fact that such an intelligentsia had a high profile under its aegis.

The collapse of the Weimar Republic appeared to contemporaries as well as to historians above all as a failure and tragedy of the left. This is the counterpart to the Marxist contention, advanced in a variety of forms, that national socialism was a product of capitalism. The contention was most strongly and unequivocally made in the Comintern's statement of 1935 that

German fascism was the most extreme and terroristic phase of monopoly capitalism. It is often quoted in the form in which it was put forward by Max Horkheimer, of the Frankfurt school of sociology, in 1939: 'Whoever does not wish to talk of capitalism should also remain silent about fascism.' It should accordingly have been the task of the left, of the proletariat, its parties and leaders, to prevent capitalism from developing into fascism.

Failure rebounds therefore upon the SPD, for long the united and powerful representation of the German working class. Apart from the specific sins of omission already referred to during the period of revolution, when the German body politic was at its most malleable, the general charge is that the SPD failed to carry out the revolution to which it had declared itself firmly committed for so long. The answer to this charge is that German society was already far too developed in 1918 to be capable of being revolutionised. Revolutions have never occurred in highly industrialised, politically developed societies. They have occurred either in pre-industrial societies, for example France in 1789, or in countries not yet industrialised, like Russia in 1917. In Germany a dictatorship of the proletariat would have deprived the German worker of rights he had enjoyed for at least a generation. The 'anti-chaos reflex' of the SPD leaders and of much of the population, even if sometimes exaggerated, was entirely natural, for a profound social upheaval would probably have led to Allied intervention and would have produced starvation and destitution for millions. From this it can be argued that it was the utopian left that through its unrealistic pursuit of all-out revolution pushed developments further to the right than need have been the case.

The continued sharp divisions of the left throughout the Weimar period have been much blamed for the fact that the labour movement proved impotent in the face of national socialism. There are two components to this argument. The first is that the division itself was fatally weakening, particularly in the form it took in the last years of the Weimar Republic. The KPD, its policy largely dictated by the exigencies of Soviet foreign policy, wasted its potential in futile, self-destructive attacks on the SPD. Blind Marxist determinism led it into the belief that the destruction of democracy would inevitably bring about the triumph of communism.

The second major consequence of the division of the German labour movement, was its effect on the SPD itself. There can be little doubt that the SPD's ideological immobilism, its failure to break out of the proletarian electoral ghetto, were largely the result of the competition from the KPD. For a time the SPD lost much of its following to the USPD and it had to fear that such losses might recur, as indeed they did, to the KPD in the closing years of the republic. From this it can be argued that it was not so much the specific nature of the KPD that was damaging as the mere existence of a more extreme left-wing alternative to the SPD.

That such an alternative existed was almost inevitable and the vision of a unified German labour movement was always an illusion. It became even more of an illusion in the final years of the republic, when the KPD and the SPD attracted different sections of the working class. It was this as much as the Moscow line of the KPD that divided the two parties. The existence of the extreme left always made it more difficult for the SPD to collaborate with the bourgeois parties, a collaboration that was essential for the health of the republic and which was achieved most of the time in Prussia. The fact that this collaboration broke down at crucial junctures, in 1923 and more conclusively in 1930, was, however, less the fault of the SPD and more due to the DVP and the pressure from its industrial wing.

Like all historical failures that of Weimar was the product not only of the republic's weaknesses and of the misjudgments of republican politicians, but of the strength and success of the republic's opponents. The anti-republican, anti-democratic, anti-parliamentary, anti-Semitic, anti-liberal stream was very broad and diverse in Germany after 1918. Many sectional groups, artisans, shopkeepers, white-collar employees, peasants, land-owners, house owners, heavy industry, the *Mittelstand* generally, fashioned for themselves ideologies that were loosely related to each other and to anti-republicanism.

Beyond such interest groups there were the many elements that were committed to fascist or proto-fascist ideas, the veterans of the Stahlhelm, the ex-Freikorps soldiers, the university students in search of nationalist solidarity, youth committed to post-romantic, anti-bourgeois pseudo-revolution. There was a whole intellectual industry, roughly labelled the Conservative Revolution, that produced the ideological images for all these groups. The cultural pessimism of Oswald Spengler, the militarist asceticism of Ernst Jünger, the anti-individualist corporatism of Othmar Spann, all this and much else entered into the broad stream of illiberalism.

Anti-Semitism was usually part of this package and formed a kind of seismograph for this sector of opinion. Weimar Germany had a numerically small and highly assimilated Jewish community, overwhelmingly urban and middle class. The German–Jewish relationship was not without tensions and the liberal expectation that the problem would simply disappear was mistaken. Nevertheless official discrimination ceased after 1918 and the trend was towards secularisation and assimilation. Some individual Jews had a high profile in the Weimar period, but they came from all camps and persuasions and their Jewishness was often tenuous. Yet many 'national' Germans, even apart from the rabid anti-Semites, thought there was a 'Jewish question'. It was an indication of their troubled state rather than of the reality of the question. Anti-Semitism did not, however, play a very major role in turning Nazism from a sect into a mass movement after 1929.

There was until the final years of the republic little reason to suppose that the diverse and ill-assorted 'national' oppposition could be formed into a battering ram to destroy the republic. It needed the extreme pressure of the great depression, following so rapidly upon the previous crisis, to marshal these diverse forces and ideas behind national socialism and Hitler. The personality of the Führer became a significant historical factor. Without his combination of demagogic gifts and political instinct the unified battering ram could hardly have come into operation. Luck was also with him, mainly because all the other players in the field turned out to be so inadequate and mistaken in their judgments.

The erosion of the political system from March 1930 onwards had made such personal factors exceptionally important. The power vacuum which rendered the machinations of political personalities significant could not, however, disguise the fact that a mass society could no longer be controlled by the élites or unrepresentative individuals. Hitler appeared to be the only personality in the political spectrum outside the left who could command large masses. By the summer of 1932 everything seemed to revolve round the question how he and his mass following could be used to make government viable again without handing him total and irrevocable power. The attempts to square this circle failed disastrously, partly because the erosion of other power centres had progressed too far, partly because the chances of taming Hitler were fatally misjudged. It was not sufficiently clearly and widely perceived that power in his hands would prove uncontrollable. Within a few years Hitler was able to unleash the Second World War and there was nothing left to act as a brake on him. The war, besides its many global consequences, was to lead to the destruction of the German state.

Appendices

ELECTIONS TO THE NATIONAL ASSEMBLY (1919) AND THE REICHSTAG (1920–33): VOTES FOR EACH PARTY %

	19 Jan. 1919	6 June 1920	4 May 1924	7 Dec. 1924	20 May 1928	14 Sept. 1930	31 July 1932	6 Nov. 1932	5 Mar. 1933
Turn-out	83.0	79.2	77.4	78.8	75.6	82.0	84.1	80.6	88.8
KPD	–	2.1	12.6	9.0	10.6	13.1	14.5	16.9	12.3
USPD	7.6	17.9	0.8	0.3	0.1	0.0	–	–	–
SPD	37.9	21.7	20.5	26.0	29.8	24.5	21.6	20.4	18.3
DDP[1]	18.6	8.3	5.7	6.3	4.9	3.8	1.0	1.0	0.9
Zentrum	15.9	13.6	13.4	13.6	12.1	11.8	12.5	11.9	11.2
BVP	3.8	4.2	3.2	3.8	3.1	3.0	3.7	3.4	2.7
DVP	4.4	13.9	9.2	10.1	8.7	4.7	1.2	1.9	1.1
DNVP[2]	10.3	15.1	19.5	20.5	14.2	7.0	6.2	8.9	8.0
NSDAP[3]	–	–	6.5	3.0	2.6	18.3	37.4	33.1	43.9
Others[4]	1.6	3.3	8.6	7.5	13.9	13.8	2.0	2.6	1.6

Source: J. Falter, T. Lindenberger, S. Schumann (eds), *Wahlen und Abstimmungen in der Weimarer Republik* (Munich: C. H. Beck, 1986), p. 44.

[1] From 1930 Deutsche Staatspartei.
[2] In 1933 Kampffront Schwarz-weiß-rot.
[3] In 1924 part of Völkisch-Nationaler-Block.
[4] Includes more than 36 regional and small parties, the most significant of which were the Wirtschaftspartei, the Christlich-nationale Bauern- und Landvolkpartei, and the Christlich-sozialer Volksdienst (Evangelische Bewegung).

NSDAP VOTE, 20 MAY 1928–5 MARCH 1933

Election	Date	Percentage
Reichstag	20 May 1928	2.6
Anhalt Landtag	20 May 1928	2.1
Bavaria Landtag	20 May 1928	6.1
Oldenburg Landtag	20 May 1928	7.5
Prussia Landtag	20 May 1928	1.8
Württemberg Landtag	20 May 1928	1.8
Lippe Landtag	6 January 1929	3.4
Saxony Landtag	12 May 1929	5.0
Mecklenburg-Schwerin Landtag	23 June 1929	4.1
Baden Landtag	27 October 1929	7.0
Lübeck Bürgerschaft	10 November 1929	8.1
Berlin Stadtversammlung	17 November 1929	5.8
Thuringia Landtag	8 December 1929	11.3
Saxony Landtag	22 June 1930	14.4
Reichstag	14 September 1930	18.3
Brunswick Landtag	14 September 1930	22.2
Bremen Bürgerschaft	30 November 1929	25.4
Schaumburg-Lippe Landtag	3 May 1931	27.0
Oldenburg Landtag	17 May 1931	37.2
Hamburg Bürgerschaft	27 September 1931	26.2
Hessen Landtag	15 November 1931	37.1
First Presidential Ballot	13 March 1932	30.1
Mecklenburg-Strelitz Landtag	13 March 1932	23.9
Second Presidential Ballot	10 April 1932	36.8
Anhalt Landtag	24 April 1932	40.9
Bavaria Landtag	24 April 1932	32.5
Hamburg Bürgerschaft	24 April 1932	31.2
Prussia Landtag	24 April 1932	36.3
Württemberg Landtag	24 April 1932	26.4
Oldenburg Landtag	29 May 1932	48.4
Mecklenburg-Schwerin Landtag	5 June 1932	49.0
Hessen Landtag	19 June 1932	44.0
Reichstag	31 July 1932	37.3
Thuringia Landtag	31 July 1932	42.5
Reichstag	6 November 1932	33.1
Lübeck Bürgerschaft	13 November 1932	33.1
Lippe Landtag	15 January 1933	39.5
Reichstag	5 March 1933	43.9
Prussia Landtag	5 March 1933	43.2

Sources: J. Falter *et al.*, *Wahlen und Abstimmungen; Thamer, Verführung and Gewalt. Deutschland 1933–45* (Berlin, 1986), p. 213.

328

GOVERNMENT COALITIONS AND THEIR PARLIAMENTARY SUPPORT

Appointment of Reich Chancellor	Reich Chancellor¹ of new government	Coalition parties	Per cent of Reichstag deputies in coalition parties	
13.02.1919	Philipp Scheidemann (SPD)	SPD, Z, DDP	78.1	National
21.06.1919	Gustav Bauer (SPD)	SPD, Z	60.3	Assembly
27.03.1920	Hermann Müller (SPD)	SPD, Z, DDP	78.1	
25.06.1920	Konstantin Fehrenbach (Z)	Z, DVP, DDP	36.6	
10.05.1921	Joseph Wirth (Z)	SPD, Z, DDP	44.6	
22.11.1922	Wilhelm Cuno	DVP, Z, DDP, BVP	41.2	
13.08.1923	Gustav Stresemann (DVP)	SPD, DDP, Z, DVP	58.8	
30.11.1923	Wilhelm Marx (Z)	DVP, Z, DDP	36.6	
03.06.1924	Wilhelm Marx (Z)	DVP, Z, DDP	29.2	
15.01.1925	Hans Luther	Z, DDP, DVP, BVP, DNVP	55.6	
20.01.1926	Hans Luther	Z, DDP, DVP, BVP	34.7	
16.05.1926	Wilhelm Marx (Z)	Z, DDP, DVP, BVP	34.7	
29.01.1927	Wilhelm Marx (Z)	Z, DVP, BVP, DNVP	49.1	
28.06.1928	Hermann Müller (SPD)	SPD, Z, DVP, BVP, DDP	61.5	
30.03.1930	Heinrich Brüning (Z)	Presidential Government (incl. DDP, DVP, Z, BVP, WP, KVP)	(34.9)	To 14 Sept 1930
			(27.8)	From 14 Sept 1930
01.06.1932	Franz von Papen	Presidential Government (incl. DNVP, CNBL)	(7.1)	To 31 July 1932
			(6.1)	31 July to 6 Nov 1932
			(8.9)	From 6 Nov 1932
03.12.1932	Kurt von Schleicher	Presidential Government (incl. DNVP, CNBL)	(8.9)	
30.01.1933	Adolf Hitler	NSDAP, DNVP	42.5	To 5 Mar. 1933
			52.5	From 5 Mar 1933

Source: Falter *et al.*, *Wahlen*, p. 45
¹ Until 14 Aug. 1919 Minister President.

INDEX OF INDUSTRIAL PRODUCTION (1928 = 100)

	Total	*Consumer goods*	*Capital goods*
1913	98	87	99
1919	37	–	32
1920	54	51	56
1921	65	69	65
1922	70	74	70
1923	46	57	43
1924	69	81	65
1925	81	85	80
1926	78	80	77
1927	98	103	97
1928	100	100	100
1929	100	97	102
1930	87	91	84
1931	70	82	62
1932	58	74	47
1933	66	80	56

Source: D. Petzina, W. Abelshauser, A. Faust (eds), *Sozialgeschichtliches Arbeitsbuch III. Materialien zur Statistik des Deutschen Reiches 1914–1945* (Munich, 1978), p. 61.

PER CAPITA NET NATIONAL PRODUCT AT 1913 PRICES (1928 = 100)

	Index	*Yearly growth rate (%)*
1913	93	
1925	89	
1926	88	−1.0
1927	99	12.5
1928	100	1.0
1929	95	−5.0
1930	91	−4.2
1931	80	−12.1
1932	76	−5.0
1933	86	13.2

Source: Petzina *et al.*, p. 78.

WAGES AS PROPORTION (%) OF NATIONAL INCOME

	National income in mill. (Reich)marks	Wages as %
1913	45 693	46.4
1925	59 978	58.4
1926	62 673	58.1
1927	70 754	57.6
1928	75 373	59.5
1929	73 448	59.8
1930	68 524	60.1
1931	56 466	61.9
1932	45 175	60.7
1933	46 514	59.4

Source: Petzina *et al.*, p. 102.

GERMAN INDUSTRIAL PRODUCTION: AN INTERNATIONAL COMPARISON (1913 = 100)

	1920	1925	1929	1932	1938
World	93	121	153	108	183
USA	122	148	181	94	143
Germany	59	95	117	70	149
UK	93	86	100	83	118
France	70	114	143	105	115
USSR	13	70	181	336	857
Italy	95	157	181	123	195
Japan	176	222	324	309	552
Sweden	97	113	151	141	232

Source: Société des Nations (ed.), *Industrialisation et commerce extérieure* (1945) pp. 160f (from Jürgen von Kruedener (ed.), *Economic Crisis and Political Collapse: The Weimar Republic 1924–1933* (New York/Oxford/Munich: Berg Publishers, 1990)).

REAL WAGES AND WAGE–INCOME RATIOS, BRITAIN AND GERMANY 1913–38

	Index of real hourly wage rates, 1925–9 = 100		Index of real wage earnings, 1925–9 = 100		Wage incomes as % of all industrial incomes	
	Germany	UK	Germany	UK	Germany	UK
1913	–	–	91	87	59	–
1925	90	97	93	98	58	69
1928	105	101	103	101	63	71
1929	109	102	108	103	62	70
1930	116	105	114	107	65	70
1931	119	114	115	113	68	72
1932	114	113	111	114	65	74
1933	113	112	109	114	63	73
1934	110	112	108	115	64	70
1938	106	114	113	115	59	64

Sources: E. H. Phelps Brown and Margaret H. Brown. *A Century of Pay*, London 1968, pp. 438, 446; G. Bry, *Wages in Germany, 1871–1945*, Princeton, 1960, pp. 466–7. Also see Fritz Blaich, *Der Schwarze Freitag. Inflation und Wirtschaftkrise*, Munich, 1985, pp. 69, 167; Sidney Pollard, 'Wege der Arbeitslosigkeit – Großbritannien und Schweden', *Deutsches Institut für Wirtschaftsforschung, Viertelijahrsheft* I (1984), p. 50; David Abraham, *The Collapse of the Weimar Republic*, Princeton, 1981, pp. 245–8; Dietmar Keese, 'Die volkswirtschaftlichen Gesamtgrößen für das Deutsche Reich in den Jahren 1925–1936', in W. Conze and H. Raupach (eds), *Die Staats-und Wirtschaftkrise des Deutschen Reiches 1929–33*, Stuttgart, 1967, p. 45. Skiba shows lower increases: R. Skiba and H. Adam, *Das westdeutsche Lohnniveau zwischen den beiden Weltkriegen und nach der Währungsreform*, Cologne, 1974, pp. 117, 123, 186, 191–2 (from Kruedener (ed.), *Economic Crisis*).

EMPLOYMENT STRUCTURE (a) AND UNEMPLOYMENT (b)

(a)

	Per cent of earning population employed in:		Tertiary sector			
	Agriculture and forestry	Industry and crafts	Total	Trade and commerce	Public and private service	Domestic service
1907	35.2	40.1	24.8	12.4	6.2	6.2
1925	30.5	42.1	27.4	16.4	6.6	4.4
1933	28.9	40.4	30.7	18.5	8.3	3.9

Source: Petzina *et al.*, p. 55.

(b) (Yearly Averages)

	Earning population (in 000s)	Unemployed (in 000s)	Per cent of trades unionists unemployed	Per cent of earners unemployed
1913	14 556	–	2.9	–
1919	16 950	–	3.7	–
1920	18 367	–	3.8	–
1921	19 126	346	2.8	1.8
1922	20 184	215	1.5	1.1
1923	20 000	818	9.6	4.1
1924	19 122	927	13.5	4.9
1925	20 176	682	6.7	3.4
1926	20 287	2 025	18.0	10.0
1927	21 207	1 312	8.7	6.2
1928	21 995	1 391	8.4	6.3
1929	22 418	1 899	13.1	8.5
1930	21 916	3 076	22.2	14.0
1931	20 616	4 520	33.7	21.9
1932	18 711	5 603	43.7	29.9
1933	18 540	4 804	(46.3)[1]	25.9

[1] For the first six months.

Source: Petzina *et al.*, p. 119.

COMPARATIVE MOVEMENTS OF THE GERMAN WHOLESALE PRICE INDEX AND THE DOLLAR/MARK EXCHANGE RATE 1914–23
(1913=1) (E=EXCHANGE RATE INDEX; W=WHOLESALE PRICE INDEX)

Month	1914		1915		1916		1917		1918	
	E	W	E	W	E	W	E	W	E	W
January	1.002	0.96	1.10	1.26	1.27	1.50	1.38	1.56	1.24	2.04
February	1.001	0.96	1.12	1.33	1.28	1.51	1.40	1.58	1.26	1.98
March	1.000	0.96	1.15	1.39	1.32	1.48	1.39	1.59	1.24	1.98
April	0.999	0.95	1.16	1.42	1.30	1.49	1.54	1.63	1.22	2.04
May	0.999	0.97	1.15	1.39	1.24	1.51	1.56	1.63	1.22	2.03
June	0.998	0.99	1.16	1.39	1.26	1.52	1.69	1.65	1.28	2.09
July	0.999	0.99	1.17	1.50	1.31	1.61	1.70	1.72	1.38	2.08
August	0.998	1.09	1.17	1.46	1.33	1.59	1.70	2.03	1.45	2.35
September	0.997	1.11	1.16	1.45	1.37	1.54	1.72	1.99	1.57	2.30
October	1.043	1.18	1.16	1.47	1.36	1.53	1.74	2.01	1.57	2.34
November	1.097	1.23	1.18	1.47	1.38	1.51	1.65	2.03	1.77	2.34
December	1.072	1.25	1.23	1.48	1.36	1.51	1.35	2.03	1.97	2.45
Annual Average	1.017	1.05	1.16	1.42	1.32	1.52	1.57	1.79	1.43	2.17

Continued overleaf

Month	1919		1920		1921		1922		1923	
	E	W	E	W	E	W	E	W	E	W
January	1.95	2.62	15.43	12.56	15.46	14.39	45.69	36.65	4 281	2 783
February	2.17	2.70	23.60	16.85	14.60	13.76	45.91	41.03	6 650	5 585
March	2.48	2.74	19.97	17.09	14.87	13.38	67.70	54.33	5 048	4 888
April	3.00	2.86	14.20	15.67	15.13	13.26	69.32	63.55	5 826	5 212
May	3.06	2.97	11.07	15.08	14.83	13.08	69.11	64.58	11 355	8 170
June	3.34	3.08	9.32	13.82	16.51	13.66	75.62	70.30	26 202	19 385
July	3.59	3.39	9.40	13.67	18.26	14.28	117.49	100.59	84 186	74 787
August	4.48	4.22	11.37	14.50	20.07	19.17	270.26	192.00	1 100 632 (in mill.)	944 041 (in mill.)
September	5.73	4.93	13.81	14.98	24.98	20.67	349.18	287.00	23.5 (in bn.)	23.9 (in bn.)
October	6.39	5.62	16.23	14.66	35.76	24.60	757.73	566.00	6.0	7.1
November	9.12	6.78	18.39	15.09	62.64	34.16	1 711.08	1 154.00	522	725.7
December	11.14	8.03	17.38	14.40	45.72	34.87	1 807.83	1 475.00	1 000	1 261.6
Annual Average	4.70	4.15	15.01	14.86	24.91	19.11	449.21	341.82		

Source: Statistisches Reichsamt: *Zahlen zur Geldentwertung in Deutschland 1914 bis 1923* (Berlin, 1925), pp. 6, 16, 17 (from Carl-Ludwig Holtfrerich, *The German Inflation 1914–1923: Cause and Effects in International Perspective* (Berlin/New York: Verlag Walter de Guyter and Co., 1986)).

GERMAN FEDERAL REVENUE AND EXPENDITURE, JANUARY 1923–MAY 1924

	Expenditure	*Revenue*	*Revenue (%)*[1]
1923[2]			
Jan.	162 480	43 375	28.5
Feb.	484 544	150 509	31.0
Mar.	848 311	41 289	4.9
Apr.	777 930	175 000	22.5
May	705 782	600 348	85.0
June	1 795 432	226 578	12.6
July	5 376 483	259 508	4.1
Aug.	61 191 000	1 791 000	2.9
Sept.	1 302 812 000	49 905 000	3.8
Oct.	43 230 293 800	393 366 434	0.9
Nov.	57 901 569 000 000	53 449 000 000	0.09
Dec.	179 898 893 000 000	32 786 037 000 000	18.2
1924[3]			
Jan.	443 425 770	437 871 555	99.0
Feb.	478 630 013	339 759 047	71.0
Mar.	485 472 028	526 983 881	109.0
Apr.	472 100 000	396 400 000	84.0
May	511 000 000	449 500 000	88.0

[1] Revenue expressed as percentage of expenditure.
[2] First ten days of month, expenditure and revenue in million paper marks.
[3] Whole month, expenditure and revenue in Reichsmarks.

Sources: Department of Overseas Trade, *Report on the Economic and Financial Conditions in Germany Revised to April 1924, by Mr. J. W. F. Threlfall, together with a Report on the Occupied Territories by Mr. C. J. Kavanagh* (London, 1924) and *Report on the Economic and Financial Conditions in Germany* (London, 1925) (from Bruce Kent, *The Spoils of War: The Politics, Economics and Diplomacy of Reparations 1918–1932* (Oxford: Clarendon Press)).

AVERAGE ANNUAL GROWTH RATES OF INDUSTRIAL
OUTPUT IN INTER-WAR GERMANY (%)

	1913–38	*1913–25*	*1925–9*	*1929–32*
Metal Production	0.8	−2.9	5.1	−28.1
Pig Iron	−0.1	−2.9	5.3	−13.8
Steel	1.0	−3.0	7.3	−29.4
Metal Working	4.2	2.3	6.7	−20.9
Stone and Earth	0.8	0.6	5.9	−31.3
extractive industries				
Hard Coal	−0.1	−2.9	5.3	−13.8
Brown Coal	3.3	4.0	9.6	−11.0
Chemical	5.0	2.4	8.8	−9.4
Oil Refining	10.5	1.9	17.0	11.6
Rubber	8.7	7.1	3.4	−3.8
Sulphuric Acid	0.3	−2.8	8.7	−18.1
Soda	2.2	−0.1	10.4	−8.4
Nitrates	8.5	35.2	11.0	−8.4
Artificial Fabrics	7.1	15.5	24.2	−0.5
Textiles	0.1	−1.7	−0.4	−6.8
Clothing	1.6	−0.1	−2.1	−0.9
Leather	−0.8	−1.8	−2.4	−4.0
Gas, Water, and	5.8	5.8	7.7	−7.8
Electricity				
Building industries	0.2	−	−	−29.9

Source: Calculated from W. G. Hoffmann, *Das Wachstum der deutschen Wirtschaft seit der Mitte des 19. Jahrhunderts* (Berlin, 1965), pp. 352–4, 362, 390–1 (from Harold James, *The German Slump: Politics and Economics 1924–1936* (Oxford: Clarendon Press)).

UNEMPLOYMENT STATISTICS 1928–33

	Official statistics end of previous month		Estimated numbers incl. 'hidden' unemployed	
	nos.(thou.)	*%*	*nos.(thou.)*	*%*
1928				
May	3745	10.0	1234	10.0
Feb	1862	9.5	2977	14.4
May	1218	6.0	2183	10.4
Aug.	1012	5.0	1867	8.8
Nov.	1171	5.7	1848	8.8
1929				
Feb.	2850	14.0	3710	17.7
May	1712	8.2	2282	10.7
Aug.	1251	6.0	1800	8.4
Nov.	1557	7.5	2076	9.8
1930				
Feb.	3218	15.8	3920	18.6
May	2787	13.6	3530	16.8
Aug.	2765	13.5	3605	17.1
Nov.	3252	16.2	4115	19.7
1931				
Feb.	4887	24.8	5982	29.1
May	4358	22.0	5433	26.3
Aug.	3990	20.3	5134	25.0
Nov.	4623	24.1	5943	29.2
1932				
Feb.	6042	32.2	7619	38.o
May	5739	30.5	7456	36.8
Aug.	5392	28.9	7164	35.4
Nov.	5109	27.6	6704	33.6
1933				
Feb.	6014	33.0	7781	39.4
May	5331	28.8	6987	34.9
Aug.	4464	23.9	6060	30.2
Nov.	3745	20.2	5172	26.1

Source: Falter *et al.*, *Wahlen und Abstimmungen.*

INDICES OF ECONOMIC CRISIS (1928 = 100)

	1929	1930	1931	1932	1933
Production:					
Capital goods	103	86	61	46	54
Investment goods	103	84	54	35	45
Elastic demand consumer goods	97	91	87	74	80
Inelastic demand consumer goods	101	101	95	85	88
Employment:					
Employed persons	99	92	80	71	74
Prices and wages:					
Capital goods	102	101	96	86	83
Consumer goods	98	91	80	67	64
Cost of living	102	98	90	80	78
Real wages	101	97	93	87	91

Source: Petzina *et al.*, p. 84.

PER CAPITA STATE EXPENDITURE (ALL LEVELS = REICH, LÄNDER, AND LOCAL GOVERNMENT; AT 1900 PRICES; 1913 = 100)

	1913 Mark	Index	1925 RM	Index	1929 RM	Index	1932 RM	Index
Defence and war-related (including military pensions)	25.1	100	21.9	87	27.7	110	14.2	57
Economy (including state concerns, industrial support, roads, transport)	17.0	100	15.8	93	22.1	130	18.2	107
Social sphere, of which:	20.5	100	64.7	316	101.6	496	106.3	519
social insurance	12.2	100	23.2	190	49.2	403	50.0	410
health and welfare	7.9	100	31.4	388	39.2	496	51.8	656
public housing	0.4	100	10.1	2525	13.2	3300	4.5	1125
Education	17.5	100	20.5	117	27.8	159	24.4	139
Public safety	7.7	100	12.1	157	13.7	178	14.6	190
Public administration and services	9.6	100	13.7	143	14.9	155	15.5	162
Debt	5.8	100	0.9	16	4.1	71	6.7	116

Source: Petzina *et al.*, p. 147.

Notes and References

Abbreviations

AdR = *Akten der Reichskanzlei*
CEH = *Central European History*
HZ = *Historische Zeitschrift*
ESR = *European Studies Review*
GH = *German History*
GG = *Geschichte und Gesellschaft*
HJ = *Historical Journal*
JMH = *Journal of Modern History*
UuF = *Ursachen und Folgen. Vom deutschen Zusammenbruch 1918 und 1945 bis zur staatlichen Neuordnung Deutschlands in der Gegenwart, Berlin 1958–78*
VfZ = *Vierteljahrshefte für Zeitgeschichte*

1 The Revolution

1. Susanne Miller, *Burgfrieden und Klassenkampf. Die deutsche Sozial-demokratie im Ersten Weltkrieg* (Düsseldorf, 1974); A.J. Ryder, *The German Revolution of 1918: A Study of German Socialism in War and Revolution* (Cambridge, 1967).
2. *UuF*, i, pp. 17–22; Gerald D. Feldman, *Army, Industry and Labor in Germany* (Princeton, 1966) p. 197ff; Jürgen Kocka, *Klassenge-sellschaft im Krieg. Deutsche Sozialgeschichte 1914–1918*, 2nd edn (Göttingen, 1978) (*Facing Total War. German Society 1914–1918* (Leamington Spa, 1984)).
3. Miller, *Burgfrieden*, p. 274; for Haase, see Ernest Hamburger, *Juden im öffentlichen Leben Deutschlands. Regierungsmitglieder, Beamte und Parlamentarier in der monarchischen Zeit 1948–1918, Schriftenreihe wissenschaftlicher Abhandlungen des Leo Baeck Instituts* (Tübingen, 1968) pp. 427–45.
4. Wilhelm Deist (ed.), *Militär und Innenpolitik im Weltkrieg 1914–1918*, (Düsseldorf, 1970) ii, p. 1242ff. ; E.-H. Schmidt, *Heimatheer und Revolution 1918. Die Militärischen Gewalten im Heimatgebiet zwischen Oktoberreform und Novemberrevolution* (Stuttgart, 1981).
5. Hans-Joachim Bieber, *Gewerkschaften in Krieg und Revolution. Arbeiterbewegung, Industrie, Staat und Militär in Deutschland 1914–1920* (Hamburg, 1981) ii, p. 527.

6. S. Miller, *Die Bürde der Macht. Die deutsche Sozialdemokratie 1918–1920* (Düsseldorf, 1978) pp. 29–32.

7. Gerhard A. Ritter and S. Miller (ed.), *Die deutsche Revolution 1918–1919. Dokumente* (Hamburg, 2nd edn. 1975) p. 27.

8. Erich Matthias and Rudolf Morsey (eds), *Die Regierung des Prinzen Max von Baden* (Düsseldorf, 1962) p. 220ff; Udo Bermbach, *Vorformen parlamentarischer Kabinettsbildung in Deutschland. Der Interfraktionelle Ausschuss und die Parlamentarisierung der Reichregierung* (Cologne, 1967).

9. W. Deist, 'Die Politik der Seekriegsleitung und die Rebellion der Flotte Ende Oktober 1918', *VfZ*, vol. 14 (1966) pp. 341–368.

10. Allan Mitchell, *Revolution in Bayern 1918/19* (Munich, 1967) (*Revolution in Bavaria 1918/19* (Princeton, 1965) p. 65ff.

11. *Regierung des Prinzen Max*, p. 561.

12. Ritter and Miller, 71.

13. Prinz Max von Baden, *Erinnerungen und Dokumente* (Stuttgart, 1968) p. 596ff.

14. Heinrich A. Winkler, *Von der Revolution zur Stabilisierung. Arbeiter und Arbeiterbewegung in der Weimarer Republik 1918 bis 1924*, 2nd edn. (Berlin/Bonn, 1985) p. 44ff; Ulrich Kluge, *Die deutsche Revolution 1918/19* (Frankfurt, 1985) p. 54ff.

15. Winkler, *Revolution*, p. 57.

16. Wilhelm Groener, *Lebenserinnerungen* (Göttingen, 1957) pp. 467–8; for Groener and other personalities see Wolfgang Benz and Hermann Graml, *Biographisches Lexikon zur Weimarer Republik* (Munich, 1988).

17. Ritter and Miller, p. 101f.

18. Eberhard Kolb, *Die Arbeiterräte in der deutschen Innenpolitik 1918–1919* (Düsseldorf, 1972); U. Kluge, *Soldatenräte und Revolution. Studien zur Militärpolitik in Deutschland 1918–19* (Göttingen, 1975); Reinhard Rürup, *Probleme der Revolution in Deutschland 1918/19* (Wiesbaden, 1968).

19. Ritter and Miller, pp. 245–8; Ludwig Preller, *Sozialpolitik in der Weimarer Republik*, 2nd edn (Kronberg/Düsseldorf, 1978) p. 230ff.

20. Winkler, *Revolution*, pp. 76–80; G. D. Feldman, 'The Origins of the Stinnes-Legien Agreement: A Documentation', *Internationale wissenschaftliche Korrespondenz zur Geschichte der deutschen Arbeiterbewegung*, vol. 9 (1973) no. 19–20, pp. 45–103.

21. Bieber, *Gewerkschaften*, ii, p. 605.

22. Arthur Rosenberg, *Geschichte der Weimarer Republik* (Karlsbad, 1935) p. 9 (*A History of the Weimar Republic*, London, 1936).

23. S. Miller and Heinrich Potthoff (eds), *Die Regierung der Volksbeauftragten 1918/19* (Düsseldorf, 1979) introduction by E. Matthias, i, CLXXIV.

24. Kluge, *Revolution*, p. 138ff; Winkler, *Revolution*, p. 70.

25. Ritter and Miller, p. 155f; Kluge, *Soldatenräte*, p. 252.
26. Winkler, *Revolution*, p. 100ff.
27. Rosenberg, *Geschichte*, p. 51.
28. Winkler, *Revolution*, p. 114ff; Hermann Weber, *Kommunismus in Deutschland 1918–1945*, (Darmstadt, 1983).
29. Hermann Weber (ed.), *Der deutsche Kommunismus, Dokumente* (Cologne, 1963) p. 41f.
30. *UuF*, iii, p. 61; Winkler, *Revolution*, p. 120f; Miller, *Bürde*, p. 225ff; J. P. Nettl, *Rosa Luxemburg* (London, 1966) ii, p. 749.
31. Robert G. L. Waite, *Vanguard of Nazism. The Free Corps Movement in Postwar Germany 1918–1923* (Cambridge, Mass., 1952); Hagen Schulze, *Freikorps und Republik 1918–1920* (Boppard, 1969); James M. Diehl, *Paramilitary Politics in Weimar Germany* (Bloomington, 1977).
32. *Hamburger Echo*, no. 50, 31 January 1919, quoted in Miller, *Bürde*, pp. 234–5.
33. Miller *Bürde*, p. 231f; Winkler, *Revolution*, p. 126f.
34. *Die Freiheit*, no. 23, 14 January 1919, quoted in Winkler, *Revolution*, p. 130; Gustav Noske, *Von Kiel bis Kapp* (Berlin, 1920) p. 67ff.
35. *UuF*, iii, pp. 204f, 207ff; Lewis Hertzman, *DNVP: Right-Wing Opposition in the Weimar Republik, 1918–1924* (Lincoln, 1963); Gerhard A. Ritter, 'Kontinuität und Umformung des deutschen Parteiensystems 1918–1920', in *Arbeiterbewegung, Parteien und Parlamentarismus. Aufsätze zur deutschen Sozial-und Verfassungsgeschichte des 19. und 20. Jahrhunderts* (Göttingen, 1976) pp. 116–157; Horst Möller, *Weimar. Die unvollendete Demokratie*, 2nd edn (Munich, 1987) p. 89ff.
36. Ritter and Miller, p. 302ff; Rudolf Morsey, *Die deutsche Zentrumspartei 1917–1923* (Düsseldorf, 1966); Klaus Epstein, *Matthias Erzberger and the Dilemma of German Democracy* (Princeton, 1959).
37. Karl Dietrich Erdmann, *Adenauer in der Rheinlandpolitik nach dem Ersten Weltkrieg* (Stuttgart, 1966) p. 21ff.
38. Lothar Albertin, *Liberalismus und Demokratie am Anfang der Weimarer Republik. Eine vergleichende Analyse der Deutschen Demokratischen Partei und Deutschen Volkspartei* (Düsseldorf, 1972); Larry Eugene Jones, *German Liberalism and the Dissolution of the Weimar Party System 1918–1933* (Chapel Hill and London, 1988).
39. Henry Ashby Turner, *Stresemann and the Politics of the Weimar Republic* (Princeton, 1963); Lothar Döhn, *Politik und Interesse. Die Interessenstruktur der Deutschen Volkspartei* (Meisenheim, 1970).
40. Winkler, *Revolution*, p. 136. Election results are quoted from Jürgen Falter, Thomas Lindenberger und Siegfried Schumann, *Wahlen und Abstimmungen in der Weimarer Republik. Materialien zum Wahlverhalten 1919–1933* (Munich, 1986).

41. R. Rürup, 'Entstehung und Grundlagen der Weimarer Verfassung', in E. Kolb (ed.), *Vom Kaiserreich zur Weimarer Republik* (Cologne, 1972) pp. 218–243; Ernst Rudolf Huber, *Deutsche Verfassungsgeschichte seit 1789*, vol. 5: *Weltkrieg, Revolution und Reichserneuerung 1914–1919* (Stuttgart, 1978) pp. 1075–92; Othmar Bühler, *Die Reichsverfassung, vom 11. August 1919*, 2nd edn (Leipzig, 1927).

42. Reinhard Schiffers, *Elemente direkter Demokratie im Weimarer Regierungssystem* (Düsseldorf, 1971) pp. 117–54.

43. Peter Haungs, *Reichspräsident und parlamentarische Kabinettsregierung. Eine Studie zum Regierungssystem der Weimarer Republik in den Jahren 1924 bis 1929* (Cologne, 1968); Hans Boldt, 'Der Artikel 48 in der Weimarer Reichsverfassung', in Michael Stürmer (ed.) *Die Weimarer Republik. Belagerte Civitas*, (Königstein, 1980) pp. 288–309.

44. Eberhard Schanbacher, *Parlamentarische Wahlen und Wahlsystem in der Weimarer Republik. Wahlgesetzgebung und Wahlreform im Reich und in den Landern* (Düsseldorf, 1982); Huber, *Verfassungsgeschichte*, vol. 6: *Die Weimarer Reichsverfassung* (Stuttgart, 1981) pp. 143–50.

45. Detlev J. K. Peukert, *Die Weimarer Republik. Krisenjahre der klassischen Moderne* (Frankfurt, 1987) p. 134 (*The Weimar Republic*, London, 1992); D. Peukert, 'The Weimar Republic – Old and New Perspectives', *GH*, vol. 6 (1988) pp. 133–44.

46. Huber, *Verfassungsgeschichte*, vi, pp. 429–34.

47. Klaus Schwabe, *Deutsche Revolution und Wilson-Frieden* (Düsseldorf, 1971).

48. Gerhard Schulz, *Revolutionen und Friedensschlüsse 1917–1920* (Munich, 1980); Leo Haupts, *Deutsche Friedenspolitik 1918–19* (Düsseldorf, 1980); Peter Krüger, *Versailles. Deutsche Aussenpolitik zwischen Revisionismus und Friedenssicherung* (Munich, 1986).

49. Quoted in Hagen Schulze, *Weimar. Deutschland 1917–1933* (Berlin, 1982) p. 196.

50. Peter Krüger, *Deutschland und die Reparationen 1918/19* (Stuttgart, 1973).

51. Schulze, *Weimar*, p. 198ff; Morsey, *Zentrumspartei*, pp. 180–92; Jürgen C. Hess, *'Das ganze Deutschland soll es sein.' Demokratischer Nationalismus in der Weimarer Republik am Beispiel der Deutschen Demokratischen Partei)* (Stuttgart, 1978) pp. 76–111; Ulrich Heinemann, *Die verdrängte Niederlage. Politische Öffentlichkeit und Kriegsschuldfrage in der Weimarer Republik* (Göttingen, 1983).

52. *UuF*, iii, 388–415; Stanley Suval, *The Anschluss Question in the Weimar Era. A Study of Nationalism in Germany and Austria, 1918–1932* (Baltimore, 1974) pp. 3–20.

53. Michael Salewski, *Entwaffnung und Militärkontrolle in Deutschland 1918–1927* (Munich, 1966).

54. Krüger, *Versailles*, p. 89f.

55. Ernst Troeltsch, *Spektator-Briefe. Aufsätze über die deutsche Revolution und die Weltpolitik 1918/22* (Tübingen, 1924) (reprint Aalen, 1966) p. 52f, 23 May 1919.

56. Walter McDougall, *France's Rhineland Diplomacy, 1914–1924* (Princeton, 1978); Henning Köhler, *Adenauer und die rheinische Republik. Der erste Anlauf 1918–1924* (Opladen, 1986).

57. Harald von Rieckhoff, *German-Polish relations, 1918–1933* (Baltimore, 1971); John W. Hiden, *The Baltic states and Weimar Ostpolitik* (Cambridge, 1987).

58. Wolfgang J. Mommsen, 'The German Revolution 1918–1920: Political Revolution and Social Protest Movement', in Richard J. Bessel and Edgar J. Feuchtwanger, *Social change and political development in Weimar Germany* (London, 1981) pp. 21–54.

59. Winkler, *Revolution*, p. 159ff; Peter von Oertzen, *Betriebsräte in der Novemberrevolution. Eine politik-wissenschaftliche Untersuchung über Ideengehalt und Struktur der betrieblichen und wirtschaftlichen Arbeiterräte in der deutschen Revolution 1918/19* (Düsseldorf, 1963) p. 113ff; R. Rürup (ed.), *Arbeiter-und Soldatenräte im rheinisch-westfalischen Industriegebiet. Studien zur Geschichte der Revolution 1918/19*, (Wuppertal, 1975); Jürgen Reulecke (ed.), *Arbeiterbewegung an Rhein und Ruhr* (Wuppertal, 1974); Martin Müller-Aenis, *Sozialdemokratie und Rätebewegung in der Provinz. Schwaben und Mittelfranken in der bayerischen Revolution* (Munich, 1980).

60. David W. Morgan, *The Socialist Left and the German Revolution. A History of the German Independent Social Democratic Party, 1917–1922* (London, 1975) p. 230ff; Miller, *Bürde*, pp. 257–59.

61. Miller, *Bürde*, p. 260ff.

62. Falk Wiesemann, 'Kurt Eisner. Studie zu seiner politischen Biographie', in Karl Bosl (ed.), *Bayern im Umbruch. Die Revolution von 1918, ihre Voraussetzungen, ihr Verlauf und ihre Folgen* (Munich, 1969) p. 387ff.

63. Mitchell, *Revolution in Bayern*, p. 242ff.

64. Winkler, *Revolution*, p. 243ff.

65. Troeltsch, *Spektator-Briefe*, vol. 79, 10 August 1919.

66. Winkler, *Revolution*, pp. 191ff; Richard Breitman, *German Socialism and Weimar Democracy* (Chapel Hill, 1981) pp. 59–73; Oswald Spengler, *Preussentum und Sozialismus* (Munich, 1920).

67. Winkler, *Revolution*, p. 283ff.

68. Fritz Blaich, *Der Schwarze Freitag. Inflation und Wirtschaftskrise*, 2nd edn (Munich, 1990) p. 23ff; Carl-Ludwig Holtfrerich, *The German Inflation 1914–1923: Causes and Effects in International Perspective* (Berlin/New York 1986) p. 17.

69. Johannes Erger, *Der Kapp-Lüttwitz Putsch* (Düsseldorf, 1967); Francis L. Carsten, *Reichswehr und Politik* (Cologne/Berlin, 1964) p. 89ff. (*Reichswehr and Politics*, Oxford, 1966).

70. *UuF*, iv, p. 7f.
71. Schulze, *Weimar*, p. 209ff.
72. Miller, *Bürde*, pp. 77–8.
73. Winkler, *Revolution*, p. 309; H. Potthoff, *Freie Gewerkschaften 1918–1933. Der Allgemeine Deutsche Gewerkschaftsbund in der Weimarer Republik* (Düsseldorf, 1987).
74. Otto Gessler, *Reichswehrpolitik in der Weimarer Zeit* (Stuttgart, 1958), p. 130f; Carsten, *Reichswehr*, p. 115ff.
75. Winkler, *Revolution*, p. 323.
76. Hans Fenske, *Konservativismus und Rechtsradikalismus in Bayern nach 1918* (Bad Homburg, 1969).
77. George Eliasberg, *Der Ruhrkrieg von 1920* (Bonn, 1974); Erhard Lucas, *Märzrevolution im Ruhrgebiet* (Frankfurt, 1970–1978) iii, p. 353ff.
78. Huber, *Verfassungsgeschichte*, vol 7: *Ausbau, Schutz und Untergang der Weimarer Republik* (Stuttgart, 1984) pp. 121–2.
79. Rudolf Heberle, *Landbevölkerung und Nationalsozialismus. Eine soziologische Untersuchung der politischen Willensbildung in Schleswig-Holstein 1918–1932* (Stuttgart, 1963) (English edn, *From Democracy to Nazism*, New York, 1970).
80. Miller, *Bürde*, p. 405.
81. Michael Stürmer, *Koalition und Opposition in der Weimarer Republik 1924–1928* (Düsseldorf, 1967).
82. Horst Möller, *Parlamentarismus in Preussen 1919–1932* (Düsseldorf, 1985); D. Orlow, *Weimar Prussia 1918–1925. The Unlikely Rock of Democracy* (Pittsburgh, 1986).
83. Klaus Schönhoven, *Die Bayerische Volkspartei 1924–1932* (Düsseldorf, 1972).
84. Eberhard Kolb, *Die Weimarer Republik* (Munich, 1984) p. 72ff. (*The Weimar Republic*, London, 1988).
85. Huber, *Verfassungsgeschichte*, vii, p. 144ff.

2 The Time of Troubles

1. Charles S. Maier, *Recasting bourgeois Europe: Stabilization in France, Germany and Italy in the Decade after World War I* (Princeton, 1975); Bruce Kent, *The Spoils of War. The Politics, Economics, and Diplomacy of Reparations 1918–1932* (Oxford, 1989).
2. German edn, J. M. Keynes, *Die wirtschaftlichen Folgen des Krieges*, translated by M. J. Bonn and C. Brinkmann (Munich, 1920).
3. G. D. Feldman, 'The Political Economy of Germany's Relative Stabilization during the 1921/22 World Depression', in Feldman *et al.* (eds), *Die Deutsche Inflation. Eine Zwischenbilanz* (Berlin, 1982) pp. 180–206.

4. Peter Wulf, *Hugo Stinnes: Wirtschaft und Politik 1918–1924* (Stuttgart, 1979) p. 205ff; Wolfgang Michalka und Gottfried Niedhart (eds), *Die ungeliebte Republik* (Munich, 1980) p. 108f.

5. Horst Günther Linke, *Deutsch–sowjetische Beziehungen bis Rapallo*, 2nd edn (Cologne, 1972).

6. Marc Trachtenberg, *Reparation in World Politics: France and European Economic Diplomacy, 1916–1923* (New York, 1980); P. Krüger, *Die Aussenpolitik der Republik von Weimar* (Darmstadt, 1985) p. 138ff.

7. Peter-Christian Witt, 'Finanzpolitik und sozialer Wandel in Krieg und Inflation 1918–1924', in Hans Mommsen, Dieter Petzina, Bernd Weisbrod (eds), *Industrielles System und politische Entwicklung in der Weimarer Republik* (Düsseldorf, 1974) i, pp. 395–426.

8. Georges Soutou, 'Die deutschen Reparationen und das Seydoux-Projekt 1920/21', *VfZ*, vol. 23 (1975) pp. 237–70; Bernd Dohrmann, *Die englische Europapolitik in der Wirtschaftskrise 1921–23* (Munich, 1980).

9. F. Gregory Campbell, 'The struggle for Upper Silesia 1919–1922', *JMH* (1970) pp. 361–85; Krüger, *Aussenpolitik*, pp. 134ff.

10. Hess, *Das ganze Deutschland* (note I. 51) p. 125.

11. *UuF*, iv, p. 344ff (Reichstag debate).

12. Holtfrerich, *Inflation*, p. 17.

13. L. Albertin, 'Die Verantwortung der liberalen Parteien für das Scheitern der grossen Koalition im Herbst 1921', *HZ*, vol. 205 (1967) pp. 566–627; Wulf, *Stinnes*, p. 266ff.

14. Carole Fink, *The Genoa Conference. European diplomacy, 1921–22* (Chapel Hill, 1984).

15. Hermann Graml, 'Die Rapallo-Politik im Urteil der westdeutschen Forschung', *VfZ*, vol. 18 (1970) pp. 366–91; Hartmut Pogge von Strandmann, 'Grossindustrie und Rapallopolitik', *HZ*, vol. 222 (1976) pp. 265–341.

16. David Felix, *Walther Rathenau and the Weimar Republic. The Politics of Reparations* (Baltimore, 1970); Ernst Schulin, *Walther Rathenau. Repräsentant, Kritiker und Opfer seiner Zeit* (Göttingen, 1979); James Joll, 'Walther Rathenau – Intellectual or Industrialist', in Volker R. Berghahn and Martin Kitchen (eds), *Germany in the Age of Total War* (London, 1981) pp. 46–62.

17. Holtfrerich, *Inflation*, p. 17; Blaich, *Schwarze Freitag*, p. 27f.

18. Winkler, *Revolution*, p. 468ff.

19. Werner Angress, *Stillborn Revolution* (Princeton, 1963); Sigrid Koch-Baumgarten, *Aufstand der Avantgarde. Die Märzaktion der KPD 1921* (Frankfurt/New York, 1986).

20. Winkler, *Revolution*, p. 482ff; Jones, *Liberalism*, p. 134ff.

21. Hans-Peter Ullmann, *Interessenverbände in Deutschland* (Frankfurt, 1988) p. 124ff; John G. Williamson, *Karl Helfferich, 1872–1924. Economist, Financier, Politician* (Princeton, 1977) p. 344ff.

22. Kurt Sontheimer, *Antidemokratisches Denken in der Weimarer Republik. Die politischen Ideen des deutschen Nationalismus zwischen 1918 und 1933*, 2nd edn (Munich, 1968); Klemens von Klemperer, *Germany's New Conservatism: Its History and Dilemma in the Twentieth Century* (Princeton, 1957); Jost Hermand, *Der alte Traum vom neuen Reich. Völkische Utopien und Nationalsozialismus* (Frankfurt, 1988).

23. Wolfgang Benz, *Süddeutschland in der Weimarer Republik. Ein Beitrag zur deutschen Innenpolitik 1918–1923* (Berlin, 1970); Anthony J. Nicholls, 'Hitler and the Bavarian background to National Socialism', in A.J. Nicholls and E. Matthias, *German Democracy and the Triumph of Hitler* (London, 1971) p. 99ff.

24. H. A. Winkler, 'Die deutsche Gesellschaft der Weimarer Republik und der Antisemitismus', in Bernd Martin and E. Schulin (eds), *Die Juden als Minderheit in der Geschichte* (Munich, 1981) pp. 271–89; Donald L. Niewyk, *The Jews in Weimar Germany* (Manchester, 1980); Werner E. Mosse(ed.), *Deutsches Judentum in Krieg und Revolution 1916–1923* (Tübingen, 1971).

25. Dietrich Orlow, *The History of the Nazi Party*, vol I: *1919–1933* (Newton Abbot, 1971); Georg Franz-Willing, *Die Hitlerbewegung. Der Ursprung 1919 bis 1922* (Hamburg, 1962); Karl Dietrich Bracher, *The German Dictatorship* (London, 1973), p. 72ff; Paul Madden, 'Some Social Characteristics of Early Nazi Party Members', *CEH*, vol. 15 (1982) pp. 34–56; Alan Bullock, *Hitler: A Study in Tyranny* (London, 1962); Joachim C. Fest, *Hitler* (London, 1974); Albrecht Tyrell, *Vom 'Trommler' zum 'Führer'. Der Wandel von Hitlers Selbstverständnis zwischen 1919 und 1924 und die Entwicklung der NSDAP* (Munich, 1975); Eberhard Jaeckel, *Hitler's World View. A Blueprint for Power* (Cambridge, Mass., 1981).

26. Harold J. Gordon, *Hitler and the Beer Hall Putsch* (Princeton, 1972).

27. V. R. Berghahn, *Der Stahlhelm. Bund der Frontsoldaten 1918–1935* (Düsseldorf, 1966); Alexander Kessler, *Der Jungdeutsche Orden auf dem Weg zur Deutschen Staatspartei* (Munich, 1980).

28. Gordon, *Beer Hall Putsch*, p. 104ff.

29. Wolfgang Zorn, *Bayerns Geschichte im 20. Jahrhundert* (Munich, 1986) p. 227ff.

30. W. Rathenau, *Tagebuch 1907–1922*, ed. Hartmut Pogge von Strandmann (Düsseldorf, 1967); Huber, *Verfassungsgeschichte*, vii, p. 249ff.

31. P. Krüger, 'Das Reparationsproblem der Weimarer Republik in fragwürdiger Sicht. Kritische Überlegungen zur neuesten Forschung', *VfZ*, vol. 29 (1981) pp. 21–47.

32. Blaich, *Schwarze Freitag*, 29; Holtfrerich, *Inflation*, p. 17.

33. Manfred Franke, *Albert Leo Schlageter. Der erste Soldat des 3. Reiches. Entmythologisierung eines Helden* (Cologne, 1981).

34. Jacques Bariéty, *Les relations franco–allemandes aprés la premiere guerre mondiale* (Paris, 1977).
35. Marie-Luise Goldbach, *Karl Radek und die deutsch–sowjetischen Beziehungen 1918–1923* (Bonn, 1973) p. 119ff; Otto-Ernst Schüddekopf, *Linke Leute von rechts. Nationalbolschewismus in Deutschland 1918–1933* (Stuttgart, 1960); Conan Fischer, *The German Communists and the Rise of Nazism* (London, 1991) p. 55.
36. Gordon, *Beer Hall Putsch*, p. 194ff.
37. Carsten, *Reichswehr*, p. 165f; Waite, *Vanguard*, p. 239ff; Thilo Vogelsang, *Reichswehr, Staat und NSDAP* (Stuttgart, 1962) pp. 33–4, 407.
38. Winkler, *Revolution*, p. 619ff; Donald B. Pryce, 'The Reich Government versus Saxony, 1923: The Decision to Intervene', *CEH*, vol. 10 (1977) pp. 112–47.
39. Hermann Rupieper, *The Cuno Government and Reparations 1922–1923: Politics and Economics* (The Hague, 1979).
40. Krüger, *Aussenpolitik*, p. 207ff; Kent, *Spoils*, p. 223f.
41. Gustav Stresemann, *Vermächtnis* (ed. Henry Bernard), 3 vols. (Berlin, 1932–3) i, p. 106ff.
42. Gordon, *Beer Hall Putsch*, p. 212ff.
43. Carsten, *Reichswehr*, p. 185.
44. *AdR, Die Kabinette Stresemann I und II*, (eds. K. D. Erdmann and Martin Vogt) (Boppard, 1978) ii, p. 935ff.
45. Ernst Deuerlein (ed.), *Der Hitler-Putsch. Bayerische Dokumente zum 8./9. November 1923* (Stuttgart, 1962); Gordon, *Beer Hall Putsch*, p. 270ff.
46. Bariéty, *Relations franco–allemandes*, p. 261ff; McDougall, *Rhineland Diplomacy*, ch. 8.
47. Klaus Schwabe (ed.), *Die Ruhrkrise 1923* (Paderborn, 1985); Erdmann, *Rheinlandpolitik* (note I. 37) p. 121ff; Henning Köhler, *Adenauer und die Rheinische Republik*, 174ff; F. L. Carsten, *Britain and the Weimar Republic. The British Documents* (London, 1984) p. 158ff; K. P. Jones, 'Stresemann, the Ruhr Crisis and Rhenish Separatism: A case study of *Westpolitik*', *ESR*, vol. 7 (1977) pp. 311–40; Norbert Ranft, 'Erwerbslosenfürsorge, Ruhrkampf und Kommunen. Die Trendwende in der Sozialpolitik im Jahre 1923', in G. D. Feldman, C.-L. Holtfrerich, G. A. Ritter, P.-C. Witt (eds), *Die Anpassung an die Inflation* (Berlin/New York, 1986) pp. 163–201.
48. G. D. Feldman, *Iron and Steel in the German Inflation* (Princeton, 1977) 405ff; Werner Link, *Die amerikanische Stabilisierungspolitik in Deutschland 1921–1932* (Düsseldorf, 1970) p. 136ff.
49. Hjalmar Schacht, *The Stabilization of the Mark* (London, 1927).
50. Stefan Zweig, *Die unsichtbare Sammlung. Eine Episode aus der deutschen Inflation*, in *Ausgewählte Novellen* (Stockholm, 1947) pp. 525–46.
51. Blaich, *Schwarze Freitag*, p. 56.

52. Holtfrerich, *Inflation*, table 41, p. 233f.
53. Andreas Kunz, 'Stand versus Klasse: Beamtenschaft und Gewerkschaften im Konflikt um den Peronalabbau 1923/24', *GG*, vol. 8 (1982) pp. 55–86.
54. Wolfram Fischer, 'Die Weimarer Republik unter den weltwirtschaftlichen Bedingungen der Zwischenkriegszeit', in Mommsen *et al.*, *Industrielles System*, p. 27ff.

3 The Golden Years

1. Carsten, *Reichswehr*, p. 208; Hans Meier-Welcker, *Seeckt* (Frankfurt, 1967); Friedrich von Rabenau, *Hans von Seeckt. Aus seinem Leben 1918–1936* (Leipzig, 1940); O.-E. Schüddekopf, *Das Heeer und die Republik. Quellen zur Politik der Reichswehrfuhrung 1918–1933* (Frankfurt, 1955).
2. Claus-Dieter Krohn, *Stabilisierung und ökonomische Interessen: Die Finanzpolitik des Deutschen Reiches 1923–1927* (Düsseldorf, 1974); Harold James, *The Reichsbank and Public Finance in Germany: 1924–1933* (Frankfurt, 1985).
3. Andreas Kunz, *Civil Servants and the Politics of Inflation in Germany 1914–1924* (Berlin 1986); Jane Caplan, *Government without Administration. State and Civil Service in Weimar and Nazi Germany* (Oxford, 1988).
4. *AdR, Kabinette Stresemann*, i, LXVII; Kent, *Spoils*, p. 239.
5. Krüger, *Aussenpolitik*, pp. 210–11.
6. Huber, *Verfassungsgeschichte*, vii, p. 478ff.
7. Peter Manstein, *Die Mitglieder und Wähler der NSDAP 1919–1933. Untersuchungen zu ihrer schichtmässigen Zusammensetzung*, 2nd edn (Frankfurt, 1989) p. 11ff; Rainer Hambrecht, *Der Aufstieg der NSDAP in Mittel-und Oberfranken (1925–1933)* (Nuremberg, 1976).
8. Attila A. Chanady, 'The Disintegration of the German National People's Party, 1924–1930', *JMH*, vol. 39 (1967) pp. 65–91; Robert P. Grathwohl, *Stresemann and the DNVP; Reconciliation or Revenge in German Foreign Policy* (Lawrence, 1980).
9. Knut Borchardt, *Wachstum, Krisen, Handlungsspielräume der Wirtschaftspolitik. Studien zur Wirtschaftsgeschichte des 19. und 20. Jahrhunderts* (Göttingen, 1982) pp. 165–182; C.-L. Holtfrerich, 'Zu hohe Löhne in der Weimarer Republik? Bemerkungen zur Borchhardt-These', *GG*, vol. 10 (1984) pp. 122–41; Jürgen von Kruedener (ed.), *Economic Crisis and Political Collapse, The Weimar Republik 1924–1933* (New York/Oxford/Munich, 1990); Ian Kershaw (ed.), *Weimar: Why did German democracy fail* (London, 1990).
10. Werner Abelshauser (ed.), *Die Weimarer Republik als Wohlfahrtsstaat. Zum Verhältnis von Wirtschafts-und Sozialpolitik in der Industriegesellschaft* (Stuttgart, 1987; K. Schönhoven, *Reformismus und*

Radikalismus. Gespaltene Arbeiterbewegung im Weimarer Sozialstaat (Munich, 1989); Potthoff, *Gewerkschaften*, p. 93ff.

11. Harold James, 'Rudolf Hilferding and the Application of the Political Economy of the Second International', *HJ* vol. 24 (1981), pp. 847–69.

12. H. A. Winkler, *Der Schein der Normalität. Arbeiter und Arbeiterbewegung in der Weimarer Republik 1924 bis 1930* (Berlin/Bonn, 1985) p. 472ff; Johannes Bahr, 'Sozialer Staat und industrieller Konflikt. Das Schlichtungswesen zwischen Inflation und Weltwirtschaftskrise', in Abelshauser, *Wohlfahrtsstaat*, pp. 185–203.

13. Preller, *Sozialpolitik*, 286ff., 332ff., 384ff; Michael Ruck, 'Der Wohnungsbau-Schnittpunkt von Sozial-und Wirtschaftspolitik. Probleme der öffentlichen Wohnungspolitik in der Hauszinssteuerara 1924/25-1930/31', in Abelshauser, *Wohlfahrtsstaat*, 91–123; Martin Schumacher, 'Hausbesitz, Mittelstand und Wirtschaftspartei', in Mommsen *et al.*, *Industrielles System*, ii, 823–35.

14. G. A. Ritter, *Sozialversicherung in Deutschland und England. Enstehung und Grundzüge im Vergleich* (Munich, 1983); Hans Günther Hockerts, 'Hundert Jahre Sozialversicherung in Deutschland. Ein Bericht über die neuere Forschung', *HZ*, vol. 237 (1983) pp. 361–84.

15. Winkler, *Normalität*, p. 36f; Harold James, *The German Slump. Politics and Economics 1924–1936* (Oxford, 1986) p. 110ff.

16. Bernd Weisbrod, *Schwerindustrie in der Weimarer Republik. Interessenpolitik zwischen Stabilisierung und Krise* (Wuppertal, 1978).

17. Dieter Gessner, *Agrarverbände in der Weimarer Republik. Wirtschaftliche und soziale Voraussetzungen agrarkonservativer Politik vor 1933* (Düsseldorf, 1976).

18. M Schumacher, *Mittelstandsfront und Republik. Die Wirtschaftspartei – Reichspartei des deutschen Mittelstands 1919–1933* (Düsseldorf, 1972); H. A. Winkler, *Mittelstand, Demokratie und Nationalsozialismus. Die politische Entwicklung von Handwerk und Kleinhandel in der Weimarer Republik* (Cologne, 1972).

19. J. Kocka,, 'Zur Problematik der deutschen Angestellten 1914–1933', in Mommsen *et. al*, *Industrielles System*, ii, pp. 792–823.

20. David. B. Southern, 'The Impact of Inflation: Inflation, the Courts and Revaluation', in Richard Bessel and Edgar J. Feuchtwanger, *Social Change and Political Development in Weimar Germany* (London, 1981) pp. 55–76.

21. M. Stürmer, *Koalition*, p. 84ff.

22. Erich Eyck, *Geschichte der Weimarer Republik*, (Erlenbach, 1956) i, p. 430ff; Andreas Dorpalen, *Hindenburg and the Weimar Republic* (Princeton, 1964); Gerhard Schulz, *Deutschland am Vorabend der Grossen Krise* (Berlin/New York, 1987), p. 253f; P.-C. Witt,

Friedrich Ebert. Parteiführer, Reichskanzler, Volksbeauftragter, Reichspräsident (Bonn, 1982).

23. Anne Orde, *Great Britain and international security, 1920–1926* (London, 1978) p. 83ff.

24. Jon Jacobson, *Locarno Diplomacy. Germany and the West, 1925–1929* (Princeton, 1972).

25. W. Link, 'Grundzüge des deutsch-amerikanischen Verhältnisses in der Stabilisierungsphase 1925–29', in Wolfgang Michalka/ Marshall Lee (eds), *Gustav Stresemann* (Darmstadt, 1982); Klaus Hildebrand, *Das Deutsche Reich und die Sowjetunion im internationalen System, 1918–1932* (Wiesbaden, 1977).

26. Winkler, *Normalität*, p. 258f.

27. Krüger, *Aussenpolitik*, p. 356ff; Martin Walsdorff, *Westorientierung und Ostpolitik. Stresemanns Russlandpolitik in der Locarno-Ära* (Bremen, 1971).

28. Ulrich Schuren, *Der Volksentscheid zur Fürstenenteignung 1926* (Düsseldorf, 1978); Schulz, *Vorabend*, p. 245ff.

29. Stürmer, *Koalition*, p. 152ff.

30. Michael Geyer, *Aufrüstung oder Sicherheit. Die Reichswehr in der Krise der Machtpolitik 1924–1936* (Wiesbaden, 1980) p. 112ff; Klaus-Jürgen Müller and Eckhardt Opitz (eds), *Militär und Militarismus in der Weimarer Republik* (Düsseldorf, 1978).

31. Ellen L. Evans, *The German Center Party 1870–1933. A Study in Political Catholicism* (Carbondale, 1981) p. 316ff; Winifried Becker (ed.), *Die Minderheit als Mitte. Die deutsche Zentrumspartei in der Innenpolitik des Reiches 1871–1933* (Paderborn, 1979); Manfred Dörr, *Die Deutschnationale Volkspartei 1925 bis 1928* (Marburg, 1964) p. 265ff.

32. Werner Schneider, *Die Deutsche Demokratische Partei in der Weimarer Republik 1924–1930* (Munich, 1978) p. 97ff; D.J.K. Peukert, 'Der Schund und Schmutzkampf als "Sozialpolitik der Seele". Eine Vorgeschichte der Bücherverbrennung ?', in Walter Huder *et. al* (eds), *Bücherverbrennung Deutschland 1933: Voraussetzungen und Folgen* (Berlin, 1983) (catalogue of an exhibition opened in Berlin in May 1983) pp. 51–64; Modris Eksteins, *The Limits of Reason: the German Democratic Press and the Collapse of Weimar Democracy* (Oxford, 1975).

33. J. Hermand and Frank Trommler, *Die Kultur der Weimarer Republik* (Munich, 1978); Walter Laqueur, *Weimar. A Cultural History 1918–1933* (London, 1974); Peter Gay, *Weimar Culture: the Outsider as Insider* (New York, 1968); John Willet, *The Weimar Years: a culture cut short* (London, 1984); Corona Hepp, *Avantgarde. Moderne Kunst, Kulturkritik und Reformbewegungen nach der Jahrhundertwende* (Munich, 1987); H. Lethen, *Neue Sachlichkeit 1924–1932* (Stuttgart, 1975).

34. Reinhard Neebe, *Grossindustrie, Staat und NSDAP 1930–1933. Paul Silverberg und der Reichsverband der Deutschen Industrie in der Krise der Weimarer Republik*, (Göttingen, 1981) p. 35ff; David Abraham, *The Collapse of the Weimar Republic: Political Economy and Crisis*, 2nd edn (New York/London, 1986) p. 128ff.

35. Gerhard Stoltenberg, *Politische Strömungen im schleswig-holsteinischen Landvolk 1918–1933: Ein Beitrag zur politischen Meinungsbildung in der Weimarer Republik* (Düsseldorf, 1962).

36. Winkler, *Normalität*, p. 315.

37. James, *Slump*, p. 218f; Kent, *Spoils*, p. 272f.

38. Günter Grünthal, *Reichsschulgesetz und Zentrumspartei in der Weimarer Republik* (Düsseldorf, 1968); Werner Stephan, *Aufstieg und Verfall des Linksliberalismus. Geschichte der Deutschen Demokratischen Partei* (Göttingen, 1973); Hartmut Schustereit, *Linksliberalismus und Sozialdemokratie in der Weimarer Republik. Eine vergleichende Betrachtung der Politik von DDP und SPD 1919–1930* (Düsseldorf, 1975); Jonathan R. C. Wright, *Above Parties. The Political Attitudes of the German Protestant Church Leadership 1918–1933* (Oxford, 1974) p. 55f; Kurt Nowak, 'Protestantismus und Weimarer Republik. Politische Wegmarken in der evangelischen Kirche 1918–1932', in K. D. Bracher, Manfred Funke, Hans-Adolf Jacobsen (eds), *Die Weimarer Republik 1918–1933. Politik. Wirtschaft. Gesellschaft* (Düsseldorf, 1987) pp. 218–37.

39. Anthony Glees, 'Albert C. Grzesinski and the Politics of Prussia 1926–1930', *EHR*, vol. 89 (1974) pp. 814–34.

40. Karl Rohe, *Das Reichsbanner Schwarz-Rot-Gold* (Düsseldorf, 1966).

41. Winkler, *Normalität*, p. 365ff.

42. Hermann Weber, *Kommunismus in Deutschland 1918–1945* (Darmstadt, 1983); Ben Fowkes, *Communism in Germany under the Weimar Republic* (London, 1984); Bernd Rother, *Die Sozialdemokratie im Land Braunschweig 1918 bis 1933* (Bonn, 1990).

43. Gessner, *Agrarverbände*, p. 108ff.

44. Gotthardt Jasper, *Der Schutz der Republik. Studien zur staatlichen Sicherung der Demokratie in der Weimarer Republik 1922–1930* (Tübingen, 1963); ibid., 'Justiz und Politik der Weimarer Republik', *VfZ*, vol. 30 (1982), 167–205; Heinrich Hannover and Elisabeth Hannover-Druck, *Politische Justiz 1918–1933*, 2nd edn (Frankfurt, 1977); Hans Hattenhauer, 'Zur Lage der Justiz in der Weimarer Republik', in K. D. Erdmann and H. Schulze, *Weimar. Selbstpreisgabe einer Demokratie* (Düsseldorf, 1980) pp. 169–76; Theo Rasehorn, 'Rechtspolitik und Rechtssprechung. Ein Beitrag zur Ideologie der 'Dritten Gewalt'', in Bracher/Funke/Jacobsen, *Weimarer Republik*, p. 411ff.

45. Orlow, *Nazi Party*, i, p. 46ff; Jeremy Noakes, *The Nazi Party in Lower Saxony, 1921–1933* (Oxford, 1971); Geoffrey Pridham,

Hitler's Rise to Power. The Nazi Movement in Bavaria 1923–1933 (London, 1973).

46. Werner Jochmann (ed.), *Im Kampf um die Macht – Hitlers Rede vor dem Hamburger Nationalklub von 1919* (Frankfurt, 1960); William Carr, *Hitler. A Study in Personality and Politics* (London, 1978) p. 22ff; Ian Kershaw, *Hitler* (London, 1991); Michael H. Kater, *The Nazi Party. A Social Profile of Members and Leaders 1919–1945* (Cambridge, Mass., 1983); Reinhard Kühnl, *Die nationalsozialistische Linke 1925–1930* (Meisenheim, 1966).

47. R. Bessel, *Political Violence and the Rise of Nazism. The Storm Troopers in Eastern Germany, 1925–1935* (New Haven, 1984); Peter H. Merkl, *Political Violence under the Swastika. 581 Early Nazis* (Princeton, 1975).

48. Berghahn, *Stahlhelm*, p. 103ff.

49. Klemperer, *New Conservatism*; W. Laqueur, *Die deutsche Jugendbewegung. Eine historische Studie* (Cologne, 1962); Felix Rabe, *Die Bündische Jugend. Ein Beitrag zur Geschichte der Weimarer Republik* (Stuttgart, 1961); D. J. K. Peukert, *Jugend zwischen Krieg und Krise. Lebenswelten von Arbeiterjungen in der Weimarer Republik* (Cologne, 1987).

50. Berghahn, *Stahlhelm*, p. 75ff.

51. Jones, *Liberalism*, p. 271ff; Schneider, *Demokratische Partei*, p. 249ff.

52. Winkler, *Normalität*, p. 521ff; Heberle, *Democracy to Nazism*, p. 99.

4   Crisis, Collapse and the Coming of Hitler

1. Otto Braun, *Von Weimar zu Hitler*, 2nd edn (New York 1940) p. 245ff; H. Schulze, *Otto Braun oder Preussens demokratische Sendung. Eine Biographie* (Frankfurt, a.M., 1977) p. 539ff; G. Schulz, *Zwischen Demokratie und Diktatur. Verfassungspolitik und Reichsreform in der Weimarer Republik*, vol. I (Berlin, 1963).

2. Wolfgang Wacker, *Der Bau des Panzerschiffs 'A' und der Reichstag* (Tübingen, 1959); Geyer, *Aufrüstung* p. 198ff; above, i, p. 135f.

3. Huber, *Verfassungsgeschichte*, vii, p. 615ff; Arnold Brecht, *Mit der Kraft des Geistes. Lebenserinnerungen. Zweite Hälfte 1927–1967* (Frankfurt, 1967) pp. 49–55.

4. Carsten, *Reichswehr*, p. 320ff; *AdR*, Martin Vogt (ed.), *Das Kabinett Müller II* (Boppard, 1970) pp. 62–4; Theodor Eschenburg, 'Die Rolle der Persönlichkeit in der Krise der Weimarer Republik. Hindenburg, Bruning, Groener, Schleicher', *VfZ*, vol. 9 (1961), pp. 1–29.

5. Wacker, *Panzerschiff*, p. 104ff.

6. Ursula Hüllbüsch, 'Der Ruhreisenstreit in gewerkschaftlicher Sicht', in Mommsen *et al.*, *Industrielles System*, i, pp. 271–289.

7. Weisbrod, *Schwerindustrie*, p. 415ff.

8. Ernst Fraenkel, 'Der Ruhreisenstreit 1928–1929 in historisch-politischer Sicht', in Ferdinand A. Hermens and Theodor Schieder (eds), *Staat, Wirtschaft und Politik in der Weimarer Republik. Festschrift für Heinrich Brüning* (Berlin, 1967) pp. 97–117.

9. Ilse Maurer, *Reichsfinanzen und grosse Koalition. Zur Geschichte des Reichskabinetts Müller (1928–1930)* (Bern, 1973).

10. John A. Leopold, *Alfred Hugenberg. The Radical Nationalist Campaign against the Weimar Republic* (New Haven, 1977).

11. Josef Becker, 'Die Deutsche Zentrumspartei 1918–1933', in Oswald Hauser (ed.), *Politische Parteien in Deutschland und Frankreich 1918 bis 1939* (Wiesbaden, 1969) p. 59ff.

12. H. Weber, *Die Wandlung des deutschen Kommunismus. Die Stalinisierung der KPD in der Weimarer Republik* (Frankfurt, 1969) i, p. 195ff; Eve Rosenhaft, 'Working-Class Life and Working-Class Politics: Communists, Nazis and the State in the Battle for the Streets, Berlin 1928–1932', in Bessel and Feuchtwanger (eds), *Social Change*, p. 224ff; Conan Fischer, *The German Communists and the Rise of Nazism* (London, 1991) p. 102ff.

13. Eyck, *Geschichte*, ii, p. 279ff; Gotthard Jasper, 'Zur innenpolitischen Lage in Deutschland im Herbst 1929', *VfZ*, vol. 8 (1960) p. 280ff.

14. M. Vogt, 'Die Stellung der Koalitionsparteien zur Finanzpolitik', in Mommsen *et al.*, *Industrielles System*, i, p. 439ff; Winkler, *Normalität*, p. 738ff; Helga Timm, *Die deutsche Sozialpolitik und der Bruch der grossen Koalition im Marz 1930*, 2nd edn (Düsseldorf, 1982) p. 149ff.

15. Carl Schmitt, *Die geistesgeschichtliche Lage des heutigen Parlamentarismus* (Munich, 1923); *Der Hüter der Verfassung* (Tübingen, 1931).

16. Werner Conze, 'Die Krise des Parteienstaates in Deutschland 1929/30', *HZ*, vol. 178 (1954) pp. 47–83; K. D. Bracher, *Die Auflösung der Weimarer Republik. Eine Studie zum Problem des Machtverfalls in der Demokratie*, 2nd edn (Stuttgart, 1957) p. 296ff.

17. Krüger, *Aussenpolitik*, p. 500ff.

18. G. Schulz, Introduction to I. Maurer and Udo Wengst, *Politik und Wirtschaft in der Krise 1930–1932. Quellen zur Ära Brüning* (Düsseldorf, 1980) i, XXXIIff; Bracher, *Auflösung*, p. 303ff.

19. H. A. Winkler, *Der Weg in die Katastrophe. Arbeiter und Arbeiterbewegung in der Weimarer Republik 1930 bis 1933* (Berlin/Bonn, 1987) p. 158ff.

20. M. H. Kater, *Studentenschaft und Rechtsradikalismus in Deutschland 1918–1933* (Hamburg, 1975).

21. Peter Bucher, *Der Reichswehrprozess. Der Hochverrat der Ulmer Reichswehroffiziere 1929/30* (Boppard, 1967).

22. *UuF*, viii, p. 224f.

23. Ludwig Bergsträsser, *Geschichte der politischen Parteien in Deutschland*, 6th edn (Mannheim etc., 1932) p. 182ff; Sigmund Neumann, *Die deutschen Parteien* (Berlin, 1932) (reprinted 1965); Erasmus Jonas, *Die Volkskonservativen 1928–1933. Entwicklung, Struktur, Standort und staatspolitische Zielsetzung* (Düsseldorf, 1965); Günther Opitz, *Der Christlich-soziale Volksdienst. Versuch einer protestantischen Partei in der Weimarer Republik* (Düsseldorf, 1969).

24. Alexander Kessler, *Der Jungdeutsche Orden in den Jahren der Entscheidung 1928–1930* (I) (Munich, 1975); Bruce B. Frye, *Liberal Democrats in the Weimar Republic: The History of the German Democratic Party and the German State Party* (Carbondale, 1985); B. B. Frye, 'The German Democratic Party and the 'Jewish Problem' in the Weimar Republic', *Year Book of the Leo Baeck Institute* 21 (1976) pp. 143–72; P. B. Wiener, 'Die Parteien der Mitte', in Mosse and Paucker (eds), *Entscheidungsjahr*, p. 289ff; Peter Pulzer, *Jews and the German State. The Political History of a Minority, 1848–1933* (Oxford, 1992) p. 291ff; A. Paucker, *Der jüdische Abwehrkampf gegen Antisemitismus und Nationalsozialismus in den letzten Jahren der Weimarer Republik*, 2nd edn (Hamburg, 1969).

25. Thomas Childers, *The Nazi Voter. The Social Foundations of German Fascism 1918–1933* (Chapel Hill/London, 1983); (ed.) *The Formation of the Nazi Constituency* (London, 1983); Richard F. Hamilton, *Who voted for Hitler?* (New York, 1983); Dirk Hänisch, *Sozialstrukturelle Bestimmungsgründe des Wahlverhaltens in der Weimarer Republik. Eine Aggregatdatenanalyse der Ergebnisse der Reichstagwahlen 1924–1933* (Duisburg, 1983); M. H. Kater, *Nazi Party* (note III, 46); Max H. Kele, *Nazis and Workers. National Socialist Appeals to German Labor 1919–1933* (Chapel Hill, 1972); P. Manstein, *Mitglieder und Wahler der NSDAP* (note III. 7); William S. Allen, *The Nazi Seizure of Power. The Experience of a single German Town 1930–1935* (London, 1966); Hans-Ulrich Thamer, *Verführung und Gewalt. Deutschland 1933–1945* (Berlin, 1986) p. 172ff; Martin Broszat, 'National Socialism, its Social Basis and Psychological Impact', in E. J. Feuchtwanger (ed.), *Upheaval and Continuity. A Century of German History* (London, 1983) pp. 134–51.

26. John E. Farquharson, *The Plough and the Swastika: National Socialist Farm Policy 1928–1933* (London, 1979); David Welch (ed.), *Nazi Propaganda. The Power and the Limitations*, Totowa 1983; W. E. Mosse, *Jews in the German Economy. The German–Jewish Economic Elite 1820–1935* (Oxford, 1987) p. 190ff. (Tietz and Wertheim).

27. P. D. Stachura, *Gregor Strasser and the Rise of Nazism* (London, 1983).

28. Gerhard Schreiber, *Hitler – Interpretationen 1923–1983. Ergebnisse, Methoden und Probleme der Forschung*, 2nd edn (Darmstadt, 1988);

Rainer Zitelmann, *Hitler. Selbstverständnis eines Revolutionärs.* (Hamburg etc., 1987).

29. Winkler, *Katastrophe*, p. 207ff; Braun, *Von Weimar zu Hitler*, p. 309ff.
30. Breitman, *Socialism*, p. 161ff; Hans-Peter Ehni, *Bollwerk Preussen? Preussen-Regierung, Reich-Länder-Problem und Sozialdemokratie 1928–1932* (Bonn, 1975) p. 183ff.
31. Heinrich Brüning, *Memoiren, 1918–1934* (Stuttgart, 1970) p. 456.
32. H. James, 'Economic Reasons for the Collapse of the Weimar Republic', in Kershaw (ed.), *Weimar*, pp. 30–57; Sidney Pollard, 'German Trade Union Policy 1929–1933 in the Light of the British Experience', in Kruedener (ed.), *Economic Crisis*, pp. 21–44.
33. Krüger, *Aussenpolitik*, p. 531ff; Dorte Doering, 'Deutsch-oesterreichische Aussenhandelsverflechtung während der Weltwirtschaftskrise', in Mommsen *et. al, Industrielles System*, ii, pp. 514–30.
34. Hermann Pünder, *Politik in der Reichskanzlei. Aufzeichnungen aus den Jahren 1929–1932* (Stuttgart, 1961) p. 60ff; Ernst Feder, *Heute sprach ich mit. . . Tagebücher eines Berliner Publizisten* (eds. Cecile Löwenthal-Hensel and A. Paucker) (Stuttgart, 1971) p. 268ff.
35. Winkler, *Katastrophe*, p. 274; Gotthard Jasper, *Die gescheiterte Zähmung. Wege zur Machtergreifung Hitlers 1930–1934* (Frankfurt, 1986) p. 67f.
36. Vogelsang, *Reichswehr*, p. 117f.
37. Winkler, *Katastrophe*, p. 254; M. Eksteins, 'War, Memory and Politics: The Fate of the Film *All Quiet on the Western Front*', *CEH*, vol. 13 (1980) pp. 60–82.
38. Pünder, *Reichskanzlei*, p. 62; Brüning, *Memoiren*, p. 186f.
39. Huber, *Verfassungsgeschichte*, vii, p. 810f.
40. Winkler, *Katastrophe*, p. 288ff.
41. Arnold Brecht, *Mit der Kraft des Geistes*, p. 139ff; Carl Severing, *Mein Lebensweg* (Cologne, 1950) ii, p. 283ff.
42. Eve Rosenhaft, *Beating the Fascists? The German Communists and Political Violence 1929–1933* (Cambridge, 1983).
43. C. J. Fischer, *Stormtroopers: A Social, Economic and Ideological Analysis 1929–1935* (London, 1983); Orlow, *Nazi Party*, i, p. 217f.
44. Edward W. Bennett, *Germany and the Diplomacy of the Financial Crisis, 1931* (Cambridge, Mass., 1962); Kent, *Spoils*, p. 336f.
45. Karl-Erich Born, *Die deutsche Bankenkrise 1931. Finanzen und Politik* (Munich, 1967); *AdR, Kabinette Brüning*, introduction by Tilman Koops, i, XXXff; *Ära Brüning*, i, p. 617f; *UuF*, viii, p. 160ff.
46. David Marquand, *Ramsay Macdonald* (London, 1977) p. 604ff; Bruning, *Memoiren*, p. 278ff.
47. Bundesarchiv Koblenz, *Nachlass Dingeldey*, vol. 36, p. 79–85, 13 June 1931.

48. James, *Slump*, p. 295ff.
49. C.-L. Holtfrerich, 'Economic Policy Options and the End of the Weimar Republic', in Kershaw (ed.), *Weimar*, pp. 58–91; K. Borchardt, 'A Decade of Debate about Brüning's Economic Policy', in Kruedener (ed.), *Economic Crisis*, 99–151.
50. Berghahn, *Stahlhelm*, pp. 156ff, 169ff.
51. H. Möller, *Parlamentarismus in Preussen*, 315ff; Ehni, *Bollwerk*, p. 198ff.
52. Carsten, *Reichswehr*, p. 326ff; Geyer, *Aufrüstung*, p. 247ff.
53. Winkler, *Katastrophe*, p. 422f; Neebe, *Grossindustrie*, p. 99ff.
54. Huber, *Verfassungsgeschichte*, vii, p. 874ff.
55. Johann Wachtler, *Zwischen Revolutionserwartung und Untergang. Die Vorbereitung der KPD auf die Illegalität in den Jahren 1929–1933* (Frankfurt, 1983).
56. Carsten, *Reichswehr*, p. 371.
57. Leopold, *Hugenberg*, p. 97ff; Bracher, *Auflösung*, *407ff*; *UuF*, viii, p. 367ff.
58. Brüning, *Memoiren*, p. 450ff.
59. K.-D. Godau-Schuttke, *Rechtsverwalter des Reiches Staatssekretär Dr. Curt Joel* (Frankfurt, 1981); Jasper, *Zähmung*, p. 72f.
60. Rudolf Morsey, 'Beamtenschaft und Verwaltung zwischen Republik und 'Neuem Staat'', in Erdmann and Schulze (eds), *Weimar*, pp. 151–168.
61. See note 46 of Chapter 3.
62. See note 115 below, also note 49 above.
63. *UuF*, viii, p. 320ff.
64. Richard Evans and Dick Geary (eds), *The German Unemployed. Experiences and Consequences of Mass Unemployment from the Weimar Republic to the Third Reich* (London, 1987); P. D. Stachura, *Unemployment and the Great Depression in Germany 1929–1933* (London, 1986).
65. Vogelsang, *Reichswehr*, p. 147ff; *UuF*, viii, p. 383ff.
66. *UuF*, viii, p. 401.
67. *UuF*, viii, p. 398ff.
68. Pünder, *Reichskanzlei*, p. 115.
69. Neebe, *Grossindustrie*, p. 120ff; Henry A. Turner, *German Big Business and the Rise of Hitler* (New York, 1985).
70. Winkler, *Katastrophe*, pp. 519ff and 528ff.
71. Rohe, *Reichsbanner*, p. 392ff.
72. Carsten, *Reichswehr*, p. 376ff; Vogelsang, *Reichswehr*, p. 161ff; G. Schulz, *Aufstieg des Nationalsozialismus. Krise und Revolution in Deutschland* (Frankfurt, 1975) p. 676ff.
73. Möller, *Preussen*, p. 555ff; Braun, *Von Weimar zu Hitler*, p. 374ff.
74. Kent, *Spoils*, p. 353ff.
75. *ibid.* 361; *Ära Brüning*, ii, p. 1179ff; *UuF*, viii, p. 204.

76. Krüger, *Aussenpolitik*, p. 546ff; Geyer, *Aufrüstung*, p. 270f; Vogelsang, *Reichswehr*, p. 180ff; Werner Conze, 'Zum Sturz Brunings', *VfZ*, vol. 1 (1953) pp. 261–88.
77. Winkler, *Katastrophe*, p. 494ff; James, *Slump*, p. 239ff.
78. D. Gessner, *Agrardepression und Prasidialregierungen in Deutschland 1930 1933* (Düsseldorf, 1977) p. 146ff; Heinrich Muth, 'Agrarpolitik und Parteipolitik im Fruhjahr 1932', in Hermens and Schieder, *Festschrift für Brüning*, pp. 317–360; Pünder, *Reichskanzlei*, p. 120ff; Bruning, *Memoiren*, p. 597ff.
79. Kolb, *Weimarer Republik*, p. 199ff.
80. Bundesarchiv Koblenz, Nachlass Dingeldey, vol. 36, pp. 117–133, typed copy of *Niederschrift über die Entwicklung der Krise und Demission des Kabinetts Brüning*, signed by Hindenburg and Meissner, 10 June 1932 (printed in Vogelsang, *Reichswehr*, p. 459ff).
81. *Ära Brüning*, ii, p. 1470.
82. Winkler, *Katastrophe*, pp. 627–8.
83. Heinrich Muth, *Carl Schmitt in der Innenpolitik des Sommers 1932*, Beiheft 1 der *HZ*, 1971.
84. Huber, *Verfassungsgeschichte*, vii. 1001.
85. E. W. Bennett, *German rearmament and the West, 1932–1933* (Princeton, 1979).
86. E. Matthias and R. Morsey, 'Die Deutsche Staatspartei', in Matthias and Morsey (eds), *Das Ende der Parteien 1933* (Düsseldorf, 1960) pp. 31–97; Jones, *Liberalism*, p. 456ff.
87. Peter Hayes, ' "A Question Mark with Epaulettes"? Kurt von Schleicher and Weimar Politics', *JMH*, vol. 52 (1980) pp. 35–65; Axel Schildt, 'Militärische Ratio und Integration der Gewerkschaften. Zur Querfrontkonzeption der Reichswehrführung am Ende der Weimarer Republik', in Richard Saage (ed.), *Solidargemeinschaft und Klassenkampf. Politische Konzeptionen der Sozialdemokratie zwischen den Weltkriegen* (Frankfurt, 1986); Friedrich Karl von Plehwe, *Reichskanzler Kurt von Schleicher. Weimars letzte Chance gegen Hitler* (Esslingen, 1983).
88. Bracher, *Auflösung*, p. 578f.
89. Möller, *Preussen*, p. 565ff; Wolfgang Benz, 'Papens 'Preussenschlag' und die Länder', *VfZ*, vol. 18 (1970) pp. 320–38; Severing, *Lebensweg*, ii, p. 347; Andrew McElligott, 'Street Politics in Hamburg, 1932–3', *History Workshop* 16 (1983), 83–90; Ursula Büttner, *Hamburg, in der Staats-und Wirtschaftskrise 1928–1931* (Hamburg, 1982).
90. Rohe, *Reichsbanner*, p. 426ff; Peter Lessmann, *Die preussische Schutzpolizei in der Weimarer Republik. Streifendienst und Strassenkampf* (Düsseldorf, 1989); Hsi-Huey Liang, *The Berlin Police Force in the Weimar Republic* (Berkeley, 1970); Christoph Graf, *Politische Polizei*

zwischen Demokratie und Diktatur. Die Entwicklung der preussischen Politischen Polizei vom Staatsschutzorgan der Weimarer Republik zum Geheimen Staatspolizeiamt des Dritten Reiches (Berlin, 1983) p. 54ff; Erich D. Köhler, 'The Crisis in the Prussian Schutzpolizei 1930–1932', in George L. Mosse (ed.), *Police Forces in History* (London, 1975); Albert Grzesinski, *Inside Germany* (New York, 1939); H. Schulze (ed.), *Anpassung oder Widerstand, Aus den Akten des Parteivorstands der deutschen Sozialdemokratie 1932/33* (Bonn, 1975).

91. R. Morsey, *Der Untergang des Politischen Katholizismus. Die Zentrumspartei zwischen christlichem Selbstverständnis und 'Nationaler Erhebung' 1932/33* (Zürich, 1977) p. 56ff; Günter Plum, *Gesellschaftsstruktur und politisches Bewusstsein in einer katholischen Region. Untersuchung am Beispiel des Regierungsbezirks Aachen* (Stuttgart, 1972) p. 139ff; Ulrich von Hehl, 'Staatsverständnis und Strategie des politischen Katholizismus', in Bracher/Funke/Jacobsen, *Weimarer Republik* (note III, 38) pp. 238–253.

92. *UuF*, viii, p. 613ff.

93. Pünder, *Reichskanzlei*, p. 149 (8 Oct. 1932).

94. R. Bessel, 'The Potempa Murder', *CEH*, vol. 10 (1977) pp. 241–54.

95. James, *Slump*, p. 184f; Abraham, *Collapse of the Weimar Republic*, p. 207ff.

96. Joseph Goebbels, *Vom Kaiserhof zur Reichskanzlei* (Munich, 1934).

97. Huber, *Verfassungsgeschichte*, vii, p. 1120ff.

98. Geyer, *Aufrüstung*, p. 286ff; Vogelsang, *Reichswehr*, p. 285ff.

99. *UuF*, viii, p. 658.

100. Winkler, *Katastrophe*, p. 748.

101. Neebe, *Grossindustrie*, p. 131ff.

102. Winkler, *Katastrophe*, p. 765ff; Schulze, *Weimar*, p. 387; Goebbels, *Kaiserhof*, 196ff; Volker Kratzenberg, *Arbeiter auf dem Weg zu Hitler? Die Nationalsozialistische Betriebszellen-Organisation. Ihre Entstehung, ihre Programmatik, ihr Scheitern 1927–1934* (Frankfurt, 1987); Siegfried Bahne, *Die KPD und das Ende von Weimar. Das Scheitern einer Politik 1932–1935* (Frankfurt, 1976).

103. Winkler, *Katastrophe*, p. 802ff.

104. *UuF*, viii, p. 685 (Meissner's record of Hitler's interview with Hindenburg, 19 Nov. 1932).

105. Neebe, *Grossindustrie*, p. 137; Turner, *Big Business*, p. 302ff; Volker Hentschel, *Weimars letzte Monate. Hitler und der Untergang der Republik* (Düsseldorf, 1978) p. 102ff; *UuF*, viii, p. 672 (Schacht to Hitler, 12 Nov. 1932).

106. Vogelsang, *Reichswehr*, p. 318ff. and documents 36–8; Carsten, *Reichswehr*, p. 431ff.

107. Huber, *Verfassungsgeschichte*, vii, p. 1166ff.

108. Udo Kissenkötter, *Gregor Strasser und die NSDAP* (Munich, 1978) p. 170ff.
109. Winkler, *Katastrophe*, p. 817ff.
110. *UuF*, viii, p. 724ff. (Schleicher's radio address of 15 Dec. 1932); *UuF*, viii, p. 512 (Reichslandbund); Schulze, *Weimar*, p. 403f.
111. Hentschel, *Letzte Monate*, p. 86ff; Franz von Papen, *Der Wahrheit eine Gasse* (Munich, 1952) p. 255f.; Braun, *Von Weimar zu Hitler*, p. 437.
112. Jutta Ciolek-Kumper, *Wahlkampf in Lippe* (Munich, 1976).
113. *UuF*, viii, p. 750f. (attitude of DNVP); Papen, *Wahrheit*, p. 265ff.
114. Hentschel, *Letzte Monate*, p. 94ff; Winkler, *Katastrophe*, p. 843f. (Osthilfe scandal).
115. Thamer, *Verführung*, p. 222 (Blomberg); *UuF*, viii, p. 756ff. (Schleicher putsch); Morsey, *Untergang des Politischen Katholizismus*, p. 82ff; Bracher, *Auflösung*, 733ff. (Hammerstein's memorandum).
116. Winkler, *Katastrophe*, p. 867ff.
117. T. Eschenburg, 'Rolle der Persönlichkeit' (note 4); Jasper, *Zähmung*, p. 115ff.
118. K. D. Bracher/W. Sauer/G. Schulz, *Die nationalsozialistische Machtergreifung. Studien zur Errichtung des totalitären Herrschaftssystems in Deutschland 1933/34*, 2nd edn (Cologne, 1962) p. 158ff.

Notes on the
English-Language Literature

There are two bibliographies on the Weimar republic in English: P. D. Stachura, *The Weimar Era and Hitler* (Oxford, 1977) and the more recent ABC-Clio Information Services (ed.), *The Weimar Republic. A Historical Bibliography*, (Santa Barbara/Denver/Oxford, 1984).

E. Kolb (note 84, Chapter 1) contains an extended bibliography; the book provides an excellent survey of the period as well as a report on the current state of research. D.J.K. Peukert (note 45, Chapter 1) is another recent highly interesting interpretative German survey now available in translation.

There is a new third edition of Anthony J. Nicholls, *Weimar and the Rise of Hitler* (London, 1992), which is still the best succinct introduction. The final phase of the republic is excellently summarised in M. Broszat, *Hitler and the Collapse of Weimar Germany* (Oxford and New York, 1987), first published in German under the title *Die Machtergreifung* in 1984. Erich Eyck's two-volume history (note 22, Chapter 1) (English edn, London, 1962–4) and Arthur Rosenberg's history (note 22, Chapter 1) are still valuable because of the first-hand knowledge of their authors.

There are many distinguished surveys in English of German history over a more extended period, such as Gordon A. Craig, *Germany 1866–1945* (Oxford, 1978). There is nothing in English to match the vast printed collections of documents available in German. The new revised three-volume edition of Jeremy Noakes and Geoffrey Pridham, *Nazism, 1919–1945* (Exeter, 1984) deserves its popularity, but is not specifically orientated towards the Weimar period.

The area most fully served by printed collections of documents in English is foreign policy, but the English series *Documents on German Foreign Policy* at present covers mainly the Third Reich. A number of memoirs important for the Weimar period were written in or are available in English, for example Viscount d'Abernon, *An Ambassador of Peace* (3 vols, London, 1929); Arnold Brecht, *Prelude to Silence* (New York, 1944); and Albert Grzesinski (note 90, Chapter 4).

Apart from foreign policy, where there is an abundance of work in English, historians writing in English have made a notable contribution to this phase of German domestic history. The history of the German labour movement and of the SPD is well covered in works such as W. L. Guttsman, *The German Social Democratic Party 1875–1933* (London, 1981);

R. N. Hunt, *German Social Democracy 1918–1933* (2nd edn, Chicago 1976), and translations such as Helga Grebing, *The History of the German Labour Movement. A Survey* (Leamington Spa, 1985) as well as in the books cited above: A. J. Ryder (note1, Chapter 1), D. W. Morgan (note 60, Chapter 1), A. Mitchell (note 10, Chapter 1) and W. Angress (note 19, Chapter 1). There are a large number of books about national socialism and in the postwar era non-Germans have sometimes found it easier to write about it than Germans, as the many excellent books on Hitler from Bullock (note 25, Chapter 2) to Kershaw (note 46, Chapter 3) testify. There are important regional studies on the rise of Nazism by J. Noakes (note 45, Chapter 3), G. Pridham (note 45, Chapter 3) and W. S. Allen (note 25, Chapter 4); works on the SA by R. Bessel (note 47, Chapter 3) and C. Fischer (note 43, Chapter 4); on the Nazi party and voters by D. Orlow (note 25, Chapter 2), M. H. Kater (note 46, Chapter 2), T. Childers (note 25, Chapter 4) and R. F. Hamilton (note 25, Chapter 4).

The debate on the Weimar's economic health has generated major contributions by H. James (note 2 and 15, Chapter 3), G. D. Feldman (note 2, Chapter 1 and note 48, Chapter 2), H. A. Turner (note 69, Chapter 4) and P. D. Stachura (note 64, Chapter 4). A number of symposia contain valuable papers on specific topics: Nicholls and Matthias (note 23, Chapter 2), Bessel and Feuchtwanger (note 58, Chapter 1), I. Kershaw (note 9, Chapter 3), J. v. Kruedener (note 9, Chapter 3), R. Evans and D. Geary (note 64, Chapter 4).

The Weimar cultural scene is excellently portrayed in the books by Gay, Laqueur and Willet (note 33, Chapter 3) and Richard J. Evans in *The Feminist Movement in Germany 1894–1933* (London, 1976) deals with another theme significant in the Weimar era and scarcely touched on here.

There are major works on the position of German Jews and on anti-Semitism, by Pulzer (note 24, Chapter 4) Mosse (note 26, Chapter 4) and Paucker (note 24, Chapter 4). Journals frequently mentioned in the notes, such as *Central European History* and the *Journal of Modern History*, contain a wealth of useful articles beyond those cited here.

Index